Windows 2000 Pro

THE MISSING MANUAL

*The book that
should have been
in the box*

Windows 2000 Pro

THE MISSING MANUAL

Sharon Crawford

POGUE PRESS™
O'REILLY®

Beijing • Cambridge • Farnham • Köln • Paris • Sebastopol • Taipei • Tokyo

Windows 2000 Pro: The Missing Manual
by Sharon Crawford

Copyright © 2000 Pogue Press, LLC. All rights reserved.
Printed in the United States of America.

Published by Pogue Press/O'Reilly & Associates, Inc., 101 Morris Street, Sebastopol, CA 95472.

November 2000: First Edition.
March 2001:   Second printing.

Missing Manual and the Missing Manual logo are registered trademarks of Pogue Press, LLC.

Many of the designations used by manufacturers and sellers to distinguish their products are claimed as trademarks. Where those designations appear in this book, and Pogue Press was aware of a trademark claim, the designations have been capitalized.

While every precaution has been taken in the preparation of this book, the publisher assumes no responsibility for errors or omissions, or for damages resulting from the use of the information contained herein.

ISBN: 0-596-00010-3   [3/01]
[M]

Table of Contents

Part Two: The Components of Windows 2000

TABLE OF CONTENTS

Part Five: Managing Your Computer

The Missing Credits

About the Author

Sharon Crawford came to computers in a roundabout way. In the early '80s, she was an electrician repairing subway cars in New York City. Though it seems astonishing that anyone would want to leave such a glamorous job, she did, in order to return home to California.

After arriving in California, she went back to school to study the finer points of electronics, and in 1988, armed with a degree and some ingenious lies, she landed her first technical writing job.

After a couple of years, Sharon was fortunate enough to get a job in the technical department of a computer-book publishing house. After a few months, she convinced a gullible acquisitions editor to give her a shot at writing a book. Since then, Sharon has written about two dozen books, on her own and with collaborators. The most recent include *Windows 2000 Server Administrator's Companion* (Microsoft Press) with Charlie Russel, *ABCs of Windows 98* (Sybex), and *Windows 2000 Professional for Dummies* (IDG) with Andy Rathbone.

About the Creative Team

Jason Gerend (contributing author) graduated from the University of Washington with a degree in psychology, but dodged graduate school and psychology research to be a freelance author of computer books. Jason worked with Sharon on her bestselling *Windows 2000 Server Administrator's Companion* and has contributed to 14 other computer books, including coauthoring the *Effective Executive's Guide To FrontPage Web Sites* and the *Effective Executive's Guide to Dreamweaver Web Sites* (Redmond Technology Press). Jason has been a professional Webmaster since 1995 and is also a Microsoft Certified Professional.

Craig Zacker (technical editor, contributing author) began his computing experience in the halcyon days of teletypes and paper tape. After earning a master's degree in English and American Literature from New York University, he worked as a network administrator and Windows NT integrator, and as a technical writer and webmaster for a large software company. Craig has authored or contributed to many books on networking, operating systems, and PC hardware, written articles for publications like *Windows NT Magazine* and *Network World,* and developed several Web-based training courses. Résumé and writing samples await at *www.zacker.com,* or via email at *craig@zacker.com.*

David Pogue (editor, indexer), creator of the Missing Manual series, is the personal-technology columnist for the *New York Times.* He's the author or coauthor of 15 computer, humor, and music books, including *PalmPilot: The Ultimate Guide;*

Mac OS 9: The Missing Manual; and six books in the *...for Dummies* series (including *Magic, Opera,* and *Classical Music*). He welcomes feedback on this book or any other in the Missing Manual series at *david@pogueman.com.* (If you're seeking technical help, however, please refer to the help sources listed in Chapter 19.) Web site: *www.davidpogue.com.*

Maarten Reilingh (copy editor) is from Red Hook, NY. A former university theater professor, reference writer, and academic journal editor, Maarty has edited nonfiction works of all kinds, including computer-related titles for IDG Books and McGraw-Hill. Besides his family, the theater, and clear expression, Maarty's passion extends to the martial art of Tang Soo Do. On the Web: *www.ulster.net/~janmaart.*

Rod Trent (technical reviewer) is a network engineer for a Big 5 Accounting Firm. He writes technical articles, scripts, and utilities on Microsoft Systems Management Server (SMS) for SWYNK.com *(www.swynk.com/trent),* where he's a contributing editor. He's also the managing editor for MyCEDevice.com and MyPocketPC.com. Rod is the author of several books and white papers on Systems Management, including *Microsoft SMS Installer* from Admin911: SMS. Rod writes freelance from the Cincinnati, OH area, where he lives with his wife and three kids.

David A. Freedman created the cover design for the Missing Manual series. From his studio in Carlisle, Massachusetts *(df301@aol.com),* David also designs logos and other graphics. Prior to establishing his design business, David worked for 20 years with Milton Glaser in New York City.

Rose Cassano (cover padlock illustration) has worked as an independent designer and illustrator for 20 years. Assignments have spanned the nonprofit sector to corporate clientele. She is lives in beautiful Southern Oregon, grateful for the miracles of technology that make living and working there a reality. Email: *cassano@cdsnet.net.* Web: *www.rosecassano.com.*

Phil Simpson (book design and layout) has been involved with computer graphics since 1977, when he worked with one of the first graphics-generating computers—an offspring of flight-simulation technology. He now works out of his office in Stamford, CT *(pmsimpson@earthlink.net),* where he has had his graphic design business for 18 years. He's experienced in many facets of graphic design, including corporate identity, publication design, corporate and medical communications.

Publisher's Acknowledgments

The Missing Manual series is a joint venture between Pogue Press—the dream team introduced on these pages—and O'Reilly & Associates. In particular, this book owes its existence to Tim O'Reilly, Cathy Record, Edie Freedman, Allen Noren, Laura Schmier, Glenn Harden, Sue Willing, Mark Brokering, Dana Furby, and Sara Winge. Special thanks, too, to agent David Rogelberg and to Elizabeth "Eagle Eye" Tonis, this book's beta reader, who pulled out every stop to exterminate lingering typos.

The Missing Manual Series

Missing Manual books are designed to be authoritative, superbly written guides to popular computer products that don't come with printed manuals (which is just about all of them). Each book features a hand-crafted index; cross-references to specific page numbers (not just "See Chapter 14"); and RepKover, a detached-spine binding that lets the book lie perfectly flat without the assistance of weights or cinder blocks.

Recent and upcoming Missing Manual titles include:

- *Windows Me: The Missing Manual* by David Pogue
- *DreamWeaver 4: The Missing Manual* by Dave McFarland
- *Mac OS 9: The Missing Manual* by David Pogue
- *AppleWorks 6: The Missing Manual* by Jim Elferdink and David Reynolds
- *iMovie: The Missing Manual* by David Pogue
- *iMovie 2: The Missing Manual* by David Pogue
- *Office 2001 for Macintosh: The Missing Manual* by Nan Barber and David Reynolds
- *Mac OS X: The Missing Manual* by David Pogue

THE MISSING CREDITS

Introduction

Although it may be hard to believe, until recently, hundred-year floods really happened only every hundred years, and a million dollars was considered a *major* lottery prize. But these days, everything's faster, bigger, and more expensive than ever. Windows 2000 is the latest computer marvel to be faster, bigger, and yes, more expensive.

Windows 2000 Professional is the successor to Windows NT Workstation 4. Like Windows NT Workstation, it's designed specifically for business applications and is a key component in a Windows Server-based network. (Windows 2000 Server is the even more expensive, complex, and powerful version of Windows 2000 designed for corporate networks.) Windows 2000 Pro is the ideal operating system to use on a Windows 2000 Server network, but it's also an excellent operating system to use on standalone computers or members of a workgroup.

On a Windows 2000 *domain* (the most common kind of business network), administrators can manage Windows 2000 Professional computers remotely; you can use programs that have been installed elsewhere on the network; and the network administrator's bag of tricks gains a number of highly technical capabilities.

Although Microsoft has continued revising the Windows 95/98 line (which includes Windows Me), these systems are designed for use at home. They're not the first choices for the workplace. Yes, they can hook up to Windows 2000 networks, and you can upgrade them to access Active Directory (see page 22), but they also lack many of the attributes that make a good business operating system.

For example, Windows 2000 Professional makes your PC remarkably stable, even more than Windows NT Workstation. System security is customizable; you can make your computer's security very loose or extremely tight. Windows 2000 is also built for speed; technically speaking, it features an efficient 32-bit, fully multithreaded, preemptive multitasking and symmetric multiprocessing (SMP) enabled kernel, which lets you run more applications and run those applications faster. Computers with multiple processors and software written to take advantage of SMP can make use of a second processor—a feature not available in Windows 95/98/Me. In short, most programs run significantly faster in Windows 2000 than in Windows 95 or its descendants.

Note: Although Windows 2000 is designed for use in business, it makes an excellent home operating system, too. Besides being stable and fast for standard productivity programs, it also makes a killer gaming platform (if your games and equipment support Windows 2000, of course).

About this Book

Despite the many improvements in Windows over the years, one feature hasn't improved a bit: Microsoft's documentation. With Windows 2000 Pro, in fact, you get no printed user guide at all. To learn about the thousands of pieces of software that make up this operating system, you're expected to read the Windows online help screens.

Unfortunately, as you'll quickly discover, these help screens are tersely written, can be overwhelmingly technical, and lack examples and illustrations. You can't even mark your place, underline, or read them in the bathroom.

The purpose of this book, then, is to serve as the manual that should have accompanied Windows 2000 Pro. In this book's pages, you'll find step-by-step instructions for using almost every important Windows 2000 Pro feature: managing files and folders, getting online, using email, setting up a small network, and so on.

The primary discussions are written for advanced-beginner or intermediate PC users. But if you're a first-time Windows user, special sidebar articles called Up To Speed provide the introductory information you need to understand the topic at hand. If you're an advanced PC user, on the other hand, keep your eye out for similar shaded boxes called Power Users' Clinic. They offer more technical tips, tricks, and shortcuts for the veteran PC fan.

About the Outline

This book is divided into six parts, each containing several chapters:

- Part 1, **Getting Started,** covers everything you see on the screen when you turn on a Windows 2000 computer: the login screen, icons, windows, menus, scroll bars, the Recycle Bin, shortcuts, the Start menu, shortcut menus, and so on.

- Part 2, **The Components of Windows 2000,** is dedicated to the proposition that an operating system is little more than a launch pad for *programs*—the actual applications you use in your everyday work, such as email programs, Web brows-

---

ers, word processors, and so on. Chapter 7, for example, describes how to w
with applications in Windows—how to launch them, switch among them
data between them, and so on.

This part also offers an item-by-item discussion of the individual software nug
gets that make up this operating system: not just the items in your Control Panel
folder, but also the long list of free programs that Microsoft threw in, including
Windows Media Player, Paint, WordPad, and Fax.

- Part 3, **Windows Online,** covers all the special Internet-related features of Windows, including the wizards that set up your Internet account, the Internet Explorer Web browser, and the Outlook Express email and newsgroup program.

- Part 4, **Network Survival,** is designed for two kinds of people: those whose PCs
connect to an office network that's been set up by somebody else (usually a *domain* network) and those who'd like to set up a smaller, less complex network (a
peer-to-peer network) themselves. These chapters show you how to dial in to your
computer from the road, use files and programs that reside on other networked
computers, share a single Internet connection among several PCs, and so on.

- Part 5, **Managing Your Computer,** guides you through troubleshooting, upgrading, maintaining, and administering the user accounts on your machine.

At the end of the book, an appendix provides detailed guidance in installing this
operating system.

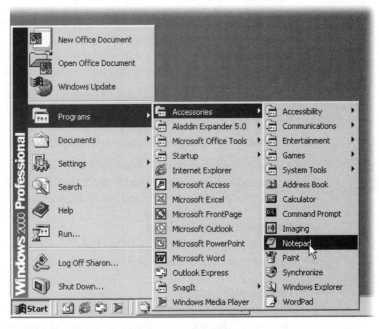

Figure I-1:
*In this book, arrow
notations help to simplify
folder and menu instruc-
tions. For example,
"Choose Start→
Programs→Accessories→
Notepad" is a more
compact way of saying,
"Click the Start button,
then slide up to the
Programs command; now,
without clicking, slide to
the right onto the
Accessories submenu; in
that submenu, click
Notepad," as shown here.*

About→These→Arrows

Throughout this book, and throughout the Missing Manual series, you'll find sentences like this one: "Open the My Computer→C: drive→WINNT folder." That's shorthand for a much longer instruction that directs you to open three nested folders in sequence, like this: "On your desktop, you'll find an icon called My Computer. Open that. Inside the My Computer window is a disk icon labeled C:; double-click it to open it. Inside that window is yet another one called Windows. Double-click to open it, too."

Similarly, this kind of arrow shorthand helps to simplify the business of choosing commands in menus, as shown in Figure I-1.

About MissingManual.com

You're invited and encouraged to submit corrections and updates on this book's Web page at *www.missingmanual.com*. In an effort to keep the book as up-to-date and accurate as possible, each time we print more copies of this book, we'll make any confirmed corrections you've suggested. We'll also note such changes on the Web site, so that other readers can mark important corrections into their own copies of the book, if they like.

In the meantime, we'd love to hear your own suggestions for new books in the Missing Manual line. There's a place for that on the Web site, too, as well as a place to sign up for free email notification of new titles in the series.

What's New in Windows 2000 Pro

The big news about Windows 2000 Professional—as compared to Windows NT 4 Workstation—is how much better it is at recognizing hardware and at running on laptops. This is especially good news when you bear in mind that Windows 2000 Pro hasn't lost a step when it comes to reliability and stability.

Anyone who has used Windows 95, Windows 98, Windows Me, or Windows NT 4 will find much that's familiar in Windows 2000. The basic look and feel are quite similar; in fact, plenty of people describe Windows 2000 as a marriage of Windows 98's look with Windows NT's networking and reliability features.

A large part of learning Windows 2000 Professional is simply discovering the new names and locations for old functions. This section briefly reviews, for people who are used to Windows NT, the features that have changed and new features.

Changes on the Desktop

When you log on to a Windows 2000 Pro computer, the desktop may seem familiar, but there are both cosmetic and functional changes.

Customizable toolbars

As described in Chapter 4, you can now create your own toolbars (short strips on the Taskbar that house the icons of programs, documents, disks, and folders you use frequently). The Quick Launch toolbar is especially useful; you can install any icon onto it just by dragging it there.

Briefcase

My Briefcase, a default presence on the desktop of Windows NT 4.0, no longer appears until you right-click the desktop and choose New→Briefcase from the shortcut menu. Windows creates a briefcase on the desktop.

If you are a happy user of Briefcase, you'll be glad to know that it works exactly as it always did (see page 325). If you tried Briefcase and found it wanting, you'll probably be much happier with Offline Files, a new feature covered in Chapter 16.

DOS Prompt is now the Command Prompt

The Command Prompt (called the DOS Prompt in Windows 95, 98, and Me) has been moved to the Start→Accessories menu. See page 197 for more information.

Tip: You can now change the color, font, and other options for the Command Prompt by right-clicking the Command Prompt title bar and selecting Defaults from the shortcut menu. (And if you run a program that requires a different look, you can set these options for a single session by right-clicking the Command Prompt title bar and selecting Properties.)

Find is now Search

In Windows 2000, the Find function has been renamed Search, gained an Explorer-style interface, and moved to the Start menu. You can also get to it just by clicking the Search toolbar button in any desktop window; the Search controls appear instantly at the left side of the window. And searching for the words *inside* files can be extremely fast if you use the new Indexing Service feature. (See Chapter 3 for details on all of these features.)

My Documents is on the desktop

While the My Documents folder has been around for some time, Windows 2000 now features its icon right on the desktop. This is the folder into which most programs propose storing newly saved files. Inside is My Pictures, a new folder that many Windows programs propose for storing graphics files; its window offers some special tools for previewing, rotating, and slide-showing the pictures within.

Network Neighborhood is now My Network Places

My Network Places, the replacement for Network Neighborhood, is the desktop icon that's your portal to the shared computers, files and folders, printers, and other resources on the network to which your computer is connected. Chapters 13, 14, and 15 are all about working on a network.

To open the Network and Dial-Up Connections window, right-click My Network Places and choose Properties from the shortcut menu. (Network and Dial-up Connections is a combination of the Network control panel and the Dial-up Networking window from previous versions of Windows. You use it to configure both your network and modem connections.)

Personalized Menus

Windows 2000 uses Personalized Menus for the Start menu and its offshoots. In other words, Windows 2000 keeps track of how often you access items on the menu and arranges the menu accordingly; after you've used a menu six times, you'll discover that the most infrequently used commands have disappeared. Figure 3-17 (page 51) shows the idea.

Some people find that this feature frees them from hunting through commands that they don't use much. Others find it disconcerting that Personalized Menus makes the Start menu and other menus *change* frequently, making it difficult to get used to the positions of familiar items. If you're in the second category, you can turn off Personalized Menus by right-clicking the Taskbar and choosing Properties from the shortcut menu. Clear the Personalized Menus checkbox and click OK.

Start menu

The Start menu isn't new, but it has undergone some changes from Windows NT 4.0. For one thing, the logoff command is no longer on the Start menu by default. To add it, follow these steps:

1. **Click Start→Settings→Taskbar & Start Menu.**

   The Taskbar & Start Menu Properties dialog box appears.

2. **Click the Advanced tab. Turn on Display Logoff.**

   While you're on the Advanced tab, note the other additions that you can make to the Start menu: For example, you can drag shortcut icons onto the Start button to add items to the menu, drag items up and down the menu to change their order, right-click them to rename them, and so on. Chapter 3 covers the ways to customize the Start menu.

3. **Click OK to close the dialog box.**

   The Log Off [Your Name] command now appears just above the Start→Shut Down command.

Options is now Folder Options

In Windows 2000, the Options command has been renamed Folder Options. You'll find it in the Tools menu of many windows, including My Computer, My Documents, My Network Places, Windows Explorer, Control Panel, and folders that you've created yourself. Use the Folder Options command to change the appearance of your desktop and folder windows, and specify how folders open. (More than everything you ever wanted to know about folder options fills Chapter 4.)

Windows NT Explorer is now Windows Explorer

The Windows NT Explorer is now called Windows Explorer; it's listed in the Start→Accessories menu. Except for the name change, it's nearly identical to the Windows Explorer in Windows NT 4 and in Windows 98.

New Save File and Open File dialog boxes

As shown in Figure I-2, the buttons at the left side of the new Save As and Open dialog boxes (which appear when you choose File→Save As or File→Open) give you quick access to the folders where you're most likely to want to stash newly created documents: the My Documents folder, the desktop, and so on.

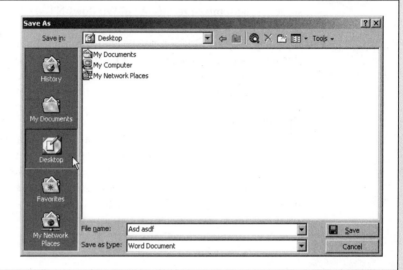

Figure I-2:
Using the "Save in" drop-down menu at the top of the screen, you can choose any folder you like—or click one of the shortcut buttons at the left side.

Changes behind the Desktop

The most dramatic changes from Windows NT 4 to Windows 2000 are on the server side. However, even experienced users of Windows NT Workstation will find (or be unable to find) some features that are quite different or in unexpected locations.

More mobile-computing features

Laptop luggers and home telecommuters are in much better shape with Windows 2000 Pro than they were with Windows NT, thanks to two new technologies: Offline Files and ACPI.

Offline Files, described on page 315, helps you keep straight which versions of the files you've copied from the network to your laptop are the most recent. ACPI (Advanced Configuration and Power Interface) is a set of technologies that let modern laptops extend their battery life and give you more control over their power consumption. (If your older laptop doesn't have the necessary circuitry for ACPI, Windows 2000 offers the older Advanced Power Management features described on page 163.)

Clipboard Viewer is now ClipBook Viewer

In the beginning, Windows had a place in memory called the Clipboard. When you copied something (such as a paragraph from your word processor), that's where the something was stored, so that you could paste it into a new location. The Clipboard had room for only one something at a time; when you copied something else, the first item was overwritten. To see what was stored on the Clipboard, you opened the Clipboard Viewer. Simple enough.

Since those halcyon days, however, the Clipboard has undergone several cosmetic surgeries, with mixed results. As in Windows NT 4, Clipboard Viewer has been renamed ClipBook Viewer (and is no longer available from a menu). ClipBook Viewer still shows any information you've copied to the Clipboard. But now you can store this information permanently in a Local ClipBook and share it with other people. The Local ClipBook opens when you start ClipBook Viewer. To open ClipBook Viewer, choose Start→Run, type *clipbrd,* then press Enter.

Computers Near Me

If your Windows 2000 Professional PC is a member of a *workgroup* (a small number of computers that are networked but don't require a server), a Computers Near Me icon appears inside the My Network Places window. The Computers Near Me window shows icons for the computers and other resources that are accessible by members of your workgroup. (You don't get a Computers Near Me icon when Windows 2000 is installed on a machine that is a member of a *domain* [a larger group of networked computers that are administered as a unit].) See page 289 for more on Computers Near Me.

Devices is now Device Manager

The Device Manager, one of the most useful utilities of Windows 95/98/Me that *wasn't* included in Windows NT 4, is now part of Windows 2000; it's one of the components of the Computer Management application. To open Device Manager, right-click My Computer and select Properties from the shortcut menu, and then click the Hardware tab. (See Chapter 16 for more on Device Manager.)

Dial-up Networking

You can open the Dial-up Networking by choosing Start→Control Panel→Network and Dial-up Connections, or by right-clicking My Network Places and choosing Properties from the shortcut menu.

Unless you're logged on as an administrator (page 369), some features of Network and Dial-up Connections will not be available. Setting up and using a dial-up connection is covered in Chapter 11.

Networking settings

In Windows 2000, the settings that were once in the Network control panel have been divided among three tools: System, Network and Dial-up Connections, and Device Manager, which are all in the Control Panel. This table shows you where the important tabs of the Network control panel in Windows 98 and Windows NT 4 are now found in Windows 2000.

Settings on this tab of the Windows 98 Network control panel	Or this tab in the Windows NT 4 Network control panel	Are here in Windows 2000
Configuration		Network and Dial-up Connections
Identification	Identification	Network Identification tab in System
Access Control		Network and Dial-Up Connections
	Services	Network and Dial-Up Connections
	Protocols	Network and Dial-Up Connections
	Adapters	Device Manager
	Bindings	Network and Dial-Up Connections

Disk Administrator is now Disk Management

Disk Administrator has been renamed Disk Management. If you're technically inclined, you can use this tool to manage disks and volumes. It supports partitions, logical drives, new dynamic volumes, and remote disk management.

To open Disk Management, right-click My Computer and select Manage from the shortcut menu. In the left pane, click Storage and then Disk Management. Information on managing and configuring disks awaits in Chapter 19.

Event Viewer

The *event log* can be a useful way of tracking down problems on your system. Event Viewer, the program that shows you the event log, is now located in the Administrative Tools control panel. To open Event Viewer, choose Start→Settings→Control Panel. Double-click Administrative Tools, and then double-click Event Viewer.

For help on interpreting what you see in the Event Viewer, refer to Chapter 19.

System Information

The System Information program displays technical information about your computer's configuration. To open it, right-click My Computer and choose Manage from the shortcut menu. In the left pane, click System Tools and then System Information.

TCP/IP

In Windows NT 4, you installed and configured networking *protocols* (communications languages for networked computers) through the Network control panel. The procedure has changed only slightly in Windows 2000.

To install, remove, or configure TCP/IP, for example, select Start→Settings→Network and Dial-up Connections. Right-click the icon for your connection and choose Properties from the shortcut menu. There's more on configuring TCP/IP in Chapter 15, which is about setting up your own network.

User Manager is now Local Users and Groups

In Windows 2000, the User Manager program has been renamed Local Users and Groups and moved into the Computer Management tool. To view and edit your settings, right-click My Computer and select Manage from the shortcut menu.

New hardware standards

Windows 2000 comes ready to recognize new kinds of add-on gadgets and connectors, including USB, FireWire (IEEE 1394), DVD, and Zip drives.

Tip: The Windows 2000 installer gives you the new DVD Player program only if your PC has a DVD drive. To launch DVD Player, just insert a DVD disc. (You can also choose Start→Programs→Accessories→ Entertainment→DVD Player.) You'll see a standard set of controls, such as Play, Stop, and Fast Forward, as well as an Options button that lets you change languages or set up parental controls.

Part One:
Getting Started

1

A Welcome to Windows 2000

W ay back in the computer Pleistocene era (that is, about ten years ago), PCs were unimpressive creatures, to be sure. Their capacity was limited, their processing was slow, and their interface was all text. Nevertheless, they were great at tasks that were difficult, time-consuming, and boring for humans. In most businesses, PCs rapidly took over the data manipulation, calculation, and word-processing chores that people hated doing. And the more the PC could do, the more was demanded of it. Hardware and software both had to improve rapidly to meet that demand.

In those early and dark ages, the PC's basic operating system was some version of DOS (Disk Operating System). Like all other operating systems, DOS is software that acts as an internal traffic cop—allotting memory, disk space, and central processing unit (CPU) time to applications, networking software, or peripheral (add-on) equipment. The operating system also keeps track of your files and does all the other behind-the-scenes chores necessary to keep a complicated piece of machinery running.

DOS had weaknesses, including a very limited memory space and a remarkable single-mindedness: Only one small application could run at a time. An early attempt to make the PC friendlier was Microsoft Windows. The less said about the early versions, the better, but Microsoft stuck with it. Windows 3.1 actually worked—most of the time—though at heart, it was still just a dressed-up version of DOS. Windows 95, Windows 98, and Windows Me were additional steps toward transcending DOS restrictions.

Right about the time of Windows 3.1, Microsoft embarked on a parallel path to develop an operating system suitable for the more demanding corporate environment: Windows NT. The first version of NT (version 3.1) was also pretty feeble. Few businesses adopted Windows NT until version 3.5, and Windows NT 4 was the first version to be adopted in large numbers for corporate networks.

Microsoft's operating-system efforts have proceeded along two parallel tracks, because each Windows series is built on a different base of computer code. The tracks can work together and communicate with each other, but their basic kernels are not the same.

- **Windows 3.0, Windows 3.1, Windows 95, Windows 98, Windows Millennium Edition (Windows Me).** Microsoft's goal in developing what it now considers its "consumer" versions of Windows was to make them as compatible (with games, add-ons, and older programs) as possible. When that design goal interferes with security and stability, compatibility wins. Thousands upon thousands of different programs run on these operating systems.

- **Windows NT 3.1, Windows NT 3.5 and 3.51, Windows NT 4.0, Windows 2000.** What Microsoft now describes as its "business" Windows versions are designed for maximum stability and security. When those design goals conflict with compatibility, stability and security win. For example, every version of Windows NT worked with fewer applications than the Windows 95 family. (Fortunately, compatibility is less of an issue in Windows 2000.)

In short, Windows 2000 server is the successor to Windows NT 4 server, and Windows 2000 Professional is the successor to Windows NT 4 Workstation.

Windows 2000 Professional

Windows 2000 comes in four versions, three of which are designed for use on network *servers* (central computers that provide services for the ordinary PCs—the *workstations*—in the company). These more expensive Windows 2000 editions (called Windows 2000 Server, Advanced Server, and Datacenter Server) *look* almost exactly like Windows 2000 Professional. In fact, you might not even be able to tell the difference when running your favorite programs. However, the Windows 2000 server editions include a large collection of networking features that generally require a professional network administrator to understand, install, set up, and maintain.

The fourth version, Windows 2000 *Professional*, is the subject of this book. Windows 2000 Pro's primary role is to operate a workstation on a network—preferably a network served by computers running Windows 2000 Server. Windows 2000 Pro, in other words, is the software that drives the PCs on most employees' desks.

Windows 2000 Professional also works very well on workstations in a *peer-to-peer workgroup* (a less complex network that you can set up yourself, without buying a server computer; see Chapter 15). Some people, welcoming its stability, even use Windows 2000 Pro on standalone (non-networked) computers at home or in a business, although the heavy-duty security features of Windows 2000 Pro aren't usually necessary in a home setting.

Getting Ready for Windows

To get the most out of Windows with the least frustration, it helps to become familiar with the following concepts and terms. You'll encounter these words and phrases over and over again—in the built-in Windows help, in computer magazines, and in this book. For example:

Using the Right Mouse Button

One of the most important features of Windows isn't on the screen—it's under your hand. The standard mouse has two mouse buttons. You use the left one to click onscreen buttons, highlight text, and drag things around on the screen.

When you click the right button, however, a *shortcut menu* appears on the screen, like the ones shown in Figure 1-1. Get into the habit of right-clicking things—icons, folders, disks, text in your word processor, buttons on your menu bar, pictures on a Web page, and so on. The commands that appear on the shortcut menu will make you much more productive and lead you to discover handy functions whose existence you may never even have suspected.

Tip: If you're left-handed, you can swap the functions of the right and left mouse buttons easily enough. Click Start→Settings→Control Panel. Then double-click the Mouse icon.

When the Mouse Properties dialog box opens, click the Basics tab, and where it says "Select the mouse button you want to use for most tasks," click Right, then click OK. Windows automatically assumes that you therefore want to use the *left* mouse button as the one that produces shortcut menus.

Figure 1-1:
Shortcut menus (also called context menus*) sometimes list commands that aren't in the menus at the top of the window. Here, for example, are the commands that appear when you right-click a disk icon (left), a document (middle), and a date square in a calendar program (right). Once the shortcut menu has appeared, left-click the command you want.*

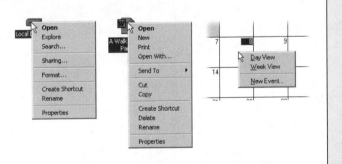

There's More than One Way To Do Everything

No matter what setting you want to adjust, no matter what program you want to open, Microsoft has provided five or six different ways to do it. To delete a file, for example, you can press the Delete key, choose Delete from the menu at the top of a window, use the *DEL* command at the Command Prompt, drag the icon onto the Recycle Bin, or right-click the icon and choose Delete from the shortcut menu.

Optimists point out that this abundance of approaches means that almost everyone will find, and settle on, a satisfying method for each task. Pessimists grumble that there are too many paths to every destination, making it much more difficult to learn Windows. Whenever you find a task has become irksome, remember you have other options.

Windows Wizards Smooth the Way

A *wizard* is a series of screens that walks you through the task you're trying to complete. Wizards make configuration and installation tasks easier by breaking them down into smaller, more easily digested steps. Figure 1-2 shows an example.

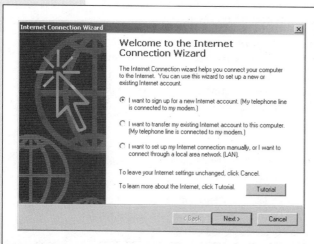

Figure 1-2:
Wizards—interview screens—are everywhere in Windows. On each of the screens, you're supposed to answer a question about your computer or your preferences, and then click a Next button. When you click Finish on the final screen, Windows whirls into action, automatically completing the installation or setup.

UP TO SPEED

Dialog Box Basics

To the joy of the powerful Computer Keyboard lobby, you can manipulate almost every element of a Windows dialog box by pressing keys on the keyboard. If you're among those who feel that using the mouse takes longer to do something, you're in luck.

The rule for navigating a dialog box is simple: Press Tab to jump from one set of options to another, or Shift+Tab to move backward. (If the dialog box has multiple *tabs,* like the one shown here, press Ctrl+Tab to "click" the next tab, or Ctrl+Shift+Tab to "click" the previous one.)

Each time you press Tab, you shift the PC's *focus* to a different control or set of controls. Windows shows you what element has the focus using text highlighting (if it's a text box or drop-down menu) or a dotted-line outline (if it's a button). You can shift the focus in your Web browser or on the desktop, too.

Once you've highlighted a button or checkbox, you can press the Space bar or Enter key to "click" it. If you've highlighted a drop-down menu or set of mutually exclusive *radio buttons* (like the Orientation buttons in the Print dialog box), press the up or down arrow key.

You Could Spend a Lifetime Changing Properties

You can change almost every aspect of the way Windows looks and works. For example, you can replace the gray backdrop of the screen with your favorite photograph, change the typeface used for the names of your icons, or set up a particular program to launch automatically every time you turn on the PC.

When you want to change some *general* behavior of your computer, such as how it connects to the Internet, how soon the screen goes black to save power, and how quickly a letter repeats on the screen when you hold down a key, you use the Control Panel window (see Chapter 8).

Many other times, however, you may want to adjust the settings of only one *particular* element of the machine, such as the hard drive, the Recycle Bin, or a particular application. In those cases, you right-click the corresponding icon. In the resulting

Figure 1-3:
Left: One quick way to find out how much space is left on your hard drive is to right-click it and choose the Properties command.

Right: The Properties dialog box appears, featuring a handy disk-space graph.

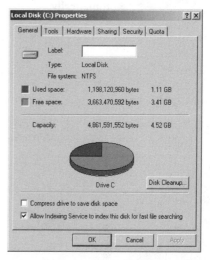

Underlined Letters in Menus

In Windows 95, 98, and Me, there are little underlines in the names of menu commands. I used to be able to open a menu by pressing the underlined letter along with the Alt key, and then trigger a command by pressing its underlined-letter key once the menu is open. I got pretty used to this system—but what happened to it in Windows 2000?

The underlines still appear in your *application* menus; Microsoft hid these keyboard-shortcut indicators only at the Windows 2000 desktop, in an effort to clean up the look of its flagship corporate software. Now they appear only when you press the Alt key.

If you miss the days when the underlines were ever present, choose Start→Settings→Control Panel. Open the Display icon, click the Effects tab, and turn off "Hide keyboard navigation indicators until I use the Alt key." When you click OK, you'll see that the underlines have returned.

shortcut menu, you'll often find a command called Properties. When you click it, a dialog box appears containing settings or information displays about that object, as shown in Figure 1-3.

Every Piece of Hardware Requires Software

A *driver* is the software that translates between your PC's brain and the equipment attached to it. Windows requires a driver for anything you might attach to, or install inside, your computer—the mouse, keyboard, screen, floppy drive, CD-ROM drive, networking circuitry, modem, scanner, digital camera, and PalmPilot, among others. Without the driver software, the corresponding piece of equipment doesn't work at all.

You can read much more about drivers in Chapter 16. For now, it's worth noting that unlike Windows NT, Windows 2000 uses Plug and Play, a system that lets you connect a new gadget to your PC without even having to think about the driver software. In most cases, Windows locates and installs the appropriate software driver automatically.

Starting Up, Logging On, and Shutting Down

Starting and shutting down a computer running Windows 2000 Professional is not simply a matter of turning the machine on and off. If your computer is part of a network, you must *log on* and *log off*. Even if your computer isn't part of a network, there's more to shutting it down properly than just cutting the power.

Logging On

When you *log on to* a Windows 2000 PC, you introduce yourself with a name and password.

What separates Windows 2000 (and Windows NT) from all the other versions of Windows (95, 98, Me) is the element of security. Because Windows 2000 is designed primarily for the business market, you can configure its security to be very tight.

A basic element of network security is the ability to keep out anyone who doesn't belong. Also important is the ability to control who gets to see what folders and files are on the network and who gets to access them. For example, in most companies, the payroll records, profit and loss statements, and customer list are not available for inspection by just anyone on the network.

One way to control access is through the use of *user accounts*. When you log on with a password, Windows 2000 checks your name and password against a user database, either on your PC or a network server, to see if you have an authorized account. Your account specifies what you can do and see on the network.

On many networks, this log-on-to-your-account system confers a second terrific benefit: You can get at your files from any machine on the network (if you've set up your files to be *shared* in this way). You can sit down at the Micron in Manufacturing or the Dell in Design, and still open, and work with, all of the files and folders that are, technically speaking, sitting on your Compaq in Communications. (More on networking in Chapter 13, and user accounts in Chapter 17.)

Note: The logging-on system has the additional effect of making it possible for a central administrator to track everything you do on the network, including which programs you're using and which Web sites you're visiting. This power is mostly used for benign purposes—to track errors and network traffic patterns—but it's something to be aware of. As long as you're logged on, you are on the network (even if you're not sitting at your own computer).

The Log On Dialog Boxes

If you work on a corporate network, the Windows 2000 loading process presents a Welcome to Windows dialog box. Follow the advice now on the screen: Press the Ctrl, Alt, and Delete keys simultaneously.

If you're used to Windows 95 or 98, you're probably used to that "three-fingered salute" serving as an emergency exit from a program that's crashed. At the Welcome to Windows dialog box, however, it summons the Log On to Windows dialog box. Enter your username and password in the boxes provided, and then click OK. (*After* you're logged on, the Ctrl+Alt+Delete combination has a different function; it opens the Windows Security dialog box, from which you can lock your computer, change your password, shut down, or, yes, exit a crashed program.)

UP TO SPEED

When You Don't Need Ctrl+Alt+Delete

If your PC is one of the rare Windows 2000 machines that's not connected to a network, you don't have to begin your day by pressing Ctrl+Alt+Delete at the welcome screen. In fact, when you installed Windows 2000 on such a machine, you were offered a choice: "Users must enter a user name and password to use this computer" or "Windows always assumes the following user has logged on to this computer." If you chose the second option, you don't have to enter a name and password at all.

In other words, on non-networked machines, it's possible that you don't have to log on, or that you can do so without pressing Ctrl+Alt+Delete. (And if you *do* have to type your name and password each time you turn on your non-networked machine, you can eliminate this requirement as described on page 170.)

But if you're among the majority using Windows 2000 Pro on a corporate network, Ctrl+Alt+Delete is part of your morning ritual.

Windows now compares the name and password you typed with a list of authorized user accounts. If you turn out to be an authorized network citizen, your own personalized Windows 2000 desktop appears, as shown on page 28. Otherwise, you're prompted to enter your username and password again—correctly, this time.

Caution: If you enter an incorrect password several times (sometimes as few as three times, depending on the password policy in effect on your network), the system locks you out. You'll have to go to a network administrator to get your password reset—most embarrassing.

Domain vs. Local Machine

If your computer is connected to a Windows 2000 or Windows NT *domain* (see the sidebar box below), the "Log on to:" drop-down menu at the bottom of the Log On dialog box offers an important choice. You can specify whether you want to log on to the *domain* (the whole network) or just to your *local* computer. (If you don't see this drop-down menu, click the Options button.)

Most people almost always choose the domain option; it lets you use the files, printers, and other goodies on the network. If you choose the local option, you can use

---

UP TO SPEED

Network Lingo

If your computer is connected to a network (as most machines running Windows 2000 are), you're likely to be exposed to some perplexing networking terms. You can't avoid them, either in this book or in your Windows 2000 life; here's a crash course in definitions.

A *domain* is a collection of computers, named as a group, that shares the same security policy and has a particular list of users in common. Unless an administrator has specified otherwise, you can log on at any computer in the domain with your user name and password. When you do so, you'll have the same network resources—printers, files, storage space—available to you as you did at your own computer. (You may also hear the term *domain* in discussions about to the Internet. Your Internet email address, for example, includes a domain name [the part after the @ symbol], for example, as do Web addresses. This type of domain is generally completely different from a Windows 2000 domain; be careful not to confuse the two.)

Most small to medium businesses—under a hundred computers—have a single domain. Larger businesses, or those with branch offices, may have several domains, organized into a *tree*. Extremely large businesses may have multiple trees, combined in what's logically called a *forest*, or even multiple forests. However, you'll most likely spend your time in a single domain; if your work involves multiple domains, you'll be told about it.

A *workgroup,* on the other hand, is a group of computers linked by network cables but without a single security policy or list of users. As noted above, in a domain, all the workstations recognize the authority of a domain controller. But in a workgroup, all workstations are considered equal; you have to configure all of the settings for user accounts and shared folders on each computer. If you've got more than about ten computers on your network, setting up accounts for everyone on each computer can quickly become an administrative nightmare (see Chapter 15).

Another term you'll hear frequently is *server*. A server is a computer that supplies certain features—programs or databases, for example—to a *client* computer (your PC).

For example, a computer that controls one or more printers on the network is called a *print server*. A print server knows which printouts go to which printer and whose printouts get priority. Somewhere on the Internet, servers dish out your email and Web pages, too.

Servers are also often hidden away in a back room (although on a smaller network, a server can also perform double duty as a workstation). All the computers in a domain that aren't controllers or servers are called *workstations* (another term for clients). These are the computers used by mere mortals.

---

your computer as though it's cut off from the network. (You *must* log on to the local machine to perform many system configuration tasks and install new hardware.) However, note that this drop-down menu remembers its setting from logon to logon. If someone logged onto your computer locally earlier today, you may inadvertently log on to your local computer account, too. (You'll notice the problem soon enough, when your PC doesn't "see" the network.) To make sure that you are indeed logging onto the domain, click the Options button, and select your domain from the "Log on to:" drop-down list box.

Logging Off

When it's time to bid farewell to your computer for some time, it's advisable to *log off* to secure your computer against unauthorized access.

Active Directory

On a network driven by Windows 2000 *Server*, the various Windows 2000 network entities, such as domains, trees, and forests, are listed, organized, and maintained in a centralized database on your network called the *Active Directory*. The average Windows 2000 Professional user may not even be aware of Active Directory, but it's the single most important new feature of Windows 2000 Server. It's a *directory service*, a database of the hardware, software, and people on a network.

On a network that uses Active Directory, every computer, printer, and user is represented by an *object* in the database. Each object is composed of *attributes* (properties) that describe it. For example, a user object's attributes specify her name, location, telephone number, email address, and other more technical elements.

Active Directory enables network administrators to create, troubleshoot, and maintain an enormous hierarchy of computers, if necessary, encompassing virtually any number of users, computers, and domains. Windows 2000 Server configures relationships between the domains automatically. A multinational corporation with tens of thousands of users in offices all over the world can all be part of one Active Directory, consisting of servers distributed in hundreds of locations, all connected by wide-area networking links.

The Active Directory information is stored on Windows 2000 Server systems that have been designated as domain controllers. A *domain controller* is a computer that stores all or part of the Active Directory database and keeps track of who is allowed to log on, who *is* logged on, and what each user is allowed to do on the network. When you log on to the domain, your system communicates with a domain controller, which verifies your credentials and permits (or denies) you access. The domain controllers on a network communicate with each other constantly, in order to keep their information updated. Even a small domain usually has at least two domain controllers, in case one should fail; larger domains can have many more. Even though they look just like Windows 2000 Professional systems, the computers that act as domain controllers usually aren't used as ordinary workstations for everyday work. In fact, they're often secreted away somewhere, such as a server closet or a data center; only administrators have physical access to them.

Unless you're a highly-paid network guru, you don't have to worry about any of this Active Directory activity; it all goes on behind the scenes. You're likely to hear it mentioned only rarely, such as when your administrator shows you how to use it for finding information about other users in the company using the Search program described in Chapter 3.

The easiest way to log off is to press Ctrl+Alt+Delete to summon the Windows Security dialog box; then click the Logoff button. Windows 2000 Pro asks if you're sure; if you are, click Yes (or press Enter). You'll be logged off after a few seconds.

Alternatively, you can choose Start→Shut Down; in the resulting dialog box, choose Log Off [Your Name] from the drop-down menu, and then click OK (or press Enter).

When you log off the system, Windows 2000 closes any applications that you may have left running. However, the *services* running on the machine continue to operate. A service is a program that runs in the background whenever Windows 2000 is running. For example, the function that makes your chosen files and folders available to other people on the network is called the *Server* service. They can continue to access the files on your machine, even after you've logged off.

Tip: If you're going away from your desk for only a short time, you can set up a password-protected screen saver. When the screen saver activates, you're still logged on, but your desktop is protected. You can return to it by simply entering the password. For details, see page 141.

Or, for more security and less waiting, press Ctrl+Alt+Delete to summon the Windows Security dialog box, and then click Lock Computer.

Shutting Down

Logging off means that *you* are no longer on the computer, but the *computer* is still turned on. Before turning the computer off at the power switch, you should run the shutdown procedure, so that Windows has a chance to sort itself out, save changes, quit open programs, and close connections to other computers.

You can shut down by pressing Ctrl+Alt+Delete (to summon the Windows Security dialog box) and then clicking the Shutdown button. Or you can choose Start→Shut Down. Either way, the Shut Down Windows dialog box (Figure 2-1) appears on your screen.

Figure 2-1:
Click the drop-down list button for the shutdown choices. Choose Shut Down to turn the computer off, or Restart to exit Windows and then restart Windows without turning the computer off. You can add "Stand by" and "Hibernate" options, if your PC offers them, using the Power Options control panel (see page 163). (These commands are primarily used on laptops.)

Tip: If other people on the network require access to files or folders that you've shared on your machine, log off instead of shutting down. That way, your PC's shared files remain available to others on the network, but the machine is still safe from inspection by somebody who sits down at your desk while you're away.

The drop-down menu offers these options:

- **Log Off [Your Name]** leaves the computer on, awaiting the next person who logs on.

- **Shut Down** quits all open programs, offers you the opportunity to save any unsaved documents, and then exits Windows. Most modern PCs then turn off automatically. If yours doesn't, you see a message on the screen telling you it's safe to turn off your computer; only now should you manually flip off the power switch.

  If you don't run the shutdown procedure, you won't get any complaints from Windows. In fact, when you turn the power back on, Windows 2000 Pro will start up, usually without a quibble. But shutting off the power without using the Shut Down command can result in lost data, and will cause severe unhappiness to anyone on the network who's connected to your computer.

- **Restart** quits all open programs, and then starts Windows again automatically. The computer doesn't turn off. (You might do this to "refresh" your computer when you notice that it's responding sluggishly, for example.)

- **Standby** puts your computer to "sleep." This special state of PC consciousness reduces the amount of electricity the computer uses. The machine remains in suspended animation until you use the mouse or keyboard to begin working again. That's a handy feature when, for example, you're on a plane; you can take a food break without closing all your programs and shutting down your laptop—and still avoid running down the battery.

  Note that your PC offers a Standby option only if (a) your computer's circuitry offers this feature, and (b) you activate it using the APM (Advanced Power Management) tab of the Power Options control panel (see page 163).

- **Hibernate**, a new feature in Windows 2000, shuts down the machine after it *memorizes* the state of your software, including all open operating system files, applications, and documents. Behind the scenes, it saves all this memorized information into a file on your hard disk. (As a result, the Hibernate command doesn't work unless you have free disk space equal to the amount of RAM in your computer.)

  You can configure your computer to hibernate automatically after a period of inactivity, and to require a password to bring it out of hibernation. See page 164.

  The beauty of this feature is that when you start the computer again, everything returns to the way it was when you shut down—*fast*. The same documents appear, the same programs are running, and so on. Hibernate, in other words, offers the speed and convenience of Standby, with the safety of Shut Down.

Note: The Hibernate command doesn't appear in the Shut Down Options dialog box until you put it there. Do so by visiting Power Options (see page 162), clicking the Hibernate tab, and turning on "Enable hibernate support."

Furthermore, some older computers don't come with the necessary circuitry (technically, *BIOS support*) for the Hibernate command. In that case, the Hibernate choice doesn't appear as a tab in the Power Options tool.

The Desktop and Start Menu

The first time you turn on a PC after installing Windows 2000 (or after unpacking a new PC that has Windows 2000 preinstalled), you encounter a Getting Started wizard that offers three choices:

- **Register Now.** Register your copy of Windows 2000 with Microsoft, so that you're eligible for exciting new streams of junk mail.

- **Discover Windows.** Take a quick tour of Windows 2000 features (you'll be asked to insert your installation CD).

- **Connect to the Internet.** Sign up for an Internet account using the Internet Connection Wizard (see page 220).

Once you're beyond this big hello, however, you encounter the digital vista shown in Figure 3-1, a screen that greets tens of millions of people every morning: the Windows *desktop*.

The Windows 2000 Desktop

The desktop is the backdrop for all activities in Windows 2000. The desktop is a virtual desk that holds virtual folders and files while you work; depending on your personality type, it can attract lots of junk.

The standard Windows 2000 Pro installation puts these icons on your desktop:

- **My Documents.** The My Documents folder is a handy storage place for your letters, memos, and other work files. Most modern programs propose saving any new files you create into this folder.

On some networks, you may be required to place *all* your work in this folder, so that your files will be included when the network performs a system-wide backup. On other networks, you may be required to put you files anyplace *except* My Documents.

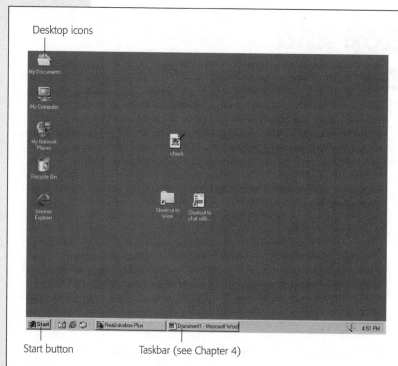

Desktop icons

Start button

Taskbar (see Chapter 4)

Figure 3-1:
Everything you'll ever do on a Windows 2000 Pro computer begins with a click on one of these three elements: a desktop icon, the Start button, or the Taskbar, which is described in Chapter 4. Some people find this default desktop too cluttered already, and promptly delete some of the icons they'll never use. Others place even more icons on the desktop—favorite programs and documents—for quicker access. Let your personality be your guide.

• **My Computer** is the trunk lid, the doorway to every single shred of software on your machine. When you double-click My Computer, a window opens to reveal icons that represent each disk drive in your machine, as shown in Figure 3-2. (Note to power users: Technically, My Computer shows a different icon for each hard drive *partition*.)

By double-clicking, for example, your hard drive icon, and then the various folders on it, you can eventually see the icons for every single file and folder on your computer.

Note: The My Computer window shows you an icon for each disk drive in your machine—floppy drive, Zip drive, CD-ROM drive, and so on—whether or not there's actually a disk in that drive. If you try to double-click one of these icons when the corresponding drive is empty, you'll get nothing but a confusing error message. (It tells you that the drive "isn't ready," which isn't the problem at all.)

• **Internet Explorer** opens the Internet browser that comes with Windows (see Chapter 11).

- **Recycle Bin.** You delete a file or folder by dragging it onto this icon. You can read more about this special icon on page 96.

Figure 3-2:
This computer has one floppy drive, one hard drive, and one CD-ROM drive. For your convenience, you also get a link to the Control Panel folder (see Chapter 8). If you click an icon to select it, Windows politely shows you a description on the left side of the window. If there's a disk in the CD-ROM drive, you get to see its name, not just its drive letter.

How to Find the Desktop on Your Hard Drive

Although the Windows 2000 desktop is easy to see both in Windows Explorer and, well, on your desktop, it's actually represented by a *folder* on your hard drive. Windows 2000 maintains a separate set of settings—a *user profile*—for each person who uses your PC. This profile includes the information that describes the icons that you like to leave lying on the desktop, the way you've arranged your Start menu, the picture you've plastered across your desktop, and so on. (See page 374 for more on user profiles.)

Windows 2000 keeps each person's user profile in the My Computer→C:→Documents and Settings folder, as shown here.

The desktop *folder* is inside the subfolder corresponding to your user profile. (You'll also find folders here that represent the contents of your Start menu, My Documents folder, Favorites folder, and so on—all of which are unique to *your* user profile.) One way to place a shortcut on the desktop, therefore, is simply to copy it to the Desktop folder in your user profile folder.

- **My Network Places** provides links to other machines on your network, as well as tools for making those links. For more on networking and using this icon, see Chapters 13, 14, and 15.

- **Outlook Express** is an email program you can use to send and receive email and read the messages on Internet *newsgroups* (bulletin boards). See Chapter 12 for more on Outlook Express.

- **Connect to the Internet** launches the Internet Connection Wizard described in Chapter 11.

Some people maintain that the desktop is best kept clean, and that all document files should be put away in their proper locations (such as the My Documents folder). Other people believe that every useful icon (or its *shortcut*—see page 101) should be placed on the desktop for easy access. Needless to say, the second approach leads to a fair amount of clutter and can make finding things difficult—just like a messy desk. However, if things become too chaotic, you can always right-click a blank spot on the desktop (assuming you can find one) and choose Arrange Icons or Line Up Icons from the shortcut menu. Doing so doesn't make your desktop any less cluttered, but at least it nudges all of your desktop icons so that they all line up nicely.

The Start Menu

If you're willing to double-click 65 times in succession, opening folder after folder, the disk icons in the My Computer window eventually lead you to every single file in your computer. The vast majority of the files and folders you'll encounter are utterly useless to you personally; they're support files, there for behind-the-scenes use by Windows and your applications.

That's why the Start menu is so important—it lists almost every *useful* piece of software on your computer, including commands, programs, and files you've been working on recently. You can use the Start menu to open your applications, install new software, configure hardware, get help, find files, and much more.

When you click the Start button, the Start menu pops open, fading into view. Its contents depend on which options you (or your network administrator) selected when installing Windows, but Figure 3-3 shows a representative example.

Tip: If you're a keyboard-shortcut lover, you can open the Start menu by pressing the Windows-logo key that's usually on the top or bottom row of your keyboard. (If you're using one of those antique, kerosene-powered keyboards that lack a Windows key, press Ctrl+Esc instead.)

In fact, if your mouse ever stops working, you can always use one of these keyboard methods to get to the Shut Down command on the Start menu. Then press the up or down arrow keys to highlight the Start-menu commands; press Enter to "click" that command.

Start menu items graced by a right-pointing triangle arrow (such as Settings in Figure 3-3) have *submenus*. As you move your mouse pointer over an item that has such an arrow, the submenu, listing additional options, pops out to the right (you don't have to click). Many submenu items have arrows of their own, indicating *additional* submenus.

This discussion describes the items in the Start menu from the bottom up, the way your mouse encounters them as it moves up from the Start button.

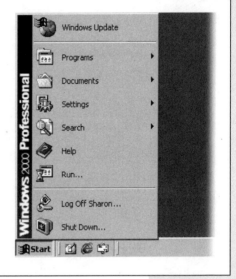

Figure 3-3:
Thin etched lines divide the sections of the Start Menu. In the beginning, the top section holds only Windows Update (a link to Microsoft's software-updates Web page); but you can add your own favorite programs and documents to this list, and such programs as Microsoft Office and Corel Suite also install commands here. The main section contains the items you'll use most. The bottom section is conveniently located for a quick logoff or shutdown.

Start→Shut Down

The Shut Down menu item is more powerful than its name implies. Choosing it opens a dialog box that offers several variations on "off," as described at the end of the previous chapter.

Tip: You can also summon the Shut Down dialog box by clicking the desktop and then pressing Alt+F4, or by pressing Ctrl+Alt+Delete and then clicking Shut Down.

Start→Run

Use the Run menu item to summon a dialog box containing a *command line*, as shown in Figure 3-4. A command line is a text-based method of performing a task. You type a command and click OK; something happens as a result. (The Run dialog is the functional equivalent of the Command Prompt, except with a graphical interface that enables you to browse for a particular file, if you like.)

Working at the command line is becoming a lost art in the world of Windows, because most people prefer to issue commands by choosing from menus using the mouse.

However, some old-timers still love the command line, and even mouse-lovers encounter situations where a typed command is the *only* way to do something.

If you're a PC veteran, your head probably teems with neat Run commands you've picked up over the years. If you're new to this idea, however, here are a few of the useful and timesaving things you can do with the Run box:

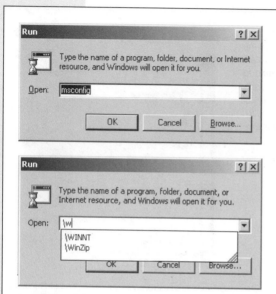

Figure 3-4:
Top: The last Run command you entered appears automatically in the Open text box. You can use the drop-down list to see a list of commands you've previously entered.

Bottom: The Run command knows the names of all of your folders. As you type, you're shown the best match for the characters you're typing. When the name of the folder you're trying to open appears in the list, click it to avoid having to type the rest of the entry.

Launch a Program

As noted later in this discussion, one of the most important Start menu commands is the Programs submenu, where you'll find the name of almost every application on your computer. You can open one of these programs by typing its *program file name* in the Open box and then pressing Enter. That's an extremely useful shortcut for both pros and novices alike, because it's frequently faster to launch a program this way than to use the Start→Programs menu.

Unfortunately, the program file name isn't the same as its plain-English name; it's an abbreviated version. For example, if you want to open Microsoft Word, you must type *winword*. That's the actual name of the Word program icon as it sits in your My Computer→C: drive→Program Files→Microsoft Office→Office folder. Some other common program-file names are shown here:

Program's real name	Program's familiar name
iexplore	Internet Explorer
msworks	Microsoft Works
msinm	Outlook Express
wmplayer	Windows Media Player
palm	Palm Desktop
sol	Solitaire
regedit	Registry Editor
calc	Calculator
…and so on.	

Tip: To discover the program file name of a favorite program, see "Which One's the Program?" on page 55.

If, like efficiency freaks worldwide, you believe that it's generally faster and more efficient to use the keyboard rather than the mouse, get this: You can perform this entire application-launching stunt without using the mouse at all. Just follow these steps in rapid succession:

1. **Press the Windows-logo key on the bottom or top row of your keyboard.**

   Doing so makes the Start menu pop open.

2. **Press the letter R key.**

   That's the underlined letter for the Run command, whose box now opens.

3. **Type the program file's name.**

   If you've typed it before, just type a couple of letters; Windows fills in the rest of the name automatically.

4. **Press Enter.**

   Windows opens the requested program instantly. Keystrokes: 4, Mouse: 0.

Launch Any Program or Document

Using the Run dialog box is handy for launching favorite applications, because it requires so few keystrokes. But you can also use the Run dialog box to open *any* file on the computer—if you're willing to do some additional typing.

The trick here is to type in the entire *path* of the program or document you want. (See the sidebar box on page 32 if you're new to the idea of file paths.) For example, to open the budget spreadsheet that's in your Projections folder, you might type *c:\projections\budget*.

Tip: Typing the path in this way is also useful for launching applications that don't appear in the Start→Programs menu. For example, some advanced Windows utilities (including *RegEdit*, an advanced program described in Chapter 19) are accessible only through the command line. (If a program doesn't appear in the Start menu, you may have to type its entire path name.)

You can also use the Run command to open some older DOS programs that don't come with a listing in the Programs menu. (On the other hand, making a shortcut to such a program, as described in Chapter 5, is probably easier.)

Open a Drive Window

When you double-click the My Computer icon on your desktop, you'll discover that Windows assigns a letter of the alphabet to each disk drive attached to your machine—the hard drive, CD-ROM drive, floppy drive, and so on. The floppy drive is always A:, one hard drive is always C:, and so on. (There hasn't been a drive B: since the demise of the two-floppy computer.)

By typing a drive letter followed by a colon (for example, *c:*) into the Run box and pressing Enter, you make a window pop open, displaying the contents of that drive.

Open a Folder Window

You can also use the Run dialog box to open the window for any folder on your machine. To do so, type a backslash followed by the name of a folder (see Figure 3-5, bottom). You might type, for example, *\Downloads* to see your downloaded files. To open a folder whose name includes spaces (such as Program Files), enclose the entire command in quotes (*"\Program Files"*), or include the drive letter (*c:\Program Files*).

Note: The Run command assumes that you're opening a folder on Drive C. If you want to open a folder on a different drive, or if you have identically-named folders on two or more drives, add the drive letter and a colon before the name of the folder (for example, *D:\data*).

Furthermore, if the folder you want to display is nested several layers deep, you must specify the entire path to that folder from the root of the drive, as in *\Downloads\Music\MP3*—not just *\MP3*.

You can even open a folder that's sitting on some other computer on the network. To do so, you use the folder's UNC path name: type two backslashes, the computer's name, and the shared folder's name. For instance, to access a shared folder called Budgets on a computer named Admin, enter *\\admin\budgets.* (See Chapters 13 and 15 for more on sharing folders over the network; see page 32 for more on UNC path notation.)

Tip: In any of these cases, if you don't remember the precise name of a file or folder you want to open in the Run dialog box, click the Browse button to display the Browse dialog box, as shown in Figure 3-5.

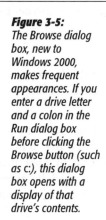

Figure 3-5:
The Browse dialog box, new to Windows 2000, makes frequent appearances. If you enter a drive letter and a colon in the Run dialog box before clicking the Browse button (such as c:), this dialog box opens with a display of that drive's contents.

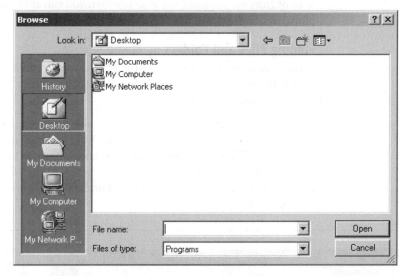

Connect to a Web Page

Here's another use for the Run dialog box: You can launch your Web browser (such as Internet Explorer) and jump directly to a specific Web page by typing its Web address (URL), such as *www.realbigcompany.com,* and then pressing Enter.

Again, you may not have to type very much; the pop-up list in the Run box lists every URL you've previously entered. Click one (or press the down arrow to highlight the one you want, and then press Enter) to go there.

Start→Help

Choosing Start→Help opens the Windows Help window, which is described in Chapter 6.

Tip: Speed fans have an alternative to using the mouse to open the Help window—just click the desktop (to make sure it has the focus) and then press the F1 key.

Start→Search

The humble Search command looks no more special than anything else on the Start menu. But in fact, it's a powerhouse, and you'll probably use it often. The Search function (which was called Find in Windows NT, 95, and 98) can quickly find all kinds of computery things: file and folder icons, computers on your network, email addresses and phone numbers, Web sites, and even maps that pinpoint any address in the United States and Canada.

If the Search program looks vaguely familiar, that's because it's actually a component of Internet Explorer, the Web browser. You can read more about Internet Explorer in Chapter 11.

Finding Files and Folders by Name

If you save your new files only in the My Documents folder on the desktop, you'll have little need to use the Search function to locate your files. You'll always know where they are—right in that folder.

Every now and then, however, you won't be able to remember where you filed something, or you'll download something from the Internet and not be able to find it again, or you'll install something and not know where to look for it. In those situations, the Search program, shown in Figure 3-6, is just what you need. It lets you look for a particular file or folder based on its description—by its name, size, date stamp, and so on.

Figure 3-6:
When you're looking for files, the Search feature is like having a bloodhound available. You can use as much information as you manage to remember to initiate a search, and it doesn't matter if you can't remember the exact name of the file that's gone missing. The Search feature ordinarily finds both folder titles and filenames; to search only for files, add .* to the end of the name you're looking for (for example, memo.*).

Setting up the search

A typical search goes like this:

1. **Choose Start→Search→For Files and Folders.**

   The Search window appears, as shown in Figure 3-6.

2. **Specify what disk you want to search, using the "Look in:" drop-down menu.**

   Every disk attached to your PC at that moment—your hard drive, Zip disk, CD-ROM, and so on—shows up here in this list. Most of the time, you just want to search your C: drive; ensure that "Local Hard Drives (C:)" appears in the "Look in:" box, and then proceed.

Tip: If you know that the file or folder you're looking for is on a particular disk or in a certain folder, double-click the icon for that disk or folder, and then press the F3 key at the top of the keyboard. Doing so splits the disk or folder window in half—the left half now contains the Search controls, which are already set up to search only inside that disk or folder window. In other words, you're spared the first two steps of this search setup business. (Press F3 again to remove the Search panel.)

You can also limit your search to a specific folder on your hard drive by typing its path into the "Look in:" blank.

---

3. **To find a file whose name you know, type its name into the top field.**

   You don't have to type the entire filename—only enough of it to distinguish it from the other files on your computer. Capitals don't matter, and neither does the position of the letters you type—if you type *John,* Windows will find files with names Johnson, Peterjohn, and DiJohnson.

   You can also search for all files of a specific type, such as all Word files, by typing **.doc*—that is, an asterisk, a period, and then the three-letter filename extension of the kind of file you want. In this context, the asterisk is a wildcard meaning, "any text at all."

   To narrow the search, you can enter both a partial name *and* an extension, such as *mom*.doc,* which will turn up Word files named Mom's Finances.doc, Moment of Truth.doc, and so on.

4. **Restrict the search even more by clicking Search Options, if you like.**

   Searching for a file by typing in a few letters of its name is by far the most frequently used Search function. But in certain circumstances, you may want to narrow the search by confining it to only files you created yesterday, for example.

   When you click Search Options, you get the panel shown in Figure 3-7. The **Date** controls let you find only files or folders you created or changed in a certain date range; the **Type** checkbox restricts your search to a particular *type* of file (Acrobat documents, applications, JPG images, and so on); and the **Size** checkbox lets you screen out files larger or smaller than a number of KB you specify.

Finally, if you turn on the Advanced Options checkbox, you're offered three final choices. **Search subfolders** makes Windows look inside all folders *inside* the disk or folder you've specified. Turn this option off only when you know for sure that the file you need is in the disk or folder you're starting with, but *not* within any subfolders there. Skipping the subfolders makes the search process much faster. **Case sensitive** instructs the Search program to match the capitalization of the characters you enter; searching for files containing "dentist appointment" won't find files containing "Dentist appointment" (with a capital D). **Search slow files** refers to files on removable storage devices—optical or tape drives. Without turning on this option, you may have to copy these files to other, faster disks (like a hard drive) before you can search them.

Windows uses the criteria you enter in these fields *in addition* to any data you entered into the basic search fields.

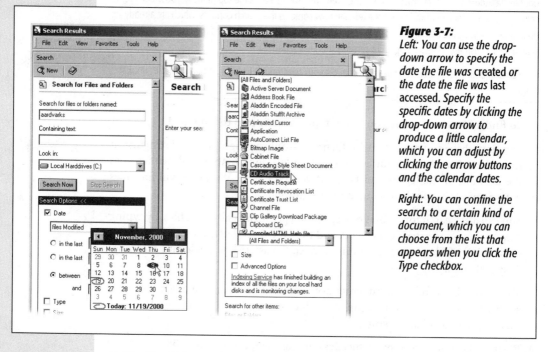

Figure 3-7:
Left: You can use the drop-down arrow to specify the date the file was created or the date the file was last accessed. Specify the specific dates by clicking the drop-down arrow to produce a little calendar, which you can adjust by clicking the arrow buttons and the calendar dates.

Right: You can confine the search to a certain kind of document, which you can choose from the list that appears when you click the Type checkbox.

5. **Finally, click Search Now (or press Enter).**

   A couple of seconds later, the screen changes. On the right side of the screen, you now see a list of files and folders whose names contain what you typed in the blank. (Figure 3-8 shows this list.)

Using your search results

Figure 3-8 shows the splendor of the Search Results window. At this point, you can proceed in many different ways:

- **Read the complete name.** If the Name column is too narrow to show the entire name of a file, use your arrow cursor to point to it without clicking. A pop-up *tooltip* appears, showing the complete name.

- **Read all about it.** If you click the name of a found icon, the top part of the window displays a little paragraph identifying the file's path, full name, and modification date and time. (This feature is shown in Figure 3-8.)

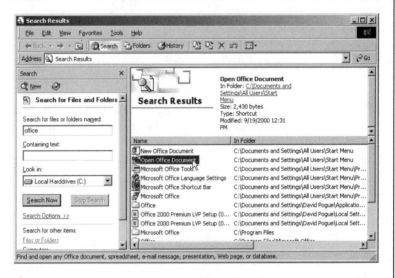

Figure 3-8:
You can manipulate the found files much the way you'd approach files in a standard folder window. For example, you can highlight something in the list by typing the first few of letters of its name or by pressing the arrow keys. You can also highlight multiple icons: Highlight all by choosing Edit→Select All, highlight individual items by clicking with the Ctrl key pressed, drag vertically to enclose a cluster of them, and so on.

- **Find out where something is.** The column just to the right of an icon's name shows you exactly where it is on your machine, using the standard Windows path notation described on page 32. (You may have to widen the column to see the complete path name; to do so, drag the dividing line at the top of the column, to the right of the In Folder column heading.)

- **Open the file.** If one of the found files is the one you were looking for, double-click it to open it. This, in fact, is what most people do most of the time when using the Search program. In many cases, you'll never even know or care *where* the file was—you just want to get into it.

- **Jump to an icon in its home folder.** If you want to get your mouse on the icon itself, without opening it yet, you can use a new Windows feature. Right-click the icon in the Search window and choose Open Containing Folder from the short-cut menu. The Search window instantly retreats to the background, as Windows highlights the actual icon in question, sitting there in its window wherever it happens to be on your hard drive.

- **Move, copy, or delete the file.** You can drag an item directly out of the found-files list onto the desktop, directly onto the Recycle Bin icon, or into a different folder, window, or disk. (If you press Ctrl as you drag, you make a *copy* of the file. For more on copying and moving icons, and the hazards thereof, see Chapter 5.)

- **Send To, Rename, or Create Shortcut.** After highlighting an icon (or icons) in the list of found files, you can use any of the commands in the File menu: Send To (which lets you move the icon to one of several standard folders), Rename, and so on. (See page 101 for more on shortcuts.)

Tip: You can right-click a found icon to copy, move, rename, or create a shortcut of it. Just choose from the resulting shortcut menu.

- **Adjust the list.** By clicking the column headings of the results window, you can sort the list of found files in various ways: by name, size, date, and so on. (You can reverse the order by clicking the column heading a second time.) You can also adjust the relative widths of the columns by dragging the column-name dividers. (You can also drag the lower-right corner of the window to make it bigger or smaller.)

Tip: Press the F3 key to hide the search-criteria panel that occupies the left part of the window. The results portion of the window now fills the screen, making it easier for you to see what you've got. Press F3 a second time to restore the criteria panel.

- **Save the search setup.** By choosing File→Save Search, you can immortalize the search you've just set up. You might use this feature if you perform the same search each day—if, for example, you like to round up all the documents you created yesterday for backing up.

  Windows automatically names the search file with a description it derives from the criteria you entered into the search fields, and adds the extension *.fnd* (for example, *files named News.fnd*). You can save the resulting search icon anywhere you like.

GEM IN THE ROUGH

Using Search to Clean Up Your Drive

You don't have to restrict your use of the Search feature to finding files you can't locate on your own. You can use its power to gather files for general hard-drive housekeeping.

If you have files about the same subject scattered in a variety of folders, you can use the Search command to gather them together. For example, search for all files with the word "budget" in the filename. Create a new folder, select all the found files in the Search Results Pane (documents, spreadsheets, accounting reports, and so on), and drag any *one* of them into the new folder to move them en masse.

You can also search for the backup files your software creates, such as files with the extensions *.xlk* (Microsoft Excel) or *.wbk* (Microsoft Word). They take up disk space, and you'll probably never use them. You can round them up using the Search command, and then delete them as a group from the Search Results window.

To use the search criteria again, double-click the saved .fnd file. The Search window opens, with your data already entered. Click Search Now to put the canned search underway.

Tip: You can make searching for words much faster by turning on the Indexing Service (see the sidebar below).

Searching for Computers

If you type in the name of a computer, the Search program tries to find it on the network. If you enter *part* of the computer's name, the search function locates all matching characters; for example, if you search for *ac,* the search will turn up *accounts, packages,* and so on. There's no browse function; you have to know at least part of the name of the computer you want to find.

Of course, if you're trying to find another PC on the network, you can simply double-click the My Network Places desktop icon, which shows you icons representing all the computers on your network. So why would you ever use the Search function to find a computer? Because it sometimes finds computers that My Network Places can't.

Searching the Internet

Because the Search feature is, behind the scenes, Internet Explorer, it's already set up to search for information on the World Wide Web (if you have an Internet account). See Chapter 11 for much more about the Internet and surfing the Web.

GEM IN THE ROUGH

Using the Indexing Service

The Windows 2000 Search command can locate words inside your files—a handy feature when you're trying to turn up a document whose contents you know, but whose name you can't remember. Unfortunately, this searching-for-words function is painfully slow.

If you're willing to sacrifice some disk space in the name of faster word searching, Windows 2000's *Indexing Service* may be the answer.

It works by reading and cataloging your text-based documents: text files, HTML documents, Microsoft Office files, and Internet email. (You can make the Indexing Service understand other kinds of documents, too, if you buy additional filters made by third-party software companies.) Once Windows 2000 has created this index, it can pinpoint text or file properties with impressive speed.

To index your files, choose Start→Search→For Files or Folders. Click the Search Options hyperlink and then click Indexing Service. A dialog box asks if you wish to enable Indexing Service. Click Yes, and then click OK. The Indexing service starts and works automatically in the background, creating a file that takes up about 25 percent as much disk space as the documents it indexes. (It tosses out unhelpful words like *the, of,* and *a,* and performs other compression tricks to reduce the index file size.)

Once the Indexing Service has completed its analysis of the files on your machine, you don't need to do anything special when searching for words inside your files. Just enjoy the amazing speed with which your Search program can now round up files according to their contents or properties—and enjoy the fact that the Indexing Service will *continue* to keep itself up to date, automatically indexing any files you create or edit.

If the Search window is open, you can click the Internet button shown at its lower left corner. If not, choose Start→Search→On the Internet.

Either way, there's an area to type in what you're looking for on the left side of the window, as shown in Figure 3-9. If you click Customize, you see a list of popular *search engines* or *search providers*—Web pages that search the Internet, such as Yahoo or AltaVista. And if you turn on the "Use the Search Assistant for smart searching" button at the top of the Customize dialog box, you can even set up a search of more than one search engine simultaneously. That's especially handy when you realize that each Internet search engine actually "knows about" only 30 percent of the world's Web pages.

To conduct a search, first select the kind of search you want. The list at the top left corner of this window offers several options (see Figure 3-9):

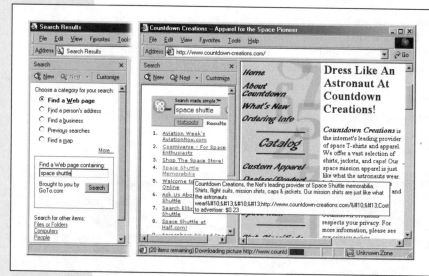

Figure 3-9:
Left: Windows is prepared to search the entire World Wide Web for "space shuttle."

Right: The matching Web pages. Point to one without clicking to read the first paragraph on that page, as shown here, or click the name of a page to view the actual Web site.

Find a Web page

This is the function you might expect when you choose Start→Search→Internet. It lets you search the World Wide Web for a particular phrase, such as *space shuttle* or *Harry Potter*. After typing the phrase, click Search Now (or press Enter).

If you're online (or have set up your PC to dial the Internet automatically, as described on page 225), Windows now sends your search request to the selected Web pages. After a moment, you get a list of results on the left side of the window (Figure 3-9, right). Here's what you can do with one of these results:

- **Read the first paragraph.** Using your arrow cursor, point to one of the Web pages listed in the search results; as shown in Figure 3-9, Windows shows you the first paragraph or so of text that appears on that Web page. This blurb is a useful preview that can save you the effort of opening (and waiting for) that Web page, only to find that it's not what you were looking for.

- **Go to the Web page.** Click one of the listings to view the actual page in the larger right portion of the window.

Find a person's address

This function makes Windows send your search request to an Internet "White Pages" Web site, exactly as described in the next section. This time, however, you can search several of these sites simultaneously, which greatly increases the odds that you'll find the person you're looking for.

To do so, click the Customize button. The Customize dialog box appears, as shown in Figure 3-10. Scroll down to see the checkboxes for the "Find a Person's Address" category; turn on as many as you'd like. Click OK.

From the Search For drop-down menu, specify what you're looking for—"mailing address" or "email address"—and then type in the first name, last name, and (if you know it) city and state or province. When you click Search (or press Enter), Windows returns a list of matches. Click one to view that person's complete address and phone number.

Figure 3-10:
When you use the Search command to find Internet-based information, you're actually searching several Web sites simultaneously. The Customize dialog box lets you specify which ones you want the command to search. If you scroll down far enough, you'll see similar checkboxes for the other kinds of Web searches, such as "Find a business" and "Find a map."

Find a business

Think of this option as a worldwide Yellow Pages directory. Click Customize to view a list of the Yellow-Pages Web sites that Windows is prepared to search. For the best odds of turning up the company you want to find, turn on *all* of the checkboxes.

This time, type in the name or type a business (depending on your selection from the Search By drop-down list), such as *auto glass* or *pediatricians*. Specify the city and state or province you want to search, and then press Enter. This function works remarkably well; it comes in especially handy when you're traveling in a strange city and find yourself in sudden, desperate need of a drugstore, hospital, or bowling alley.

Previous searches

Click this button to view a tidy list of the Internet searches you've most recently performed. Click one to repeat that search; the Internet is constantly changing, and you're likely to turn up different results each time you search.

Find a map

It's one of the miracles of the Internet: You can type in almost any street address in the United States or Canada, and get a map, as detailed as you want it (see Figure 3-11). It's free, and it's all built right into the Windows search function.

Figure 3-11:
Once Windows shows you the map of the address you specified, click the Zoom Level controls to magnify or reduce the scale of the map. You can also view adjacent chunks of the map by clicking the Map Mover arrow buttons.

Tip: As great as the Search feature is, invoking it is a lot of work. You have to click, for example, Start→Search→On the Internet; by Windows standards, that's a colossal expenditure of energy.

Fortunately, there are faster ways to summon the Search feature. While holding down the Windows-logo key, you can press the letter-F key. You can also click the Search button on the toolbar of any folder or disk window—or, if there's no toolbar, you can choose File→Search.

Searching for People

This tantalizing option lets you type in somebody's name; the Search program can consult any of several "White Pages" Web sites online in an attempt to track down that person's email address and telephone number. It can also search your own Windows address book when you want to check someone's phone number or other information.

To try out this feature, choose Start→Search→People. The dialog box shown in Figure 3-12 appears.

Searching your address book

The Start→Search→People command brings up the dialog box shown in Figure 3-12. Windows 2000 assumes that you want to search your network's Active Directory (see page 22) for a certain name or phone number, but you can use the drop-down menu to confine your search to your own PC's address book instead. Enter information in one or more fields, and then click Find Now. All matching entries appear at the bottom of the window, also shown in Figure 3-12.

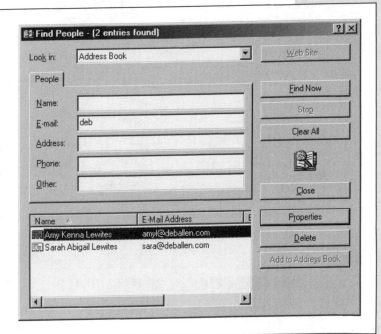

Figure 3-12:
Fill in whatever you know about the person you want to find (top). You can use partial words. The Search command produces a list of all matches (bottom). As shown here, if you're trying to find an email address for somebody at a company, you don't even have to know the company's full domain name. Select the entry that matches your quest, and then click Properties to see all the information you've collected about that person.

Searching phone books on the Internet

No matter how social a person you are, it's theoretically possible somebody out there has managed to elude your Address Book or your company's Active Directory. There may be times that you want to look up the phone number or email address of someone who's not even in the local phone book. Fortunately, you live in the Internet age where a number of Web sites serve as worldwide White Pages. The Search→People command can access these Web sites automatically.

Use the "Look in:" drop-down menu (see Figure 3-13) to display a list of these people-finding Web sites. Choose a search service to try; as a little experimentation will quickly demonstrate, some of these sites work better than others.

You must be connected to the Internet to use this feature (or your browser must be configured to start your Internet connection automatically when it opens; see page 225). The dialog box that appears has two tabs:

- The **People** tab provides a place to enter a name, email address, or both. Use this tab if you know that information, and need a street address or a telephone number.

- The **Advanced** tab lets you narrow your search. As you can see in Figure 3-13, you can make some very fine distinctions as you describe the person you're trying to find.

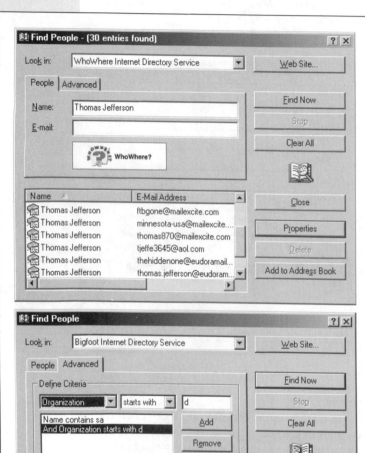

Figure 3-13:
Top: A straight-ahead name search by no means turns up every one of the 200 million Internet citizens, but it's occasionally successful in turning up a few matches for the name you specify. Bottom: On the Advanced tab, you can use the categories and choices in the drop-down lists to provide as many details as possible to the Internet search engine. Here, for example, you're looking for a company whose name you vaguely remember, begins with a D, and contains sa. Delessa, Dilessa, or something like that; if you're lucky, the Web site will find it.

When you're finished setting up your search, click Find Now. The Search program uses your existing Internet connection to send the query off to the chosen Web site. After a few minutes, you'll get a response, even if it's "No response."

Unfortunately, the technology gods don't smile on this feature. You'll probably discover that Internet phone book sites fail to find someone more often than they succeed.

Tip: Instead of using the Find People dialog box, it's frequently more productive to work directly on the directory Web page. After choosing the search engine you want to use from the drop-down list, click Web Site. In a flash (or in a few minutes, depending on the speed of your Internet connection), you're on the Internet and the browser window displays the search engine you selected. Working directly on the Web, instead of using the Search feature as an intermediary, offers more powerful choices for searching.

Start→Settings

The Start→Settings command offers four commands: Control Panel (see Chapter 8), Network and Dial-Up connections (Chapters 13, 14, and 15), Printers (Chapter 7), and Taskbar & Start menu (later in this chapter). These last three items are also represented in the Start→Settings→Control Panel window. But most people use them so frequently that Microsoft put them on the Settings submenu to save a step.

Start→Documents

The Documents submenu lists the My Documents folder (which is also represented by an icon on the desktop) and a cascading list of the last 15 documents you've opened. Using the My Documents command can be useful when your other windows cover the My Documents folder icon. And using the list of recent documents can save you time when you want to reopen something you've been working on recently, but you're not in the mood to go burrowing through desktop folders to find its icon.

Note, however, that:

- Documents appear on the "recently used" list only if your applications are smart enough to update it. Most modern programs (including all Microsoft programs) perform this administrative task, but not all do.

- The Documents list doesn't know when you've deleted a document or moved it to another folder or disk; it continues to list the file even after it's gone. In that event, clicking the document's listing produces an error message.

Tip: There's another easy way to open a document you've recently worked on: Start by launching the program you used to create it. Many programs maintain a list of recent documents at the bottom of the File menu; choose one of these names to open the corresponding file.

Start→Programs

For most people, the Start→Programs command is the most important function of the Start menu. It's the master list of every program on your computer. You can jump directly to your word processor, calendar, or favorite game, for example, just by choosing its name from the Start→Programs menu.

When you install a software program, it usually installs either a *program item* or a *program group* on the Start→Programs menu, as shown in Figure 3-14.

Accessories

This folder lists (and lets you open) the free add-on programs that came with Windows 2000. You'll find them described in Chapter 9.

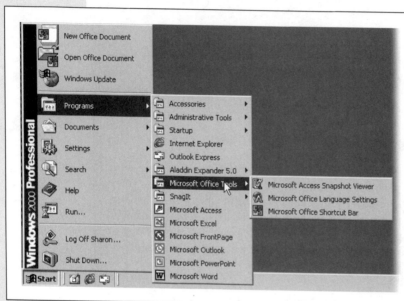

Figure 3-14:
The Start→Program may list the actual application (such as Microsoft Word), which you can click to launch the program. But it may also list a program group, a submenu that lists everything in a particular application folder. Sometimes an application's folder contains commands for launching the software, uninstalling the software, running specific utilities, opening the help files, and so on.

Administrative Tools

See page 378 for a summary of these advanced technical tools.

Startup

The Start→Programs menu also lists the *Startup folder,* a folder (program group) of programs that load automatically every time you start Windows 2000. This can be a very useful feature; if you check your email or calendar every morning, you may as well save yourself a few mouse clicks by putting a *shortcut* (see page 101) of the corresponding program into the Startup folder.

In fact, what you put into the Startup folder doesn't have to be an application. It can just as well be a certain document you work on every day. It can even be a folder or disk icon whose window you'd like to find open and waiting each time you turn on the PC. (The My Documents folder is a natural example.)

Of course, you may be interested in the Startup folder for different reason: to *stop* some program from launching itself, unbidden, every time you turn the machine on (such as the startup utilities installed by Microsoft Office or Quicken).

Fortunately, it's easy to either add or remove items from the Startup folder:

1. **Click the Start button. Slide the cursor up to Programs. Right-click Startup, and choose Open from the shortcut menu.**

   The Startup window opens, revealing whatever is inside it at the moment.

   To delete an icon from this folder, just right-click it and choose Delete from the shortcut menu. Close all the windows you've opened and enjoy your newfound freedom from self-launching software.

   To add a *new* icon to the Startup folder, on the other hand, read on.

2. **Navigate to the disk, folder, application, or document icon you want to add to the Startup folder.**

   Doing so requires familiarity with one of two folder-navigation schemes: My Computer or Windows Explorer. Both are fully described in the next chapter.

3. **Using the right mouse button, drag the icon directly into the Startup window, as shown in Figure 3-15.**

   When you release the button, a shortcut menu appears.

4. **Choose Create Shortcut(s) Here from the shortcut menu.**

   Close all the windows you've opened. For now on, each time you turn on or restart your computer, the program, file, disk, or folder you dragged will open by itself.

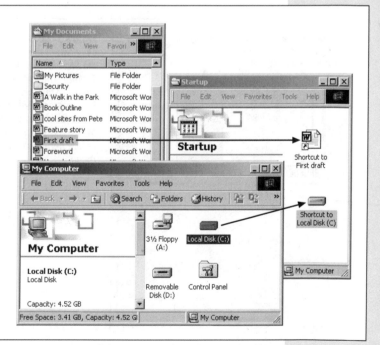

Figure 3-15:
It's easy—and useful—to add a program or document icon to your Startup folder, so that it launches automatically every time you turn on the computer. Here, a document from the My Documents folder is being added. So is the icon for the hard drive, which ensures that the hard drive window will be ready and open each time the computer starts up.

Customizing the Start Menu

As millions of Windows users illustrate, it's perfectly possible to live a long and happy life without ever tampering with the Start menu; for many people, the idea of making it look or work differently comes dangerously close to nerd territory. (It's true that listing your favorite files there gives you quicker access to them—but it's even easier to use the Quick Launch toolbar, as described on page 78.)

Still, knowing how to manipulate the Start menu listings may come in handy someday. It also provides an interesting glimpse into the way Windows works.

Note: Any Start menu changes apply only to the person that's currently logged on to this computer. When you log on, Windows loads *your* customized Start menu, as stored in your user profile; when the next person logs on, he'll see his own version of the Start menu.

Changing the Basic Start Menu Settings

Microsoft offers a fascinating set of Start menu customization options. It's hard to tell whether these options were selected by a scientific usability study or by a dartboard, but you're likely to find something that suits you.

To view and change the basic options, right-click a blank spot on the Taskbar; choose Properties from the shortcut menu. Alternatively, choose Start→Settings→Taskbar & Start Menu. Either way, the Taskbar and Start Menu Properties dialog box opens, as seen in Figure 3-16.

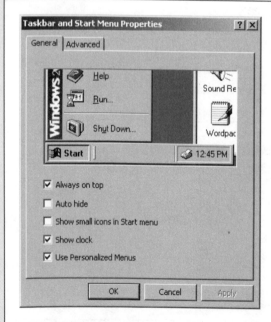

Figure 3-16:
Only two of the options on the General tab apply to the Start Menu; the rest are for configuring the Taskbar. The two Start Menu items, "Show small icons in Start menu" and "Use Personalized Menus," have a great deal of influence over the way the Start menu looks and behaves. Because of their importance, you should try changing the settings for each before deciding on a final configuration for the Start menu.

Only two of the checkboxes in this dialog box pertain to the Start menu: "Show small icons in Start menu" and "Use personalized menus."

- **Show small icons in Start menu.** Turning on this checkbox gives you smaller icons next to the commands in the Start menu. As a result, the Start menu is more compact.

- **Use Personalized Menus.** When the Use Personalized Menus checkbox is on, Windows watches you and studies your behavior (that is, even more than usual). If it notices that you haven't been using certain Start menu commands, Windows hides them, making the menu listing shorter. Figure 3-17 shows the idea.

Figure 3-17:
Left: A Programs menu displaying only those you've used recently. Click the arrow at the bottom of the menu (or just point to it and wait) to see the full menu, as shown at right. The previously displayed items announce their favored status by appearing in a darker shade of gray.

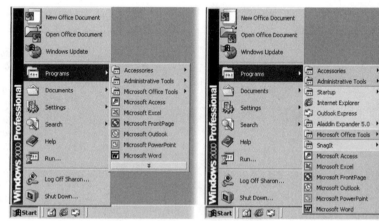

Figure 3-18:
The bottom of the Advanced tab contains a list of on/off options for the Start Menu. The list is about five times the height of the window, so you'll have to scroll down to see all the options.

As noted in Chapter 1, you may find either that Personalized Menus makes it harder to find commands (because they keep moving around), or that it makes life easier because you don't have to sift through commands you never use.

The Advanced tab

Click the Advanced tab (Figure 3-16) to see the dialog box shown in Figure 3-18. At the bottom of the dialog box, you'll find a long scrolling list of checkboxes. Some affect the Taskbar, and are described in the next chapter; the rest, described here, affect the Start menu in interesting ways:

- **Display Administrative Tools.** This command adds a listing for Administrative Tools (a folder of troubleshooting and maintenance tools described in Chapter 19) to your Start→Programs menu.

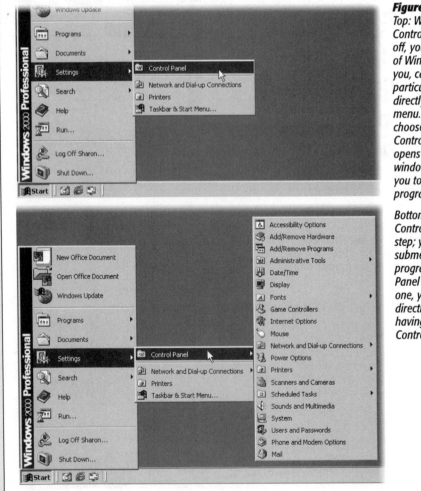

Figure 3-19:

Top: When Expand Control Panel is turned off, you, like generations of Windows users before you, can't open a particular Control panel directly from the Start menu. Instead, you must choose Start→Settings→ Control Panel, which opens the Control Panel window, where it's up to you to open the settings program you want.

Bottom: Expanding the Control Panel saves you a step; you now get a submenu that lists each program in the Control Panel folder. By clicking one, you can open it directly, without ever having to open the Control Panel window.

- **Favorites.** This option adds a Favorites command to the Start Menu that lists your favorite Web sites, the same ones you've "bookmarked" when using Internet Explorer (see page 233). Thereafter, you can use the Start Menu to launch Internet Explorer and travel directly to the selected site.

- **Display Logoff.** This option hides or shows the Logoff item on the Start Menu, which saves you a traipse to the Shut Down dialog box when you want to sign out of your PC without actually shutting it down.

- **Expand** options. *Expanding* means that instead of simply listing the name of a folder (such as Control Panel), your Start menu sprouts a submenu listing the *contents* of that folder. As illustrated in Figure 3-19, this new Windows 2000 feature saves you the trouble of having to open a folder window (such as Control Panel or My Documents), double-click an icon inside it, and then close the window again.

  The Taskbar and Start Menu Properties dialog box offers individual checkboxes for expanding these Start menu folder names: Control Panel, My Documents, Network and Dial-Up Connections, and Printers.

- **Scroll the Programs menu.** This option changes how the Start→Programs menu looks when there are too many programs listed there to fit on the screen. Ordinarily when this situation arises, a second Programs menu appears to the right of the first one, continuing the list. But if you turn on this checkbox, all your programs appear instead on one massive, scrolling Programs list. As you scroll down past the last visible name, the top of the Programs menu scrolls off the screen.

FREQUENTLY ASKED QUESTION

Opening the Control Panel Window When You Can't

OK, I'm with you—I turned on the Expand Control Panel checkbox, so now I can open any control panel program directly from my Start menu. Trouble is, now I can't open the Control Panel window! Nothing happens when I click the Start→Settings→Control Panel command. How do I open the Control Panel window?

Ah, there's a troublemaker in every class.

Click the Start button to open the menu, slide up to Settings, and then *right-click* Control Panel. Choose Open from the shortcut menu. You're back in business.

Adding Icons to the Start Menu

Usually, when you install a new program, its installer inserts the program's name and icon in your Start→Programs menu automatically. There may be times, however, when you want to add something to the Start menu yourself, such as a folder, a document, or even a disk—not to mention applications whose installers don't add their names automatically.

Note: You're not allowed to touch the body of the Start menu—the list of commands between Shut Down and Documents. You can move things, remove things, or add things only in the listings *above* the Programs command—and among the items in the Programs submenu. (The two legal areas are indicated in Figure 3-20.) In other words, Windows won't let you drag, say, the Shut Down or Help commands into oblivion.

Microsoft wouldn't be Microsoft if it didn't provide at least 437 different ways to do this job. Here are three of the world's favorites.

Drag an icon directly onto the Start menu

Nothing could be easier:

1. **Locate the icon you want to add to your Start menu.**

   It can be an application (see the sidebar on page 55), a document you've created, a folder you frequently access, one of the programs in your Control Panels folder, or even your hard drive or floppy drive. (Adding disks and folders to the Start menu is especially handy, because it lets you dive directly into their contents without having to drill down through the My Computer window.)

Tip: Adding an application name to your Programs menu requires that you find the program *file*, as described on page 55. To do so, either use the Search command described earlier in this chapter, or use the Windows Explorer window described in Chapter 5. You'll find your program files in the My Computer→C: drive→Program Files folder.

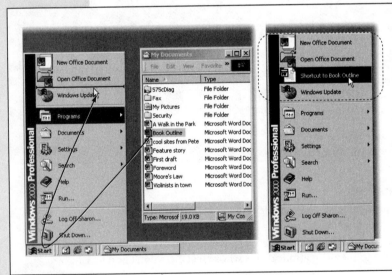

Figure 3-20:
Left: You can add something to the top of your Start menu by dragging it, from whatever folder it's in, onto the Start button to open the Start menu, and then directly up into position. When you release the mouse, you'll find that it's been happily ensconced where you dropped it (right). Once the menu is open, you can drag commands up or down in the circled area of the menu at right.

2. Drag it directly onto the Start button.

If you release the mouse now, Windows adds the name of the icon you've just dragged to the top of the menu, as shown at right in Figure 3-20.

But if you prefer some additional control over the placement of the icon, continue the drag upward to the top section of the menu (above the Programs command). You're free to drop it exactly where you want it among the items listed there (Figure 3-20, left).

Similarly, if you drag to the Start button and then up to the Programs command without releasing the mouse, you can place it exactly where you want it in the Start→Program submenu.

FREQUENTLY ASKED QUESTION

Which One's the Program?

I want to add a program to my Start menu like you said. But where is its icon?

To discover the program file name of a favorite program, open your My Computer→C: drive→Program Files folder. Inside you'll find folders containing all of your applications— and inside each of *these* folders, you'll find icons for each application's components. Right-click the window, choose View→Details from the shortcut menu, and look for an icon whose Type column says "application."

OK, I did that. But in the program's folder, there are 15 million little files that all say they're applications. How do I know which is the actual application file?

First, you can usually recognize which application is the primary one both by its short-form name and by its icon. *WinWord* is probably a good hint that you've found Word for Windows, for example.

Second, the instructions from the software company may tell you which file to click.

Use the Add Listing wizard

If dragging icons around isn't your thing, you can use one of Microsoft's famous wizards for the same purpose. If you choose Start→Settings→Taskbar & Start Menu, click the Advanced tab, and then the Add button, the Add Shortcut wizard walks you through the process of choosing a file to add.

Use the Start Menu folder

To open your Start menu folder, right-click the Start button and select Open. Instead of the fancy icon-adding wizards and drag-and-drop schemes described in this section, you may prefer to fine-tune your Start menu the low-tech way: Just open your Start Menu folder. (Or, if you'd like the newly installed item to show up on *everyone's* Start menu—everyone who uses your PC—right-click the Start button and select All Users.) You can add, remove, or rename shortcuts in your Start menu just by manipulating the shortcuts in this folder (or the Programs folder inside it).

Removing Icons from the Programs Menu

It's easy to remove most applications from your PC—at least those whose programmers have read the *Emily Post Big Book of Programming Etiquette*. Just choose Start→ Settings→Control Panel→Add/Remove Programs; you get a list of every program installed on your machine (except for those supplied with Windows 2000). You can then make a selection from this list and click Add/Remove to delete the software from your life. (More on Add/Remove Programs in Chapter 7.)

In some cases, however, Add/Remove Programs fails to remove the program's name from the Start menu, or you may have to manually uninstall an application that doesn't register itself with Add/Remove Programs at all. Over time, the Programs menu can become extremely crowded, and therefore harder to navigate. Error messages become increasingly frequent as you choose the names of these dearly departed applications, perhaps forgetting that you've sent them to the great CompUSA in the sky.

Fortunately, you can remove these unwanted names—or any other program, file, folder, or disk name—from your Start menu, by one of these two methods.

Note: When you delete an item from one of the menus on the Start menu, you're only deleting the *shortcut* that appears on the menu. Deleting items from the Start menu doesn't actually uninstall any software.

Drag it off the menu

Here's the world's easiest method for ditching a file, program, folder, or disk name from your Start menu. Click the Start menu to open it, and then simply *drag* the name in question off of the top of the menu (or from the Programs submenu)— onto the desktop, for example, or even directly onto the Recycle Bin icon.

Use the shortcut menu

Here's the second easiest way to clean up the Start menu: Click the Start menu to open it. Then right-click the file, folder, program, or disk name and choose Delete from the shortcut menu. It disappears instantly.

Tip: Speaking of the shortcut menu, you can also *rename* something you've added to your Start or Start→Programs menu. Click the Start menu to open it, right-click the name of the item you want to rename, and choose Rename from the shortcut menu. You'll be offered the Rename dialog box, where you can edit the name and then click OK.

Reorganizing the Programs Menu

To change the order of the Start→Programs listings, click the Start menu to open it, slide up to the word Programs, and simply drag the folder, document, disk, or program name up or down as you see fit. As you drag an item through the list of programs, a black line appears to show you the resulting location of your dragging action. Release the mouse when the black line is where you want the relocated icon to appear. If you change your mind while you're dragging, press the Esc key to leave everything as it was.

Tip: To sort your Start→Programs submenu alphabetically, right-click anywhere on the Programs submenu and choose Sort By Name from the shortcut menu.

Add folders to hold submenus

Many listings Start→Programs menu listings are folders (those accompanied by a right-facing arrow). For example, clicking Start→Programs→ Accessories→Games reveals a submenu that lists the games that come with Windows.

Without all these folders consolidating the Start→Programs menu, you'd need one of those very expensive 95-inch monitors to see the entire list of applications. Fortunately, you can create Programs-menu folders of your own, and stock them with whatever icons you like. For instance, you may want to create a folder for CD-ROM-based games, eliminating those long lists from the Programs menu.

To add a folder to the Programs menu, follow these steps:

1. **Right-click the Start button; choose Explore from the shortcut menu.**

   The Start Menu Explorer window appears.

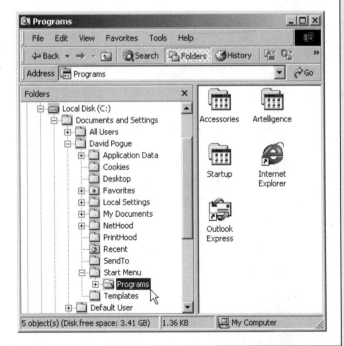

Figure 3-21:
The listings on the Programs menu appear in the right pane. Notice that some of the items have folder icons. These folders create submenus in your Programs menu.

2. **Click the Programs folder.**

   Its contents are listed in the right pane, as shown in Figure 3-21.

3. **Choose File→New→Folder.**

   Or, if your right mouse button hasn't been getting enough exercise, right-click a blank spot in the right pane, and then choose New→Folder from the shortcut menu.

4. **When the new folder item appears, type a folder name and then press Enter.**

5. **Close the Start Menu window. Click OK to close the dialog box.**

   Your new folder appears at the bottom of the Start→Programs menu. Feel free to drag your new folder to the location you choose on the menu.

Now you can put favorite file, folder, disk, or application icons *into* this new folder. To do so, drag an icon onto the Start→Programs menu, and then onto the new folder/submenu you created. Of course, the first time you do this, your newly created folder submenu just says "Empty"; drag the icon onto that "Empty" notation to install it into your submenu. Then drag as many other icons as you like into this new folder.

You can even create folders *within* folders in your Start→Programs menu. Just repeat the instructions above—but following step 2, click the + sign next to the first folder you added. Then continue with step 3.

Start→Windows Update

Choosing this command connects to the Internet and checks Microsoft's Web site for any Windows 2000 updates. (You can't use this feature unless you have administrative privileges, as described on page 369.)

Windows, Folders, and the Taskbar

Windows got its name from the rectangles on the screen—the *windows*—in which every computer activity takes place. You look at a Web page in a window, type short stories in a window, read email in a window, and look at the contents of a folder in a window—sometimes all at once.

This overlapping-windows scheme makes using a computer much easier than windowless operating systems like DOS. But it has a downside of its own, as any Windows veteran can tell you: As you create more files, stash them in more folders, and launch more programs, it's easy to wind up paralyzed before a screen awash with cluttered, overlapping rectangles.

Fortunately, Windows is crawling with icons, buttons, and other inventions to help you keep these windows under control.

Windows in Windows

There are two categories of windows in Windows: *desktop* windows (which open when you double-click a disk or folder icon) and *application* windows (which appear when you're working on a document or in a program, such as Word or Internet Explorer). Nonetheless, all of these windows have certain components in common. Figure 4-1 shows a representative example: the window that appears when you double-click the My Documents icon on your desktop.

- **Title bar.** This top strip displays the name of the window. It's also the "handle" that you drag when you want to *move* the window on the screen.

• **Minimize button.** Click this button to temporarily hide a window; it shrinks down into the form of a button on your *Taskbar* (see page 76). (You can open it again by clicking that icon.) *Keyboard shortcut:* Press Alt+Space bar, then N.

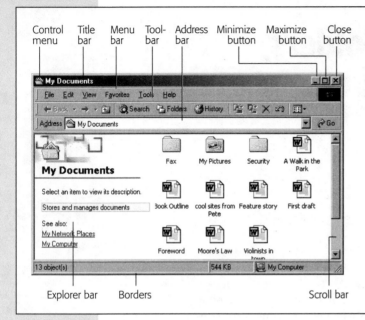

Control menu | Title bar | Menu bar | Tool-bar | Address bar | Minimize button | Maximize button | Close button

Figure 4-1:
All windows have the same basic ingredients, making it easy to become an expert in window manipulation. This figure shows a desktop window—a disk or folder; but you'll encounter the same elements in application windows.

Explorer bar   Borders   Scroll bar

• **Maximize button.** Click this button to enlarge the window so that it fills the screen. (*Keyboard shortcut:* Press Alt+Space bar, then X.) At this point, the Maximize button turns into a Restore button (whose icon shows two overlapping rectangles), which you can click to return the window to its previous size.

Tip: You can also maximize a window by double-clicking its title bar. Double-clicking the title bar on a maximized window returns it to its previous size.

• **Close button.** Click the X to close the window. *Keyboard shortcut:* Press Alt+F4; or press Alt+Space bar, then C.

• **Menu bar.** Click one of these words (such as File or Edit) to open a menu, which shows a list of commands available in this window.

• **Toolbar.** Some windows have these special strips that hold one-click shortcut buttons, which are equivalents for menu commands Microsoft thinks you'll use frequently. (More on toolbars at the end of this chapter.)

• **Scroll bar.** A scroll bar appears if the window isn't large enough to show all its contents, as described in the sidebar box on the next page.

• **Address bar.** This bar lets you type in a Web address, or even the address of a folder on your PC; when you press Enter, that Web page or a list of the contents of the folder appears on the screen. (This bar shows up in desktop windows and Web browsers, not in application windows. See page 228 for details.)

- **Control icon.** The icon next to the title is actually a menu that offers commands for sizing, moving, and closing the window. You can double-click it to close a window; otherwise, it's not very useful, because its commands duplicate the other doodads described here.

- **Borders.** You can change the size of a window by dragging these borders. Position your pointer over any border until the pointer turns into a double-headed arrow. Then drag inward or outward to reshape the window. (To resize a full-screen window, click the Restore button first.)

Tip: If you drag the corner of a window, you can resize it in both dimensions at once. The diagonally striped ribs of the lower-right corner may suggest that that's the *only* corner you can drag, but it's not; all four corners work the same way.

- **Explorer bar.** This special left-side-of-the-window panel shows information about the window, or about whatever icon you click.

    But using the View→Explorer Bar command, you can fill this half of the window with your choice of several other kinds of information: the Search pane described on page 36, your list of Favorite icons and Web sites, the History list (folders you've opened recently), or Folders (the Windows Explorer-like folder tree described on page 86). You can even choose Tip of the Day (to see a helpful Windows trick at the bottom of the window) or, if you're online, Discuss (to open a chat window).

UP TO SPEED

Scroll-Bar Crash Course

Scroll bars are the strips at the right side and bottom of a window. Some windows have both, some have only one, and a few have none. The scroll bar signals you that the window isn't big enough to show you all of its contents.

Click the arrows at each end of a scroll bar to move slowly through the window, or drag the square handle (called the *thumb*) to move faster. (The position of the thumb relative to the entire scroll bar reflects your relative position in the entire window or document.) You can quickly move to a specific part of the window by holding the mouse button down on the scroll bar where you want the thumb to be. The scroll bar rapidly scrolls to the desired location and then stops.

If you have a mouse that's equipped with a wheel, such as the Microsoft IntelliMouse, you can scroll (in most programs) just by turning the wheel with your finger, even if your cursor is nowhere near the scroll bar. You can also scroll by clicking the wheel inside the window to create an *origin mark* in the scroll bar, and then moving the mouse (without clicking) upward or downward. The farther you move the mouse away from the origin mark, the faster the window scrolls. Click the wheel again to leave AutoScroll mode.

Finally, you can scroll without using the mouse at all. Press the Page Up or Page Down keys to scroll the window by one window-full, or use the up- and down-arrow keys to scroll one line at a time. Ctrl+Home brings you to the top of the window; Ctrl+End to the bottom.

Sizing, Moving, and Closing Windows

It's easy enough to resize and reposition your desktop windows—an especially useful feature when more than one are open.

Sizing a window

Every Windows window falls into one of these three categories:

- **Maximized** means that the window fills the screen; its edges are glued to the boundaries of your monitor, and you can't see anything behind it. It gets that way when you click its Maximize button. This is a great condition for your window when you're surfing the Web or working on a document for hours at a stretch, because the largest possible window means the least possible scrolling.

Tip: When a window is maximized, you can *restore* it (as described below) by pressing Alt+Space bar, then R.

- When you click a window's **Minimize** button (Figure 4-1), the window disappears from sight. It hasn't actually closed, however; it's simply reincarnated as a button on the Taskbar strip at the bottom of the screen. You can bring the window back by clicking this Taskbar button, which bears the window's name. Minimizing a window is a great tactic when you want to see what's in the window behind it.

- A **restored** window is neither maximized nor minimized; it's a loose cannon, floating around on your screen as an independent rectangle. Because its edges aren't attached to the walls of your monitor like a maximized window, you can make it any size you like by dragging its borders.

Tip: Double-clicking the title bar makes a window alternate between its maximized (full-screen) and restored conditions.

Moving a window

Moving a window is easy—just drag the title bar.

Most of the time, you move a window to get it out of the way when you're trying to see what's *behind* it. However, moving windows around is also handy if you're moving or copying data between programs, or moving or copying files between drives or folders, as shown in Figure 4-2.

Closing a window

You can close a window in any of several ways:

- Click the Close button (the X in the upper-right corner of the window).

- Click the icon in the upper-left corner, and then choose Close from the drop-down menu.

- Press Alt+F4.

- Right-click the window's Taskbar button (see page 76), and then choose Close from the shortcut menu.

- In application windows, choose File→Exit.

- In desktop windows, choose File→Close.

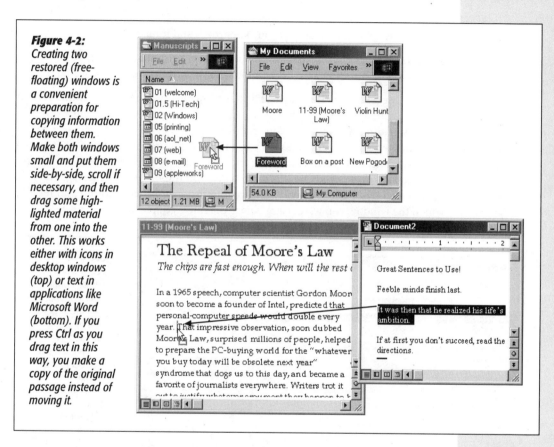

Figure 4-2:
Creating two restored (free-floating) windows is a convenient preparation for copying information between them. Make both windows small and put them side-by-side, scroll if necessary, and then drag some high-lighted material from one into the other. This works either with icons in desktop windows (top) or text in applications like Microsoft Word (bottom). If you press Ctrl as you drag text in this way, you make a copy of the original passage instead of moving it.

When you close a document window in one of your programs, no matter which action you use, you're given an opportunity to save your work before the window closes. Be careful, too—in many programs, including Internet Explorer, closing the window also quits the program entirely.

Working with Multiple Windows

Many people routinely keep four or five programs open at once—a calendar, word processor, Web browser, and email program, for example. Others (such as computer book authors) regularly work in just one program, but have several document windows open at once (representing several chapters, for example). Learning how to manage and navigate among a flurry of overlapping windows is an essential Windows survival skill.

Active and inactive windows

When you have multiple windows open on your screen, only one window is *active,* which means that:

- It's in the foreground, *in front* of all other windows.

- It's the window that reacts to your keystrokes and mouse clicks.

The title bar of the active window is blue; the background (inactive) window title bars are gray. (You can change this color scheme, as described on page 142.)

Just because a window is in the background, by the way, doesn't mean that it can't continue with whatever assignment you gave it. For example, when your word processor is printing a document, your email program may be collecting mail, or your Web browser can be loading a Web page. If a background program needs to pass a message up to you (such as an error message), it automatically pops to the foreground, becoming the active program. When you respond to the message (usually by clicking OK), Windows sends the program *back* to the background and returns you to the window you were using before the message appeared.

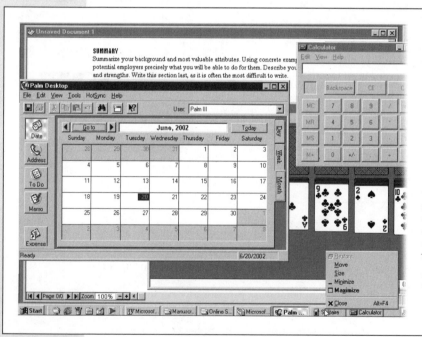

Figure 4-3:
There's a word processor buried in this morass, and without the Taskbar buttons at the bottom edge, it would take a lot of blind clicks to find it and make it the active window. Sometimes you need to bring a particular window into the foreground in a big hurry, especially if the boss arrives when you're playing Solitaire.

Manipulating Windows with the Taskbar

The *Taskbar* (Figure 4-3) can be a helpful assistant when you're working with multiple windows. It provides one-click window-manipulation commands. As you can see in Figure 4-3, it's not always easy to find a particular window.

- To bring a window to the foreground, making it the active window, click its button on the Taskbar.

- To minimize, maximize, restore, or close a window, even if you can't see it on the screen, right-click its button on the Taskbar and choose the appropriate command from the shortcut menu (Figure 4-3, bottom).

- To arrange all open windows in an overlapping pattern (except those you've minimized), as shown in Figure 4-4, right-click a blank spot on the Taskbar and choose Cascade Windows from the shortcut menu.

- To arrange all nonminimized windows in neat little boxes, each getting an equal rectangular chunk of your screen, right-click a blank spot on the Taskbar and choose Tile Vertically or Tile Horizontally from the shortcut menu.

- To minimize all the windows in one fell swoop, right-click a blank spot on the Taskbar and choose Minimize All Windows from the shortcut menu.

If you change your mind, the Taskbar shortcut menu always includes an Undo command for the last Taskbar command you invoked. (Its wording changes to reflect your most recent action—Undo Minimize All, for example.)

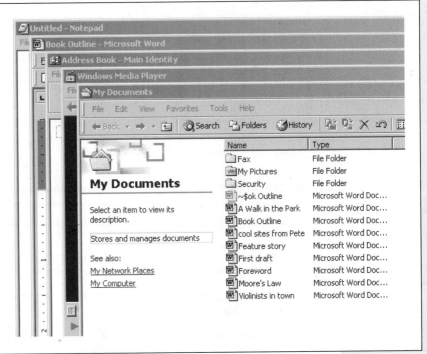

Figure 4-4:
Cascading windows are neatly arranged so you can see the title bar for each window. Click any title bar to bring that window to the foreground as the active window. After you've clicked a few title bars and worked in several windows, you'll have to choose the Cascade Windows command again to rearrange all your open windows.

There is, however, a trick to closing multiple *desktop* windows: While pressing the Shift key, click the X in the upper-right corner of the last window you opened. Doing so doesn't close all open desktop windows, but it closes all the ones that sprang from a single "parent" disk or folder. For example, if you opened My Computer, then your C: drive, then your Program Files folder, the Shift trick closes all those windows. But if you had also opened the My Documents folder on the desktop, it stays open, because it wasn't part of the My Computer→C: drive→Program Files series.

Configuring Desktop Windows

Windows windows look just fine as they come from the factory; all the edges are straight, and the text is perfectly legible. Still, if you're going to stare at this computer screen for half of your waking hours, you may as well investigate some of the ways these windows can be enhanced for better looks and greater efficiency. As it turns out, there's no end to the tweaks Microsoft lets you perform.

Icon and List Views

You can view the files and folders in a desktop window in any of several ways: as small icons, as jumbo icons, as a tidy list, and so on. Each window remembers its view settings independently.

To change this view setting for a particular open window, choose one of these commands from its View menu: Large Icons, Small Icons, List, Details, or Thumbnails. (Figure 4-5 illustrates each of these options.)

Changing the sorting order

Windows starts out arranging the icons alphabetically, with folders in one A-to-Z group and the list of loose files in a second group. To change the sorting criterion, choose View→Arrange Icons, and then select one of these options:

- **By Name** arranges the icons alphabetically by name.

- **By Type** arranges the files in the window alphabetically by file *type*, such as Word documents, applications, JPEG files, and so on.

Tip: The file type is determined by the file's *filename extension* (see page 122), but selecting this option sorts the files by the name *assigned* to the type. For example, the extension .psd denotes Adobe Photoshop documents, but Windows sorts these files under A (for Adobe), not P (for PSD).

- **By Size** arranges the files in the window by size, starting with the smallest file. (Folders are unaffected; Windows never shows you the sizes of folders.)

- **By Date** sorts the files in the window by creation date (not modified date), starting with the oldest file.

- **Auto Arrange,** which is available only in icon views, isn't actually a sorting method;

it's a straightening-up method. It rearranges the icons so they're equally spaced and neat. (You can use this command on the desktop, too, which is one way to avoid Cluttered Windows Desktop Syndrome.)

Note: You can't reverse the sort *order* of your icons (from Z to A, for example) except in Details view, described next.

Manipulating the Details view

The Details view provides some unique characteristics that make it more powerful than the other views. First, there's the obvious advantage of being able to see the size and date of the objects in neat columns, as shown in Figure 4-5. Second, you can sort the contents by file size, type, or date simply by clicking the appropriate column heading.

Figure 4-5:
*The five ways you can view the contents of a folder window. In **Large Icons** view (top), a large icon, with its label beneath, represents each file or folder. This is the default view. In **Small Icons** view (middle left, shown without its left-side panel), a small icon (label to the right) represents each file or folder; the icons are arranged in rows. (The alphabetical progression goes from left to right, rather than top to bottom.) The **List** view is similar, except the contents are arranged in columns (middle right). **Details** view (lower left) is the same as List view, except that you get additional columns of information that reveal the size, icon type, and the date and time the object was last modified. (This view, a familiar one to Macintosh fans, is growing in popularity.) Finally, in **Thumbnails** view (lower right), each icon is enclosed in a tiny picture frame. Graphics files are actually shown in the frame, so this view is really only useful for windows that contain graphics files. (Thumbnails view is not available in the My Computer window).*

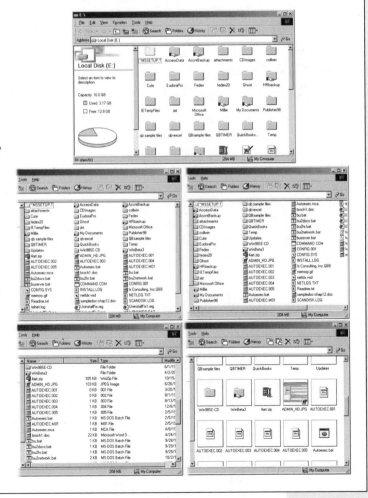

Tip: If you click the same column heading again, the sorting order is reversed. For instance, clicking the Modified column once places your files into oldest-files-first sequence; a second click arranges the files with the *newest* file first. A small arrow appears on the column heading that points up or down to indicate the order of the sort.

Finally, you can add more columns to the window—up to 28 columns of information about each icon. Start by choosing View→Choose Columns to open the Column Settings dialog box shown in Figure 4-6. Click the checkboxes to turn the columns on or off. To rearrange the sequence of columns, click the name of a checked column and use the Move Up and Move Down buttons. The top-to-bottom list in the dialog box becomes the left-to-right display in the window.

Tip: You can change the width of a column by editing the number at the bottom of the Column Settings window (Figure 4-6). But that's much too unnatural. Instead, position your cursor on the vertical line between column headings in a Details-view window. When the pointer turns into a double-headed arrow, drag the vertical line horizontally.

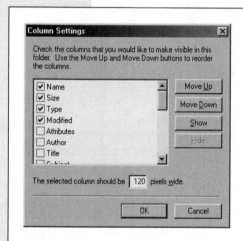

Figure 4-6:
The range of information you can display about objects in the window is robust enough to satisfy even the terminally curious. Some of the characteristics listed here are for specific types of files; you won't need a column for Audio Format, for example, in a folder that holds word-processing documents.

Web View vs. Classic View

When you first run Windows, desktop windows show up with many visual attributes of a Web page, as shown in Figure 4-7.

The *classic* view, on the other hand, simply displays the contents of the folder, omitting the graphics on the left side of the Web-type window and packing a lot more info into your window. (Figure 4-8 shows this view.) Switching to the classic view is a system-wide alteration, affecting all desktop windows. To accomplish this change, open any folder window, and then:

1. **Choose Tools→Folder Options.**

   The Folder Options dialog box appears.

2. Turn on "Use Windows classic folders," and then click OK.

Now your windows look more like Figure 4-8, which shows the same folder that appears in Figure 4-7.

Tip: After you've tweaked your system windows into a perfectly beautiful and efficient configuration, you don't have to go through all of that work for each folder. Windows can make all your changes the new default for *all* your desktop windows.

Choose Tools→Folder Options→View tab. Click the Like Current Folder button. Windows asks if you're sure you know what you're doing. Click Yes.

Figure 4-7:
Opening My Documents reveals a graphical display of contents and a Web-like layout, including underlined links, an address bar, and Back/Forward buttons on the toolbar. There's even a background graphic like the ones that sometimes lurk as the backdrops of Web pages. This background adds nothing to the features of the window, but it may satisfy some artistic yearning in you.

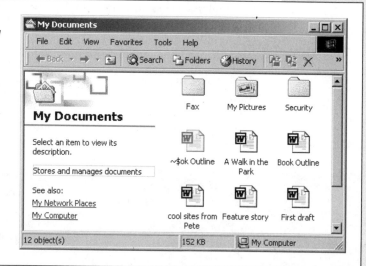

Figure 4-8:
Microsoft dubs this the "classic" view, meaning the way folders looked before the Web-type display was built into desktop windows. That should mean that folder windows look like "out-of-the box" Windows 95 or Windows NT 4 windows. However, a "classic" window is actually a melding of the classic Windows design and the newer Web style; it can still incorporate an address bar and Back/Forward buttons.

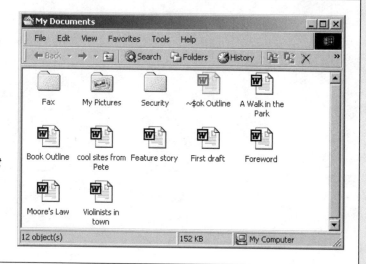

The Four Window Toolbars

On the day it's born, a desktop window has two *toolbars* across the top (see Figure 4-9). (That doesn't include the strip that says File, Edit, View, and so on. That's not a toolbar; it's the *menu bar.*)

But by choosing View→Toolbars, or right-clicking a blank spot on a toolbar and choosing toolbar names from the shortcut menu, you can add or hide whichever toolbars you like, on a window-by-window basis. There are four toolbars from which to choose, called the Standard Buttons, Address Bar, Links, and Radio toolbars. (Only the first two appear when you first open a window in Windows.)

The Standard Buttons toolbar

If you think the Standard Buttons toolbar looks suspiciously like a toolbar from a Web browser, you're right. Microsoft redesigned this toolbar to reflect the growing emphasis in Windows toward erasing the differences between your desktop and the Internet. It starts out with these buttons:

- **Back, Forward.** These buttons resemble those in a Web browser that let you return to Web pages you've just seen. This time, however, they show you the contents of a disk or folder you've just seen. If you're using one-window-at-a-time mode (see "Uni-window vs. Multi-Window" in the next section), these buttons are your sole means of getting around as you burrow through your folders.

POWER USERS' CLINIC

Customizing and Decorating Web-Style Windows

As you may have noticed, the Web-style desktop windows in Windows look a bit like Web pages, complete with a colorful graphic and links at the left side (see Figure 4-8). Using a special wizard, you can change the look of this left-side window portion. You can change the picture that appears here, the color of the background or the icon labels, the message that appears that describes the folder contents, and so on. (No, this feature is nothing to write home about, but some lucky Microsoft intern worked very hard on it.)

To get started, choose View→Customize This Folder from any desktop window (except the My Computer window). When the wizard appears, click Next. The wizard offers to help you do any of the following tasks:

- Choose a different *HTML template* for the window. This option, for people who know the HTML

Web-programming language, lets you specify the font, color, size, and other characteristics of the design of the left-side pane. If you click "I want to edit this template," the wizard will open the actual HTML code in the Notepad (see page 198), where you can go to town changing its look.

- Choose a new background color for the window, as well as a contrasting color for the text inside it.

- Add a comment (to explain what the folder is for and what's in it).

After you use the wizard to customize your Web-based windows, the next time you launch the wizard, you'll be offered a new option: Remove Customizations. The wizard lists the customizations you've made, and you can remove one or all of them.

- **Up.** Click this button to move up one level in the folder hierarchy. For example, if you're viewing your My Pictures folder, clicking this button opens the My Documents folder that contains it.

- **Search.** Opens the Search panel described on page 36.

Configuring
Desktop Windows

GEM IN THE ROUGH

Eliminating Double-Clicks

If you like the Web-like window display shown in Figure 4-7, you can take the Web paradigm a step further so that *one* click, not two, opens an icon.

To accomplish this setup, choose Tools→Folder Options. Select "Single-click to open an item" on the General tab to enable single-clicks to open folders and files. Then turn the icon names into links by selecting "Underline all icon titles" or "Underline an icon title when I point to it."

If a single click opens an icon, you're entitled to wonder: Then how does one *select* an icon (which you'd normally

do with a single click)? Answer: Just point to it, letting the mouse hover over the icon without clicking. To make multiple selections, press the Ctrl key as you point to additional icons.

If you're an experienced Windows user, this option will probably feel extremely unnatural. (Microsoft made this behavior the standard setting in prototype versions of Windows 98. The public's response to it was overwhelmingly negative; it's been an optional feature ever since.)

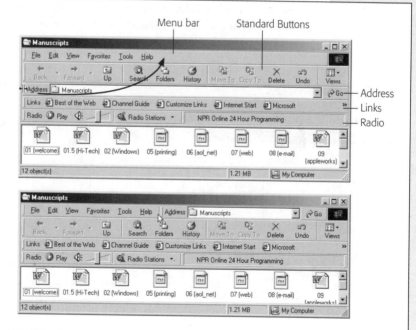

Figure 4-9:
Top: The four basic toolbars that you can summon independently for any desktop window.

Bottom: By dragging the vertical left-side handle of a toolbar, you can make the displays more compact by placing two or more bars on the same row. You can even drag one directly up into the menu bar, as shown here, saving even more vertical space.

- **Folders.** Hides or shows the master map of disks and folders at the left side of the window, simulating the two-panel Windows Explorer navigational display described in the next chapter.

- **History.** Opens a new panel at the left side of the window that shows every Web site and network computer you've visited recently.

- **Move To, Copy To.** These buttons are available only when you've highlighted an icon or icons in a folder or disk window. Clicking the Move To or Copy To button summons a "Browse for Folder" window that lets you choose a different folder or disk on your computer. If you then click OK, you move or copy the highlighted icon or icons to the specified location.

- **Delete.** Gives the highlighted icon or icons a fast trip into the Recycle Bin. (The icon may not disappear until you close and reopen the window you were looking at.)

- **Undo.** Takes back the last thing you did, such as clicking the Move To, Copy To, or Delete button.

- **Views.** Opens a short menu listing the five basic ways a window can display its icon contents—as large icons, small icons, and so on. (You can also use the View menu on the menu bar for the same purpose.) For details on these views, see page 66.

These are just the buttons that Microsoft proposes; you're free to add any of several other buttons to the toolbar, or get rid of ones you never use. To begin the customizing process, choose View→Toolbars→Customize to open the dialog box shown in Figure 4-10.

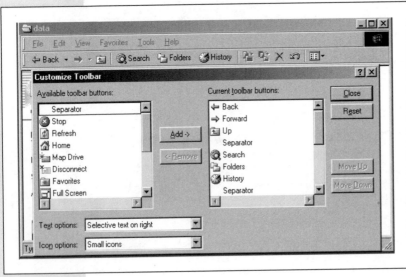

Figure 4-10:
Select a button from the list at left; click Add to add it to the toolbar. Click Delete to remove a button from the list at right. To reorganize the toolbar, select a button and use the Move Up and Move Down buttons. You can also add separators to creates groups of buttons in the same toolbar. Any changes you make to this toolbar affect all windows.

Tip: Setting all folders to the same view or resetting all folders to their default views doesn't reset the Standard Buttons toolbar. To return a modified toolbar to its original state, you must open the dialog box shown in Figure 4-10 and click the Reset button.

The Address bar toolbar

The Address Bar toolbar (Figure 4-9) may look like the white strip at the top of your Web browser, where you type the URL (Web address) of a Web site you want to visit. But the Address Bar accepts more than Web addresses. After all, Web addresses are just locations of particular files on particular computers, so it's not much of a stretch to see how it lets you open any file on your machine or any files on your network (that you have permission to see) by typing its address here.

You can type any of the following information into the Address Bar text box:

- **A Web address.** Skip the *http://* part. Just type the body of the Web address, such as *www.microsoft.com,* in this box. When you click Go or press Enter, the actual web page you selected will appear in the window.

- **A search phrase.** If you type some text into this strip that isn't obviously a Web address, Windows assumes that you're telling it, "Go onto the Internet and search for this phrase." From here, it works exactly as though you've used the Internet search feature described in Chapter 3.

- **A folder name.** You can also type one of several important folder names into this strip, such as *My Computer, My Documents, My Network Places, My Pictures*, and so on. When you click Go or press Enter, you open that folder window.

- **A program or path name.** Type in the path to a folder or file on your own computer or on your network. For a file or folder on your own machine, you specify the drive letter and folder name. On the network, you'll need the *UNC* name (page 32), which looks something like *\\server_name\foldername\subfolder.*

In each case, as soon as you begin to type, a pop-up list of recently visited Web sites, files, or folders appears below the Address bar. Windows is trying to save you some typing. If you see what you're looking for, click it with the mouse, or press the down arrow key to highlight the one you want and then press Enter.

The Links toolbar

This toolbar offers buttons representing your favorite Web sites—the ones you the added to your Favorites→Links folder in Internet Explorer (see page 229).

The Radio toolbar

The Radio toolbar came into existence with Internet Explorer 5. It's an odd tool, but great fun, because it lets you use your Internet connection to listen to radio stations locally or internationally. (For starters, try Radio Pogoda, an oldies station in Warsaw. Radio Bleue from Tahiti has its weird charms, as well. To program the Radio toolbar, see page 194.)

Uni-Window vs. Multi-Window

When you double-click a folder, Windows can react in one of two ways:

- **It can open a new window.** Now you've got two windows on the screen, one overlapping the other. Moving or copying an icon from one into the other is a piece of cake, as shown in Figure 4-2. Trouble is, if your double-clicking craze continues much longer, your screen will eventually be overrun with windows, which you must now painstakingly close again.

- **It can replace the original window with a new one.** This only-one-window-at-all-times behavior (the default) keeps your desktop from becoming crowded with windows. If you need to return to the previous window, the Back button takes you there. Of course, you'll have to use a different method to move or copy icons from one folder to another using this method, because you can't drag and drop.

Which system you adopt is a matter of preference and experience. Whatever you decide, here's how you tell Windows which behavior you'd like:

1. **Choose Tools→Folder Options in any desktop window.**

   It doesn't matter what window you start in; the change you're about to make affects every window. The Folder Options dialog box appears.

2. **On the General tab, click "Open each folder in the same window" or "Open each folder in its own window," as suits your fancy, and then click OK.**

Tip: You can override these choices on a case-by-case basis by pressing *Shift* as you open a folder. Doing so reverses the status of the chosen setting described in step 2 above.

The Folder Options Options

If you choose Tools→Folder Options from any folder window, and then click the View tab (see Figure 4-11), you see an array of options that affect all of the folder windows on your PC. When assessing the impact of these controls, *earth-shattering* isn't the adjective that springs to mind; still, you may find one or two of them useful:

- **Display compressed files and folders with alternate color.** As described on page 396, Windows 2000 lets you compress certain files and folders to conserve disk space. This option makes their icons change color, so you'll know at a glance which have been compressed.

- **Display the full path in the address bar.** When this option is on, Windows shows the exact location of the current window in the Address bar (if it's showing)—for example, *C:\Documents and Settings\Sharon\My Documents\Outlines*. Seeing the path can be useful when you're not sure which disk a folder is on, for example.

- **Display the full path in the title bar.** Same idea, but this time the path of the open folder or file shows up in the *title bar* of the window.

- **Hidden files and folders; Hide protected operating system files.** Windows hides certain files and information that, if deleted or changed by mistake, could damage the operating system and cause you hours of troubleshooting grief. Yes, Big Brother is watching you, but he means well. (See page 207 for details on this feature.) You'll have the smoothest computing career if you leave these options untouched.

- **Hide file extensions for known file types.** Windows normally hides the three-letter *filename extension* on standard kinds of files and documents (Word files, Excel files, and so on), in an effort to make Windows seem less technical and intimidating. If you prefer, however, you can make these extensions reappear by turning this option off; see page 207 for more on this topic.

- **Launch folder windows in a separate process.** Use this last-resort feature only if you have programs that refuse to play nicely with one another. That is, whenever they're open, your system locks up, slows down, or displays other peculiar behavior. Using this option keeps each program in its own memory space, eliminating conflicts.

- **Remember each folder's view settings.** This checkbox makes every folder window open using whatever view it showed last (Details, Large Icons, or whatever).

  You might assume, then, that *removing* the checkmark would make every folder open with some standard default view, regardless of the last view you used. But for some reason known only to its diabolic creators, clearing this checkbox produces a much more complicated scheme:

  The first folder you open (in the My Computer or Windows Explorer window) appears in the view it used most recently—the *saved* view. Any additional folders you open also appear using this view.

  If you change the view of the *first* window—from Large Icons to Details, for example—you've just changed the saved view. Subsequent folders you open also inherit Details view, and when you reopen Windows Explorer or My Computer, Details view will prevail.

  But if you switch the *second* folder you open (or a later one) to Details view, you affect the default window view only during *this* folder-opening session. When you next reopen Windows Explorer or My Computer, you'll be back in Large Icons view. In other words, *when* you change views determines whether the View setting "sticks" for future openings of Windows Explorer or My Computer.

- **Show My Documents on the Desktop.** You're not allowed to throw away the My Documents desktop icon, but you can make it disappear by turning off this checkbox.

- **Show pop-up description for folder and desktop items.** If you point to (but don't click) an icon, a Taskbar button, and so on, you get a *tooltip*: a floating yellow label that helps identify what you're pointing to. If you find these Tooltips distracting, turn off this checkbox.

Note: The changes you make in the Folder Options settings are global; they affect *all* desktop windows.

The Taskbar

Windows 2000 is a *multitasking* operating system, which in English means that you can run multiple programs at the same time; the computer divides its processing power among them. This makes it easy to work on a letter or spreadsheet while an email program is open and operating, or while downloading a file from the Internet. However, when multiple windows or programs are open, they start to overlap and hide each other, sometimes making it difficult to find the window you want. The *Taskbar* alleviates this problem (Figure 4-12) by representing all currently open programs or windows as labeled buttons.

The Taskbar has several important functions:

- **It shows you what's happening.** The right end of the Taskbar—the *Tray*—contains little status icons that show you the time, whether or not you're online, whether or not your laptop's plugged in, and so on.

- **It lists every open window and program.** Each time you launch an application or open a desktop window, a new button appears on the Taskbar. A single click makes that window pop to the front—a terrific tool in your fight against window clutter.

- **It gives you quick access to buried functions.** The left end of the Taskbar—the

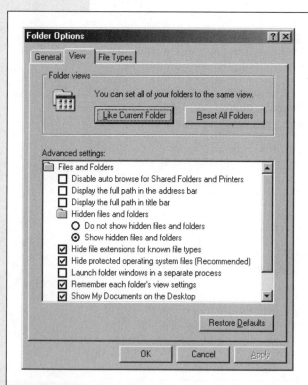

Figure 4-11:
Use the list in this dialog box to choose what you want to see and how you want to see it. Don't make important system files visible unless you're confident that you'd never accidentally delete them during a cleaning frenzy.

Quick Launch toolbar—lists the icons of programs, folders, disks, and files you use a lot.

This section covers each of these features in turn.

System Tray

The *System Tray* is the small area on the far right side of the Taskbar where you see the current time, a speaker icon, and other icons. Windows 2000 and various small programs maintain unobtrusive status displays here, or icons whose shortcut menus can configure the system or a program. Here are some of the icons you may find:

- The current **time,** which, when double-clicked, opens to display the Date/Time control panel programs.

Tip: If you point to the time and wait a moment without clicking, a pop-up balloon appears that tells you the day of the week and today's date.

- Click the **speaker** icon to summon a slider that you can use to adjust the volume of your speakers. Double-click the icon to open a dialog box that controls speaker balance and the volume level for all sound devices.

- A **display** icon, which you can use to change the resolution of your screen.

- A **battery meter** icon, which shows how much battery power your laptop has left.

- A **network** icon (two overlapping monitors), which appears while you're connected to the Internet.

- A **printer** icon, which appears while you're printing something.

- A **fax** icon, which appears while you're sending or getting a fax.

In addition, instant messaging, music players, and other programs may place their own icons in the System Tray.

Tip: Some computer manufacturers preinstall icons in the Tray, most of which you'll rarely use. Unfortunately, you may have to hunt for their Off switches. Sometimes you can right-click the icon to open a configuration dialog box; sometimes you may have to configure the options of the responsible application itself; and sometimes you may have to remove a shortcut to the application from your Start→ Programs→Startup folder, as described in Chapter 3.

Figure 4-12:
The Taskbar is usually divided into three chunks, according to its three functions. To identify an icon, point without clicking to view an identifying tooltip.

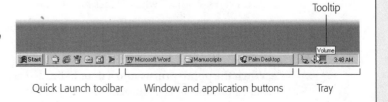

Quick Launch toolbar   Window and application buttons   Tray

Window Buttons

The Taskbar buttons make it easy to switch between open programs and windows; just click one to bring its associated window into the foreground, even if it had been minimized (see page 60).

Some programs, such as Microsoft Word, also display the name of the document you're working on. However, the button is almost always too small to show the full document name. The solution: Use the cursor to point to the button without click-ing. A tooltip pops up to identify the full name of the document.

You can also manipulate windows directly from the Taskbar button. Right-click the button to see the Control menu, which offers Minimize, Maximize, Close, and other useful window-control functions. It's a real time-saver to close a window without having to first bring it into the foreground.

The Quick Launch Toolbar

The left end of the Taskbar shows little icons that represent files, programs, and Windows you open frequently (see Figure 4-12); one click does the trick. For details on this toolbar and the others in Windows, see page 81.

Customizing the Taskbar

You're not stuck with the Taskbar as it came from Microsoft. You can resize it, move it, or hide it completely.

Moving the Taskbar

You can move the Taskbar to the top of your monitor, or, if you're a true rebel, to either side. To do so, just drag it there, using any blank spot in the central section as a handle. Release the mouse when you see a red line appear near the edge.

When the Taskbar is on the left or right edge of the screen, Windows widens it auto-matically. That's because the Taskbar buttons are horizontal; if you're expected to read their names, you need the added width.

Tip: No matter which edge of the screen holds your Taskbar, most applications adjust their own windows to make sure the Taskbar is visible. In other words, your Word document will shift sideways so that it doesn't overlap the Taskbar you've dragged to the side of the screen.

Resizing the Taskbar

When the Taskbar accumulates a lot of buttons and icons, you may want to enlarge it so you can see what's what. Here's how to adjust its size:

1. **Position your pointer on the inside edge of the taskbar.**

   That is, use the edge that's closest to the desktop.

2. **When the pointer turns into a double-headed arrow, drag the edge of the Task-bar in the appropriate direction.**

Drag it toward the desktop to enlarge the Taskbar, or toward the edge of your monitor to make it smaller.

Note: *If you're resizing a Taskbar that's on the top or bottom of the screen, the Taskbar automatically changes its size in increments of its original size. You can't fine-tune the height; you can only double or triple it, for example. If it's on the left or right edge of your screen, however, you can resize the Taskbar freely.*

Setting Taskbar Properties

You can further adjust the Taskbar's behavior in some interesting ways; for example, you can make it invisible until you request it. To do so, choose Start→Settings→ Taskbar and Start Menu. (Or right-click a blank spot on the Taskbar, and then choose Properties from the shortcut menu.)

The Taskbar and Start Menu Properties dialog box appears, offering these options:

• **Always on top.** This option makes sure that no other window can cover up the Taskbar. Your programs automatically shrink their own windows as necessary to accommodate the screen bulk of the Taskbar. (If you deselect this option, full-screen application windows don't make room for the Taskbar; they overlap it.)

You may find it useful to turn this option off when you need extra screen space, such as when you're running games and graphics programs. Some people like the additional lines they gain in a word processing window, or the additional Web-page space they can see in a Web browser.

Tip: *To open the Taskbar when it's not visible, just press Ctrl+Esc, or press the Windows-logo key on your keyboard.*

• **Auto hide.** This feature makes the Taskbar disappear whenever you're not using it. This is a clever way to give your entire screen to application windows, and yet have the Taskbar at your cursor-tip when you need it.

When Auto hide is enabled, the Taskbar disappears when you click anywhere else, or when your cursor has moved a short distance from the Taskbar. You can

---

GEM IN THE ROUGH

The Taskbar Shortcut Menu

The Taskbar has its own, very useful shortcut menu, which you can summon by right-clicking any blank spot on the Taskbar. It offers several commands for organizing swarms of open windows (see "Manipulating Windows with the Taskbar" on page 65), as well as a Toolbars command that lets you show and hide the four Windows Taskbar tool-bars. (See page 70 for more on these toolbars.)

Furthermore, in some applications, you'll see additional commands on the Taskbar button shortcut menu. For example, the Taskbar button shortcut menu for Eudora offers a command to check for new email.

---

see a thin line along the edge of your screen, which represents the edge of the Taskbar. As soon as your pointer moves close to that black line, the Taskbar reappears. (This feature can be inconvenient when one of your programs comes complete with its own toolbar or status bar at the bottom of the screen; you may keep inadvertently activating the Taskbar instead of the application control you need.)

- **Show clock.** The "Show clock" option shows or hides the current time from the Taskbar Tray.

Hiding the Taskbar manually

You may occasionally want to dedicate all your desktop space to an application window. Perhaps you're designing a complicated set of graphics, or you need to see more rows in a spreadsheet. In these situations, you can hide the Taskbar like this:

1. **Position your mouse pointer on the inside edge of the Taskbar.**

   When you reach the right spot, the pointer turns into a double-headed arrow.

2. **Drag the Taskbar edge toward the edge of the monitor.**

   When the Taskbar disappears, you can see a thin line representing the hidden edge. To bring the Taskbar back, move your mouse toward this line until the usual cursor turns into a double-headed arrow, then drag the Taskbar back onto the screen.

Taskbar Toolbars

Windows offers four canned Taskbar *toolbars:* separate, recessed-looking areas on the Taskbar containing special-function features (see Figure 4-13). You can add icons to any toolbar, and you can also create your own toolbars (see the next section).

To make these toolbars appear or disappear, right-click a blank spot on the Taskbar and choose from the list of toolbars that appears. The ones with checkmarks are the ones you're seeing now; choose one with a checkmark to make the toolbar disappear.

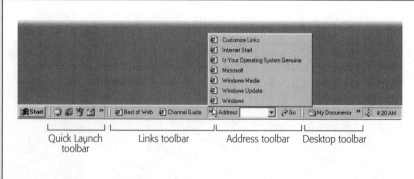

Figure 4-13:
Toolbars eat into your Taskbar space; use them sparingly. If you've added too many icons to the toolbar, an arrow appears at its right end. Click it to expose a list of the commands or icons that didn't fit.

Quick Launch Toolbar

For sheer convenience, the Quick Launch toolbar puts the Start menu to shame. Maybe that's why it's the only toolbar that appears on your Taskbar automatically. It contains icons for functions that Microsoft assumes you'll use most often:

- **Show Desktop**, a one-click way to minimize (hide) *all* the windows on your screen to make your desktop visible. Don't forget about this button the next time you need to burrow through some folders, put something in the Recycle Bin, or perform some other activity in your desktop folders. *Keyboard shortcut:* Windows key+D.

- **Launch Internet Explorer**, for one-click access to the Web browser included with Windows.

- **Launch Outlook Express**, for one-click access to the email program included with Windows (see Chapter 12).

But you should consider those buttons only hints of this toolbar's power. What makes it great is how easy it is to add your *own* icons, those you use frequently. There's no faster or easier way to get them open, no matter what you're doing on your PC—the Taskbar is always visible and showing your favorite icons.

To add an icon there, simply drag it from whatever desktop window it's in (or from the Start menu, or even the desktop itself) onto the Quick Launch toolbar area, as shown in Figure 4-14. To remove an icon, right-click it and choose Delete from the shortcut menu. (You're removing only its image from the Quick Launch toolbar; you're not actually removing any software from your computer.) If you don't use Outlook Express for email, for example, remove it from the Quick Launch toolbar.

Desktop Toolbar

The Desktop toolbar (Figure 4-13) is a row of icons representing the icons sitting on your desktop: My Computer, My Documents, and so on. This toolbar can make

Figure 4-14:
You can add almost any kind of icon to the Quick Launch toolbar (an application, document file, disk, folder, control panel, or whatever) just by dragging it there (top); the thick vertical bar shows you where it'll appear. The only challenge is to find the window that houses the icon you want to add. If it's an application, see page 55 for hints on finding the actual icon of the program in question.

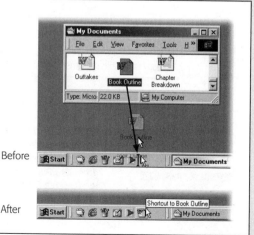

Before

After

your Taskbar very crowded. You can ease the crowding by right-clicking the toolbar and deselecting Show Text. Naturally, this creates a new problem—without the text all the icons may not be easily identifiable.

Consider avoiding this space-hungry toolbar. Instead, when you need to access one of the icons on your desktop, click the Show Desktop icon on the Quick Launch toolbar.

Address Toolbar, Links Toolbar

These toolbars are exactly the same as the window toolbars described on page 73. Those toolbars, however, appear only in the windows in which you've summoned them; these appear on the Taskbar at all times.

Redesigning Your Toolbars

To change the look of a toolbar, right-click a blank spot on that toolbar to display its shortcut menu. The shortcut menu offers these choices, depending on the toolbar:

- **View** lets you change the size of the icons on the toolbar.

- **Show Text** identifies each toolbar icon with a text label.

- **Refresh** redraws the Links or Desktop toolbar if it needs updating. For example, suppose you drag an icon onto your desktop. The Desktop toolbar doesn't change to list the new icon—until you use this Refresh command.

- **Open** works only with the Quick Launch and Links toolbars. It opens a window that lists what's in the toolbar, so that you can delete or rename the icons conveniently. (Of course, you can also delete or rename something on these toolbars by right-clicking an icon and choosing Delete or Rename from the shortcut menu. But using the Open command can be useful when you're performing extensive changes to the toolbar; it opens a window, where the icons are larger and you have more working room.)

- **Show Title** makes the toolbar's name (such as "Quick Launch" or "Desktop") appear on the toolbar.

Tip: You can enlarge an individual toolbar by placing your mouse pointer on either edge of the toolbar. When the pointer changes to a double-headed arrow, drag to the right to make the toolbar wider. (Doing so may make the other toolbars smaller, however.)

Figure 4-15:
Top: To park a toolbar in a different location, drag upward on the ridge at the left edge. Bottom: What you get is a strange sort of floating toolbar; it's now an on-screen, perpetually available launcher. (Use Tooltips, or choose Show Text from its shortcut menu, to identify the icons.) If you drag the toolbar to an edge of the screen, it becomes glued there like a second Taskbar.

Moving toolbars

You don't have to keep toolbars at the bottom of the screen; you can move them anywhere on your screen you find handy, as shown in Figure 4-15. To return a toolbar to its original location, drag its title bar back onto the Taskbar.

The disadvantage to moving a toolbar off the Taskbar is that you're using screen real estate that might be better used by your document windows. In addition, any windows you open *cover* the on-screen toolbar, rendering it useless. Of course, you can minimize all the windows to get to the toolbar, but that seems more like work than convenience.

Creating toolbars

The Quick Launch area of the Taskbar is such a delight that you might wish you could create several *different* Quick Launch toolbars, each stocked with the icons for a different project or person. One could contain icons for all the chapters of a book you're writing; another could list only your games.

Fortunately, Microsoft has anticipated your craving. It's easy to create as many different custom toolbars as you like, each of which behaves exactly like the Quick Launch toolbar.

Windows creates toolbars from *folders;* so the first step is to fill a folder with the icons (or shortcuts) that you'll want to add to the custom toolbar. Just drag this folder's icon onto the Taskbar; when you release the mouse, it instantly becomes a toolbar of its own.

Feel free to tailor it as described in the previous discussions—by changing its icon sizes, hiding or showing the icon labels, or adding new icons to it by dragging them from other desktop windows.

FREQUENTLY ASKED QUESTION

The Not-So-Amazing Disappearing Toolbar

I made a custom toolbar, and actually spent quite a lot of time on it. And then, when I needed more space on my Taskbar, I right-clicked it and chose Close from shortcut menu.

And now I want it back. But when I right-click a blank area on the Taskbar and choose Toolbars, my custom toolbar isn't listed there! How do I get it back?

You've discovered an unfortunate little quirk of custom toolbars: They don't really exist. All you've done is added a folder listing to your Taskbar, as fleeting as the morning dew. If you close a custom toolbar, it's gone forever.

The folder from which you created it, however, is still hanging around. If you want your toolbar back, just drag the corresponding folder back to the Taskbar.

Icons, Shortcuts, and the Recycle Bin

Every disk, folder, file, application, printer, and networked computer, on or attached to your PC, is represented on your screen by an icon and a name. To avoid spraying your screen with hundreds of thousands of overlapping icons, Windows organizes them into folders, and put those folders into *other* folders, and so on, until only a handful of icons actually appears on your screen.

This folders-in-folders scheme works beautifully at reducing screen clutter, but it means that you've got some hunting to do whenever you want to open a particular icon. You've got to *open* folder after folder until you corner your quarry.

Making this navigation process easy and understandable is one of the primary design goals of Windows—and of this chapter.

Tip: To create a new folder to hold your own icons, right-click where you want the folder to appear (on the desktop or in any desktop window except My Computer), and choose New→Folder from shortcut menu. The new folder appears, its temporary "New Folder" name highlighted. Type a new name for the folder and then press Enter.

Two Ways to Navigate

Windows offers two key ways to navigate your folders:

- **My Computer.** Using this scheme, you double-click one folder after another, leaving a trail of open windows behind you, burrowing ever deeper into the folders-within-folders.

• **Windows Explorer.** You do all of your navigating in a single window, where all the folders appear in a vertical list that looks something like an outline.

Each method has its advantages, as described in this section; you'll probably settle on using one or the other most of the time.

Navigating the My Computer Icon

When you double-click the My Computer icon in the upper-left corner of the screen, you see icons that represent the disk drives attached to, or installed inside, your computer (see Figure 5-1, top). By double-clicking one of these icons, you open a window that lists the folders and files on it (Figure 5-1, bottom). Frequently, you have to open folders *within* folders (subfolders) to find the actual icon you're looking for.

Tip: As you navigate your folders, keep in mind the power of the Backspace key. Each time you press it, you jump to the parent window of the one you're now looking at—the one that contains it. For example, if you're perusing a folder inside My Documents, pressing Backspace opens the My Documents window.

Likewise, the Alt key, pressed with the right and left arrow keys, serves as a Back and Forward button. Use this trick to "walk" backward or forward through the list of windows you've most recently opened.

For example, if you double-click your C: drive icon, here are three of the most important folders you'll find:

• **Documents and Settings.** This folder contains a subfolder for each person who's been authorized to use this PC. Each folder stores the preferences of the account holder: what's on his desktop, what his Start and Favorites menus look like, and what's in his My Documents folder. (The My Documents icon on the desktop is only a *shortcut* to this folder [see page 29], which is where your files are actually stored.)

It also contains a folder called All Users; anything in *its* Desktop, Documents, Favorites, and Start Menu folders show up on *everyone's* desktop, My Documents folder, Favorites, and Start menu. Unless you have administrative rights, you'll be able to open only your own folders in Documents and Settings.

• **Program Files.** This folder contains all of your applications—Word, Excel, Internet Explorer, your games, and so on.

• **WINNT.** This most hallowed folder contains Windows itself, the thousands of little files that make Windows Windows. Most of these folders and files have cryptic names that appeal to cryptic people. In general, the healthiest PC is one whose WINNT folder has been left alone.

Navigating with Windows Explorer

One of the most efficient means of seeing what's on your hard drive is the Windows Explorer window. Because many Windows veterans prefer the Explorer browsing scheme to My Computer, Microsoft provides at least five ways to open it:

- Choose Start→Programs→Accessories→Windows Explorer.

- Right-click a disk or folder icon and choose Explore from the shortcut menu.

- Shift-double-click any disk or folder icon.

- Choose Start→Run, type *explorer,* and then press Enter.

- Press the Windows-logo key+E.

As shown in Figure 5-2, the hierarchy of folders appears on the left. Because you get to see every folder on the machine at once, you're less likely to lose your bearings using Windows Explorer than when simply burrowing through folder after folder as described in the previous section.

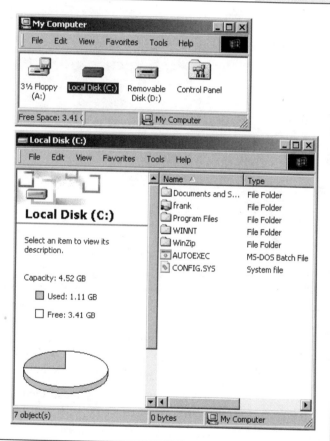

Figure 5-1:
Top: The My Computer window is the starting point for any folder-digging you want to do. It shows the "top-level" folders: the disk drives of your PC, plus shortcuts of other drives on the network that your administrator may have set up here. If you double-click the icon of a removable-disk drive, such as your CD-ROM drive, Zip drive, or Jaz drive, you get only an error message unless there's actually a disk in the drive.

Bottom: The contents of a typical hard drive (C: drive) after you've clicked the "View the entire contents of this drive" link (not shown).

In the left pane, each folder may have a + or – button next to it. A + button next to a folder means that it contains subfolders; click the + button to *expand* the list of subfolders. At this point, the plus sign turns into a – sign, which you can click to collapse the folder listing.

Slide the scroll bar for the left pane all the way to the top. If you expand My Computer, you'll see that the disks associated with your PC (hard drives, floppy, CD-ROM, and so on) appear under My Computer. At the top is the folder called Desktop. In the Explorer's terms, the Desktop is the top of the hierarchy (see Figure 5-2), with My Documents, My Computer, and other pieces connected to it.

Tip: You may find it easier to move around a number of files or folders if you open *two* copies of the Explorer. Just right-click two different icons (or the same one twice), and choose Explore from the shortcut menu each time.

Then, to arrange the Explorer windows so you can access them easily, right-click the Taskbar and select Tile Windows Horizontally, Tile Windows Vertically, or Cascade Windows. Windows adjusts the size and position of both incarnations of the Explorer window (and any other open windows) so that they're fully visible.

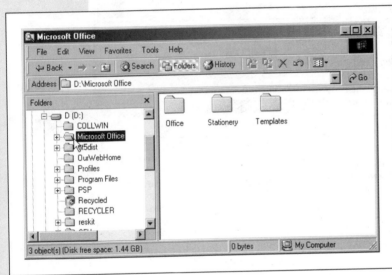

Figure 5-2:
If you look closely, you can see that one of the folders in the left column is open. The contents of the open folder are displayed in the right-hand pane. You use the scroll bars on either side to move up and down through the listing.

Viewing folder contents

To see what's in one of the disks or folders listed at the left side of the Explorer window, you can use any of these techniques:

- Click a folder in the left pane of the Explorer; the contents appear in the right pane.

- Double-click a folder in the left pane, or click the + button next to its name. The branch expands in the left pane.

- Right-click a folder in the left pane and select Open from the shortcut menu. A new window opens, displaying the contents of the folder you clicked. (To open a *program or document* that appears in either side of the window, double-click it as usual.)

The right-side pane of the Explorer window behaves exactly like any folder window; don't forget that you can change it to an icon view or list view, for example, using the View menu as usual.

Keyboard shortcuts

If you arrive home one day to discover that your mouse has been stolen, or if you just like doing things with the keyboard, you'll enjoy the shortcuts that work in the Explorer window:

left-arrow	Collapses the highlighted folder—or, if it's already collapsed, highlights its "parent" folder.
right-arrow	Expands a highlighted folder, or if it's already expanded, highlights the first folder inside it.
F6 or Tab	Highlights the other half of the window.
Alt+left arrow	Highlights whatever folder you last highlighted.
Backspace	Highlights the "parent" disk or folder of whatever you've got highlighted.
Ctrl+Z	Undoes whatever you just did in this Explorer window.
A, B, C...	Highlights the first visible file or folder in the left-pane hierarchy that matches the letter you typed. Type the same letter again to highlight the *next* matching icon.

You can also press the letter keys to highlight a folder or file that begins with that letter, or the up and down arrow keys to "walk" up and down the list.

When the panel is too narrow

As shown by the D: drive in Figure 5-2, clicking the + button to expand a folder gives you a new indented list of folders inside it. If you expand folders within folders to a deep enough level, the indentation may push the folder names so far to the right that you can't read them. You can remedy this problem with any of the following actions:

• Adjust the relative sizes of the window halves by dragging the vertical bar between them.

• Position your mouse pointer over a folder whose name is being chopped off. A tooltip appears to display the full name of the folder.

• Use the horizontal scroll bar at the bottom of the left pane to shift the contents.

Life with Icons

Both of the navigational schemes described so far in this chapter have only one goal in life: to help you manage your icons. Windows displays every piece of software and hardware on your PC as an independent icon. You could spend your entire workday just mastering the techniques of naming, copying, moving, and deleting these icons—and plenty of people do.

How to Name Your Icons

To rename a file, folder, printer, or disk icon, begin like this:

- Click carefully, just once, on the icon's name (not the icon itself).

- Click its icon and then press F2.

- Right-click the icon and choose Rename from the shortcut menu.

A "renaming rectangle" now appears around the current name; type the new name you want, and then press Enter. If another icon in the folder has the same name, or if you included an illegal character (described next), Windows beeps and makes you choose a different name.

A folder or file name can be up to 255 characters long, including spaces and the *file extension* (the three-letter suffix that identifies the type of file). Windows won't let you use the following symbols in a filename, however (because they're reserved for behind-the-scenes use by Windows itself): \ / : * ? " < > |

Even so, it's not a good idea to create names that approach the 255-character maximum length, because you'll have trouble reading their names in Windows Explorer and in dialog boxes. Furthermore, some of your older applications (those that aren't certified for Windows 2000) may not be able to open files with extremely long filenames.

You can give more than one file or folder the same name, as long as they're not in the same folder. For example, you can have as many files named "Letter to Smith" as you wish, as long as each is in a different folder.

Icon Properties

As you may have read in Chapter 1, *properties* are a big deal in Windows. Properties are preference settings, and you can change them independently for every icon on your machine.

To view the Properties dialog box (Figure 5-3) for an icon, choose your favorite technique:

- Right-click the icon; choose Properties from the shortcut menu.

- While pressing Alt, double-click the icon.

- Highlight the icon, and then press Alt+Enter.

- Highlight the icon, and then click the Properties button on the Standard Buttons window toolbar (if you see it).

But these settings aren't the same for every kind of icon. Here's what you can expect from opening the Properties dialog boxes for various kinds of desktop icons (see Figure 5-3).

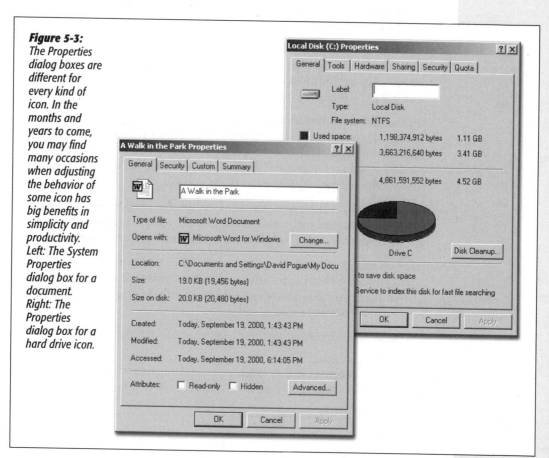

Figure 5-3:
The Properties dialog boxes are different for every kind of icon. In the months and years to come, you may find many occasions when adjusting the behavior of some icon has big benefits in simplicity and productivity.
Left: The System Properties dialog box for a document.
Right: The Properties dialog box for a hard drive icon.

- **My Computer.** This Properties dialog box is packed with useful information about your machine. For example, the **General** tab (shown in Figure 5-3) tells you what kind of processor is inside, how much memory (RAM) your PC has, and what version of Windows you've got. The **Network Identification** tab shows your PC's name and workgroup, as it shows up on the network. The **Hardware** tab offers access to several equipment-related tools, such as the Device Manager and the Hardware Wizard (see Chapter 16).

  The **User Profiles** tab shows the list of people who've been given accounts on this machine; you can use the buttons here to change their *type* (see page 374), to copy their settings, or to delete them. Finally, the **Advanced** tab provides some very technical options pertaining to the computer's virtual memory, environment, startup options, and system-failure options.

- **Disks.** On the **General** tab, you get to see the disk's name (which you can change), its capacity (which you can't change), and how much of it is full. The **Tools** tab offers quick access to such disk-maintenance tools as Backup and the disk defragmenter (see Chapter 19); **Hardware** tells you the brand and model names for your disks; the **Sharing** tab (if you have it) controls who can access this disk over the network (see Chapter 15).

- **Data files.** The **General** properties for a plain old file, such as one of your documents, control special file-system properties known as *attributes*. For example, the *read-only* attribute locks the document; you can open it and read it, but you can't make any changes to it. *Hidden* makes the icon invisible.

  The **Custom** and **Summary** tabs, if available, let you type in descriptive information about the file for easier searching and tracking. (The Custom tab is part of the Microsoft Office Fast Find feature, and shows up only on Office documents; Windows 2000 uses the information on the Summary tab to assist its Indexing Service, which is described on page 41.)

- **Folders.** Here you get the same checkbox options described for data files. But you may also see a separate tab called **Sharing**, which lets you make this folder available for invasion by other people on your office network (see Chapter 13).

- **Program files.** A program file offers many of the same options as data files (including the same General, Security, and Summary tabs). It also offers a **Version** tab that stores a considerable wealth of detail about the program's version number, corporate parent, language, and so on.

- **Shortcuts.** You can read about these useful controls at the end of this chapter.

Tip: The Properties dialog boxes for disks, folders, and data files may also offer a Security tab, which gives you control over which network citizens are allowed to meddle with this information. Details on pages 303-304.

Copying and Moving Folders and Files

Moving folders and files from one disk or folder to another is a snap. Windows offers two different techniques: dragging icons and using the Copy and Paste commands.

No matter which method you use, however, you start by showing Windows which icons you want to copy or move. And you do that by *highlighting* them.

Highlighting Icons

To highlight one icon, you just click it once. But you don't have to move or copy one icon at a time; you can select multiple icons in the same folder or disk window. For example, you can move a bunch of documents from one folder in your My Documents folder to another, or copy a group of them onto a backup disk.

Tip: It's easier to work with multiple icons in Details view (page 67), where all the icons are displayed in a single column.

To highlight multiple files in preparation for moving or copying, use one of these techniques:

To highlight all the icons

To select all the icons in a window, press Ctrl+A (the keyboard equivalent of the Edit→Select All command).

To highlight several icons in a list

If you're looking at the contents of a window in Details view, you can drag vertically over the file and folder names to highlight a group of consecutive icons.

Alternatively, click the first icon you want to highlight, and then press Shift as you click the last file. All the files in between are automatically selected, along with the two icons you clicked.

To highlight several icons in Icon view

If you're looking at the contents of a window in Large or Small icon view, you can highlight a group of neighboring icons just by dragging across them. Start with your cursor above and to one side of the icons; drag diagonally. As you drag, you create a temporary dotted-line rectangle. Any icon that falls within this rectangle darkens to show that it's selected.

Tip: If you include a particular icon in your diagonally dragged group by mistake, click it while pressing Ctrl. That removes it from the selected cluster.

To highlight only specific icons

If you want to highlight only, for example, the first, third, and seventh icons in the list, start by clicking icon No. 1. Then, while pressing the Ctrl key, click each of the others. (If you click a selected icon *again* while pressing Ctrl, you *de*select it. You can use this trick when you've just highlighted an icon by accident.)

Tip: The Ctrl-key trick is especially handy if you want to select *almost* all the icons in a window. Press Ctrl+A to select everything in the folder, then hold down the Ctrl key while you click any unwanted sub-folders to deselect them.

Copying by Dragging Icons

You can drag icons from one folder to another, from one drive to another, from a drive to a folder on another drive, and so on. (When you've selected several icons, drag any *one* of them; the others go along for the ride.)

Here's what happens when you drag icons in the usual way (using the left mouse button):

- Dragging to another folder on the same disk *moves* the icon.

- Holding down the Ctrl key while dragging to another folder on the same disk *copies* the icon. (If you do so within a single window, you get a duplicate of the file called "Copy of [whatever its name was].")

- Dragging an icon from one disk to another *copies* the folder or file.

- Pressing Shift while dragging from one disk to another *moves* the folder or file (without leaving a copy behind).

Tip: You can move or copy icons by dragging them either into an open window or directly onto a disk or folder *icon.*

Figure 5-4:
Right-dragging icons is much easier, and much safer, than left-dragging when you want to move or copy something, thanks to this shortcut menu.

The right-mouse button trick

Instead of trying to remember all of those possibilities, consider using the *right* mouse button as you drag. When you release the button, the menu shown in Figure 5-4 appears.

Tip: You can cancel a dragging operation at any time by pressing the Esc key.

Dragging icons in Windows Explorer

You may find it easier to copy or move icons in Windows Explorer, because the two-pane display format makes easier to see where your files are and where they're going. (Remember, you can add the Explorer-like folder-list hierarchy to *any* window by choosing View→Explorer Bar→Folders.)

1. **If necessary, click the + button next to the appropriate icon in the left pane to make the destination folder visible.**

   For example, if you want to copy an icon into a certain folder, expand the drive (by clicking the + button) so that you can see its list of folders. If the destination is a folder *within* that folder, expand its parent folder as necessary.

2. **Click the *icon* (not the + button) of the disk or folder that contains the icon you want to manipulate.**

   Its contents appear in the right pane.

3. **Locate the icon you want to move in the right pane; drag it to the appropriate folder in the left pane (see Figure 5-5).**

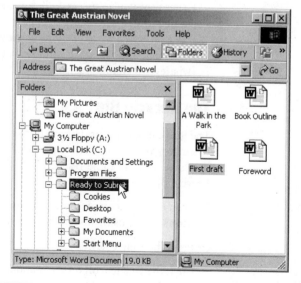

Figure 5-5:
The file First Draft, located in My Documents→The Great Austrian Novel, is being dragged to the folder named Ready to Submit. As the mouse pointer moves over any folder in the left pane, that folder's name is highlighted automatically. When you arrive at the correct target folder, release the mouse button.

Copying by Using Copy and Paste

Dragging icons to copy or move them may feel good, because it's so direct: You actually see your arrow cursor pushing the icons into the new location.

But you pay a price for this satisfying illusion: You may have to spend a moment or two fiddling with your windows, or clicking buttons in the Explorer folder hierarchy, so that you have a clear "line of drag" between the icon to be moved and the destination folder.

Fortunately, there's a better way: You can use the Cut, Copy, and Paste commands to move icons from one window into another. The routine goes like this:

1. **Highlight the icon or icons you want to move.**

2. **Right-click one of the icons. Choose Cut or Copy from the shortcut menu.**

   Alternatively, you can choose Edit→Cut or Edit→Copy, using the menu bar at the top of the window. (Eventually, you may want to learn the keyboard shortcuts for these commands: Ctrl+C for Copy, Ctrl+X for Cut.)

   The Cut command makes the highlighted icons disappear from the window. You've stashed them on the invisible Windows Clipboard, as described in Chapter 7.

   The Copy command also places copies of the files on the Clipboard, but doesn't disturb the originals.

3. **Right-click the window, folder icon, or disk icon where you want to put the icons. Choose Paste from the shortcut menu.**

   Once again, you may prefer to use the menu bar: Choose Edit→Paste. *Keyboard equivalent:* Ctrl+V.

   Either way, you've successfully transferred the icons. If you pasted into an open window, you'll see the icons appear there. If you pasted onto a closed folder or disk icon, you have to open the icon's window to see the results. And if you pasted right back into the same window, you get a duplicate of the file called "Copy of [whatever its name was]."

The Recycle Bin

The Recycle Bin is your desktop trash basket. This is where you put files and folders when they've outlived their usefulness; it's the waiting room for data oblivion. There they stay, waiting to be rescued by being dragged out again, until you *empty* the Recycle Bin.

You can drag an icon on top of the Recycle Bin icon, or move highlighted folder or file icons into it using one of these techniques:

• Press the Delete key.

• Click the Delete icon on the Standard Buttons toolbar.

- Choose File→Delete.

- Right-click a highlighted icon and choose Delete from the shortcut menu.

You can put unwanted files or folders into the Recycle Bin from any folder window, from within Windows Explorer, or even inside the Open File dialog box of Windows applications.

Note: All of these methods put icons from your *hard drive* into the Recycle Bin. But deleting an icon from a removable drive (floppy, Jaz, or Zip drives, for example) or from other computers on the network, does *not* involve the Recycle Bin, and gives you no opportunity to retrieve them.

POWER USERS' CLINIC

Secrets of the Send To Command

If you find yourself copying or moving certain icons to certain folders or disks with certain regularity, it's time to exploit the File→Send To command that lurks in every folder window (and in the shortcut menu for almost every icon).

This command's submenus offer a quick way to copy and move highlighted icons to popular destinations. For example, you can teleport a copy of a highlighted file directly to a floppy disk by choosing File→Send To→3 1/2 Floppy. You're spared the tedium of choosing Copy, selecting the floppy drive, and choosing Paste. Another useful command is "Send To→Desktop (create shortcut)," which dumps a shortcut icon onto your desktop background. Then there's the Send To→Mail Recipient, which bundles the highlighted icon as an email attachment that's ready to send.

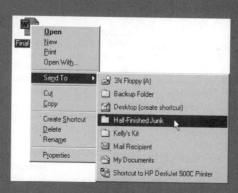

But the real power of the Send To command is its ability to accommodate your *own* favorite or frequently used folders. Lurking in your My Computer→C: drive→Documents and Settings→[Your Name] folder is a folder called SendTo. Any shortcut icon you place here shows up instantly in the File→Send To menus (and shortcut menus) of your desktop folders (and icons).

This folder, alas, is among those that Microsoft considers inappropriate for inspection by novices. As a result, the SendTo folder comes hidden in Windows. To make it appear, open any folder window; choose Tools→Folder Options; click the View menu; and turn on "Show hidden files and folders." Click OK. Now, when you open the My Computer→C: drive→Documents and Settings→[Your Name] folder, you'll see the SendTo folder.

Most people create shortcuts here for folders and disks (such as your favorite backup disk). When you highlight an icon and then choose Send To→My Documents, for example, Windows copies that icon to the My Documents folder. (If you press Shift while you do so, you *move* the icon to the other disk or folder.)

But you can even add shortcuts of applications (program files) to the SendTo folder. By adding WinZip to this Send To menu, for example, you'll be able to drop-kick a highlighted icon onto the WinZip icon (for decompressing) just by choosing Send To→WinZip. You can even create shortcuts of your printer or fax modem; thereafter, you can print or fax a document just by highlighting its icon and choosing File→Send To→[your printer or fax modem's name].

You'll be asked to confirm if you want to send the files to the Recycle Bin. After you click Yes, Windows moves the icons there (see Figure 5-6). Now the Recycle Bin icon changes: The container appears to be brimming over with paper.

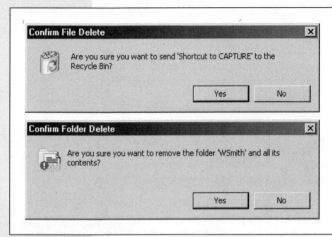

Figure 5-6:
It's easy to tell when a deletion is headed for the Recycle Bin—the confirming dialog box looks like the one shown here at top. If the deleted icon is being permanently and irrevocably deleted, the dialog box has a different icon (bottom), complete with an attention-getting exclamation point.

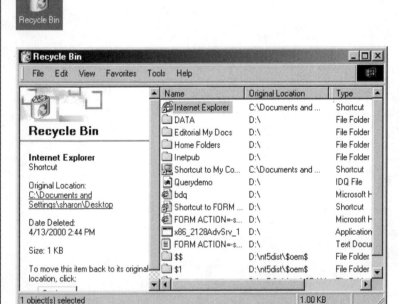

Figure 5-7:
When you double-click the Recycle Bin (top), the Recycle Bin window (bottom) displays information about each folder and file it holds. You can sort the contents, making it easier to find a deleted icon, by clicking the gray column heading for the type of sort you need.

Restoring Deleted Files and Folders

If you change your mind about sending something to the software graveyard, open the Recycle Bin by double-clicking. A window like the one in Figure 5-7 opens.

To restore a file or a folder, right-click its listing and choose Restore from the short-cut menu. To restore multiple files, select them using any of the techniques described on page 93. Then right-click any *one* selected file and choose Restore from the short-cut menu. And to put everything back, of course, just click the Restore All button (at the bottom of the left-side Recycle Bin window pane).

Restored, in this case, means returned to the folder from whence it came, wherever on your hard drive it was when you deleted it. If you restore an icon whose original folder has been deleted in the meantime, Windows re-creates that folder to hold the restored file(s).

Tip: You don't have to put icons back into their original folders. If you *drag* them out of the Recycle Bin window, you can put them back into any folder you like.

Emptying the Recycle Bin

While there's an advantage in the Recycle Bin (you get to undo your mistakes), there's also a downside: The files in the Recycle Bin occupy as much disk space as they did when they were stored in folders. Deleting files doesn't gain you any additional disk space until you *empty* the Recycle Bin.

That's why most people, sooner or later, follow up an icon's journey to the Recycle Bin with one of these two cleanup operations:

• Right-click the Recycle Bin icon and choose Empty Recycle Bin from the short-cut menu.

• Choose File→Empty Recycle Bin, or click the Empty Recycle Bin button in the window.

• Open the Recycle Bin window. Highlight only the icons you want to get rid of. Click the Delete button on the toolbar (if it's there), or press the Delete key. (This method lets you empty only *part* of the Recycle Bin.)

• Wait. When the Recycle Bin accumulates so much stuff that it occupies a significant percentage of your hard drive space, Windows empties it automatically, as described in the next section.

All of these procedures produce "Are you sure?" messages.

Customizing the Recycle Bin

You can make several useful changes to the behavior of the Recycle Bin. Right-click its icon and choose Properties from the shortcut menu. The Recycle Bin Properties dialog box appears (see Figure 5-8).

Skip the confirmation

On the Global tab of the Recycle Bin Properties panel, a checkbox controls the confirmation notice that opens every time you delete a file or folder.

If you like the comfort of being consulted about every deletion, leave the checkmark in the box. If you clear the checkmark, files you delete will move to the Recycle Bin without asking for your confirmation. (Turning off this warning isn't much of a safety risk; after all, files aren't really being removed from your drive when you put them in the Recycle Bin.)

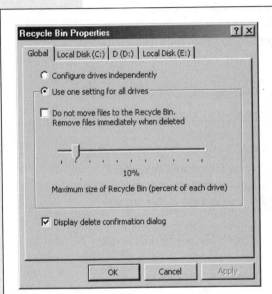

Figure 5-8:
Use the Recycle Bin Properties dialog box to govern the way the Recycle Bin works, or even if it works at all. If you have multiple hard drives, the dialog box has a tab for each of them, so that you can configure a separate and independent Recycle Bin on each drive.

Skip the Recycle Bin, always

If you, a person of steely nerve and perfect judgment, never delete a file in error, you can make your files bypass the Recycle Bin entirely when you delete them. You'll reclaim disk space instantly when you press the Delete key to vaporize a highlighted file or folder.

To set this up, turn on the "Do not move files to the Recycle Bin" checkbox (Figure 5-8). And voilà: Your safety net is gone. (Especially if you also turn off the confirmation dialog box as described above. Then you're *really* living dangerously.)

Skip the Recycle bin, just this time

If always skipping the Recycle Bin seems too extreme, consider this safety/convenience compromise: Leave the Recycle Bin safety net in place most of the time, but bypass the Recycle Bin only when it seems appropriate.

The trick to skipping the Recycle Bin on a one-shot basis is to press the Shift key while you delete a file. Doing so—and then clicking Yes in the confirmation box—

---

deletes the file permanently, skipping its layover in the Recycle Bin. (The Shift-key trick works for every method of deleting a file: pressing the Delete key, choosing Delete from the shortcut menu, and so on.)

Warning: Some older programs (those not written specifically for Windows 95 or later) let you delete files right from within the program. Files deleted this way don't get sent to the Recycle Bin. Similarly, files you delete at the DOS prompt also disappear into never-never land rather than into the Recycle Bin. Therefore, for safety's sake, you should make all your deletions through the Windows Explorer or My Computer or on the desktop. The file goes to the Recycle Bin only if Windows 2000 Pro knows about the deletion.

Adjusting reserved space

Behind the scenes, the Recycle Bin is a reserved space on your hard drive. When you delete an icon or drag it to the Recycle Bin icon, Windows actually moves it to that reserved space. (If you have more than one hard drive, each drive has its own reserved space and its own Recycle Bin icon, although opening the Recycle Bin icon always shows you all the deleted files from *all* drives.)

To adjust the size of this reserved area, open the Recycle Bin's Properties dialog box, click "Configure drives independently," and then click each drive tab in turn. Click the sliding arrow to move the percentage up or down. The field below the slider shows the percentage of the drive that's reserved. (If your drives are different sizes, you might want to make things easier for yourself by just reserving the same percentage on each drive.)

Remember that the Recycle Bin works on a "first in, first out" basis, so if you make the reserved space very small, deleted files may pass into oblivion faster than you'd like.

Creating Shortcuts

Files and folders are often in the most inconvenient places—particularly in Windows 2000 Pro, where many documents you might need are several levels down in the folder structure, or even on another computer.

Shortcuts are very small files that act as pointers to other icons; when you double-click the shortcut icon, the original disk, folder, file, or program opens (Figure 5-9). You can also set up a keystroke for a shortcut icon, so that, in effect, you can open any program or document just by pressing a certain key combination.

Shortcuts provide quick access to things you use a lot; because you can make as many shortcuts of a file as you want, and put them anywhere on your PC, you can effectively keep an important program or document in more than one folder. Just create a shortcut of each to leave on the desktop in plain sight. Or drag their icons onto the Start button or the Quick Launch toolbar (see page 78), which also works by creating shortcuts. In fact, everything listed in the Start→Programs menu is also a shortcut; the My Documents folder on the desktop is a shortcut, too (to the actual My Documents folder).

Tip: Resist the confusion that may arise from the Microsoft term *shortcut,* which refers to one of these duplicate-icon pointers, and *shortcut menu,* the context-sensitive menu that appears when you right-click almost anything in Windows. The shortcut *menu* has nothing to do with the shortcut icons feature; maybe that's why it's sometimes called the *context* menu.)

Creating and Deleting Shortcuts

To create a shortcut, you can use any of these methods:

- Right-drag an icon from its current location (Windows Explorer, a folder window, or even the Search window described on page 36) to the desktop. When you release the mouse button, choose Create Shortcut(s) Here from the menu that appears.

- If you're not in the mood for using a shortcut menu, you can also left-drag an icon while pressing Ctrl and Shift. A shortcut appears the instant you release the mouse button.

- Right-click the icon and select Create Shortcut from the shortcut menu. A shortcut to the icon you clicked appears in the same folder. You can then move the shortcut by dragging it into a new window, or by right-clicking it and choosing

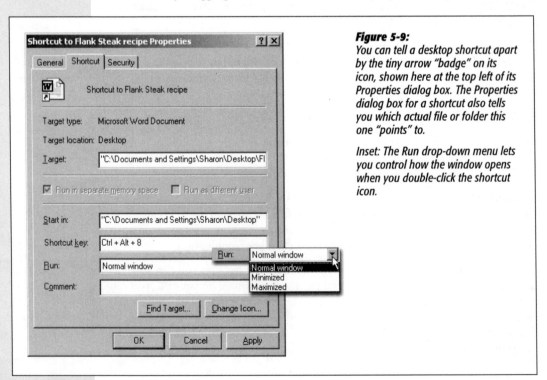

Figure 5-9:
You can tell a desktop shortcut apart by the tiny arrow "badge" on its icon, shown here at the top left of its Properties dialog box. The Properties dialog box for a shortcut also tells you which actual file or folder this one "points" to.

Inset: The Run drop-down menu lets you control how the window opens when you double-click the shortcut icon.

Cut from the shortcut menu. Then right-click where you want the shortcut to be (such as a different window) and choose Paste.

- If the original icon isn't handy or you don't want to go find it, you can right-click the desktop and select New→Shortcut. When the Create Shortcut dialog box appears, type its path (see page 32), if you know it, or click the Browse button to search your computer for the icon you want. Click Next, accept or change the name for the shortcut, and click Finish. The shortcut appears on your desktop.

You can rename or delete a shortcut just as you'd delete any icon, as described earlier in this chapter. Neither deleting nor renaming a shortcut affects the file it points to.

What to Do with Shortcuts

The point of shortcuts is to save time and energy. Merely placing a bunch of shortcuts on your desktop is only the tip of the iceberg; here are several other ways shortcuts can be useful.

Adding a program shortcut to the Start menu

Having your favorite programs listed in the Start→Programs menu is fairly convenient, but not as convenient as having frequently used programs right at the *top* of the Start menu. To put one there, just drag a shortcut (from your desktop or from an open folder window) directly onto the Start-menu button. From now on, when you open the Start button, the program will be instantly available. (See page 50 for more on editing the Start menu.)

- **Disk drives.** Right-click a disk drive in the Windows Explorer or My Computer (see page 86) and drag it to the desktop to create a shortcut to the drive. When you double-click the shortcut icon, you'll see the disk's contents almost instantly—much faster than having to open the Explorer or My Computer window.

- **Other computers.** You can also create shortcuts to other computers—or even to individual files on them. The other computer can be on your network, or can even be a computer you connect to using Dial-Up Networking (see Chapter 14).

  Use the My Network Places icon (see page 289) to find the computer or file you want, right-drag it to your desktop (or another folder), and choose Create Shortcut(s) Here from the shortcut menu.

Unveiling a shortcut's original icon

To locate the original icon from which a shortcut was made, right-click the shortcut icon and choose Properties from the shortcut menu. As shown in Figure 5-9, the resulting box shows you where to find the "real" icon. Click Find Target; Windows opens the folder containing the original file.

Assigning a keyboard shortcut

Even after reading all of this gushing prose about the virtues of shortcuts, efficiency experts may still remain skeptical. Sure, shortcuts let you put favored icons everywhere you want them to be, such as your Start menu, Quick Launch toolbar, the desktop, and so on. But they still require clicking to open, and that still means taking your hands off the keyboard, and that, if you're a touch typist, means slowing down.

But lurking within the Shortcut Properties dialog box (Figure 5-9) is a feature with immense ramifications: the Shortcut Key box. By clicking here and then pressing a key combination, you can assign a personalized keystroke for the shortcut's file, program, folder, printer, networked computer, or disk. Thereafter, you can summon the corresponding window to your screen, no matter what you're doing on the PC, by pressing that simple keystroke.

Two rules apply as you're trying to choose keystrokes to open your favorite icons:

- They can't incorporate the Backspace, Delete, Esc, Print Screen, or Tab keys, or the Space bar.

- There are no one- or two-key combinations available here. Your combination must include either Ctrl+Alt or Ctrl+Shift *and* another key.

All of this is the operating system's attempt to prevent you from inadvertently duplicating one of the built-in Windows keyboard shortcuts, thoroughly confusing both you and your computer.

Getting Help

Fortunately, there are many sources for help in Windows 2000 Pro—in fact, so many that it's easy to get confused. This brief chapter offers some help with Help.

Built-in Windows 2000 Help

When Microsoft refers to help, it's generally referring to *online* help. (As you've noticed, Windows 2000 comes with very little in the way of printed instructions.) The following discussion starts with the simplest and most direct methods of getting online help and proceeds to more complicated ones.

Press F1

Whenever you're confused or lost in Windows 2000 Pro, press the F1 key, which always stands for Help in Windows and Windows programs. Because the help is *context sensitive*, the sort of help you'll get depends on where you are and what you're doing. If you're working in a program, the help will be for that program. If you're using some aspect of Windows 2000 Pro, the help will be the operating system's help.

Click the Right Mouse Button

Often you can find useful information if you right-click the dialog box, description, or menu that has you stymied. If a box labeled What's This? pops up, click inside it for more information (see Figure 6-1).

Click the Question Mark

In some windows and dialog boxes, you'll see a question mark on the right end of the title bar. Click the question mark then click an item in the dialog box. If instant help is available, a box opens with some explanatory text (Figure 6-1, right).

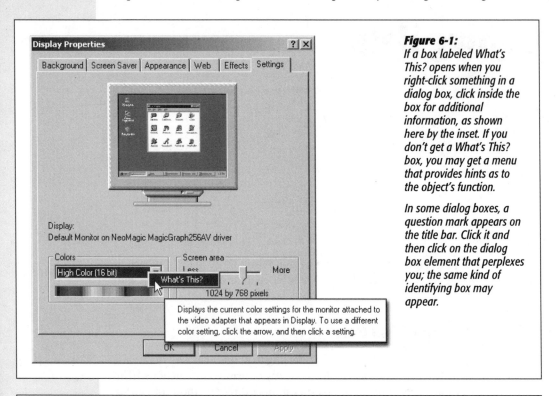

Figure 6-1:
If a box labeled What's This? opens when you right-click something in a dialog box, click inside the box for additional information, as shown here by the inset. If you don't get a What's This? box, you may get a menu that provides hints as to the object's function.

In some dialog boxes, a question mark appears on the title bar. Click it and then click on the dialog box element that perplexes you; the same kind of identifying box may appear.

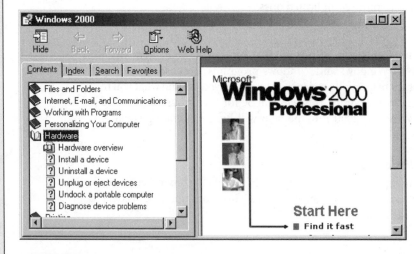

Figure 6-2:
Book icons represent topics and subtopics. Click on one to reveal the contents. The Help Viewer allows you to see the table of contents, index, or search results while you're looking at a Help topic.

Choose Help from the Menu Bar

For help with the Windows program you're using, click Help on the program's menu bar. Depending on the program, this Help menu may contain a command called Help Topics, Contents, or Contents and Index. Select it to open the Help topics specific to that program.

Choose Start→Help

To access the Help system as a whole for Windows 2000 Pro, choose Start→Help (or press F1 at the desktop). The Help Viewer opens, offering an integrated table of contents, an index, and a full-text search feature to find information easily (Figure 6-2).

The Windows 2000 Help system uses HTML (the Hypertext Markup Language that's used to create Web pages) to format and display information. As a result, many of its pages contain underlined *hyperlinks* that, when clicked, connect you either to the World Wide Web or, more often, to other topics in the Help system for additional information.

Finding a Help topic

To find a topic in the Help Viewer, click one of the tabs.

- **Contents.** The Contents tab displays a table of contents organized by subject. You can browse by clicking the book icons to reveal topics and subtopics. Click a topic to display the contents (Figure 6-2).

- **Index.** The Index tab displays the Help system's contents in alphabetical order. If you know a word that describes the subject you're looking for, type it in the field at the top of the tab. Double-click an index entry to display the topic. (Topics are frequently indexed under more than one entry.)

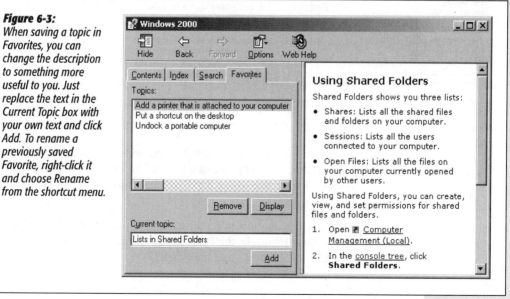

Figure 6-3:
When saving a topic in Favorites, you can change the description to something more useful to you. Just replace the text in the Current Topic box with your own text and click Add. To rename a previously saved Favorite, right-click it and choose Rename from the shortcut menu.

• **Search.** To find every instance of a word or phrase, type it on the Search tab and then click List Topics. Be as specific as possible. For example, if you're looking for information on *virtual private networking,* you get better results by searching for all three words (or *VPN*) than if you search for *networking* alone. Both searches return many results, but the *networking* search results will include dozens of entries that have nothing to do with VPN.

• **Favorites.** Once you find the information you need, you can bookmark the topic so you can find it again faster the next time. This tip is especially useful for procedures that you use regularly, but not so often that you memorize the steps.

To bookmark a help page that's currently on the screen, click the Favorites tab and then the Add button (Figure 6-3). The Help viewer adds the title to the topics list; you can return to it later by double-clicking its name in the list.

If you're connected to the Internet, you can click the Web Help button on the Help Viewer's button bar for Web-based help and technical support, as shown in Figure 6-4.

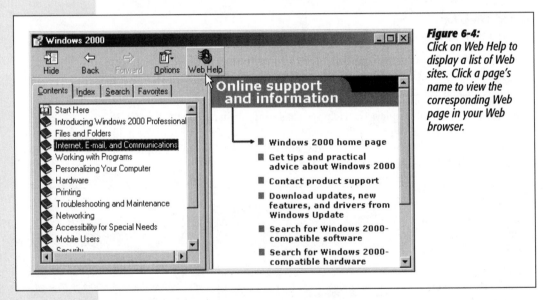

Figure 6-4:
Click on Web Help to display a list of Web sites. Click a page's name to view the corresponding Web page in your Web browser.

Printing a Help topic

To print a particular Help topic, right-click the topic window and choose Print from the shortcut menu. To print just part of a topic, use the mouse to highlight the text you want to print. Right-click in the highlighted portion, and then choose Print from the shortcut menu.

To print all the topics in a section, select the topic on the Contents tab. On the Help toolbar, click Options→Print. In the Print Topics dialog box, select Print the Selected Heading and All Subtopics, and then click OK.

Copying a Help topic

To copy information in the Help viewer to another document, follow these steps:

1. In the topic pane of the Help viewer, right-click inside the topic and then Select All from the shortcut menu.

   All of the help text is now highlighted.

2. Right-click again inside the topic window and select Copy.

   Windows 2000 copies the selected material to the invisible Clipboard.

3. Open the document to which you want to copy the topic, such as a word processing document or email message. Click where you want the topic to appear. Finally, right-click where you want the text to appear and choose Paste from the shortcut menu.

More Web Help

To get the latest documentation for Windows 2000 Pro, go to the Windows 2000 Home Page at *www.microsoft.com/windows2000*.

If you are an administrator (logged on with administrative privileges; see page 369), you can go to Windows Update (on your Start menu and at *http://windows update.microsoft.com*) to download and install the latest drivers, patches, and new help files.

Getting Help for an MS-DOS Command

To get help for an MS-DOS command, click Start→Programs→Accessories→ Command Prompt. In the command prompt window, type the name of the command followed by /? (a slash and a question mark), as shown in Figure 6-5.

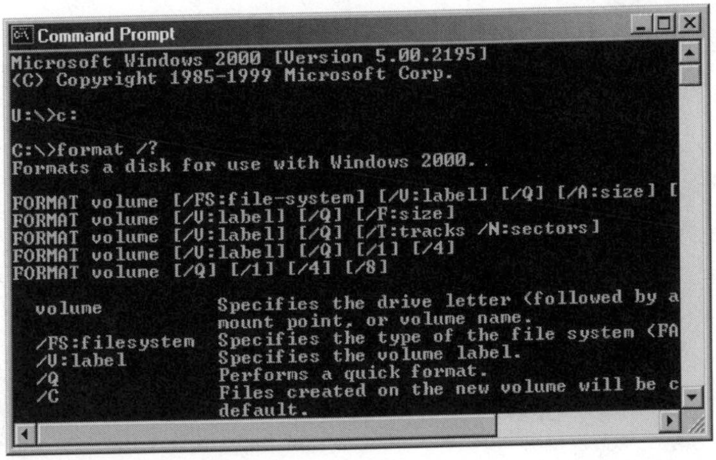

Figure 6-5:
For information on the Format command, you'd type in format /?, *as shown here. You can use the scroll bars on the window to see all the Help information.*

To see a list of all MS-DOS commands that you can use from a Windows 2000 command prompt, along with short description of what they do, simply type *help* at a command prompt, and then use the scroll bar to read the (long) list of commands.

Keyboard Commands in the Help Viewer

If you prefer using the keyboard (or your mouse isn't available), you can use the keyboard commands in the list below to navigate the various sections (*panes*) of the Help Viewer window.

Press These Keys	To Do This
F6	Switch between Help navigation pane and topic pane
Ctrl+Tab	Switch to the next tab in the navigation pane
Up Arrow	Move up one item in the Contents, Index, or Search Results pane
Down Arrow	Move down one item in the Contents, Index, or Search Results pane
Shift+F10	Open the Shortcut menu
Alt+0	Open the Options menu
Ctrl+Home	Move to the beginning of a topic
Ctrl+End	Move to the end of topic
Ctrl+A	Select all text in the pane
Alt+O, then P	Print a topic
Alt+F4	Close the Help viewer

2

Part Two:
The Components of
Windows 2000

Running Applications

While it's true that you need to be able to use your computer's operating system, the operating system isn't the reason you have a computer. The operating system is the platform, but the objective is to run *programs*.

Starting Programs

Windows 2000 Pro lets you start programs in many different ways. You'll probably use one or two of these methods all the time, and rarely use others:

- Double-click the program's icon or shortcut, wherever it may be: in the Windows Explorer window, on the desktop, in a folder, and so on. Or right-click such an icon and choose Open from the shortcut menu.

- Highlight a program (or program shortcut) icon and then press Enter.

- Choose the program's name from the Start→Programs menu.

- Click a program's icon on the Quick Launch toolbar (page 78).

- Choose Start→Run, then type the program file's name (page 55), and press Enter.

- Type the program filename and path into the Address bar in any folder window and press Enter (page 73).

- Double-click a document associated with the program.

- Use Search (page 36) to locate a program or file associated with a program and double click to start.

• Have Windows launch the program for you, either when the PC starts up (see page 48) or at a time you specify, using the Scheduled Tasks tool (see page 166).

What happens next depends on the program you're using. Most present you with a new, blank, untitled document. Some, such as FileMaker and PowerPoint, greet you with a question: Do you want to open an existing document or create a new one? A few oddball programs, such as Adobe Photoshop, don't open any window at all when first launched.

Switching Between Programs

One of the attractions of Windows 2000 is its ability to run multiple programs at the same time. For every program you open, a button appears on the Taskbar; some programs produce a button for every *document* that's open.

Switching Using the Taskbar

The easiest way to switch between programs is to click the corresponding button on the Taskbar (Figure 7-1). With each click, you make the corresponding window or program pop to the front.

Even with a lot of windows open, it's fairly easy to navigate among them simply by clicking buttons on the Taskbar. Sometimes, though, you need to clear the whole screen to get at something on the desktop. That's when you click on the desktop icon, which minimizes *all* windows, collapsing them to the Taskbar. (The desktop icon, which sits on the Quick Launch toolbar, looks like an old-fashioned blotter.)

Tip: Instead of clicking the Desktop button on the Quick Launch toolbar, you can also press Windows key+D.

Which Programs Run?

The easiest programs to use in Windows 2000 Pro are the ones made specifically for Windows 2000, but programs written for Windows NT or Windows 95/98/Me work almost identically.

Many, but not all, programs written for Windows 3-point-something (3.x) work fine in Windows 2000 Pro. Even those that work, however, may have limitations: For example, if one Windows 3.x program crashes, they all do. This crashing doesn't affect your other running non-3.x programs, but it's a nuisance. Furthermore, Windows 3.x requires all files and folders to use DOS 8.3 file names ("ltrtomom.doc" instead of "Letter to Mom"). As a result, every file you save

from a program originally designed for Windows 3.x must have a short name, and when you use the File→Open command from within one of these programs, you'll see your Windows 2000 files and folders represented by truncated names.

To see if your favorite program is *sure* to run in Windows 2000, search Microsoft's list of certified Windows 2000-compatible programs at *www.microsoft.com/windows2000/ready*. It's not a list of every 2000-compatible program on earth, but it's a good first step in your investigation.

After you've cleared the open windows to the Taskbar, you can:

- Open them all back up with another click on the Desktop icon (or another press of Windows key+D).

- Open them one at a time by clicking the buttons on the Taskbar.

- Close a window by right-clicking its Taskbar button and selecting Close from the shortcut menu.

Switching with Alt+Tab

You can also bring a different program to the front without using the mouse. If you press Alt+Tab, you summon a floating palette that displays the icons of all running programs, as shown in Figure 7-1. Each time you press Alt+Tab, you highlight the next icon; when you release the keys, the highlighted program jumps to the front.

To move *backward* through the open programs, press *Shift*+Alt+Tab.

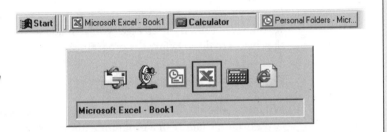

Figure 7-1:
Top: Every window has a Taskbar button.

Bottom: Press Alt+Tab to highlight successive program icons. When you release the Alt key, the highlighted program jumps to the front.

UP TO SPEED

Multitasking and Its Discontents

It has been theoretically possible to *multitask*—run multiple programs and switch among them—ever since Windows 3.0. Multitasking was dependent on the programs voluntarily sharing the time and attention of the central processing unit (CPU), an arrangement called *cooperative* multitasking.

In those days, however, neither the hardware nor the software was up to the job. Cooperative multitasking works only when applications are designed to smoothly yield processing time to other applications. The computers and programs at that time were built on *16-bit architecture* (16 bits of information handled at a time), and 16-bit programs work as if other programs don't exist. So these applications incessantly bumped into each other, sometimes resulting in a crashed program or a completely halted system, requiring a reboot.

Windows 95 was the first *32-bit* version of Windows, and the 32-bit architecture made *preemptive* multitasking possible. In preemptive multitasking, Windows has the authority to act as traffic cop, to keep applications isolated from one another, so that a badly behaved application doesn't necessarily bring down the whole system.

Now, all these years later, Windows 2000 (like Windows NT and Windows 95/98/Me) is a 32-bit system, most popular software is 32-bit, and PCs are a good deal more powerful than they were in 1991. The result is that Windows 2000 multitasks handily, with far fewer crashes.

Closing Programs

When you quit an application, the memory it uses is returned to the system for use by other Windows programs and operating subsystems. You can close it using one of these techniques:

- Choose File→Exit.

- Press Atl+F, then X.

- Click the program window's Close box (the X at the upper-right corner of the window), or double-click its Control-menu icon (the icon at the upper-left corner of the window).

Tip: If you see *two* Close boxes, the one closer to the corner of your monitor closes the *program*. The inner one closes the currently open *document,* but leaves the application running.

- Right-click the program's Taskbar button and choose Close from the shortcut menu.

If you haven't saved the changes you've made to your document, you'll be offered the chance to do so before the program shuts down all the way.

Escaping a Crashed Program

Windows 2000 Pro is very skilled at keeping itself alive. You can almost always recover from the failure of a program without losing data or facing a reboot.

Some symptoms of a crashed program include:

- The display appears to freeze—you can move the mouse pointer, but clicking has no effect.

- Some programs are working, but when you place the pointer over another, the pointer turns into an hourglass and stays that way.

- A warning dialog box tells you that a program is going to shut down (whether you like it or not).

Sometimes it's a false alarm; if you wait 30 seconds or so, everything will come back to life. But if it doesn't, follow these steps:

1. **Press Ctrl+Alt+Del.**

   The Windows Security dialog box appears.

2. **Click Task Manager.**

   Now the Windows Task Manager appears, listing all of the programs you're running at the moment.

3. **On the Applications tab, look for a program labeled Not Responding. Highlight it and click End Task.**

When the application disappears from the list, it's safe to close Task Manager and get on with your work. You can immediately restart the crashed program and get back to work, if you like.

Here are some other hints for working with Task Manager.

• When you press Ctrl+Alt+Delete, be patient. It may take a moment for the Windows Security dialog box to open.

• Sometimes when Task Manager opens, it shows all the programs as Running—even when you know that's not correct. Click Refresh Now on the View menu until Task Manager coughs up the truth.

• After you click End Task, Windows 2000 may open another dialog box claiming that "This Program is Not Responding." In that case, click the End Now button; despite an implication to the contrary, it's the only button that works.

Moving Data Between Documents

You can't paste a picture into your Web browser, and you can't paste MIDI music information into your word processor. But you can put graphics into your word processor, paste movies into your database, insert text into Photoshop, and combine a surprising variety of seemingly dissimilar kinds of data. And you can transfer text from Web pages, email messages, and word processing documents to other email and word processing files; in fact, that's one of the most frequently performed tasks in all of computing.

Cut, Copy, and Paste

Most experienced PC users have learned to trigger the Cut, Copy, and Paste commands from the keyboard, without even thinking. For example:

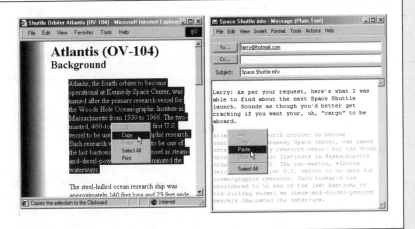

Figure 7-2:
Suppose you want to email some text you find on a Web page to a friend. Left: Start by dragging through it and then choosing Copy from the shortcut menu (or choosing Edit→Copy). Now switch to your email program, and paste it into an outgoing message (right).

1. **Highlight some material in the document before you (see Figure 7-2).**

   In most cases, this means highlighting some text (by dragging through it) in a word processor, layout program, email application, or even a Web page in your browser.

2. **Use the Cut or Copy command.**

   You can trigger these commands in any of three ways. First, you can choose the Cut and Copy commands found in the Edit menu of your document window. Second, you can press the keyboard shortcuts Ctrl+X (for Cut—think of the X as representing a pair of scissors) or Ctrl+C (for Copy). Finally, you can right-click the highlighted material and choose Cut from the shortcut menu.

   When you do so, the PC memorizes the highlighted material, socking it away on an invisible storage pad called the Clipboard. If you chose Copy, nothing visible happens. If you chose Cut, the highlighted material disappears from the original document.

   At this point, most people take it on faith that the Cut or Copy command actually worked; but if you're in doubt, choose Start→Programs→Accessories→System Tools→Clipboard Viewer. The Clipboard window appears, showing whatever you've copied.

3. **Click the cursor to indicate where you want the material to reappear.**

   This may entail switching to a different program, a different document in the same program, or simply a different place in the same document. (Using the Cut and Paste commands within a single document may be these commands' most popular function; it lets you rearrange sentences or paragraphs in your word processor.)

4. **Choose the Paste command.**

   Here again, you can do so either from a menu (choose Edit→Paste), by right-clicking and choosing Paste from the shortcut menu, or from the keyboard (press Ctrl+V). The copy of the material you had originally highlighted now appears at your cursor—that is, if you're pasting into a program that can accept that kind of information. (You won't have much luck pasting, say, a paragraph of text into Quicken.)

The most recently cut or copied material remains on your Clipboard even after you paste, making it possible to paste the same blob repeatedly. Such a trick can be useful when, for example, you've designed a business card in your drawing program and want to duplicate it enough times to fill a letter-sized printout. On the other hand, whenever you next copy or cut something, whatever was already on the Clipboard is lost forever.

Tip: Office 2000 is an exception; it doesn't wipe out the Clipboard's contents when you copy something new. In fact, it hangs onto the last *twelve* chunks of copied material. When it comes time to paste the material back into a document, you can use the Clipboard toolbar to specify which item you want to paste.

Drag-and-Drop

As useful and popular as it is, the Copy/Paste routine doesn't win any awards for speed; after all, it requires four steps. In many cases, you can replace that routine with the far more direct (and enjoyable) drag-and-drop method. Figure 7-3 shows how it works.

Tip: To drag highlighted material to a spot that's off the screen, drag the cursor until it approaches the top or bottom edge of the window. The document scrolls automatically; as you approach the destination, jerk the mouse away from the edge of the window to stop the scrolling.

Figure 7-3:
You can drag highlighted material (left) into a new spot (right).

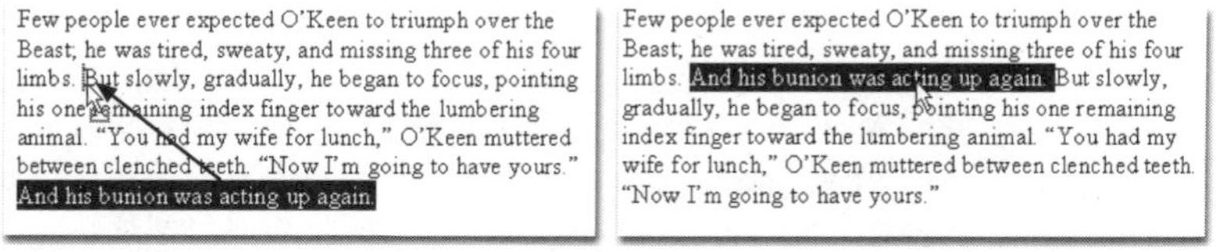

Few people ever expected O'Keen to triumph over the Beast; he was tired, sweaty, and missing three of his four limbs. But slowly, gradually, he began to focus, pointing his one remaining index finger toward the lumbering animal. "You had my wife for lunch," O'Keen muttered between clenched teeth. "Now I'm going to have yours." And his bunion was acting up again.

Few people ever expected O'Keen to triumph over the Beast; he was tired, sweaty, and missing three of his four limbs. And his bunion was acting up again. But slowly, gradually, he began to focus, pointing his one remaining index finger toward the lumbering animal. "You had my wife for lunch," O'Keen muttered between clenched teeth. "Now I'm going to have yours."

FREQUENTLY ASKED QUESTION

When Formatting is Lost

How come pasted text doesn't always look the same as what I copied?

When you copy text from, for example, Word, and then paste it into another program, such as the Notepad, you may be alarmed to note that the formatting of that text (bold, italic, the choice of font, size, and color, and so on) doesn't reappear intact. There could be several reasons for this problem.

For example, not every program *offers* text formatting; Notepad, for example, doesn't. And the Copy command in some programs (such as Web browsers) doesn't pick up the formatting along with the text; when you paste something you've copied from Internet Explorer and paste it into Word or WordPad, you get plain, unformatted text.

Finally, a note on *text wrapping:* Thanks to limitations built

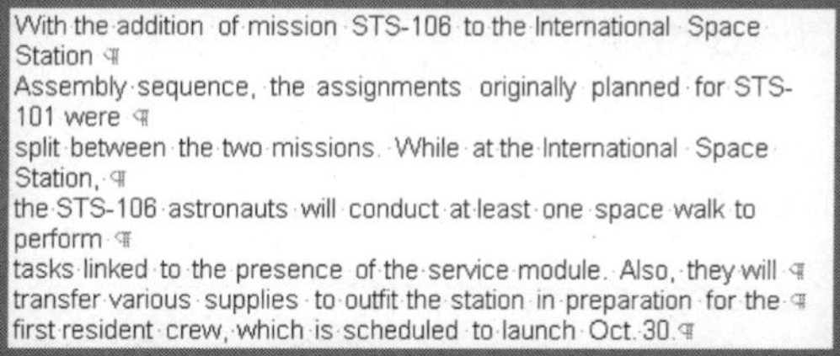

> With the addition of mission STS-106 to the International Space Station ¶
> Assembly sequence, the assignments originally planned for STS-101 were ¶
> split between the two missions. While at the International Space Station, ¶
> the STS-106 astronauts will conduct at least one space walk to perform ¶
> tasks linked to the presence of the service module. Also, they will ¶
> transfer various supplies to outfit the station in preparation for the ¶
> first resident crew, which is scheduled to launch Oct. 30. ¶

into the architecture of the Internet, email messages aren't like word processor documents. The text doesn't flow continuously from one line of a paragraph to the next, such that it reflows when you adjust the window size. Instead, email programs insert a press of the Enter key at the end of each line *within* a paragraph.

Most of the time, you don't even notice that your messages consist of dozens of one-line "paragraphs"; when you see them in the email program, you can't tell the difference. But if you paste an email message into a word processor, the difference becomes painfully apparent—especially if you then attempt to adjust the margins, as shown here.

To fix the text, you have to delete the invisible carriage return at the end of each line. Veteran PC users sometimes use the word processor's search-and-replace function for this purpose.

Several of the built-in Windows programs work with the drag-and-drop technique, including WordPad and Outlook Express. Most popular commercial programs offer the drag-and-drop feature, too, including email programs and word processors, Microsoft Office programs, and so on.

As shown in Figure 7-3, drag-and-drop is ideal for transferring material between windows or between programs. It's especially useful when you've already copied something valuable to your Clipboard, because drag-and-drop doesn't involve (and doesn't erase) the Clipboard.

The most popular use for the drag and drop technique, however, is rearranging the text in a single document. In, say, Word or WordPad, you can rearrange entire sections, paragraphs, sentences, or even individual letters, just by dragging them—a terrific editing technique.

Tip: When you use drag-and-drop to move text within a document, you *move* the highlighted text, deleting the highlighted material from its original location. If you press Ctrl as you drag, however, or when you drag text onto the desktop, you make a *copy* of the highlighted text.

Using drag-and-drop to the desktop

As shown in Figure 7-4, you can even drag text or graphics out of your document windows and directly onto the desktop. There your dragged material becomes an icon—a *Scrap file*.

When you drag a clipping from your desktop *back* into an application window, the material in that clipping reappears. Drag-and-drop, in other words, is a convenient and powerful feature; it lets you treat your desktop itself as a giant, computer-wide pasteboard, an area where you can temporarily stash pieces of text or graphics as you work.

Insert Object (OLE)

Here's yet another, much less popular relative of Copy and Paste: the Insert Object command, which is available in most Windows programs. (You may hear it referred to as Object Linking and Embedding, or OLE, or even "oh-LAY.")

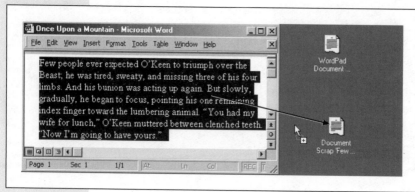

Figure 7-4:
When you drag material out of the document window and onto the desktop, you get a Scrap file. You can view a Scrap file just by double-clicking it, so that it opens into its own window.

Using OLE, you can insert material from an OLE *server* application (such as part of an Excel spreadsheet) into a document running on an OLE *client* application (such as Word). The spreadsheet material appears in the Word document, but when you click the spreadsheet in Word, the menus on your screen change to those of Excel! You can then manipulate the spreadsheet data using any of the standard Excel tools. (When you click on another part of the Word document, the menus revert to their original form.)

Some applications can function only as an OLE server or an OLE client; others can be both. Generally speaking, you'll have better results if you use two applications that are designed to share data with each other, such as Microsoft Office applications.

To insert data using OLE, choose Insert→Option in the OLE client program. You'll be prompted for the file you want to insert, or offered the chance to create a new document to embed. As the name Object Linking and Embedding implies, you can either create a *link* to another kind of document or *embed* it:

- **Linking** means that you're grabbing a material from an OLE server document (such as an Excel spreadsheet) and inserting it into a document running on an OLE client (such as Word). In this scenario, the transferred material remains

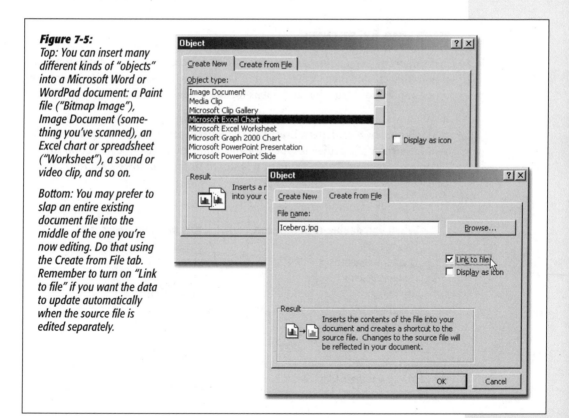

Figure 7-5:
Top: You can insert many different kinds of "objects" into a Microsoft Word or WordPad document: a Paint file ("Bitmap Image"), Image Document (something you've scanned), an Excel chart or spreadsheet ("Worksheet"), a sound or video clip, and so on.

Bottom: You may prefer to slap an entire existing document file into the middle of the one you're now editing. Do that using the Create from File tab. Remember to turn on "Link to file" if you want the data to update automatically when the source file is edited separately.

"live." If you edit the spreadsheet in Excel, the changes you make will appear in the spreadsheet portion of the Word document the next time you open it.

The advantage of this arrangement is that the linked file (the spreadsheet) isn't actually saved as part of your Word document, so the Word file doesn't grow any larger. The disadvantage is that if you move or distribute the Word document, the link gets broken, and the spreadsheet doesn't go along for the ride.

- **Embedding** inserts the OLE server material (such as the spreadsheet) directly into the client document (the Word file). The client document therefore becomes much larger; furthermore, changes you make to the server document aren't reflected in the embedded copies. The advantage of this method, however, is that you can at least email the Word document it to someone without losing the embedded spreadsheet.

Tip: OLE isn't nearly as popular as drag-and-drop or Copy/Paste, despite the apparent flexibility it provides. That's because OLE has a reputation for behaving erratically; the high hopes that Microsoft had for it as a cornerstone of its application technology haven't panned out. If you decide to use OLE, it's best to do so using Microsoft applications on a fast computer with plenty of memory.

Filename Extensions

Every operating system needs a mechanism to associate documents with the applications that created them. When you double-click a Microsoft Word document icon, for example, Word launches and opens the document.

In Windows, every file name has a suffix called a *filename extension,* which is a period followed by three letters. Every time you install a new program, the installer lets Windows know about the file types (the filename extensions) the new application is capable of opening. This information is stored in the Windows 2000 Registry (see page 405).

Here are some common examples:

When you double-click this icon	... this program opens it
Fishing trip.doc	Microsoft Word
Quarterly results.xls	Microsoft Excel
Home Page.htm	Internet Explorer
Agenda.wpd	Corel WordPerfect
A Home Movie.avi	Windows Media Player
Animation.dir	Macromedia Director

Tip: For an exhaustive list of every file extension on the planet, visit *www.whatis.com*; click the link for Every File Format in the World.

Behind the scenes, Windows maintains a massive table that lists every extension and the program that "owns" it. To see this list, choose Tools→Folder Options from the menu bar of any folder window. As shown in Figure 7-6, the Folder Options box appears; click the File Types tab.

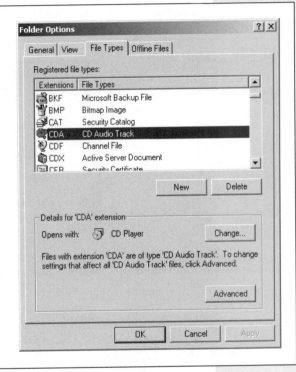

Figure 7-6:
Every software program you install must register the file types it uses. The link between the file type and the program is called an association. This dialog box displays the icon for each file type, and an explanation of the selected listing.

Making File Extensions Show Up

It's possible to live a long and happy life without knowing much about these extensions; indeed, because they don't feel very user-friendly, Microsoft designed Windows to *hide* the extensions on most icons. (See Figure 7-7.) If you're new to Windows, and haven't poked around inside the folders on your hard drive much, you may never even have seen them.

Note: Hiding file extensions also makes it harder for you to change one accidentally, which would confuse Windows and maybe even prevent you from opening open the icon to see what's in it.

Some people appreciate the way Windows hides the extensions, because the screen becomes less cluttered and less technical-looking. Others pine for the Windows 3.1 days, when every icon appeared with its suffix.

To make Windows show the file suffixes on *all* icons, choose Tools→Folder Options from any folder window's menu bar. In the Folder Options dialog box, click the View tab. Turn off "Hide file extensions for known file types," and then click OK.

Hooking up a file extension to a different program

Windows comes with several programs (Notepad and WordPad, for example) that can open text files (whose file extension is *.txt*). And Windows also comes with several programs (Paint, Imaging, Internet Explorer) that can open JPEG picture files (whose file extension is *.jpg*). So how does it decide *which* program to open when you double-click a .txt or .jpg file?

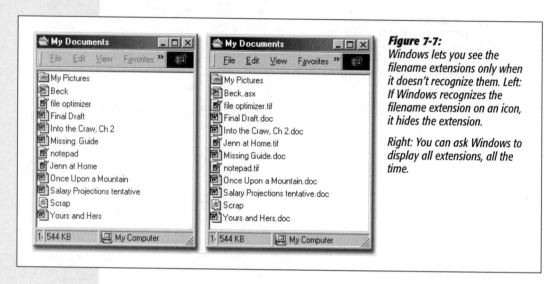

Figure 7-7:
Windows lets you see the filename extensions only when it doesn't recognize them. Left: If Windows recognizes the filename extension on an icon, it hides the extension.

Right: You can ask Windows to display all extensions, all the time.

Windows comes with its own extension-to-application pairing list, shown in Figure 7-6. But at any time, you can reassign a particular file type (filename extension) to a different application.

To do so, right-click the file's icon and choose Open With from the shortcut menu. Windows presents the Open With dialog box shown in Figure 7-8. Just find, and double-click, the name of the program you want to open this kind of file from now on.

As you do so, be sure to check the status of the checkbox below the list; it says, "Always use this program to open these files." If that checkbox is on, then *all* files of this type (.jpg, for example) will open in the newly selected application from now on. If the checkbox is off, then the new application will open only *this* .jpg file, only this once.

Tip: This technique is a good cure if you've made a file association by mistake, or when a new program you install performs a "power grab," claiming a particular file type for itself without asking you.

Creating your own file associations

Every now and then, the dialog box shown in Figure 7-8 appears unbidden. It comes up automatically whenever you try to open a file whose extension Windows doesn't recognize. Maybe you've tried to double-click a document created by an old DOS program that doesn't know about the Windows file-association feature, or maybe your company's programmers wrote a custom application that Windows doesn't yet know about.

In any case, there are two ways to teach Windows to use a particular application whenever you open similar documents in the future. First, you can open the Folder Options dialog box shown in Figure 7-6; the New button lets you associate the mystery document with an application of your choice.

Figure 7-8:
Scroll through the list of installed programs to select the one that can handle the file you're trying to open. If you select the option to use this program for every file with the same extension, you create a file association that will handle similar files in the future.

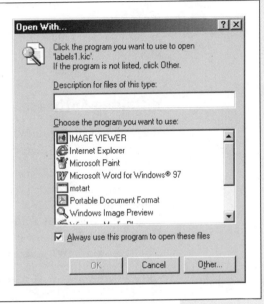

Figure 7-9:
Use this window (a cousin to the Open File dialog box pictured above) to search your system and locate the application you want to associate with a specific file type. Double-click a folder to open it, or use the icons on the left side of the window to move to a particular location. Here, a mysteriously compressed down-loaded file is about to be opened by a decompression program called Aladdin Expander.

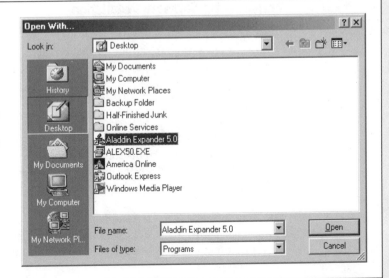

Tip: It's sometimes useful to associate a particular document type with a program that *didn't* create it. For example, if you double-click a text file, and the Open With dialog box appears, you might decide that you want such documents to open automatically into WordPad. (It's fine to set up a single application to open documents of different types—text files, Word files, and RTF files, for example.)

Second, you can use the Open With dialog box shown in Figure 7-8; this method is often simpler, because all you have to do to summon this dialog box is to double-click the mystery file.

If the program you want to take over the document-opening task doesn't show up in this list, click Other in the Open With dialog box. Windows opens the window shown in Figure 7-9. Double-click the name of the application you'll want to open this file type. Add a description of this file type, if you like.

Installing Software

Today, almost all new software comes to your PC from one of three sources: a CD, your network, or the Internet.

In general, you can't use any of these programs without first installing them using a special program provided by the software company. Besides the obvious chore of transferring the software files to your hard drive, the installer also adds the new program's name to the Start→Programs menu, tells Windows about the kinds of files (filename extensions) it can open, transfers certain required files to special locations on your drive, and makes certain changes to the Registry (see page 405).

Tip: For instructions on adding or removing components of Windows 2000 Pro itself, see page 420.

Preparing for Software Installation

Before you begin the installation process for any software, take the following safeguards:

- Exit any open programs. (One quick way: Right-click the buttons on the Taskbar, one at a time, and choose Close from the shortcut menu.)

- Temporarily disable your virus-scanning software, which may foul up the installation process.

Installing Software from a CD

The CD you received from the software company is probably a self-starter; it offers the *AutoPlay* feature, which means that as soon as you put the CD into the CD-ROM drive, the installer launches.

Installing software with CD Autoplay

If Autoplay is working, a few seconds after you insert the CD into your drive, your cursor becomes an hourglass. A few seconds later, the welcome screen for your new software appears.

The installation process is usually a wizard, so you'll be asked to answer questions, choose options, and click Next at each window. Along the way, you may be asked to type in a serial number, which is included with the product.

If the last installer window has a Finish button, click it. The installation program transfers the software files to your hard drive, and the program's name appears on your Start→Programs menu.

Installing software without Autoplay

If the installation routine doesn't begin automatically when you insert the CD, then you'll have to take matters into your own hands. One of two factors is at play:

- **There's no AutoPlay file.** If the CD wasn't designed to launch an installer automatically when it's inserted, then you'll have to follow the instructions that came with the software.

- **You've got AutoPlay turned off.** If the instructions imply that the CD *should* have Autoplay, you can manually launch the installation program. Open My Computer and double-click the icon for your CD-ROM drive. In the CD-ROM drive window, look for an icon called Setup.exe or Autorun.inf. Double-click the former; right-click the latter and choose Install from the shortcut menu.

  If you find both files, it doesn't matter which method you use. The installation now gets underway.

Installing software using Add/Remove Programs

As noted in Chapter 8, the Add/Remove Programs tool in the Control Panel is a master list of programs installed on your PC. You can also install new programs using its Add New button, like this:

1. **Choose Start→Settings→Control Panel. Double-click the Add/Remove Programs icon.**

   The Add/Remove Programs dialog box appears.

2. **Click the Add New Programs button.**

   Now the Browse window appears, so that you can choose the disk or downloaded installer.

Tip: If you click Windows Update at this point, your PC will connect you to Microsoft's update site on the Internet. Use this option only if you're looking to download and install Microsoft product updates.

---

3. **Click the CD or Floppy button. Place the CD or floppy with the program in the appropriate drive, and then click Next.**

   The wizard will search for a file named Setup.exe (the almost universal name for installer programs). When it finds the file, you'll see a dialog box like the one in Figure 7-10.

If you're installing a program you've downloaded, the wizard won't find the disk. Instead, it will offer you a Browse button, so that you can navigate to, and double-click, its Setup.exe program.

4. Click Finish.

The installer takes over. (The exact steps depend on the software in question.)

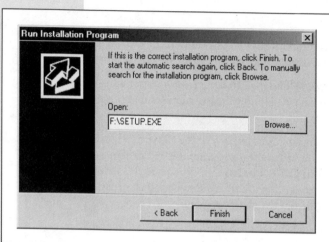

Figure 7-10:
If the program you're looking for isn't actually called Setup.exe, click the Browse button to search for the correct file. If you select a file that isn't actually an installer, the file will open, but no installation will be performed.

Installing from the Network

The typical user on a typical corporate network (if there is such a thing) almost never has the necessary permissions to install or uninstall programs. To ensure safety and security, most network administrators try to keep unauthorized applications off the company machines.

However, there may well be programs that the network administrator has "published" on the network that you can install onto your machine; she may also choose to *push* some programs onto your machine from her end—that is, to install them remotely. (If you try to delete a pushed program, it gets reinstalled automatically.)

Note: Publishing or pushing applications is entirely in the network administrator's control. She decides what features of the application are available, where you're allowed to install it, and so forth.

If your network administrator has published some programs, your Add/Remove Programs control panel offers a button called Add Programs from Your Network. Click it to look over, and choose to install, the published applications.

Installing from Another Computer

If there *is* no network administrator—that is, if you're on a peer-to-peer network (or a *very* informal client/server network)—you can set up a shared folder on one computer that can serve as an installation source for the programs you use, as shown in Figure 7-11. All of the other PCs on the network can access the installers via network. (See Chapter 13 for details on creating shared folders of this kind.)

Uninstalling Software

Removing programs from your computer is simplicity itself—*if* the program complies with Microsoft's programming suggestions (in the form of the *32-bit Windows API standard*) for installation. Programs that do comply are recorded in the Registry (see page 405) when installed, which means Windows can dependably remove them when you request it later. Applications that don't know about the 32-bit Windows API standard (including older applications, most shareware and freeware, and lots of smaller and less elaborate programs) don't bother registering, and may be more difficult to remove.

Figure 7-11:
To install a program from a central Install folder, use My Network Places as described on page 289. Open the folder for the program you want and double click the Setup.exe file.

Using Add/Remove Programs

You shouldn't remove a program from your PC just by dragging it to the Recycle Bin. Doing so may leave behind Registry information, meaning that your Registry is no longer current, and may delete important DLLs (*dynamic-link libraries*—shared bits of software code) that other programs may require. (That's why you generally can't *copy* a program to a new location, either; instead, you must uninstall it and then reinstall it.)

Instead, use the Add/Remove Programs tool in the Control Panel to delete programs you no longer want, like this:

1. Click Start→Settings→Control Panel. Double-click Add/Remove Programs.

   The Add/Remove Programs window opens.

2. **If the program is in the list of Currently Installed Programs, highlight it and click the Change/Remove button.**

   Windows asks you to confirm your decision.

3. **Answer warnings as needed.**

For example, you may be warned that one of the deleted program's files is also needed by other programs. In such cases, you're generally better off *not* deleting the file in question. Leaving it behind does no harm, but deleting it might render one of your other applications nonrunnable.

Uninstalling Manually

If your program isn't listed in Add/Remove Programs, you'll have to do your own surgery. If the program placed itself on your Start→Programs menu, choose the Uninstall option in a submenu there, if you see it. If you don't see an Uninstall command, you need to find the program's folder and delete it. Here are options to try:

• If you have a shortcut to the program either on the desktop or on the Programs menu, you can use the technique shown in Figure 7-12 to hunt down the actual program folder.

• Open Windows Explorer (page 86), then My Computer. You may have to poke around to find the application's folder. Look for a folder with your program's name or the program's manufacturer's name. Before deleting the folder, look inside to be sure you have the right one. Not sure? Run the program from the folder.

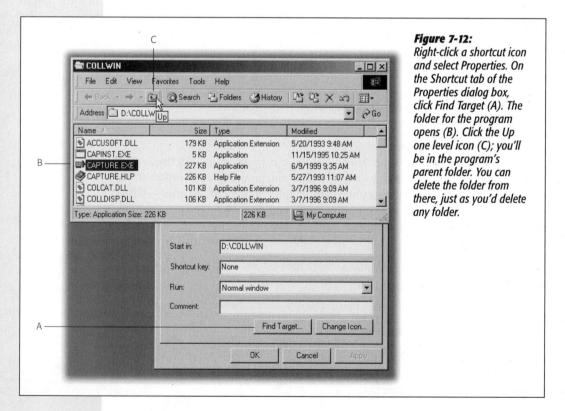

Figure 7-12:
Right-click a shortcut icon and select Properties. On the Shortcut tab of the Properties dialog box, click Find Target (A). The folder for the program opens (B). Click the Up one level icon (C); you'll be in the program's parent folder. You can delete the folder from there, just as you'd delete any folder.

- For truly devious programs that seem to elude you despite all efforts, open the My Computer→C: drive→Program Files. Look for the program folder there.

- Consider calling the software company to ask precisely which files are safe to delete.

Tip: Chapter 10 has information on locating and identifying remaining bits of programs you've deleted.

Troubleshooting Applications with System Information

When your system is acting up with mysterious symptoms, the System Information tool can tell you a lot about what's going on with your software. Many of the entries it reveals are obscure to everyone but the most expert. But even if you're not a computer professional, System Information is where you find the information asked for by the technical-support person at the other end of the phone line.

To open System Information, right-click My Computer and select Manage from the shortcut menu. Under System Tools, open the entry for System Information (Figure 7-13). The application-related information here lurks in the two folders called Software Environment and Applications. (See Chapter 19 for more on general Windows troubleshooting.)

Figure 7-13:
Double-click the Software Environment folder to read information about the software currently loaded in the computer's memory, both all running programs and their active components.

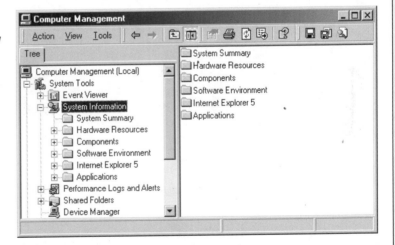

The Control Panel

C onsidering that Windows was originally designed for use in starships, it's not surprising that most important settings can be found in the Control Panel. (OK, it's true: Windows was originally designed for use on Intel 286 computers and not starships. But a Pentium III 1-GHz machine is a lot nearer to a starship than it is to the 286 8-MHz machines Windows first ran on).

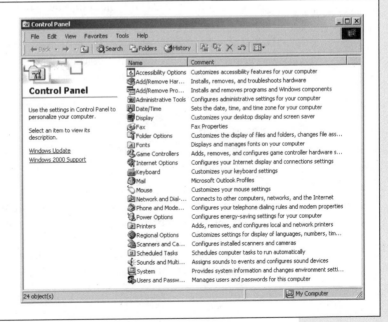

Figure 8-1:
Not everything in the Control Panel window is, in fact, a Control Panel applet; some (such as Fonts and Printers) are shortcuts to important folders, and others (such as Add/Remove Programs) are wizards that help you set up various Windows features.

The Control Panel is a collection of tools (sometimes called *applets,* because they're like miniature applications, or simply *control panels)* you can use to change Windows 2000 settings. To see your PC's collection of control panel applets, open the Control Panel window by choosing Start→Settings→Control Panel (see Figure 8-1).

Note: Some hardware devices, such as display adapters, network cards, cameras, scanners, and sound cards, install their own tools in the Control Panel, as do many programs, such as antivirus programs and media players like Apple QuickTime and RealNetworks RealPlayer. Don't be surprised if your Control Panel doesn't match the one pictured in this chapter.

As you explore the Control Panel, you may discover that you can't change some of the settings in the various control panels without administrative privileges on your PC (see page 369); most people on a corporate domain network don't have this kind of privileges. To access these controls, you can either log onto your computer using the Administrator account, or configure your domain user account to be a member of the local Administrators group, using the Users and Passwords control panel (as described later in this chapter).

Accessibility Options

Windows 2000 comes with a number of tools that can be useful for people who have sight, sound, or movement impairments. Some are available through this Accessibility Options control panel (Figure 8-2); additional tools are on the Start menu under Start→Programs→Accessories→Accessibility (see page 171).

The range of accessibility options is truly amazing—you can adjust almost every aspect of your interaction with the computer, whether it's audio, visual, or tactile.

Tip: The Accessibility Options are a good beginning, but if you're going to be at the computer a lot, investigate more advanced utilities for daily use. Microsoft's accessible-technology Web site at *www.microsoft.com/enable* offers information on what's available now and what's being developed. It's an excellent resource.

Keyboard Tab
The Keyboard tab offers a set of helpful adjustments that make it easier to type without causing errors.

- **StickyKeys** is useful for people who have difficulty pressing two keys at once—such as triggering Ctrl, Alt, and Shift key combinations. Once you've turned this feature on, you can press each key of such combinations one at a time instead of simultaneously. To do so, press the first key (Ctrl, Alt, or Shift) *twice,* which makes it "stick." Then press the second key (usually a letter key). Windows responds exactly as though you had pressed the two keys simultaneously.

- **FilterKeys.** In Windows, holding down a key for longer than a fraction of a second produces repeated keystrokes (such as TTTTTTT). When you turn this option on, Windows treats such a repeated key as a single keystroke, which can be useful if you have trouble pressing keys lightly and briefly.

- **ToggleKeys.** When you turn on this option, the computer beeps whenever you press the Caps Lock, NumLock, or Scroll Lock key.

  You don't have to be disabled to find this option attractive; the confirmation beep means that you're less likely to look up after five minutes of typing to find a page of text tHAT lOOKS lIKE tHIS.

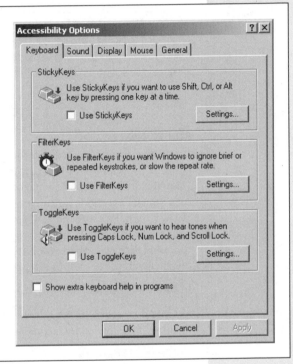

Figure 8-2:
Double-click the Accessibility Options icon to open the dialog box shown here. You start out looking at the Keyboard tab, which offers useful ways to adjust keyboard behavior. By clicking Settings, you can fine-tune many of these features, making it even easier to accommodate special computing needs.

Tip: All three of these features have built-in, system-wide On switches that don't require a visit to the Control Panel. For example, you can turn StickyKeys on or off by pressing the Shift key five times in a row, no matter what you're doing on the PC, and even if "Use StickyKeys" is turned off on the Keyboard tab.

Similarly, you can turn on FilterKeys by pressing the right-side Shift key for at least eight seconds, or turn on ToggleKeys by pressing your Num Lock key for at least five seconds.

Sound Tab

Turn on SoundSentry to tell Windows to make your screen flash or blink when a sound occurs—a useful feature if you're hearing-impaired. ShowSounds makes your applications display an explanatory caption every time they'd otherwise trigger a sound. (Not all programs work with this feature, however.)

Display Tab

If your sight is going, you may find that Use High Contrast makes text easier to read. Use the Settings button to choose white lettering on black, black on white, or any color combination you that works for you.

You can also use this dialog box to make your blinking insertion point easier to see. You can change the blink rate, the width of the blinker, or both. (Making it fatter comes in especially handy on older laptops whose screens aren't the greatest.)

Tip: One of the simplest and most powerful aids to those with failing vision is the "Windows Standard (large)" and "Windows Standard (extra large)" *Desktop Themes.* You'll find these controls in the Display control panel, on the Appearance tab, as described later in this chapter. With a single click, you can make Windows enlarge the type used in all of its dialog boxes, menus, icon names, tooltips, and so on.

Don't miss the Mouse control panel (page 157), either, where you can select much larger arrow cursors.

Mouse Tab

If you find using the mouse difficult, or if you'd like more precision when using graphics programs, consider turning on the MouseKeys feature (by turning on the "Use MouseKeys" master switch on this tab, and then pressing the NumLock key to turn MouseKeys mode on and off). It lets you use the number keypad to control the arrow cursor. Pressing the 2, 4, 6, and 8 keys on this pad moves the mouse around your screen down, left, up, and right. (Check your keyboard—you'll see the corresponding directional arrows on these keys.) The 7, 9, 1, and 3 keys move the cursor diagonally in the corresponding directions.

In MouseKeys mode, the other keys also have new assignments:

- Hold down the Ctrl key to make the cursor jump in larger increments, or Shift to move it in smaller, more precise increments.
- Use the 5 key on the numeric keypad to simulate a mouse click (left-click).
- Use the – key on the keypad to simulate a right-click.
- Use the + key on the keypad to simulate a double-click.

MouseKeys also offers a way to drag, so you can select text or move objects on the screen without using the mouse:

1. **Use the keypad arrows to position the cursor on the highlighted text, icon, or whatever you want to drag.**

2. **Press Ins (the zero key on your numeric keypad).**

   To "right-drag," press the minus-sign key, *then* Ins.

3. Use the keypad arrows to drag to the target location.

4. Press Del on the keypad to "drop" the object.

General Tab

Using the settings on the General tab, you can set Windows to turn off accessibility options if it's been awhile since anyone used them. That's a useful setup if, for example, several people share a computer and only one of them requires these options. You can also ask Windows to notify you by playing a sound or a message when options are turned on or off.

Add/Remove Hardware

As described in Chapter 16, you can use this applet to help you install the drivers for new equipment (primarily when Plug and Play doesn't work).

Add/Remove Programs

This tool not only makes it easy for you to install software from CDs, DVDs, and floppies, but it also provides a means to install software made available on your corporate network, or to add or remove optional components of Windows. The Add/Remove Programs tool is covered in Chapter 7 and Appendix A.

Administrative Tools Folder

The presence of the Administrative Tools folder depends on the kind of *account* you have (see page 369). If it's present, the folder contains tools for performing advanced administration tasks on your system, such as viewing or modifying hardware settings; see page 378 for details.

Date/Time

The Date/Time tool is, surprisingly enough, where you can set your computer's clock, calendar, and time zone information (see Figure 8-3). However, this Control Panel option is available only when you're logged on using an account with sufficient privileges—such as an administrator or power user account. (See page 369 for details on these account types.)

Tip: You can also access the Date/Time Properties dialog box by double-clicking the clock in the System Tray.

Display

The Display applet governs the way Windows appears onscreen. You can change the background for the Windows 2000 desktop, specify a screen saver, change the colors of windows and text, add self-updating Web-page information to your desktop, as well as change the resolution and color settings for your monitor(s). You make these changes using the six tabs of the Display Properties dialog box.

Tip: As a shortcut to opening this control panel, right-click the desktop and select Properties from the shortcut menu.

Background Tab

The default blue of the desktop is nice enough, but there's considerable appeal to the idea of customizing it with your own picture (called *wallpaper* in Windows parlance). Click one of the names in the "Select a background" list (Figure 8-4) to see how it looks on the miniature monitor in the dialog box. (Most of the graphics listed in the list are designed to be repeating patterns, not full-screen backdrops, which explains why they look so puny in the middle of the miniature monitor.)

If nothing in the list excites you, you can use one of your own graphic files, such as a scanned photo, as wallpaper. Click Browse to find the file you want.

Your selected wallpaper image can cover the desktop entirely (choose the Stretch setting from the Picture Display drop-down menu), repeat like tiles across the desktop (the Tile setting), or appear centered in the middle of the desktop (the Center setting).

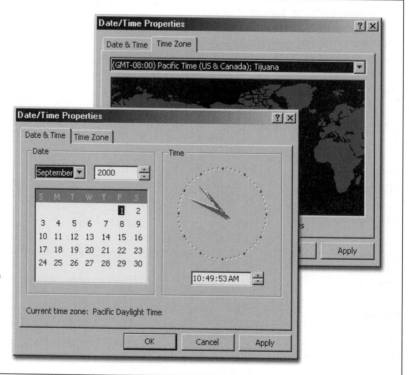

Figure 8-3:
Left: After double-clicking the Date/Time icon in the Control Panel, use the Date/Time Properties dialog box to set the time and date. On the Date & Time tab, select the current month from the first box. Enter the current year in the second box, and then click the current day on the calendar. Enter the current time in the time box.

Right: Click the Time Zone tab to select your current time zone and to tell Windows 2000 whether or not to automatically update the clock for daylight savings.

Tip: To use a two-color, repeating pattern on the desktop instead of a solid color or wallpaper, click the Pattern button and then select a pattern. If your wallpaper doesn't fill the screen, the pattern appears behind it.

If you're really obsessive, you can even click the Edit Pattern button to edit the pattern, pixel by pixel (a *pixel* is the smallest dot your monitor can display). All patterns are made up of two colors—black and the current desktop background color. (See the Changing Window Colors and Settings section later in this chapter for information on changing the background color of the desktop.)

Figure 8-4:
Choose the image you want to use as wallpaper from the list on the Background tab of the Display Properties dialog box. From the Picture Display drop-down list box, choose whether you want to Center, Tile or Stretch the image. To use an image not shown in the box, click the Browse button to select an image from elsewhere on the computer or network.

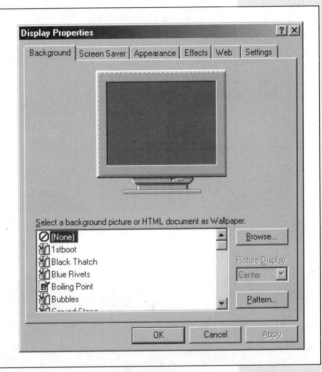

GEM IN THE ROUGH

Wallpaper File Types

In earlier versions of Windows, only bitmap images (images with the .bmp or .dib filename extension) could be used as desktop wallpaper. Fortunately, you can now also use images with any of the following file formats: JPEG (.jpg or .jpeg), GIF (.gif), or Portable Network Graphics (.png). By clicking the Browse button and selecting an HTML document, you can also use entire Web pages as wallpaper, although if you want the hyperlinks to work, you need to use Active Desktop (see page 143).

Note that any image formats except bitmap (.bmp and .dib) require the Active Desktop, which consumes a small amount of additional system memory (less than a megabyte).

If you browse the Web with Internet Explorer or a recent version of Netscape Navigator, you can take an image from the Web and use it as your wallpaper, as shown in Figure 8-5.

Figure 8-5:
To use an image you find on the Web for your desktop wallpaper, launch Internet Explorer, browse to the image you want to use, right-click the image and then choose Set As Wallpaper from the shortcut menu.

WORKAROUND WORKSHOP

When a Beautiful Picture Looks Lousy on the Desktop

Pictures that look great on the World Wide Web may not look so great as wallpaper on your desktop because of differences in *resolution*. For example, the nice ice selected in Figure 8.5 turns out to be very small when placed on the desktop. So suppose you right-click the desktop, choose Properties from the shortcut menu, set the Picture Display drop-down menu to *Stretch,* and click Apply.

Yikes! The nice ice is no more than a blur (even though it still looks OK in the Display Properties dialog box). Then problem is the result of taking a small picture and spreading it out over a large area (your screen). The solution is to find a larger picture that doesn't have to be stretched so much. Of course, you can also try the *Tile* setting—though that usually looks almost as terrible as the Stretch.

Screen Saver Tab

For a while, screen savers were one of the hottest selling software categories on the market, thanks to two factors. First, older monitors were prone to something called *phosphor burn-in* (an after-image permanently burned into the screen) when left on with an unchanging image on the screen for a long time. The second—and more important—reason is that screen savers are fun.

Screen savers have no practical use today, however, because monitors haven't been subject to burn-in for at least a decade. Furthermore, monitors made in the last few years have an energy-saving feature that turns them off after a period of inactivity. However, screen savers are still fun. To use a screen saver, click the Screen Saver tab, as shown in Figure 8-6.

If you leave your computer, whatever work you were doing is hidden behind the screen saver; passers-by can't see what's on the screen. To make the screen saver go away, move the mouse, click a mouse button, or press a key.

Figure 8-6:
Choose the screen saver you want from the Screen Saver drop-down list box. A small preview of the screen saver appears in the dialog box; click the Preview button to get a full-screen preview. Specify how many minutes to wait before displaying the screen saver in the Wait box. To change the screen saver's settings (if there are any), click the Settings button.

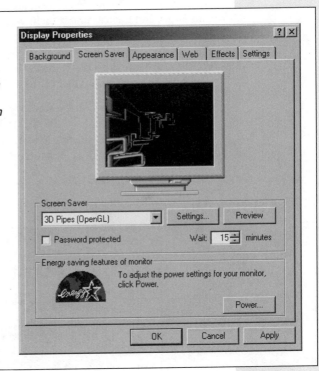

Finally, a few notes on screen savers in Windows:

- Turn on the "Password protected" checkbox to require the currently logged-on user (probably you) to log on again in order to regain access to the system.

- Screensavers are sometimes very processor-intensive. Thus, instead of allowing your computer to power down during periods of inactivity, screen savers actually increase power consumption. They also slightly decrease the amount of processing power available to any background services you may have running, such as file sharing, a Web server, or 3-D rendering. On a laptop, a screen saver may interfere with Windows 2000's power-management features, causing your battery to run down more quickly.

- There are *many* freeware or shareware screen savers available on the Internet, some of which are add-on modules for the built-in Windows screen saver. Perform a Web search for *screen savers*; you'll find more than you could ever use.

Appearance Tab

This tab, shown in Figure 8-7, lets you change the colors and text formatting for all of your windows, menus, and dialog boxes, which can make windows easier (or, in some cases, harder) to see. For example, if you're lucky enough to have a very large monitor, you may find that at its regular settings, the screen icons look like houses seen from a jet at 35,000 feet. Using the Appearance tab, you can simply make the icons larger and the text under them bolder.

You can proceed with your interior-decoration project in any of several ways:

- Use the Scheme drop-down menu to choose one of the canned themes that come with Windows. The top half of the dialog box gives you a preview of the effect.

- Change the elements of the scheme one at a time. Start by choosing from the Item drop-down menu (or by clicking a piece of the illustration, as shown in Figure 8-7). Then use the Size, Color, and Color 2 drop-down menus to tailor the chosen element—such as Desktop or Scrollbar.

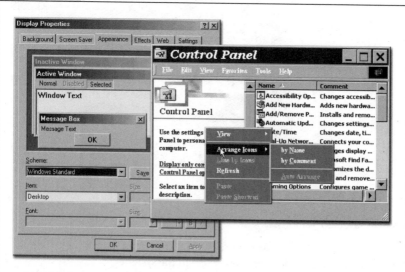

Figure 8-7:
Left: To make your own scheme, click the simulated windows in the dialog box to select an aspect of the interface to modify, then use the boxes to change the colors and fonts. You can also select a part of the interface using the Item drop-down list. Right: These controls can radically change the look of your desktop and windows.

- Some of the screen elements named in the Item drop-down menu have text associated with them: Icon, Inactive Title Bar, Menu, Message Box, ToolTip, and so on. When you choose one of these text items, the Font drop-down menu at the bottom of the dialog box comes to life. Using this menu, you can change the typeface (font, color, and size) used for any of these screen elements. If you have trouble reading the type used in tooltips, wish your icon names showed up a little bolder, or would prefer a more graceful font used in your menus, these controls offer the solution.

If you come up with an attractive combination of colors and type sizes, you can add them to the Scheme drop-down list by clicking Save As. You'll be asked to name your creation; thereafter, you'll see it listed with the "official" Microsoft schemes.

Web Tab (Active Desktop)

When the Active Desktop was introduced with Internet Explorer 4, it was supposed to be revolutionary. Microsoft imagined that everyone would have Web-page desktops filled with dynamic stock tickers and other cool stuff. Companies would create special, fancy Web pages called Channels that would be live on your desktop, keeping it up-to-date.

Active Desktop has turned out to be a good deal less popular than Microsoft expected—primarily because to be useful, it requires a permanent connection to the Internet. If you've got one, you may want to give Active Desktop a try.

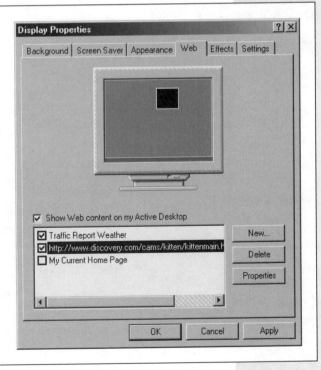

Figure 8-8:
To add a Web page to your desktop, click New. Click the Visit Gallery button to see a list of Web pages specifically designed for the Active Desktop (such as the vaunted stock ticker), or enter the location of the Web page you want in the Location box. If the picture or Web page is on your computer or network instead of the Internet, click Browse. Click OK when you're done, and then click OK in the dialog box confirming the addition of the page or image to the Active Desktop.

Adding items to the Active Desktop

Once you've got the Web tab in front of you (Figure 8-8), turn on Active Desktop like this:

1. **Turn on "Show Web content on my Active Desktop."**

2. **Turn on a checkbox in the list (such as "My Current Home Page").**

These checkboxes represent the various Web pages you'd like to see plastered across your desktop. To add to this list, click the New button, type the URL (Web address), and click OK.

You can add any kind of Web information to your Active Desktop. Frequently updated pages like stock tickers are popular, but you can also use Web pages that don't change much.

By clicking New and then Visit Gallery, in fact, you can check out the Microsoft Web site, which offers an array of newsy, constantly updating Active Desktop elements, such as sports, weather, or travel news. These aren't actually Web pages; they're blurbs that appear in their own little boxes on your living desktop.

And if you click Browse, you can choose a graphics file or HTML (Web-page) document on your hard drive for displaying on the desktop. (Using the Back-

---

GEM IN THE ROUGH

Active Desktop for Modem Fans

While Active Desktop works best if you have a full-time Internet connection, using it with a dial-up modem isn't impossible. You can set up your PC to connect at a certain time of day (just before you arrive at your desk, for example), update the Web page on your desktop, and then hang up. That way, a recent (but detached-from-the-Internet) Web page greets you each morning.

To set up this arrangement, open the Web tab of the Display control panel. Click the name of the Web page you want to self-update, and then click Properties.

A special dialog box appears. Turn on "Make this page available offline," and then click the Schedule tab. Turn on "Using the following schedule"; click Add; use the controls to indicate which time of day you want your desktop updated; name the schedule, if you like; and turn on the "automatically connect for me" checkbox at the bottom of the window.

But before you click OK, consider this: At the specified time,

your PC will dial the Internet and update the Web page on your desktop. But what then? You can read what's on the page, but you can't very well click one of the links on it. The Web page is frozen onto your desktop, disconnected from the Internet. If you click one of the links on it, you'll get only an error message.

That's the virtue of the final tab, the Download tab. The "Download pages __ links deep" option makes your PC download not just the specified Web page, but also all Web pages *connected* to it. If you change the number here to 2, then you'll also be able to click links on *those* pages; you'll have the freedom to explore the links on your Active Desktop Web page to the extent of pages-from-pages you specify. (All of these additional downloaded Web pages take up disk space, however, which is why there's a "Limit hard-disk usage" checkbox, too.)

When you're finished setting up your automatic download, click OK.

---

ground tab of the Display control panel, described earlier, is a more direct way of placing a picture on your desktop. But choice, Microsoft always says, is good.)

3. **Click Apply (to preview the Web page on your desktop) or OK (to apply it to your desktop and close the dialog box).**

Now your entire desktop becomes a Web browser.

Tip: If you have a permanent connection to the Internet, you can put a Webcam display on your Active Desktop. (A Webcam is a video camera somewhere in the world, whose video feed is broadcast to the Internet 24 hours a day.) While you're busy working, you can keep an eye on the lava lamp cam or hairless-albino-rat cam. To find a list of Webcams available for this purpose, search the Web for *webcam*. Unfortunately, the Active Desktop needs some help in dealing with Webcams. To place one on the desktop, you must first add the Web page containing the Webcam to your desktop, and then resize the "window" until it displays only the Webcam.

Rearranging and Using the Active Desktop

Active Desktop Web pages work like regular Web pages; you can click links to move from page to page. (Most links open pages in your Web browser instead of staying right there on the desktop, however.) To get back to the previous page, press the Backspace key. To open a link in a new browser window, right-click the link and choose Open In New Window from the shortcut menu.

To move an Active Desktop item, move the cursor over the top part of the item until a gray bar appears. Drag this bar to move the item (see Figure 8-9).

If you push your cursor to the top of a Web-page area, you can make a little menu bar appear, complete with commands (in a tiny, upper-left drop-down menu) that pertain to the desktop-as-Web-page feature.

POWER USERS' CLINIC

Making Your Own Active-Desktop Web Page

Any Web-page creation tool (including FrontPage Express, Word 2000, or Netscape Composer) can make a Web page for use as a desktop background. You might create, for example, a Web page that consists of a large image to cover the bulk of the desktop and give you something pretty to look at, along with links to the Web pages or documents you use most frequently.

To link to a file on your hard drive, use the *file:///* prefix; for example, on the Active Desktop tab, click the New button and enter *file:///C:\Data\desktop.html* in the Location field.

This creates a link to the C:\Data\desktop.html file on your hard drive. It only takes a couple minutes to create a basic page (and you can layer other Web pages on top of it).

The capabilities of Active Desktop will expand with the next version of Windows 2000, which is reported to integrate email, calendar information, and instant messaging into the Active Desktop. To get a sneak peak at this technology, download the MSNBC Digital Dashboard for Outlook 2000 (available from the Outlook 2000 Web site, *www.microsoft. com/office/outlook*).

Tip: When your desktop is your browser, the usual Internet Explorer menu bar doesn't appear. You won't find standard IE commands like Back, Forward, Add to Favorites, and so on.

But if you right-click the desktop, a special shortcut menu appears that contains all of the important Web-browsing commands.

If you right-click *outside* the Web-page portion of your desktop (in the unaffected desktop to either side), you get a shortcut menu bearing an Active Desktop command. (If your Active Desktop material covers the entire desktop, this is impossible—don't bother trying.) The shortcut menu's Active Desktop submenu offers several useful commands, including Show Web Content (the on/off switch for putting a Web page on your desktop); Show Desktop Icons (which hides or shows your desktop icons); and Lock Desktop Items (prevents your Active Desktop windows from moving or changing shape). At the bottom of this submenu are the names of any Web pages you've selected. Use these commands to switch your desktop from one Web page to another, like a glorified Favorites command.

Figure 8-9:
To make an Active Desktop item take up the entire screen (except for a small area on the left side for icons), click the rightmost button on the item's gray pop-up bar (shown at top right of the Ant Cam window). The other button (the one to the left) makes the item cover the whole screen. To manually resize an item, drag the window's corner.

Turning off Active Desktop

To turn off the Active Desktop, right-click a blank spot on the desktop and choose Active Desktop→Show Web Content from the shortcut menu.

Effects Tab

The dialog box shown in Figure 8-10 lets you perform several subtle cosmetic tweaks to your desktop. Some are so subtle, they're practically invisible.

Desktop icons

The top section of the dialog box lets you change the pictures that Windows uses for the important desktop icons (see Figure 8-10).

Figure 8-10:
If you can't stand the look of, say, the Recycle Bin icon, click it in this scrolling list and then click Change Icon. You'll be shown an assortment of potential replacement images; if you've created or downloaded additional miniature pictures, you can use one of those instead by clicking the Browse button and navigating to the folder that contains them. Make sure to choose All Files from the "Files of type:" drop-down list box; otherwise, the icon file may not appear.

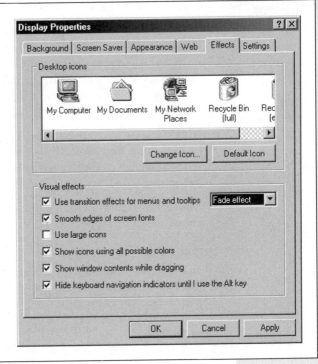

Visual effects

There's no need to change any of these settings, but they're worth reading about; some of them may be the Off switches for Windows behaviors you've found annoying:

- **Use transition effects for menus and tooltips.** Turns *transition effects* on or off when opening new menus and tooltips. The Fade Effect setting makes newly opened menus and tooltips appear by fading in gradually. The Scroll Effect setting *unrolls* a menu or tooltip. If you remove the checkmark, menus just appear, which makes menus open slightly faster. (Frankly, most people can't see a nickel's worth of difference among the three choices.)

- **Smooth edges of screen fonts.** Smoothes the jagged edges of large fonts onscreen, using a process called *anti-aliasing*. This setting works only when you've set your monitor to 16-bit color or more, as described next. This setting *does* make a difference in the look of text, even if you don't have an artist's eye.

- **Use large icons.** Makes desktop icons extra large, which can be useful on high-resolution displays being viewed with low-resolution eyes.

• **Show icons using all possible colors.** Specifies that icons use as many colors as supported by your display or by the icons themselves. In most circumstances, the difference this setting makes is marginal. However, you may get strange results if you have this option off and are using large icons. (Some of the icons may turn into black or white blobs. Even then, however, all will be well if you just reboot your system.)

• **Show window contents while dragging.** If the option is off, when you drag or resize a window, you see a faint outline of its border; you don't see all the items *in* the window coming along for the ride. As soon as you stop dragging, the contents reappear. If you enable this feature, however, as you drag a window across your screen, you see all the contents, too—which can slow the dragging process.

• **Hide keyboard navigation indicators until I use the Alt key.** When this checkbox is cleared, certain letters are underlined in menus and on dialog boxes. As described on page 17, these letters indicate that you can trigger certain commands by pressing the Alt key along with the underlined letter.

By default, Windows 2000 hides these underlines and you need to press the Alt key to make them appear.

Settings Tab

Of all the pages in the Display properties, this page has the most going on (see Figure 8-11). Here's where you can change the settings that affect your computer's display features.

Color settings

Today's monitors and video cards offer different *color depth* settings, each of which permits the screen to display a different number of colors simultaneously. The options in this drop-down menu vary depending on the amount of memory on your video adapter card and the video driver installed on your system.

Generally, you'll find three choices: *256 Colors, High Color (16-bit),* and *True Color (24-bit).* The 16- and 24-bit descriptions refer to the number of memory bits that your video adapter uses to display the color of each pixel on the screen. For example, 8-bit color provides a palette of 256 colors; 16-bit provides 65,536 colors; and 24-bit provides 16,777,216. These numbers don't refer to the actual number of colors on the screen; they indicated the palette of *possible* colors from which Windows can choose.

In the early days of computing, higher color settings required a sacrifice in speed. Today, however, there's very little downside to leaving your screen at its maximum color-depth setting ("True Color"). Photos, in particular, look best when your monitor is set to higher bit depth settings. The 256 Colors option, on the other hand, can make photos look blotchy; it's useful only for certain computer games that, having been designed to run on ancient PCs, require the lower color setting.

Changing resolutions

Monitors are described in terms of their *resolution*—the number of pixels (that is, dots) on the screen, measured in each dimension. The resolutions available on the slider under Screen Area are determined by your video adapter card and monitor.

Here are the most likely possibilities:

640 x 480   A standard VGA monitor that's 640 pixels wide by 480 pixels high.

800 x 600   A typical SVGA monitor (super VGA). Often used on laptop screens and smaller (15-inch) monitors.

1024 x 768   The upper limit for VGA and the beginning of more advanced systems, such as 8514/A and XGA. This is a very fine (that is, not grainy) resolution—but if your monitor is 15 inches or smaller, you'd better have very good eyes.

1280 x 1024   A very fine resolution suitable for larger monitors—17 to 19 inches.

Other resolutions may be available, such as 1152 x 864 or even 1600 x 1024, depending on your video hardware. As you move the slider, the display on the simulated monitor changes, giving a fairly accurate indication of how different resolutions affect the look of the screen (Figure 8-11).

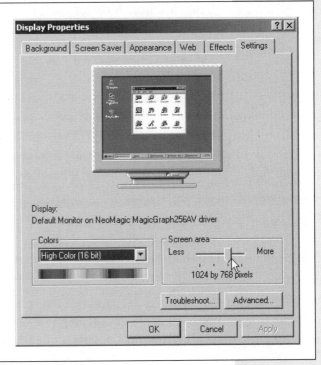

Figure 8-11:
As you move the slider toward higher resolutions, the number of colors displayed in the Color Palette box changes. As resolution numbers go up, color numbers have to go down, because they're both competing for the same video memory. That's why, if you want the most realistic color represented on your screen at a high resolution, you need a display adapter (video card) with 8 MB of memory or more.

When you use a low resolution setting, such as 640 x 480, the pixels that make up your screen image get larger, thus enlarging the picture—but showing a smaller slice of the page. Use this setting when, for example, playing a small movie so that it fills more of the screen. At higher resolutions (such as 800 x 600 or 1024 x 768), the pixels get smaller, making your windows and icons smaller but showing more over-all area. Use this kind of setting when you want to see as much screen area as possible: when working on two-page spreads in a page-layout program, for example. At the highest resolutions, screen elements are very small, so you may want to click the Advanced button and try Large Fonts from the Font Size box. (The exceptions: laptops or LCD monitors. The pixels on an LCD display are fixed in size. Changing the resolution can only make the image physically smaller by using part of the screen.)

Tip: If you change your screen resolution, you may end up with some very peculiar arrangements of your icons. They may be way too far apart, or so close together that they're difficult to use.

Fortunately, the Appearance tab has controls for the spacing of icons. Pull down the Item drop-down list and select one of the Icon Spacing choices, then use the Size control to adjust the spacing, in pixels. But it's an excellent idea to note the original settings, because it's fairly easy to make a hash of your Desktop and not remember where you started.

Using Multiple Monitors

People have one of two reactions when they hear that Windows 2000 Pro supports the use of multiple monitors. One faction says, "Who would want to do such a thing?" The other faction cries out, "Oh, boy! I can hardly wait!" If you're in that second group, read on.

Multiple monitors can greatly increase the amount of screen real estate available for work, allowing you to have more windows open, or at least be able to see more of the windows that are already open.

While it's most common to use just two monitors (with two video adapter cards), technically, Windows 2000 can support up to ten monitors. In practice, you're limited by the capacity of your system to accept extra video cards; each monitor must have its own card, unless you have a single card that supports multiple monitors. Realistically, this means that most computers can't handle more than three or four monitors.

If you're purchasing a new computer and want to use multiple monitors, don't be shy about getting the computer supplier to set it up for you. If you already have multiple monitors running under Windows 98, and you're upgrading to Windows 2000, don't count on all multiple monitors working under Windows 2000—the two operating systems deal with multiple monitors in completely different ways; multiple monitors that work under Windows 98 may not work under Windows 2000 (and occasionally vice versa).

If you do want to try setting up multiple monitors yourself, here's how to do it:

1. **Check Microsoft's Hardware Compatibility List (HCL).**

   The URL is *www.microsoft.com/hcl*. Make sure that *all* of the display cards you plan to use are multiple-monitor compatible. If your display card isn't on the list, check with the card's manufacturer for the existence of Windows 2000 drivers that support multiple monitors. If this quest also turns up negative, replace the card with one that's on the HCL.

2. **Use a jumper or DIP switch to disable the VGA output on each secondary display adapter.**

   Consult the display adapter's manual for instructions.

3. **Open the computer case; install all of the video adapters, preferably in the PCI slots closest to the AGP slot (PCI slot 0 or 1, farthest from the ISA slots).**

   The AGP slot, if there is one, is the slot for your main video adapter card. The PCI slots are the shorter of the other two possible slot types in your computer.

4. **Turn on both monitors and then turn on the computer.**

   The initial startup screen should appear on the primary monitor.

5. **Log on to Windows.**

   If luck is with you, Windows detects the video adapters and monitors automatically and installs the appropriate drivers. (You may be prompted for updated drivers, which you can provide, if available.)

6. **Right-click a blank area of the desktop, choose Properties from the shortcut menu, and then click the Settings tab.**

   Now you're ready to configure the software settings for your monitors.

7. **Select a monitor.**

   On the Settings tab of the Display Properties dialog box, click on one of the numbered monitor icons (see Figure 8-12) to modify that monitor and video adapter's properties.

8. **Enable the monitor (if it's disabled).**

   To do so, click your secondary monitor's icon and then turn on "Extend my Windows desktop onto this monitor," if it's not already on. (The primary monitor's "Extend my desktop" checkbox is always grayed out).

9. **If you like, specify which monitor is your primary monitor.**

   You do that by clicking the monitor's icon and then turning on "Use this device as the primary monitor." This setting is important for programs, such as most games, DVD players, and screen capture programs, that aren't compatible with multiple monitors.

10. **Adjust the screen area and colors.**

You can adjust the screen area, colors, and advanced properties for each monitor independently, just as you would with a single monitor; simply click each monitor's icon before making the changes.

You may want to finish up by telling Windows 2000 how your monitors are positioned relative to each other, as shown in Figure 8-12. (If a monitor is physically located on the right side, but its icon is positioned on the left, you'll have to move the mouse off the *left* side of the screen to get to windows in the monitor on the right.)

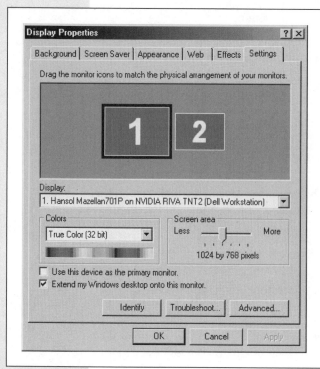

Figure 8-12:
Drag the monitor icons to match the layout of the physical monitors (to figure out which monitor is which, click the Identify button). For example, if the number two monitor is centered on the right side of the number one monitor, drag the number two icon to the right side of the number one icon. Now you'll be able to access windows on the number two monitor by moving the mouse off the right side of the screen.

Fax

The Fax icon in the Control Panel connects you to the properties pages for faxes; see page 173.

Folder Options

A double-click on Folder Options in the Control Panel opens the properties pages discussed on page 74. You can also get to this dialog box by selecting Folder Options from the Tools menu in most windows; this is just another path to the same destination.

Fonts

To see the list of fonts installed on your computer, double-click the Fonts icon in the Control Panel. The Fonts folder isn't like any ordinary folder; in the View menu, you see a new option called List Fonts by Similarity (Figure 8-13).

If your font list is very long and unwieldy, choose View→Hide Variations to hide font variations, such as italic and bold, making the list easier to look through.

In addition to the fonts that come with Windows 2000, there are thousands of others, from the sublime to the absurd, which you can buy from type companies or download for free from the Web. Windows TrueType font files (the most common font format) have a .ttf extension. You install new fonts like this:

1. **Open the Fonts control panel.**

   Do this by selecting Settings→Control Panel and double-clicking the Fonts icon.

2. **Choose File→Install New Font.**

   The Add Fonts dialog box appears.

3. **Use the Folders and Drives selectors to browse to the folder where your new TrueType font files reside.**

   In the List of Fonts box, you'll see a list of all of the fonts the applet finds in the selected folder.

4. **Select the fonts you want to install.**

   You can highlight the individual fonts you want to install, or just click the Select All button.

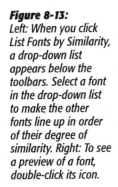

Figure 8-13:
Left: When you click List Fonts by Similarity, a drop-down list appears below the toolbars. Select a font in the drop-down list to make the other fonts line up in order of their degree of similarity. Right: To see a preview of a font, double-click its icon.

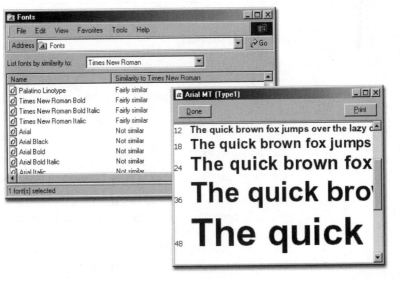

5. **Turn on "Copy fonts to Fonts folder."**

If you don't do this, your PC will access the font files from their current location, in whatever folder they're in. If, weeks later, you inadvertently delete them or their folder, the fonts will disappear from your Font menus and dialog boxes. Copying them to your Fonts folder makes it much less likely that you'll lose your fonts in this way.

6. **Click OK.**

Once the fonts are installed, you can use them in any application, just as you can the standard Windows 2000 set.

Game Controllers

If you're a serious gamer, this applet may interest you. You use it to configure and control the joysticks, steering wheels, game pads, flight yokes, and other controllers you've attached to your PC.

If Windows 2000 Pro doesn't automatically install a new controller's driver, you can use the Add button to do so. As you'll see in the resulting dialog box, there's a controller type for all occasions.

The Advanced page of Game Controllers allows you to assign IDs to multiple controllers and otherwise customize your setup.

Tip: If you're unable to add your game controller, it's possible that your game port isn't properly installed. Right-click the My Computer icon and select Manage from the shortcut menu. Double-click Device Manager, then click the + sign beside Sound, Video and Game Controllers. If Gameport Joystick is not listed, use the Add/Remove Hardware function in the Control Panel (page 347) to install it.

Internet Options

This applet opens the same dialog box that appears when you choose Tools→Internet Options in Internet Explorer. Most of the settings apply to Web browsing—and, specifically, to Internet Explorer. Its six tabs break down like this:

• **General, Security, Content.** These tabs control your home page, cache files, and history list, and let you define certain Web pages as off-limits to your kids. Details on these options are in Chapter 11.

• **Connections.** Controls when your PC modem dials; see page 225 for details.

• **Programs.** Use these drop-down menus to indicate which Internet programs you generally prefer for email, creating Web pages, and so on. For example, the email program you specify here is the one that will open automatically whenever you click an "email me!" link on a Web page. The checkbox at the bottom of the dialog box tells Windows to watch out for the day when you install a browser other than Internet Explorer; at that time, you'll be asked which program—IE or the new one—you want to use as your everyday browser.

- **Advanced.** On this tab, you'll find dozens of checkboxes, most of which are useful only in rare circumstances or affect your Web experience only in minor ways. For example, "Enable Personalized Favorites Menu" shortens your list of favorite Web sites (see page 233) over time, as Internet Explorer hides the names of sites you haven't visited in a while. "Show Go button in Address bar" lets you hide the Go button at the right of the Address bar; after you've typed a Web address (URL), you have to press Enter to open the corresponding Web page instead of clicking the actual Go button. And so on.

You can get a relatively coherent description of each by clicking the question-mark button (upper-right) and then clicking the checkbox in question.

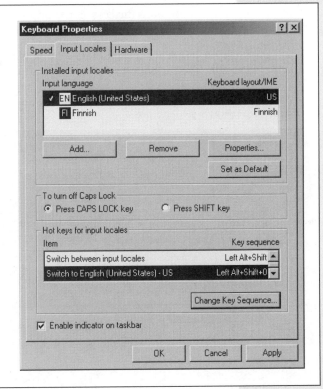

Figure 8-14:
After you've added a couple of layouts to the Language tab, specify which one you want by clicking its name and then click Set as Default. Also on this page (for some reason) is the option to be able to turn off Caps Lock by pressing the Shift key. Longtime users of the now-quaint typewriter will find this familiar.

Keyboard

The Keyboard tool offers three tabs that govern its behavior:

Speed tab

On a PC, every key repeats if you press it long enough, making it easy to type *XXXXX* or *Yippeeeee!* You control this behavior like this:

- **Repeat delay.** Determines how long a key has to be held down before it starts repeating. The difference between the Long and Short settings is about a second.

- **Repeat rate.** Determines how fast a key repeats once it starts. Click the practice area to test this and the delay setting.

- **Cursor blink rate.** This slider governs the blinking rate of the insertion point when you're editing text. A blink rate that's too slow makes it more difficult to find your insertion point in a window filled with data. A blink rate that's too fast can be distracting. The blinking cursor on the left demonstrates the setting.

Input Locales

The symbols you use when you're typing Swedish aren't the same as when you're typing English. Microsoft solved this problem by creating different *keyboard layouts,* one for each language. Each keyboard layout rearranges the letters that appear when you press the keys. For example, when you use the Swedish layout and press the semicolon key, you don't get a semicolon (;)—you get an ö.

As shown in Figure 8-14, you use this tab to add new layouts if you frequently type in different languages or use different keyboards. A special icon—a blue square bearing a two-letter country code—will appear on your Taskbar tray, a useful reminder as to why your typing is producing unexpected symbols.

FREQUENTLY ASKED QUESTION

The Windows-logo Key

I know that the Alt and Ctrl keys are used to trigger menu functions without the mouse. But my keyboard has even more keys that I don't recognize. What are they?

If your keyboard was made recently, it probably has a couple of special keys: one (actually, two identical keys) bearing the Windows logo, and another that looks like a tiny open menu. These keys offer a lot of quick ways to move around in Windows 2000.

For example, you can press the Windows-logo key to pop the Start menu open (or close it again) without having to use the mouse. And you can press that open-menu key to simulate a right-click at the current location of your mouse pointer.

Even better, the Windows logo key has a number of useful functions when it's pressed in conjunction with other keys. For example:

Minimize or restore all windows	Windows+D
Minimize all windows	Windows+M
Restore all windows	Windows+Shift+M
Switch between open windows	Windows+Tab
Open the Run dialog box (page 31)	Windows+R
Search for files/folders	Windows+F
Search for computers	Windows+Ctrl+F
Open Windows Explorer	Windows+E
Mute speaker (or turn it back on)	Windows+V
Windows Help	Windows+F1
Utility Manager (page 173)	Windows+U
System Properties	Windows+Break
Move the "focus" from Start button to QuickLaunch toolbar to Tray	Windows+Ctrl+Tab

Note: Some shortcuts don't work if StickyKeys is turned on (see page 134).

Tip: To see what your new keyboard arrangement looks like, use the Character Map program described on page 195.

Hardware Tab

You'll use this tab only for troubleshooting your keyboard. Should that be your fate, click the Troubleshooting button and follow the steps proposed by the troubleshooting wizard.

Mail

This icon doesn't appear until you've installed an email program that uses MAPI (the Messaging Application Programming Interface), such as Microsoft Outlook 2000 (but not Outlook Express). When you double-click Mail, you open the properties and settings dialog box for that email program.

Mouse

The mouse icon in the Control Panel is the gateway to all things mouselike. There are four pages of properties: Buttons, Pointers, Motion, and Hardware.

Buttons Tab

This tab offers three useful controls: button configuration, double-click speed, and ClickLock.

- **Button configuration.** If you're left handed (and keep your mouse on the left side of the keyboard), this tab lets you switch the functions of the right and left mouse buttons, so that your index finger naturally rests on the primary button (the one that selects and drags).

- **Files and Folders.** This control is a duplicate of the one described on page 71.

- **Double-click speed.** Double-clicking isn't a very natural maneuver. For example, if you double-click too slowly, the icon you're trying to open remains stubbornly closed.

  Let Windows know what you consider a double-click by adjusting this slider. The left end of the slider bar represents 0.9 seconds, and the right end represents 0.1 seconds. Each time you adjust the slider, you can test your adjustment by double-clicking the jack-in-the-box in the Test area. If the creature pops out, you've successfully double-clicked. If not, adjust the slider again.

Pointers Tab

If your fondness for the standard Windows arrow cursor begins to wane, you can assert your individuality by choosing a different pointer shape.

Selecting a pointer scheme

Windows has many more cursors than the arrow pointer. At various times, you may also see the hourglass "please wait" cursor, the I-beam cursor (which appears when you're editing text), the little pointing-finger hand (which appears when you point to a Web-page link), and so on.

All of these cursors come prepackaged into design-coordinated sets called *schemes*. To look over the cursor shapes in a different scheme, use the Scheme drop-down menu (Figure 8-15); the corresponding pointer collection appears in the scrolling list. (Some, the ones whose names include "large," offer jumbo, magnified cursors that are ideal for very large screens or failing eyesight.) When you find one that looks like an improvement over the "(None)" set, click OK.

Tip: Be wary of changing either the Precision Select or Text Select pointers. Both require a cursor that you can place with considerable accuracy—and that's not easy with a revolving barber pole or a waddling dinosaur.

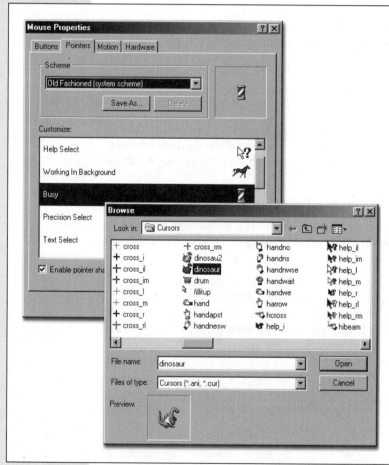

Figure 8-15:
Left: Select a scheme from the drop-down list or highlight the pointer you'd like to change then click Browse. Right: You see some of the nearly 200 cursors that come with Windows 2000 Pro. Highlight one to see it in the Preview box. Double-click to select it. If you have file extensions showing (page 124), you can easily distinguish the animated pointers (.ani) from the stationary ones (.cur).

Create your own pointer scheme

Once you've replaced a cursor shape, you've changed the scheme to which it belongs. At this point, you can either click OK to make your change take effect and get back to work, or you can save the new, improved scheme under its own name, so that you'll be able to switch back to the original when nostalgia calls. To do so, click Save As, name the scheme, and then click OK.

Motion Tab

This tab offers a few more random cursor-related functions, which depend on the type of mouse you have and the mouse driver installed on your computer. Your Mouse applet may include these options, for example:

Speed

It may surprise you that the cursor doesn't move five inches when you move the *mouse* five inches. Instead, you can set things up so that moving the mouse one millimeter moves the pointer one full inch—or vice versa—using the Speed slider.

It may come as even more surprise that the cursor doesn't generally move *proportionally* to the mouse's movement, regardless of your "Speed" setting. Instead, the cursor moves farther when you move the mouse faster. How *much* farther depends on the Acceleration setting you choose. The Fast setting is nice if you have an enormous monitor, because it means that you don't need an equally large mouse pad to get from one corner to another. The Slow setting, on the other hand, can be frustrating, because it forces you to pick up and put down the mouse a lot as you scoot across the screen.

Snap to default

Many times when you reach for your mouse, it's to click a button in a dialog box. If you, like millions of people before you, usually click the *default* (outlined) button, such as OK, Next, or Yes, the Snap to Default feature can save you the effort of positioning the cursor before clicking.

When you turn on "Move pointer to the default button" checkbox, every time a dialog box appears, your mouse pointer jumps automatically to the default button, so that all you have to do is click. (Of course, you can always press Enter to "click" the default button, regardless of the pointer's location.)

Hardware Tab

The primary feature of this tab is the Troubleshoot button, which unleashes a wizard that, in times of mouse trouble, can help you pinpoint a solution.

Network and Dial-Up Connections

A double-click of the Network and Dial-Up Connections icon opens a window that contains links to whatever connections are set up on your computer—a local area network, dial-up connections—and an icon for making new connections. You'll encounter this folder in Chapters 11, 14, and 15.

Phone and Modem Options

The Phone and Modem Options tool changes the settings for any modems attached to your computer. This is also where you make settings for the Phone Dialer (see page 185).

Phone and Modem Options opens with three tabs: Dialing Rules, Modems, and Advanced. You'll work with the first two regularly, but rarely, if ever with the Advanced tab.

Dialing Rules Tab

Dialing rules are what your computer knows about your phone line, such as whether or not you have call waiting and what area code you're in. The first time you check Phone and Modem Options, a Location Information dialog box opens, in which you're supposed to specify your country and area code. (If you filled in this information during the Windows 2000 installation process, you're spared this duty.) The Phone and Modem Options properties open with one *location* (a memorized set of area code and dialing settings) listed.

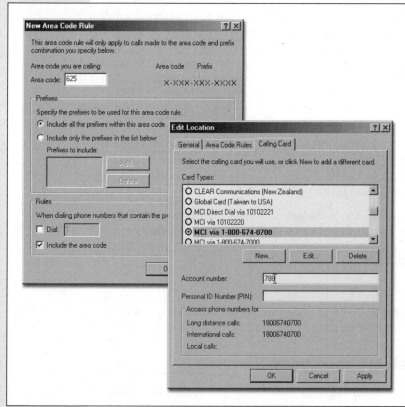

Figure 8-16:
Left: In the Area code text box, type in the area code to which the rule will apply. For example, if you have to dial an area code for all calls—even local ones—type in your area code. Under Prefixes, turn on "Include all the prefixes within this area code." In the Rules area, turn on "Include this area code."

Right: If you're lucky, your calling-card company is listed here; supply your account number and PIN code. Otherwise, click New and provide your calling card's information. You have to do all this only once—at least until the information changes.

If you travel with your computer, you can create multiple locations. For example, if you occasionally work from your beach hut in Biarritz or your manse in Mamaroneck, you can set up a location for each place so you can quickly dial up an Internet connection no matter where you are—without having to change a screenful of settings.

Editing an existing location's settings or creating a new location requires the same information. To get started, click New (or click an existing location and then click Edit) and then follow these steps:

1. **Provide a helpful name for the connection.**

   Examples: *Beach Hut/No call waiting* or *Mamaroneck, Dial 9 First.*

2. **Use the drop-down list for Country/region to specify your dialing location. Enter the area code (or country code plus area code).**

3. **Enter any dialing rules that the system needs to know about.**

   For example, if you must dial 9 to get an outside line, type 9 into the "To access an outside line for local calls" box. Also, if the line has Call Waiting, disable it by turning on the checkbox and then choosing the call waiting-disable code from the drop-down menu. The beeps from an incoming call can confuse your mo-

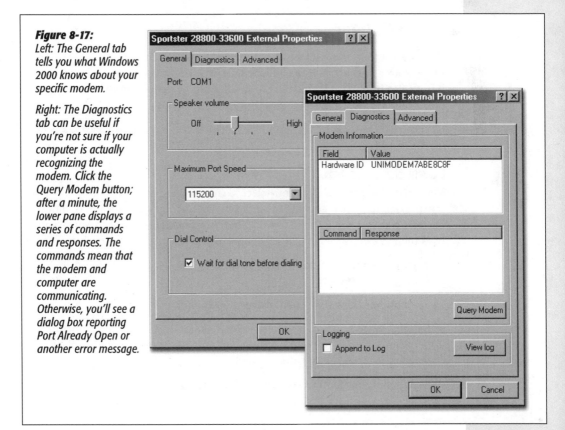

Figure 8-17:
Left: The General tab tells you what Windows 2000 knows about your specific modem.

Right: The Diagnostics tab can be useful if you're not sure if your computer is actually recognizing the modem. Click the Query Modem button; after a minute, the lower pane displays a series of commands and responses. The commands mean that the modem and computer are communicating. Otherwise, you'll see a dialog box reporting Port Already Open or another error message.

dem and cause it to disconnect. (Ask your phone company what code to use to disable call waiting just for one call; it's usually *70.)

4. **Click OK when you're finished, or go on to Area Code Rules (Figure 8-16) or the Calling Card tab (Figure 8-17).**

If you're in one of the increasing number of area codes that require the dialing of extra numbers, you need to add an area code rule. Click Add on the Area Code Rules tab to view the dialog box shown at left in Figure 8-16.

Click the Calling Card tab, on the other hand, if the calls from this location are to be charged to a calling card.

Modems Tab

To find the hardware-type settings for your modem, click the Modems tab. Highlight your modem's name and click Properties (Figure 8-17).

In general, you should change these settings only when Windows doesn't seem to recognize your modem, and you're sure a particular setting is wrong. The exception is the speaker volume, which you're free to adjust so that you don't wake the dead with the screeches made by two modems connecting at 2 a.m.

Power Options

The Power Options applet lets you manage the power consumption of your computer. Power savings is important when you're operating a laptop on battery power, but it's also important if you'd like to save money (and the environment) by cutting down on the amount of electricity your desktop PC uses.

As shown in Figure 8-18, the settings available in this control panel vary depending on the computer.

Power Schemes Tab

The Power Schemes tab lets you select, change, or create *power schemes.* A power scheme defines which components of your PC, such as your keyboard, mouse, or processor, shut down (to save power) after a certain amount of time since you last used them. Power schemes can save power using several different tricks:

- **Turn off monitor.** Your monitor goes dark, and the power light on it changes from green to yellow.

- **Turn off hard disks.** The hard drives stop spinning.

- **System standby.** The computer goes into *standby mode,* which is something like being asleep. All of its components go into reduced-power mode. (Wake it up by pressing a key or clicking the mouse.)

- **System hibernates.** Your computer hibernates (see "Hibernate Tab").

Note: The standby and hibernate options are primarily useful on laptops, and they appear only if you've turned on "Enable Advanced Power Management support," if available, on the APM tab described below. In addition, you'll be offered these controls only if your user account has been given administrative privileges, as described on page 369.

You're welcome to change the settings for any of these schemes. (If you have a laptop that offers Advanced Power Management, as described below, you can create separate settings for "Plugged in" and "Running on batteries" conditions.)

Once you've done so, you can click Save As to preserve your new settings under their own new scheme name. Finally, click OK to close the Power Options Properties dialog box and put the selected power scheme into effect.

Alarms and Power Meter Tabs: For Laptops

Notebook computers offer special options that help them conserve battery power. (You'll see these tabs only if you've turned on "Enable Advanced Power Management support," if available, on the APM tab.)

Alarms tab

When your battery starts running out of juice, your laptop shows a warning message. When it's only got a few seconds of power left, you get a second, more urgently worded message. Both messages are designed to clue you in that *now* is a good time to save whatever document you've been working on; the laptop is about to go to sleep until you've plugged the power cord into the wall.

The controls on this tab let you specify when (or whether) these messages appear, what kind of notification you want (a message, a sound, or both), and what the laptop does as a result (such as going into standby mode).

Power Meter tab

This tab is your laptop battery's fuel gauge. If your computer has two batteries, turn on "Show details for each battery"; you'll see an icon for each battery, which slowly "empties" as your power runs down.

Advanced tab

The Advanced tab, despite its impressive name, usually contains just two options. The first checkbox puts a power icon on the Taskbar tray. You can click this icon to produce a menu listing your power schemes.

If you select "Prompt for password," you're asked to enter a password. Thereafter, the PC won't wake up from standby mode until you've entered the password.

On some computers, an additional option called Power Buttons appears. It lets you choose how your computer will behave when you press the Off button. It can actually turn off—the default—or you can choose to go to Standby.

Hibernate Tab

Hibernate is designed to shorten the long delays involved in shutting down and starting up again later. If you turn on "Enable Hibernate support," you'll see a new option (Hibernate) in the Shut Down Windows dialog box (page 23). When you choose Hibernate as a shut down option, the system saves all your active work onto the hard drive, including open windows and documents—and only then shuts down. When you return to the computer and turn it on, the PC boots up as usual; if you've enabled "Prompt for password" on the Advanced tab, you'll be prompted for a password. After you provide it, the desktop opens instantly, with all programs running and documents open, exactly as you left it.

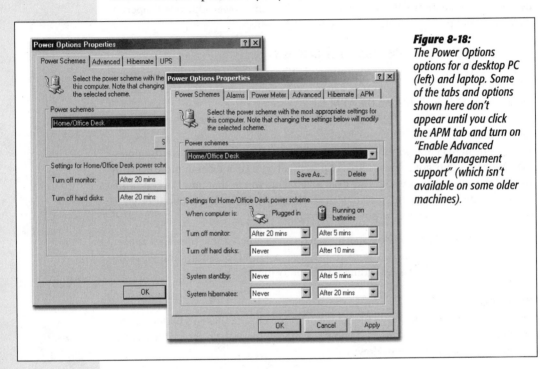

Figure 8-18:
The Power Options options for a desktop PC (left) and laptop. Some of the tabs and options shown here don't appear until you click the APM tab and turn on "Enable Advanced Power Management support" (which isn't available on some older machines).

APM Tab

APM stands for Advanced Power Management, which refers to special power-saving circuitry available in many modern PCs. This tab (if your PC has it) contains nothing but an on/off switch, "Enable Advanced Power Management support." When you turn it on, you add a few useful power-management features to your PC.

For example, turning on APM adds a new option, Stand by, to the Shut Down dialog box. (Standby mode is a low-power condition that's a lot like Off, except that the computer continues to sip a small amount of power, and "wakes up" almost instantly when you press a key or click the mouse.) Turning on APM also gives you many more options on the Power Schemes tab described above, as shown at right in Figure 8-18.

Note: If your computer is compatible with a technology standard called ACPI (Advanced Configuration and Power Interface), you won't see an APM tab. That's because ACPI *automatically* enables the APM Features, so there's no need for an APM on/off switch. (You don't need to worry about knowing which your computer is; Windows 2000 Pro detects the power capabilities automatically).

UPS Tab

A UPS (Uninterruptible Power Supply) is a device that shields your PC from power outages and fluctuations. You use this tab only if you actually have a UPS connected to your PC that Windows 2000 "sees"; you configure the UPS using the controls here. For example, you can configure your computer to display notifications at specified intervals when a power failure occurs, and to shut down after using battery power for a certain period of time. This feature lets the system shut down in a controlled manner, even when you're not around to help it.

Tip: For details on UPS devices, an excellent source of information is the UPS FAQ *(www.uga.edu/~ucns/lans/docs/ups.html)*. The commercial site eHow.com *(www.ehow.com/home/)* has simple instructions on choosing and setting up a UPS.

Printers

The Printers icon in the Control Panel opens the Printers window, which holds icons for the printers you've installed, plus an Add Printer icon. Adding and configuring printers is covered starting on page 349.

Regional Options

Regional Options lets you set date, time, number, and currency options for any number of countries and language groups. For example, if you're preparing documents for colleagues in Sweden, choose Swedish from the drop-down list on the General tab. Now Excel's "Currency" formatting option uses kronor, and the date and time stamps on your files in list-view folder windows appear in the European format.

Likewise, the Input Locales tab offers another place to specify keyboard layouts (see page 156).

Scanners and Cameras

Most scanners and cameras come with their own software, which may add icons to this folder in the Control Panel. This folder also houses an icon for the Scanners and Cameras wizard, which you need to install the software for a new scanner or camera only if the mere act of plugging a scanner or camera into a port on a computer doesn't make Windows 2000 recognize and configure it.

To open the Scanner and Camera Installation Wizard, double-click its icon and then click the Add button. Select the manufacturer and model of the device you want to install. If you have a floppy disk or CD that came with the device, click the Have Disk button.

Next, you're asked what port you want to use. If you know which port the camera or scanner is plugged into, select it. If you don't, leave Automatic Port Select highlighted and click Next. Accept the device name (or change it) and click Next again.

Windows 2000 now copies the necessary files and completes the installation. (See Chapter 16 for more on installing add-ons to your PC.)

Scheduled Tasks

The Scheduled Tasks tool lets you set up any program to run automatically at regular, scheduled intervals. Unfortunately, that's a trick that sounds more useful than it is; in many cases, Scheduled Tasks does little more than remind you that you need to run the application you've specified. It doesn't actually make the program *do* anything. You must generally type out commands to make the program do anything automatically.

To schedule a task, you double-click the Add Scheduled Task icon, which opens the Scheduled Task Wizard. The wizard walks you through the process of selecting the program that you want to, specifying how often you want to run it and when (Figure 8-19). You then specify the user account and password that you want the program to use when it runs.

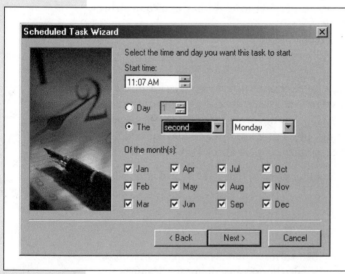

Figure 8-19:
Select the time of day and the day of the month you want the program you've selected to run. If the task is to run only during certain months, check that as well.

On the wizard's final page, you can check the "Open advanced properties" checkbox to enable further configuration after the wizard has scheduled the task. You get a dialog box that lets you specify *command-line options* (short computer-code instructions) for the program you've scheduled.

The command line capabilities of various programs vary greatly. Windows 2000's backup program (Chapter 18), for example, relies on the Scheduled Tasks tool to run its jobs, so it offers a generous collection of command-line parameters. Other programs have none at all. By examining the documentation for the program you want to schedule, you can determine whether you can fully automate the task you want to perform, and the command-line parameters you need to do it.

Sounds and Multimedia

When the first Macintosh user figured out how to produce rude sounds from a computer, PC users were positively pea-green with envy—but not for long. Soon the PC could produce an equally appalling array of noises. Today, the technology has gone much farther; now your PC can also play music and videos, which can be as pleasant as you want them to be. This applet sits at the hub of your PC's audio and visual features.

Sounds Tab

As you may have noticed, Windows plays a sound to accompany every error message. These sounds are generally innocuous beeps or clicks. Using the Sounds tab, you can get rid of the existing sounds, change them around, or set up sounds to play when triggered by all kinds of other Windows events: opening or exiting a program, opening a menu, restoring a window, and so on. Once the Sounds tab is open, follow these steps:

1. **In the Sound Events box, highlight the system or program event to which you want to assign a sound.**

   The speaker icon indicates events that already trigger sounds.

2. **Use the Name drop-down menu to select the sound that you want to play when the event occurs.**

   Click the triangular Play button to listen to a preview of the sound.

   If the sounds that you want to play aren't listed, click Browse to locate the sound files on your computer or network, or select a different sound scheme (set of preassigned sounds) from the Scheme drop-down menu.

Where the sounds are
When you click the Browse button, Windows opens the C:→WINNT→Media folder, which contains the *WAV files* that provide sounds. If you drag WAV files into this Media folder, they become available for use as Windows sound effects.

Tip: The World Wide Web is bursting with sound files. Search for *WAV files* using any search engine, and be prepared to waste many fun-filled hours with sound bits from famous movies, catch phrases of TV characters, music clips, and sound effects of all kinds. You can have Dirty Harry demanding that you "Make my day!" when you boot up in the morning. Or hear Juliet declaim, "Goodnight, sweet prince…" when you log off.

Sounds schemes

You can save an entire set of sound/event pairings as a custom sound *scheme,* or modify an existing scheme and save it. When your nerves are frazzled, for example, you might switch to a sound scheme named Silence is Golden, in which every available system or program sound is turned *off.*

Audio Tab

The Audio tab is where you select your preferred audio devices. If you, like most people, have only one sound card and microphone, you'll find this tab to be of little interest (although you can click Volume to play around with the volume settings, if it amuses you).

Hardware Tab

You can use the Troubleshoot and Properties buttons to troubleshoot sound problems. As a first step, click a device's name in the list to see if it's "working properly."

System

This advanced Control Panel applet is the same one that appears when you right-click your My Computer icon and choose Properties from the shortcut menu. It has five tabs that specify various properties of your PC (see Figure 8-20):

- **General.** You can't change anything on this screen, but that doesn't mean it's not useful (see Figure 8-20).

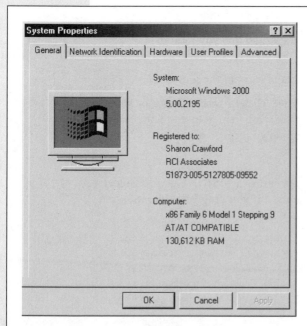

Figure 8-20:
The General tab of the System properties provides some general information about the operating system, registration, and the computer. This is one place to look to see what version of Windows 2000 Pro you're running, as well as how much RAM the system has.

- **Network Identification.** This tab tells you the name that the network uses to identify your computer. This is also the page you come to when you want your formerly freestanding computer to join a network.

- **Hardware.** Here you'll find buttons that launch various equipment-related configuration programs. For example, the Hardware Wizard button opens the Add/Remove Hardware wizard (page 347). The Device Manager button opens, of course, the Device Manager screen (page 357).

  Hardware Profiles are primarily useful on laptops; they're canned settings for different equipment settings. For example, you might create one profile for use when connected to the docking station at the office, and another for use at home; by switching profiles, you quickly inform your laptop of its new gear situation.

  To create one, click Hardware Profiles; click Copy to duplicate an existing profile; click Properties to tell Windows about your docking status, and then click OK. Now use the Device Manager (page 357) to turn the listed components on or off for the profile you've just created. From now on, when you start up your machine, Windows will ask you to specify which hardware profile you'd like to use.

- **User Profiles.** This page lists the *user profiles* (individual accounts, each with its own desktop, Start menu, and other settings) on this computer. (See Chapter 17 for more on profiles.)

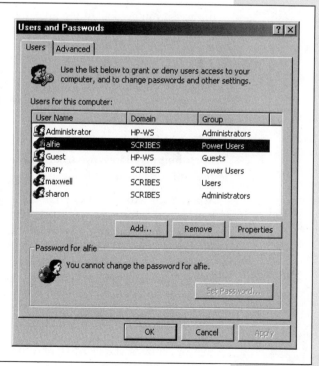

Figure 8-21:
Click the Add button to add users to the local groups on the computer. All you need is a username for each and the domain name, or you can browse through the Active Directory for user names. You also need to specify what level of access to grant the new user. Note that as a local administrator, you can change passwords for local accounts, but you can change domain user passwords only on a machine that's a domain controller (see page 22).

• **Advanced.** These buttons open several administrative programs. If your PC isn't on a network, *or* if you're the system administrator on the network, you can adjust these settings as described in Chapter 17.

Users and Passwords

This control panel shows the master list of accounts that have been set up for people who share your PC. (See Chapter 17 for more accounts, users, and groups.) You can't open the control panel at all unless you've been designated an administrator for this computer (page 369).

Users Tab

On the Users tab, you can turn off "Users must enter a user name and password to use this computer," saving you the step of logging in every time you turn on the PC. Do so, needless to say, only if you're the only one who uses your computer (it's your home PC, for example).

You can also use this tab to add users to the various local groups on the computer, providing them with access to administrative functions they'd otherwise be denied. For example, if you normally log on using your domain account, you may find it irritating to have to log off and then log in again as the local Administrator to configure certain properties of your system. The Users tab (Figure 8-21) lets you add your domain user account to the local Administrators group, so that you have the access you need all of the time. By selecting a user and clicking the Properties button, you can also specify how much freedom the user has to make changes to this PC.

Note: The Users and Passwords control panel lets you add existing users to local groups. But to create *new* user accounts, you must use the Computer Management console, as described on page 371.

Advanced Tab

These buttons address two security issues: Certificate Management (an administrative issue discussed in Chapter 17) and Secure Boot Settings.

Secure Boot Settings is the option that requires you to press Ctrl+Alt+Delete before you log on (see page 20). It's safe to remove this requirement only if your computer isn't on a network, has no permanent connection to the Internet, *and* is otherwise physically secure. (The Ctrl+Alt+Delete key combination a security precaution that prevents "snooping" programs from intercepting the password you type.) Turning this security feature off saves three keystrokes, but it's degree of protection that you're better off with than without.

The third area on the Advanced tab is called Advanced User Management. When you click this button, you get a window in which you can build *local groups,* lists of network citizens who share sets of security settings and access permissions. See Chapter 17 for details on local groups.

Programs in the Start Menu

L ike all versions of Windows before it, Windows 2000 Pro comes with a vast array of small programs to help with miscellaneous chores. Some you'll find useful—others not. This chapter covers these tools as they appear in your Start→Programs menu.

Accessibility Features

If you have trouble using your keyboard or reading small text on the screen, the programs in the Start→Programs→Accessories→Accessibility folder may be just what you need. They include:

Accessibility Wizard

The screens of this wizard ask you to describe the nature of your disability, and make changes to your Windows settings automatically, using (for example) the other Accessibility programs described here.

Magnifier

Magnifier is a floating window that shows a horizontal slice of your screen displaying an enlarged version of whatever your cursor touches as you move it around. Using its Settings control panel shown in Figure 9-1, you can specify how much magnification you get and which area of the screen gets magnified, among other parameters.

On-Screen Keyboard

If you're having trouble typing, keep the On-Screen Keyboard program in mind. It lets you type just by clicking the mouse (Figure 9-1), which you may find useful in a pinch.

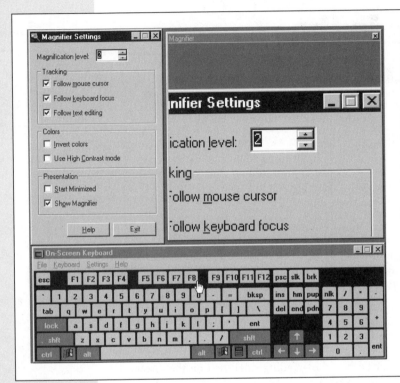

Figure 9-1:
Open Magnifier by choosing Start→ Programs→Accessories→ Accessibility→Magnifier. Top right: Don't forget that you can drag the large magnified window around to a more convenient spot on the screen, and even resize it by dragging the lower-right corner. Top left: Use the Magnifier Settings panel to choose more high-contrast colors, if you like. Bottom: The On-Screen Keyboard, meanwhile, may be just the ticket if your keyboard keys (or your hands) aren't fully functional.

Narrator

Narrator is a speech-synthesis program. (It's not in the Accessibility folder by default; you can get to it only by opening the Utility Manager, described next). Whenever it's running, you hear a middle-aged man's voice, bearing only a faint trace of Scandinavian accent, read aloud any text that's on the screen, such as dialog boxes, error messages, window titles, text you type, and menus you open. It works in most Windows 2000 programs (including Internet Explorer, WordPad, and the programs in the Control Panel), but may not operate in other applications.

If you find Narrator helpful, don't miss its Options screen (which may be hidden squarely behind the welcome screen), where you can set Narrator up to read what you type and to start up minimized. By clicking the Voice button, you can even change the voice's speed, volume, and pitch.

Utility Manager

This program, whose functions are available only if you've been given administrator privileges (see page 369), lets you control the *other* three Accessibility programs described here (Magnifier, Narrator, On-Screen Keyboard). Its most important option is the "Start automatically when Windows starts" checkbox, which can make life a lot easier for a disabled person.

Communications Features

The Start→Programs→Accessories submenu contains a handful of shortcuts to faxing, dialing, and conferencing programs. This section presents each one in turn.

Fax

Windows 2000 Pro lets you send and receive faxes directly from your desktop. All you need is a fax modem, a standard component on most modern PCs.

You can fax a document as easily as printing it. In fact, the fax modem shows up in your Printers Folder as just another printer (Figure 9-2).

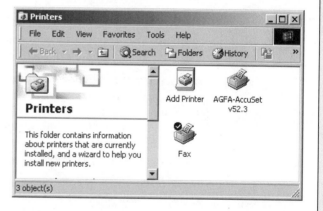

Figure 9-2:
To Windows 2000, a fax device is just another printer. It's not, however, a shared printer, meaning that you can't share your fax with others on your network.

Setting up your virtual fax machine

If your PC has a fax modem, you're already set to send faxes (see "Sending a fax" in the next section); the presence of a *fax printer* icon in your Start→Settings→Printers window tells you so. To make sure it's set up the way you like it (and to turn on your ability to *receive* faxes), proceed like this:

1. **Choose Start→Programs→Accessories→Communications→Fax→Fax Service Management.**

   As a reward for that massive mouse trek, the Fax Service Management program appears.

2. **In the console (left) pane, click Devices. In the details (right) pane, right-click your fax modem's name; select Properties from the shortcut menu.**

The fax modem's Properties dialog box appears.

3. **On the General Tab, specify whether or not you want to be able to *receive* faxes.**

The "Enable send" box is turned on by default, but you should indicate your return fax number in the TSID (transmitting station identifier) box. If you want your PC to receive incoming faxes, turn on "Enable receive." If you have a different fax number for receiving faxes, enter it in the CSID (call subscriber identifier) box.

Note: If you want your PC to receive faxes, you have two wiring options. First, you can dedicate a phone line just to your modem. Second, if you'd rather let your modem share your regular voice line, you can use the "Enable manual answer for the first device" option described on the next page.

If you allow incoming faxes, you can indicate how long the PC should wait (how many rings) before answering the phone when a fax call comes in.

4. **On the Received Faxes tab, specify how you want incoming faxes to be handled.**

If you'd like them printed automatically, turn on "Print on" and use the drop-down menu to choose a printer. If you'd rather have them saved as files on your hard drive, turn on "Save in Folder" and indicate where you want the files saved.

Finally, you can ask Windows to route incoming faxes automatically to the In box of your email program. That's a convenient setup—it helps you consolidate your communications, regardless of their sources—but it works only if you meet a long list of requirements. Unfortunately, this feature works only if you have a *MAPI-enabled* email program. Microsoft Outlook is; Outlook Express isn't. (If your email program isn't MAPI-happy, the "Send to local email inbox" checkbox is dimmed.)

5. **Click OK. Close Fax Service Management.**

Next, complete the user information for faxing. Choose Start→Control Panel, and then double-click the Fax icon to open the Fax Properties dialog box. On the User

---

POWER USERS' CLINIC

Opening Up Fax Management

Anyone can *look* at Fax Service Management settings, but you can make changes to them only if you're an administrator or have administrator privileges (see page 369). In that case, you can set other users' permissions so that they can view *and* change fax settings.

To do so, open the Fax Service Management program, as described on page 173. Right-click "Fax Service on Local Computer" (in the left half of the window) and select Properties from the shortcut menu. In the resulting dialog box, click the Security tab, click Everyone, and turn on the un-checked Allow boxes; click OK.

Information tab, type in the information you'd want to appear on the fax cover page (see Step 5 on the next page). The other Properties tabs are:

- **Cover Page.** Lists the fax cover pages you've designed. (See "Creating Cover Pages" later in this section.)

- **Status Monitor.** These checkboxes let you specify how you'd like to be notified when a fax comes in or goes out. **Display the status monitor** means that you'll see a small progress-bar dialog box; **Display icon on taskbar** adds a system Tray icon for faxing, offering quick links to the Fax Queue, your folder of faxes, and the Fax Monitor. **Play a sound,** of course, means that you'll hear a sound effect when you receive a fax. (To change the sound, open Sounds & Multimedia in Control Panel and look for Incoming Fax in the Sound Events list.)

  The **Enable manual answer for the first device** is for people who have only a single phone line for both voice and fax calls. If you turn this on, when a call comes in, an "Answer this call?" dialog box will open. If you pick up your phone handset and hear a fax tone, click Yes. Otherwise, click No, and proceed with your normal voice call. (If the caller tells you a fax is about to arrive, you can turn on the Answer Next Call checkbox in the Fax Monitor window. Your PC will answer the *next* call.)

- **Advanced Options.** This tab's buttons open the Fax Service Management Console, Fax Help, and Add a Fax Printer programs.

Sending a fax

Sending faxes couldn't be more convenient; there's no printout to throw away, no paper involved. Your PC sends the fax directly to a fax machine's brain. Here's the whole process, step by step:

1. **Open up whatever you want to fax (a word processing document, spreadsheet, or whatever). Choose File→Print.**

   The Print dialog box appears.

2. **Choose Fax in the Select Printer drop-down menu (or click the fax icon); then click OK or Print.**

   The Send Fax wizard appears. If this is the first time you've run the wizard, a dialog box asks if you want to edit your user information, as described in the previous section. If you've already done so, select "Keep the current user information" and click OK.

3. **On the Recipient and Dialing Information page, type the name and fax number of the recipient (see Figure 9-3).**

   You can also click Address Book to select someone's name in your Windows Address Book (see page 261). If your Address Book information included the recipient's fax number, you can skip to Step 5.

4. **Click Add, and then repeat this step for any additional recipients. Click Next.**

   Now you're invited to add a cover page to your outgoing fax.

5. **Turn on "Include a cover page," if you like, and then select a cover-page template from the drop-down list.**

   This list is empty unless you've designed a cover page or two (see page 178). When you choose a cover page, you can also type a subject line and note to appear on it.

6. **Click Next. On the Scheduling Transmission page, specify when you want to send the fax.**

   Add your company's billing code information, if necessary.

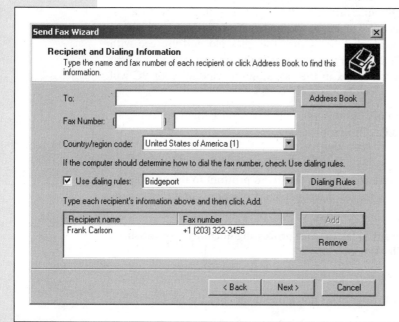

Figure 9-3:
If the fax number isn't local, turn on the Use Dialing Rules checkbox, and then choose the appropriate dialing rules from the drop-down list. (See page 160 for instructions on defining "locations" for dialing.) If you're using dialing rules and you're calling a place that doesn't require an area or city code, type the first three digits in the first Fax Number box, and the rest in the next text box.

Tip: If you find yourself frequently specifying a later time (such as off hours, to reduce interference with normal work) or a certain billing code for your faxes, consider changing the default settings for this screen. Choose Start→Settings→Printers. In the Printers window, right-click the fax printer icon; select Printing Preferences from the shortcut menu. Specify the default sending time you prefer (and billing code, if appropriate), and click OK twice. (If you duplicate the fax icon in the Printers window, you can use these techniques to give each "fax printer" different billing codes, default send times, and other settings.)

If you're wondering how Windows 2000 knows "when discount rates apply," it doesn't. You must tell it; open the Fax Service Management program. Right-click "Fax Service on Local Computer," and select Properties from the shortcut menu. On the General tab, you can set the actual discount rate times in your area.

7. **Click Next.**

The final screen shows you a summary of your outgoing fax's settings.

8. **Click Finish to send the fax (or to prepare it to wait until the time you specified).**

Windows 2000 will send the fax automatically at the specified time.

If it begins to dial at an inopportune time—or if you discover a typo just as your PC tries to send the fax—you can cancel the fax attempt by clicking the End Fax Call button in the Fax Monitor (Figure 9-4).

Your recipient is in for a treat. Faxes sent by a PC come out looking twice as crisp and clean when a real fax machine receives them (because they were never scanned in with a typical fax machine's crude scanner on your end).

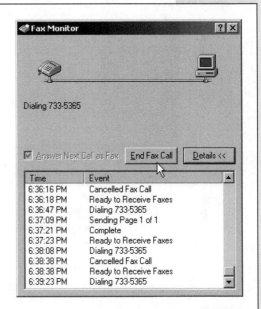

Figure 9-4:
The End Fax Call button is available when the Fax Service is dialing the number. It's grayed out as soon as the connection is made. The Fax Monitor window doesn't close on its own, by the way; close it manually by clicking its close button.

Tip: You can send a fax cover page without a document, too—a great trick when you just want to send a quick note. To do so, choose Start→Programs→Accessories→Communications→Fax→Send Cover Page Fax to open the Send Fax wizard, and then follow Steps 3 through 8.

Receiving a fax

When a fax arrives at your modem, you may or may not hear the incoming ring, depending on your modem's settings. You see a fax icon on the Tray, and a Fax Monitor window opens (Figure 9-4).

To look at or print a copy of a fax, right-click the Fax icon in the Tray, and select My Faxes from the shortcut menu. In the My Faxes folder, double-click either Received Faxes or Sent Faxes. Double-click a fax to open it in the Imaging Preview viewer program (or whatever graphic program you've associated with TIF files; see page 122). You can print out a fax just as you would any image file.

GEM IN THE ROUGH

Incomprehensible Fax Names

One would think that as clever as computers are, they'd figure out some way to list your faxes other than by a long string of meaningless letters and numbers. And the availability of a thumbnail view isn't helpful with this sort of file.

The solution is to *rename* your fax files—or at least the ones

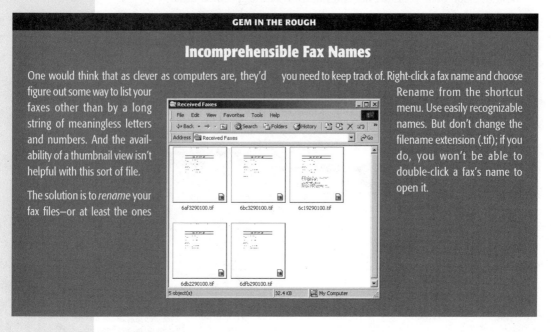

you need to keep track of. Right-click a fax name and choose Rename from the shortcut menu. Use easily recognizable names. But don't change the filename extension (.tif); if you do, you won't be able to double-click a fax's name to open it.

Creating cover pages

You can idle away many pleasant hours designing your own cover pages. You do that on the Cover Page tab of the Fax control panel.

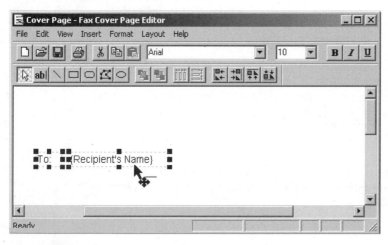

Figure 9-5:
Start by choosing Insert→Recipient→Name. A form field *appears, which you can drag anywhere on the page. When you send a fax, Windows will fill this box with the name of the person who's getting your fax. Use the other Insert commands to place other fields on your cover page, such as your own contact information, the date and time, and so on.*

In addition to placing informational fields on your cover page as shown in Figure 9-5, you can paste in graphics, such as your company logo, and dress up the page with lines and shapes, courtesy of the drawing tools at the bottom of the window.

When the cover page looks good, choose File→Save, type a memorable name, and click Save. From now on, this template will be one of your cover-page options whenever you send a fax.

Tip: Cover pages must have a .cov filename extension.

HyperTerminal

HyperTerminal is a relic from the days when all dial-up services were text-based (like an old BBS), not graphically based (like the Web). You can still use HyperTerminal for direct serial and modem connections, but now it can also serve as a *Telnet* client (a program that can access text-based systems like bulletin boards and public-library systems).

To configure a Telnet session using HyperTerminal, choose Start→Programs→Accessories→Communications→HyperTerminal. Enter a descriptive name in the New Connection box then click OK.

In the Connect To dialog box, click the Connect Using drop-down list and select TCP/IP (Winsock), as shown in Figure 9-6. Click OK to make the Telnet connection. Finally, enter your login ID and start the session.

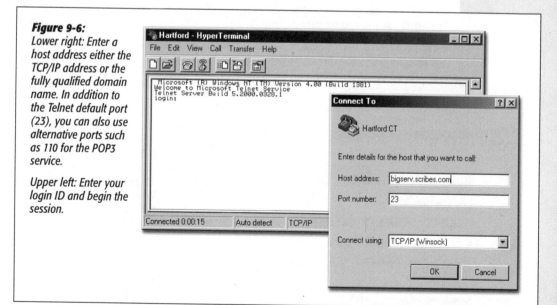

Figure 9-6:
Lower right: Enter a host address either the TCP/IP address or the fully qualified domain name. In addition to the Telnet default port (23), you can also use alternative ports such as 110 for the POP3 service.

Upper left: Enter your login ID and begin the session.

Internet Connection Wizard

This program walks you through the creation of new Internet account. Details are on page 220.

NetMeeting

This program lets you use your local network or the Internet to collaborate and communicate with other people by typing messages, sending video images back and forth, speaking to each other via microphone and speaker, drawing on a virtual "white board," and even using each other's software. All of this works best on a LAN, but it also works over the Internet if both sides have a fast connection.

Start NetMeeting by choosing Start→Programs→Accessories→Communications→NetMeeting. A wizard walks you through the process of filling in your name and email address, specifying the Internet Locator Service (ILS) directory that will list you, specifying your connection speed (such as modem or cable modem), adjusting your microphone and speaker levels, and so on.

The ILS directory is a server on the Internet with which you can register; you'll be able to communicate with any other registered user. However, you can also communicate with another NetMeeting client directly, without an intervening server, as long as you know the IP address of the other computer. While using a server is more practical on the Internet, you're better off connecting directly when using NetMeeting on an office network.

After you've set up NetMeeting, schedule a time with your collaborators, just as you might schedule a conference call. Everybody has to be on the Internet (or office network) at the same time.

Note: Each participant must have either Phone Dialer or NetMeeting open; otherwise, you'll see a message that the person you called is not able to receive Internet calls.

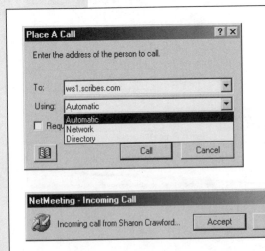

Figure 9-7:
Lower right: Enter a host address either the TCP/IP address or the fully qualified domain name. In addition to the Telnet default port (23) you can also use alternative ports such as 110 for the POP3 service. Upper left: Enter your login ID and begin the session.

Making the call

To make a call, open NetMeeting and choose Call→New Call (Figure 9-7).

After you click the Call button, your computer attempts to connect to the addressee. At the other end, the recipient sees a message like the one at right in Figure 9-7. When you're connected, you'll see a window like the one in Figure 9-8.

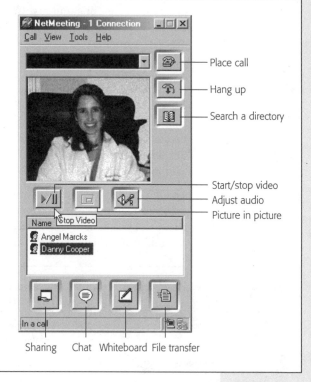

Figure 9-8:
The four buttons on the NetMeeting window don't have labels—not even tooltips. If you're lucky enough to have video equipment hooked up, you can even participate n a videoconference.

Place call
Hang up
Search a directory
Start/stop video
Adjust audio
Picture in picture
Sharing   Chat   Whiteboard   File transfer

Once your meeting is underway, you can perform four remarkable stunts, which correspond to the four icons at the bottom of the NetMeeting window (Figure 9-8). Once you figure out how they work, the amount of travel time and plane fares you can save using NetMeeting adds up quickly. Here's what they do:

Sharing Programs

Amazingly enough, other people in your meeting can use your programs—editing one of your Word documents or typing numbers into your Excel spreadsheet, for example—even if they don't have Word or Excel on their machines.

It works like this:

1. **Launch the program you want everyone to be able to use. Then click the Sharing button (the first one on the left) on the NetMeeting screen.**

   The Sharing window appears, as shown in Figure 9-9.

2. **Click the name of the program you want to share, and then click Share.**

Note, in particular, the Desktop, which is always listed in the Share Programs window. If you share it, then everybody else in the meeting can see what you see as you work in Windows. As far as NetMeeting is concerned, the Desktop is simply another program that you can share.

Under most circumstances, the other people in the meeting can just *look* at the program you're using. But if you'd like others in your meeting to be able to *control* the application—to edit the documents and use the menus, for example, proceed as follows:

3. **Click Allow Control.**

Instantly, a new window appears on the screens of the other participants, showing exactly what you see in *your* copy of the program. When you move your cursor, it moves on their screens; when you open a dialog box, they see it, too. Because your microphone is working during a NetMeeting meeting, you can use this feature to collaborate on documents, teach somebody a new program, or help somebody troubleshoot a PC.

And if you've shared your Desktop, giving away control means that other people can even manipulate your computer files and folders! They can open folders, rename or delete files, make backup copies, and perform any task that you can yourself, from wherever on the Internet to happen to be.

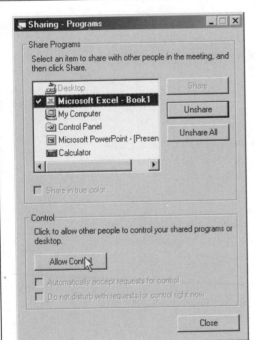

Figure 9-9:
If you want others to also be able to control the application you're sharing, click Allow Control. "Automatically accept requests for control" means that the other user can take control through the Control menu. "Do not disturb with requests for control right now" means that if anyone else asks for control, they won't get it (and you won't even have to refuse the request). If you're the one sharing the application, you can regain control simply by clicking inside the program window.

Just clicking Allow Control, however, is not enough to transfer control of a program to one of your collaborators. He must also choose Control→Request Control from his shared-program window; only then can he edit your documents or manipulate your desktop.

It's worth noting, by the way, that all of this controlling and sharing requires an enormous amount of data to be shuttled over the wires. Depending on the speed of your connection, the cursor may seem jerky and everything may feel very slow; that's normal, especially if you're connecting via standard dial-up modems.

Chat

Click the Chat button to open a window where you can type messages to others participating in the connection, exactly as in an Internet chat room. Opening the Chat window on your computer causes it to open on the screens of the other participants as well.

Select View→Options to change the look of the Chat window.

Figure 9-10:
These four windows correspond to the four buttons shown at the bottom of the previous figure. Clockwise from top left: The Sharing window, which lets other people see what you're doing on your desktop and in your applications; the Chat window; the File Transfer window; and the Whiteboard, which lets you and your comrades work together on a design.

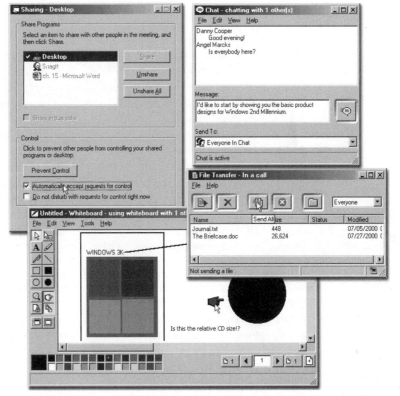

Whiteboard

Click the Whiteboard button to open a shared version of Paint (page 201). All participants can use the whiteboard—adding notes or drawings. Figure 9-10 shows the Whiteboard and Chat windows.

Tip: If you attempt to change or discard the whiteboard, you're asked to confirm the action; other people using the whiteboard will see it simply vanish without offering a chance to save the contents. In other words, check with others in the NetMeeting before closing the window.

To copy a picture or portion of another open document to the whiteboard, select Tools→Select Area. Your cursor changes to crosshairs; drag it around the area you want to capture. (You may first have to position the other document's window on the screen so that you can see the portion you want to grab.) When you release the mouse button, the selected area pops on to the whiteboard. Similarly, you can paste a whole window to the whiteboard by selecting Tools→Select Window.

If the whiteboard gets too crowded, add a page in front of the current page by selecting Edit→Insert Page Before. (Choose Insert Page After to add a page *after* the current page.)

File transfers

To send a file or files to anyone (or everyone) in the NetMeeting, click the File Transfer button. Use the drop-down menu to specify who gets the file; choose File→Add File to specify the file you want to send; finally, to send the files on their way, click the Send All files button (Figure 9-10), or right-click one file and choose Send a File from the shortcut menu.

Audio and video

If your PC has a microphone and speakers , audio is automatically turned on during a NetMeeting, so that everybody else can hear whatever you say. Note, however, that you may not be able to hear anybody else *while* you're speaking. Some sound cards don't offer this *full-duplex* audio feature; in that case, you'll get more of a CB radio effect—*half*-duplex communication—where only one person can speak at a time. (In that case, you may want to say, "Over!" after each comment.)

You can send video to only one other person in the meeting, and if you're using NetMeeting over a standard modem connection, "video" may be a generous term. You may find that the picture is jerky and grainy, more like a series of still images than a TV broadcast. However, when you connect over an office network, the image quality is much better. Click the Start Video button to begin transmitting; click Stop Video when you've had enough.

Network and Dial-up Connections

This item simply opens up your Network and Dial-up Connections folder, as described on page 306.

Phone Dialer

You can use this program to dial a phone connected to your computer, via your modem; you can even use its Edit→Add To Speed Dial List command to build up a list of numbers you dial frequently.

But Phone Dialer would be fairly uninteresting if that were all it did. (After all, practically every phone comes with a speed-dial function these days.) Phone Dialer is really another tool for *IP Telephony* (using the Internet for phone conversations) and video conferencing; its features overlap considerably with NetMeeting.

To communicate using Phone Dialer, you need a microphone and a sound card (if you want to be heard by the other participants) and a video camera (if you want to be seen). To contact one other person, you need only his modem's phone number; to contact someone else on your network (or another company's network), you need her computer name, IP address, or Internet directory name.

To place a voice call, click the Dial button in the Phone Dialer toolbar to open the Dial dialog box (Figure 9-11, top). After you click Place Call, the active call window appears on the screen (Figure 9-11, bottom).

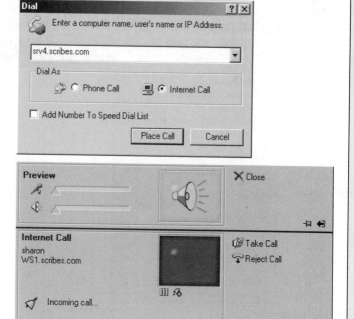

Figure 9-11:
Enter a computer name, as shown, or an IP address (in the format 192.168.1.54). You can also use Phone Dialer simply to dial your phone (if it's connected to the same line as your modem). To do so, select Phone Call and enter a telephone number. Bottom: In the Preview window at the top, you can adjust both the incoming and outgoing sound levels. Click the Take Call icon or Reject Call icon.

Receiving a call requires that you have Phone Dialer running. When you receive an incoming call, the Preview and Internet Call dialog boxes open automatically (Figure 9-11), and you may hear a sound.

Note: As with NetMeeting, the quality of your connection may be very low if you're connecting via modem—much higher if you're connecting over a LAN.

Entertainment Features

This submenu of your Start→Programs folder might be better named "Multimedia," because all four of these programs pertain to sound and video.

CD Player

The CD Player program (Figure 9-12) serves as the front panel for your computer's music CD-playing features, complete with Play, Stop, Pause, Next Track, Eject, and other familiar buttons. If you insert an audio CD into the CD drive and start CD Player, you'll be asked if you want to download information about the CD from the Internet.

Figure 9-12:
CD Player gives every CD the name "New Title," and every song on it is "Track 1," "Track 2," and so on. Fortunately, the program can consult an Internet database to download the actual CD and track names, which it fills in automatically and remembers for the next time you insert the disc. This option alone is a major improvement over the bad old days when you had to type all the track information in.

Next, the CD begins to play. Click the Track arrow to see the names (and lengths) of the tracks, as shown in Figure 9-12. You can change tracks by clicking the list; click the Disc button (or just look at the top of the window) to see the name of the CD.

The Mode menu lets you choose to play tracks at random, repeat a track until you go mad, repeat the entire CD until you go mad, or preview each track (for an amount of time you set by clicking Options→Preferences). For volume control, drag the virtual knob.

Tip: Windows Media Player, described later in this chapter, does the same thing—with many more options.

Sound Recorder

In recent years, Media Player (page 189) has taken over the sound-*playing* duties in Windows; in fact, if you double-click a WAV file (a standard Windows sound file), Media Player opens and plays it. But Sound Recorder is one simple way to *record* new sounds—and edit them. You can then associate these files with events on your computer (like booting up, shutting down, or launching a program), as described on page 167.

Recording sounds

To record a sound, follow these steps:

1. **Choose Start→Programs→Accessories→Entertainment→Sound Recorder.**

   Sound Recorder opens.

2. **Check the recording format by choosing File→Properties→Convert Now.**

   In this dialog box (Figure 9-13), you can specify the sound quality for your recording; the better the quality, the more disk space your file will consume. The default ("untitled") setting is fine for casual voice recordings, which will consume 7 K of hard drive space for every second recorded.

   For a higher quality, click the Name drop-down list (Figure 9-13). Telephone quality is slightly better than the default. Radio is even better; CD quality is the best of all, but consumes 172 K of drive space for every second recorded. Experiment to find an acceptable quality for the type of audio you're recording. Telephone quality is usually fine for voice recordings, but if you're creating a WAV file from an audio CD, you'll probably want to use a higher sound quality.

3. **To begin recording, click on the button with the dark red dot. Start the CD or start speaking into the microphone. Click the button with the black square to stop recording.**

   If you see animated sound waves in the Sound Recorder window, great; that's your VU (sound level) meter. It tells you that the PC is hearing you. If you don't see these yellow lines, however, then the sound isn't getting through. The problem is most likely that your PC control panel isn't set to record the appropriate sound source. Choose Edit→Audio Properties, and then use the Sound Recording drop-down menu to choose your microphone's name.

4. **Select Save from the File menu to save the sound clip. Name the file in the Save dialog box.**

If you want your new sound to be available in the Sounds and Multimedia control panel (so that you can make it play back to signal a Windows event), save it into the C: drive→WINNT→Media folder.

Playing sounds

To play an existing WAV file, open Sound Recorder. You can drag a WAV file from a desktop window onto the Sound Recorder window, or select File→Open and then browse for the file. Figure 9-13, bottom, shows a file being played.

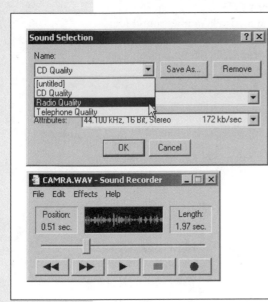

Figure 9-13:
Top: Experiment to find an acceptable quality, but bear in mind that unless you have great speakers, you won't get much benefit from using the higher quality settings. Bottom: Note that the total length of the file is displayed on the right and the current position of the playback is on the left. You can click the fast-forward and rewind buttons to jump to the end or beginning of the file.

Editing sounds

You can play with a file before you save it—adding echo or editing unwanted parts. Using the commands in the Edit menu, you can make your recording play faster or slower, add an echo effect, or even play it backward—great for finding subliminal messages in your own utterances.

To tidy up a sound file, you can edit out sound from the slider position to the beginning of the file or to the end of the file. To remove the introduction from a musical clip, for example, adjust the slider to just before the point where the good sound starts—play the file a few times, watching the position indicator to make sure you have the right spot—then choose Edit→Delete Before Current Position.

Volume Control

The controls you see in this program govern the volume and balance levels of the speakers, microphones, and sound-card elements of your PC. Every PC's sound card and other features are different, so not all of the controls may be operational on your machine, but you get the idea. Here are a few of the things you might want to do with Volume Control:

- **Shut your PC up.** By clicking "Mute all" at the lower-left corner of the window, you make your PC completely silent—a handy feature when you don't want some errant beep or squawk to let the world know that you're using your laptop in, for example, church.

- **Adjust the stereo balance of your PC speakers.** If one of the speakers is farther away from your head, you can drag the Balance sliders so that the distant speaker plays a little bit louder.

- **Fine-tune MIDI playback.** If your sound card can play back MIDI files (a compact file format for instrumental music), use the Synthesizer balance and volume controls to tweak its sound.

- **Adjust the bass and treble.** These knobs don't appear on the Volume Control screen; you have to choose Options→Advanced Controls, and then click Advanced, to see these sliders.

Media Player

Media Player has evolved from one of those Windows applets whose unimportance couldn't be overestimated into a genuinely useful and entertaining tool. In its latest incarnation, Windows Media Player can play CDs, MP3 files, sounds, digital movies, or Internet radio stations. The program can also save your favorite CD tracks to your hard drive or MP3 player. This blossoming is the result of the growth of streaming audio and video over the Internet—plus the explosion in the use of MP3 technology for music storage and distribution.

Getting Version 7

Unfortunately, the version of Media Player that came with your copy of Windows 2000 may be the older, much less useful version 6; the following discussion, and indeed *all* Media Player discussion these days, revolves around the newer version 7.

To find out which version you have, choose Start→Programs→Accessories→Entertainment→Windows Media Player. Choose Help→About Windows Media Player. If the dialog box that opens reveals that you have a version before 7.0, click OK, and then don't hesitate: Choose Go→Windows Media Player Home Page to download the latest version of Media Player for Windows 2000.

Audio CDs

For its first trick, Media Player can simulate a $200 CD player, capable of playing your music CDs while you're working at your computer. To fire it up, just insert a CD into your computer's CD-ROM drive (see Figure 9-14).

Tip: As the music plays, you get to watch psychedelic screen-saver-like displays, which Microsoft calls *visualizations,* that bounce and shimmer to the music. To try a different one, click the Next Visualization arrow (the tiny arrow button just below the shimmery display), or press Tab+Enter, or choose View→Visualizations. And if you tire of the 48 built-in displays, you can download more of them from the Internet by choosing Tools→Download Visualizations.

If the Media Player window shows names like "Track 1" and "Track 2" instead of actual song names, it's because the track data wasn't encoded on the CD by the record company. In such cases, exactly as with CD Player described earlier, you can let the Internet fill in the missing information for you. Just click the CD Audio button at the left side of the Media Player window, and then click Get Names at the top of the window. Once you're online, a wizard walks you through the steps needed to identify the album in your CD drive.

After you enter the CD and song names for a particular CD, Windows saves this information in your music library (see "Copying Music to Your Hard Drive," later in this chapter). The next time you insert this CD, the Media Player will recognize it and display the track names and album information automatically.

Figure 9-14:
Media Player automatically displays the album title and the titles of each track, if that information was encoded onto your music CD. The track that's currently playing is highlighted (along with its length) and the elapsed time appears below the scroll bar. Double-click a track name to listen to it. The controls at the bottom of the Media Player window are like the controls on a physical CD player (Pause, Play, Next Track, Volume, and so on).

Tip: If the Media Player window is taking up too much screen space, making it harder for you to do other work, press Ctrl+2, or click the Compact Mode button in the lower-right corner of the window (Figure 9-15). Either way, the Media Player reappears in the lower-right corner of your screen, a fraction of its former size, its useful controls still visible. Press Ctrl+1 to return the Media Player window to its full-size glory. (Of course, you can also just minimize Media Player, as you would any window.)

Change the skin

In hopes of riding the world's craze for MP3 files (compact, downloadable, CD-quality sound files), Microsoft has helped itself to one of MP3-playing software's most interesting features: *skins.* A skin is a design scheme that completely changes the look of Windows Media Player.

To choose a new skin, click the Skin Chooser button on the left side of the Media Player window. (If you don't like any of the designs or just want to keep looking, click More Skins to visit Microsoft's Windows Media Skin Gallery.) Then click each of the available skins to see a preview of its appearance. When you click the Apply Skin button, your player takes on the look of the skin you chose *and* shrinks down into Compact mode, as described in the previous tip.

Figure 9-15:
At full size, the Media Player window occupies a large chunk of your screen (Figure 9-14). Left: In Compact Mode, it takes up less space on your screen.

Right: Compact Mode also puts a small control window in the corner of your desktop. Click the compact window for a menu that offers, among other commands, Return to Full Mode.

Copy the CD to your hard drive

You can copy an audio CD, or selected tracks, to your hard drive in the form of stand-alone music files that play when you double-click them. Having CD songs on your hard drive affords you a number of benefits:

- You can listen to whatever songs you like, without having to hunt for the CDs they came from.

- You can listen to music even if you're using the CD-ROM drive for something else (such as a CD-based game).

- You can build your own *playlist* (set of favorite songs) consisting of cuts from different albums.

- You can compress the file in the process, so that each song takes up less disk space.

Follow these steps to copy audio from a CD to your hard drive:

1. Click the CD Audio button on the left side of the Media Player window.

The track list appears.

2. **Turn off the checkbox of any track you *don't* want to copy.**

   Before you proceed, choose Tools→Options; on the CD Audio tab, make sure that Digital Copying is selected. Click OK.

3. **Click the Copy Music button on the toolbar.**

   The button changes its name to Stop Copy, which you can click to interrupt the process. Windows now copies the selected tracks onto your hard drive.

When you perform this copying procedure, Windows goes about building a *music library,* a set of nested folders, in the C:→Documents and Settings→All Users→Documents→My Music folder. Within the My Music folder, Windows makes a folder for each performer; within the performer folder, there's a folder for each CD; and within *that* folder, you'll find icons representing the tracks you copied. To play a song, just double-click its icon.

Tip: Instead of burrowing through four folders to find a song you've copied to your hard drive, just use Windows Media Player to play them. Click the Media Library button to see the list of songs you've copied; double-click a song name to play it.

Burning your own CDs

If your PC has a CD burner attached, you can create your own audio CDs that play in any standard CD player. Candidates for this treatment are MP3 files, WAV files, and Windows Media files (.asf, .wma, and .wmv), such as the ones you've copied from a CD to your hard drive.

1. **Copy the music you'll want to your hard drive.**

   If you're using MP3 or WAV files, they're probably already on your hard drive. If you're planning to use tracks from a CD, copy them as directed in "Copy the CD to your hard drive," above. Remember that the quality settings you use will affect the sound quality of the finished disc.

2. **Create a playlist.**

   A playlist, in this case, is simply a list of the tracks you'll want on your homemade CD. To create a playlist, click the Media Library button, click New Playlist, type a name for the list. Then add tracks to the new playlist by highlighting their names (at the right side of the window) and then clicking "Add to playlist" on the toolbar; choose "Add to [your new playlist's name]" from the tiny menu. The maximum length for a CD is 74 minutes.

3. **Choose File→Copy to CD.**

   Now the Playlists list appears.

4. **Double-click the name of the playlist you want converted to a CD.**

   If the equipment gods are smiling, your CD burner now spins into action, and the messages on the screen keep you posted as the CD is created.

Tip: If you want to play the resulting CD in a standard stereo CD player, use a CD-R disc (which you can record only once); CD-RW (rewritable) discs play only in computers.

Copy the CD to a portable device

If you have a palmtop computer that's capable of playing music, such as a Diamond Rio or a Windows CE-based palmtop, you can copy your CD files there. To do so, connect the palmtop, and then click the Portable Device button on the left side of the Media Player window. Now Media Player displays a split window: the left side lists the tracks on the CD, and the right side lists the music currently installed on the palmtop. Turn on the checkboxes of the tracks you want, and then click Copy Music; Windows copies the music you selected to your portable player.

Finding music on the Internet

Your CD collection isn't the only source of music worth listening to as you work. The Internet is crawling with Web sites that harbor music files you can download and make part of your music library (or download to your palmtop).

To find them, click the Media Guide button on the Media Player window. You're shown a list of Microsoft media Web sites, where you'll find lists, search engines, and other methods for finding music.

Listening to the radio

You can use the computer itself as a radio, one that can tune in to any of hundreds of radio stations from all over the world, each brought to you by the Internet. To do so, open Windows Media Player. Click the Radio Tuner button at the left to connect to the Internet, where you can select the stations you want to hear (see Figure 9-16).

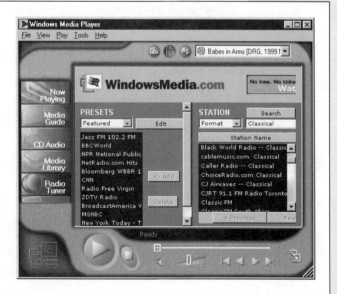

Figure 9-16:
The left side of the Radio Tuner window lists your preset stations (Microsoft features several popular stations in a collection named Featured); the right side provides search features you can use to find stations you want to add to this canned list.

To create your own list (which will replace Microsoft's Featured List), choose My Presets from the drop-down menu at the top of the left pane. Then find the stations you want to add by using the search features in the right pane. When you find a radio station you like, select it and click Add. Once you've done so, the radio station will appear automatically in the Radio toolbar that you can summon to any desktop window (see page 73). (To remove a station from your preset list, select it and click Delete.)

Watching video

Media Player can also play movie files, such as those you've downloaded from the Internet, made yourself, or grabbed from a CD-ROM. The standard Windows movie-file format is *.avi,* but Media Player can also play many other Microsoft media formats (.ask, .asx, .wav, .wma, .wm, .wmv, .wax, .wvx), Unix formats (.au, .snd), MPEG formats (.mpg, .mpeg, .m1v, .mp2, .mp2v, .mp3, .mpa, .mpe, .m3u), MIDI files (.mid, .midi, .mi), Apple QuickTime files (.qt, .aif, .aifc, .aiff, .mov), RealAudio files (.ram, .ra, .rm, .rmm), and several others (.ivf, .cda).

Note: Media Player 7 still doesn't recognize RMJ, the format of RealJukebox. If you've collected a music list in RMJ format, you won't be able to import the files into Media Player, unless you're able to convert them into a compatible format.

Games

Despite Microsoft's efforts to promote Windows 2000 as the system software for corporations, its installer endows Windows 2000 Pro with four games. In fact, there's

---

TROUBLESHOOTING MOMENT

Glitches in Streaming Music and Video

As a rule, Media Player is smart enough to adjust itself to circumstances. If data delivery slows, Media Player looks to the server for a data format that will keep the show from being interrupted, even if the quality is lower.

The last few years have seen an exponential increase in the quality of audio and video playback. Unfortunately, that's accompanied by just as big increase the quantity of streaming audio and video being used on the Internet. As a result, you can run into some really annoying glitches, skips, and assorted crud when trying to view and/or listen to streaming content. A common problem is a high volume of traffic on your local network or on the Internet as a whole.

If network slowdowns are common, sometimes increasing the buffer size can keep things flowing. To change the buffer size, choose Tools→Options→Performance. The larger the buffer, the longer it will take for your file to begin playing—but a larger buffer can help if the music or video often stops or stutters.

If a *proxy server* provides your network's Internet access (ask your network administrator), changing the proxy settings can be helpful in resolving issues when Windows Media Player stops responding (hangs), too; choose Tools→Options and then click the Network tab to access them. If you didn't set up your own proxy settings, ask your network administrator for help in changing these settings.

no way to *not* install them. (If you're on a network, however, the administrator can craft a policy that keeps you from seeing or using the games.)

You can find these four charming time-wasters under Start→Program→ Accessories→Games. They are FreeCell and Solitaire (classic card games), Minesweeper (click squares to find the mines without blowing yourself up), and Pinball (a 3-D, realistic-looking virtual pinball machine).

Complete instructions lurk within the Help menu of each game. That's fortunate, because the rules of some of these card games can seem elaborate and quirky, to say the least.

System Tools

Most of the programs included in this folder are utilities designed to keep your PC in good health. They include Backup (Chapter 18); Disk Cleanup, Disk Defragmenter, and System Information (Chapter 19); and Scheduled Tasks (Chapter 8). That leaves only Getting Started (the brief Windows 2000 tour that greeted you the first time you turned on your Windows 2000 computer) and Character Map, described next.

Character Map

In addition to the standard letters, numbers, and punctuation marks, your PC can create hundreds of different typographical symbols, such as the currency symbols for the Yen and British pound, diacritical markings for French, Spanish, and other languages, various scientific symbols, and trademark and copyright signs. Obviously, these symbols don't appear on your keyboard; instead, they're hidden behind the keys you do see.

Character Map reveals their locations. Use the upper-left drop-down menu to specify the font you want to use (every font contains a different set of symbols). Now you see every single symbol provided by the font. As you hold your mouse down on each symbol, you see a magnified version of it to help you distinguish them. See Figure 9-17 for details on transferring a particular symbol into your document.

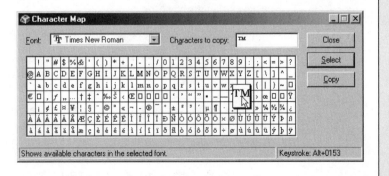

Figure 9-17:
When you find the character you want, double-click it to transfer it into the "Characters to copy" box, as shown here. (You can double-click several in a row to capture a sequence of symbols.) Click Copy, then Close. Return to your document, where you can choose Edit→Paste to insert the symbols.

Tip: In general, Internet email can't handle the fancy kinds of symbols revealed by Character Map. Don't be surprised if your copyright symbol turns into a gibberish character when received by your correspondent.

When Alt+0169 is Faster

When I click the copyright symbol in Character Map, the lower-right corner of the window says "Keystroke: Alt+0169." But when I try to enter that key sequence into my word processor, I don't get the copyright symbol!

That's absolutely right. You're leaving out two critical steps: First, you can't type those Alt+number codes unless you're in NumLock mode. If the NumLock light (usually at the top of your keyboard) isn't illuminated, press the NumLock key first.

Once you're in NumLock mode, *then* you can use the Alt-key combinations suggested by Character Map—*if* you type the numbers using the numeric keypad at the right side of your keyboard (not the numbers on the top row; if you're on a laptop without a numeric keypad, God help you). You have to keep the Alt key pressed continuously as you type the number sequence. When you release the Alt key, the symbol appears in your document.

Address Book

The Address Book is a central Windows directory for phone numbers, email addresses, and mailing addresses; you'll find a complete discussion starting on page 261.

Calculator

The Calculator application included with Windows 2000 looks like those el cheapo pocket calculators that the bank gives you when you open an account. You can operate it by clicking the buttons with your mouse or by pressing the corresponding keys on your keyboard. Most of the buttons look just like the ones on the plastic calculator that's probably in your desk drawer at this very moment, but a couple require special explanation:

- **squrt.** Finds the square root of the currently displayed number.

- **%.** Type in one number, click this button, type a second number, and click this button again to find out what percentage the first number is of the second.

Tip: Without a paper-tape feature, it's easy to get lost in the middle of long calculations. The solution is simple: Type your calculation, such as *34+(56/3)+5676+(34*2)=,* in a word processor. Highlight the calculation you've typed, choose Edit→Copy, switch to the Calculator, and then choose Edit→Paste. The previously typed numbers fly into the Calculator in sequence, finally producing the grand total on its screen. (You can then use the Edit→Copy command to copy the result back out of the Calculator, ready for pasting into another program.)

Choose View→Scientific, to turn this humble five-function calculator into a full-fledged scientific number cruncher, as shown in Figure 9-18.

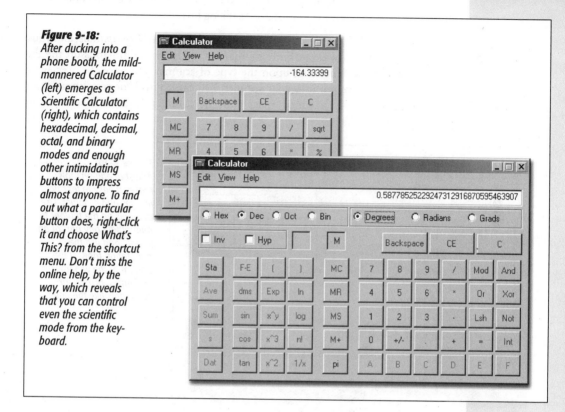

Figure 9-18:
After ducking into a phone booth, the mild-mannered Calculator (left) emerges as Scientific Calculator (right), which contains hexadecimal, decimal, octal, and binary modes and enough other intimidating buttons to impress almost anyone. To find out what a particular button does, right-click it and choose What's This? from the shortcut menu. Don't miss the online help, by the way, which reveals that you can control even the scientific mode from the keyboard.

Command Prompt

Unlike Windows 95, 98, and Me, Windows 2000 isn't built on the DOS architecture. However, Windows 2000 (and NT) still provides a simulation of the DOS prompt, which you can use to run the usual MS-DOS commands or launch other programs. You can cut and paste text to and from the Command Prompt window, use the up and down arrow keys to backtrack through the commands you previously entered, scroll up to review information that's no longer visible in the window, and use the right and left arrow keys to insert a missing letter in your current command, without having to type the whole thing over.

Imaging

Imaging, a program provided by Kodak, lets you view images, scan text or graphics, and annotate those scans or pictures (Figure 9-19). Although it doesn't provide any actual photo retouching features, Imaging can process scans and photographs in many other useful ways, such as flipping or rotating them, marking them up with lines or text labels, or changing their resolution. In addition to cropping, resizing, rotating, and decorating images, you can convert documents from one graphics file format to another with the File→Save As dialog box.

Imaging also works directly with your scanner (if it's *TWAIN-compatible*, and you'd have to look far and wide to find one that isn't). Use the commands on the File menu (which vary depending upon the type of scanner you have) to preview or scan whatever you've put into your scanner. You can control the resolution, color, size, and cropping of a scanned image with the commands in the menu and the icons on the toolbars.

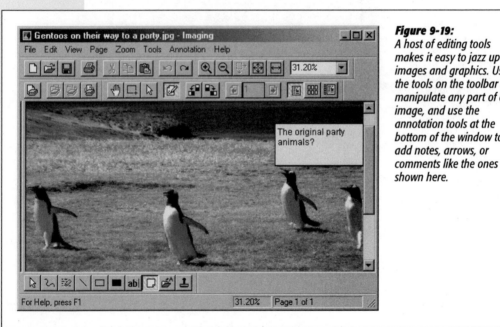

Figure 9-19:
A host of editing tools makes it easy to jazz up images and graphics. Use the tools on the toolbar to manipulate any part of an image, and use the annotation tools at the bottom of the window to add notes, arrows, or comments like the ones shown here.

Tip: If you save a file in TIF format, you can reopen the file and remove or modify the annotations later. However, if you save it as JPG or BMP, the annotations become a permanent part of the image. Imaging can open and save files in many other graphic formats, too, including PCX, GIF, DCX, WIF, and AWB.

Notepad

Notepad is the simplest form of "word processor," designed solely for the creating and viewing of text files. It has no fancy features: You can change the font, search the file for a word or phrase, or print the file—but that's it.

Nevertheless, people use the Notepad a lot (Start→Programs→Accessories→ Notepad) precisely because of its simplicity, and because text files are so common.

By default, the text in Notepad doesn't automatically wrap at the end of each line; chunks of the text may appear chopped off by the right side of the window. This "feature" evolved from Notepad's origins as a programmer's tool; when you're writing software programs, the Return key denotes the end of a command, and has nothing to do with the layout of the text. If you're not programming, you can choose Format→Word Wrap to make Notepad behave more like a "real" word processor. (Word Wrap will remain turned on until you change it.)

To print anything from Notepad that doesn't look completely goofy, you need to visit the File→Page Setup command. The document will print out according the margin settings in the Page Setup dialog box, *not* according to how it looks on the screen.

Notepad also has the quirk of printing the file's name at the top center of the page. To get rid of that, again choose File→Page Setup. When the Page Setup dialog box opens, you'll see some codes highlighted in the Header box. Press Delete to clear the box, and with it the automatic title printout. You can also clear the Footer box to get rid of the automatic page numbering.

Tip: If you press F5, the current time and date appear in the document.

GEM IN THE ROUGH

The Command Prompt at Your Command

When you open a Command Prompt window or run a DOS program, the window appears with a standard size and color. You can change these settings, either permanently or for only one session.

To do so, open the Command Prompt by choosing Start→Programs→ Accessories→Command Prompt.

Click the icon in the upper-left corner, or press Alt+ Space bar, to open the Control menu; choose Properties to open the dialog box shown here.

The Font, Layout, and Colors tabs control aspects of the appearance of the Command Prompt window. The QuickEdit and Insert Modes allow cutting and pasting and inserting text.

When you click OK, Windows 2000 asks if the changes are for this session only or for all sessions started by this shortcut (the one you chose from the Programs→Accessories menu). Click your reply, and then click OK.

Note, by the way, that you can have several *different* shortcuts to the Command Prompt, each configured differently. To duplicate the one you have (so that you can then change its settings), choose Start→Programs→ Accessories; right-click the Command Prompt, and then drag it to the desktop. Select Create Shortcut Here from the context menu. You'll find a new icon on the desktop, which you can modify (using its Properties command), rename, and then stash wherever you find convenient.

Paint

Like Notepad and other tools in this group, Paint is fairly limited. It's not a substitute for a full-featured bitmap editor like Adobe Photoshop, but it does supply some basic tools for creating and altering graphic images.

Creating Original Art

The fundamentals are simple. Launch paint by choosing Start→Programs→Accessories→Paint. Choose Image→Attributes to select the image size and whether it's to be in color or black-and-white. Then click OK.

You make your sketch or painting like this:

1. **Click a tool on the palette at the left side.**

   If you need help identifying one of these tools, point to it without clicking. A tooltip identifies the icon by name, and a help message appears at the very bottom of the window.

2. **If you've selected a painting tool, such as the paintbrush, pencil, or line tool, choose a "paint" color from the palette at the bottom of the window.**

   You may also want to change the "brush" by choosing from the options below the tool palette, such as the three spray-paint splatter sizes shown at left in Figure 9-20.

GEM IN THE ROUGH

Notepad Log Files

As stripped-down as it is, Notepad has one surprising feature not available in any other text or word processor: automated log files. When you use this feature, every time you open a certain file, Notepad automatically inserts the current date and time at the bottom of the file. Using this feature, when you type your text and save the file, you've got a tidy record of when you last worked on it—a nifty way to keep any type of a log, such as a record of expenditures or a traditional diary.

To set this up, create a new Notepad document (choose File→New). Type .*LOG* at the top of the new document. (Put nothing, not even a space, before the period.)

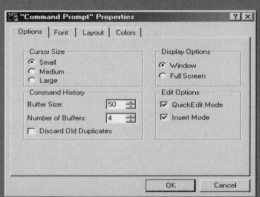

Now save the document (File→Save). Give it a name. (Notepad adds the extension .*txt* automatically.)

When you next open the file, Notepad types out the date and time automatically and puts your cursor on the next line; you're ready to type the day's entry.

To make your log file easier to read, press the Enter key to insert a blank line after each entry before saving the file.

---

3. **If you've selected one of the bottom four tools on the palette,** *right*-**click a swatch to specify the color you want to fill the** *inside* **of the shape.**

These tools all produce enclosed shapes, such as squares and circles; you can specify a different color for the border of these shapes and for the fill color inside.

4. **Finally, drag your cursor in the image area.**

As you work, don't forget the Edit→Undo command. Paint is especially forgiving; by choosing Undo three times, you can "take back" the last three painting maneuvers you made.

Tip: For detail work, click the magnifying-glass icon and then click your painting. You've just enlarged it so that every dot becomes easily visible.

When you're done with your masterpiece, you can:

- Select File→Save and give the picture a name. You can save it in one of several different kinds of bitmapped file formats. (Paint can open all the most common graphic file types, such as GIF, JPG, TIF, PCX, and BMP, but can save your work in only a few file formats.)

- Select File→Send, which will let you select an email recipient worthy of receiving your work.

- Select File→Set as Wallpaper to tile or center your work of art as the wallpaper on your screen.

Figure 9-20:
Left: The top two tools don't draw anything; instead, they select portions of the image for cutting, copying, or dragging to a new location. Middle: The photo shows a somewhat smudged penguin. Right: By choosing View→Zoom→Custom, you can choose from several zoom levels to get the degree of magnification you need. Here, the smudge is being edited away, one pixel at a time.

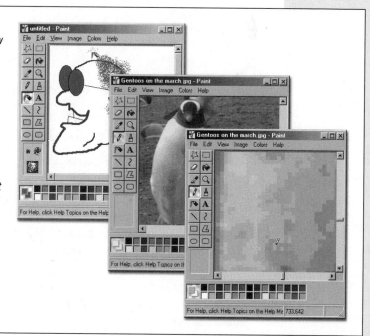

Synchronize

This program is designed to bring a folder on your PC and a folder on the network up to date with each other (when you return with your laptop from a trip, for example). For details, see page 315.

Windows Explorer

See page 86 for details on this navigational tool.

WordPad

WordPad is an odd duck: It's more elaborate than Notepad, but still falls far short of being a real word processing program like Microsoft Word. Still, it's a great help if you don't have Microsoft Word, because WordPad lets you open (and edit) Word files sent to you by other people. (If Microsoft Word isn't on your PC, then any icon with the filename extension *.doc* opens into WordPad when you double-click it. If you install Microsoft Word, however, it "takes over" the *.doc* extension, so that Word documents now open into Word.) WordPad can also open and create plain text files, Rich Text Format (RTF) documents, and Microsoft Write documents.

Tip: Like plain text files, Microsoft's Rich Text File format (RTF) is compatible with a wide variety of word processing and page-layout programs. But unlike text files, RTF files retain much of the formatting you'd find in a "pure" word-processing document, such as bold, italics, fonts, and embedded graphics. If you expect that a coworker might not have Word or WordPad, saving your documents in RTF format is a good idea.

To open WordPad, choose Start→Programs→Accessories→WordPad; you're shown an empty sheet of electronic typing paper. Just above the ruler, you'll find drop-down menus and icons that affect the formatting of your text, as shown in Figure 9-21. As in any word processor, you can apply these formats (such as bold, italic, or color) to text you've highlighted, or to text you're *about* to type. In other words, if you click the I (Italics) button, the next words you type will be italicized. Click the I button a second time to "turn off" the italics. The rightmost formatting icons affect entire paragraphs, as shown in Figure 9-21.

WordPad doesn't offer such big-gun features as spell checking, style sheets, or tables. But it does offer a surprisingly long list of Microsoft Word-like core word processing features. For example:

- **Edit→Find, Edit→Replace.** Using the Find command, you can locate a particular word or phrase instantly, even in a long document. The Replace command lets you go a step further, replacing that found phrase with another one (a great way to change the name of your main character all the way through the novel, for example).

- **Indents and Tab stops.** As shown in Figure 9-21, you can click to place Tab stops on the ruler. Each time you press the Tab key, your insertion point cursor jumps in line with the next Tab stop.

- **Object Linking and Embedding.** See page 120 for details.

- **Drag-and-drop editing.** You can drag highlighted text from place to place on the screen. See page 119 for details.

- **File→Send.** WordPad is completely integrated into Windows 2000. You can write messages in color and send them to mail recipients, who will see your messages just as you wrote them—fonts, colors, embedded objects, and all. Just prepare the message in WordPad and then choose File→Send.

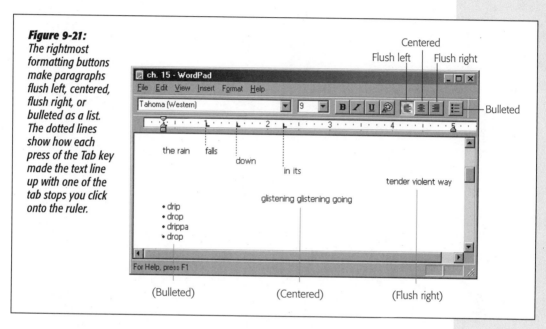

Figure 9-21:
The rightmost formatting buttons make paragraphs flush left, centered, flush right, or bulleted as a list. The dotted lines show how each press of the Tab key made the text line up with one of the tab stops you click onto the ruler.

Administrative Tools

These advanced administrative programs are described on page 378.

Startup

As described on page 48, this is the launch-at-startup folder; when you turn on the computer, Windows 2000 automatically opens any document, program, folder, or disk whose shortcut you've dragged into this folder.

Internet Explorer, Outlook Express

For details on these two cornerstones of Windows 2000's Internet suite, see Chapters 11 and 12.

The Files of Windows 2000

When you buy a new car, you generally don't expect to find the door pockets stuffed with maps or the upholstery already supplied with cookie crumbs and grease stains. However, when you buy a new computer these days, or get assigned one at work, it usually comes preloaded with thousands of software particles in every nook and cranny of your hard drive. Some of the files are parts of programs you use; on a used computer, some are left over from programs and operations long gone.

This chapter helps you figure out which files you can delete or move safely, and which you should leave in place.

What You See on the Hard Drive

Microsoft Windows 2000 Professional assumes you're the sort of person who doesn't want to be bothered by details; it hides many of its own files, and even whole folders. This maneuver has the advantage of keeping you out of areas where you could do significant damage to the computer's operation. On the other hand, if you're reading this chapter, you're probably more curious than the average user, and you want to know more about the system you're working with.

To see everything Windows 2000 has been hiding from you, you have to flip three different switches, shown in Figure 10-1.

Extensions of Known File Types

As described on page 122, most files have three-letter filename extensions that help Windows associate them with their parent applications. By default, Windows *hides* these extensions, to decrease clutter and to protect the extensions from being inadvertently changed. Nevertheless, you may experience less confusion if you make these filename extensions visible once again, as described on page 124.

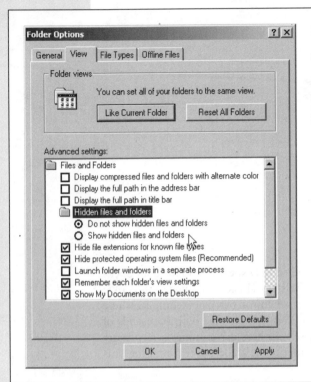

Figure 10-1:
To get at the hide/show switches, open a desktop folder window and choose Tools→Folder Options→View. In the list of checkboxes, under the heading "Hidden files and folders" (indicated here by the cursor), you'll find buttons that govern these three categories of files and folders.

Protected Operating System Files

Microsoft hides a large collection of files (mostly in the WINNT folder) that are so important, the computer can't operate without them. By clearing the "Hide protected operating system files" checkbox, you can make these protected files visible, but it's advisable not to do so; moving, renaming, or deleting any of them can make your computer unstable at best, and nonfunctional at worst. If you change or delete one, you may have to reinstall Windows 2000 Professional to make your PC well again.

The most elemental files are the boot files that let Windows 2000 start up. If you make the protected files visible, it's good to know what these files are, if only to prevent you from getting carried away and trying to delete them. These boot files sit in your C: drive's root directory (its main window), and are called Boot.ini, Ntdetect.com, and Ntldr; depending on your system's hardware configuration, you may also find Cdldr and Ntbootdd.sys there.

If you change or eliminate any of these files, you'll damage Windows so severely that your computer won't be able to start up. (The sole exception is Boot.ini, a text file that contains the *boot menu* that appears during the startup sequence. If you know what you're doing, you can make changes to this file without killing your system.)

Hidden Files and Folders

Hidden files and folders exist in a gray area between filename extensions and system files. Deleting, renaming, or moving a hidden file probably won't make your computer stop working, but it may cause parts of Windows 2000 Pro to fail or perform erratically. (Again, most of these are in the WINNT folder.)

You can make these hidden files reappear by clicking "Show hidden files and folders," as shown in Figure 10-1. When these files are hidden, you'll know of their existence by a report on the status bar (Figure 10-2, top). Even when they show up, hidden folders and files are a ghostly presence (Figure 10-2, bottom).

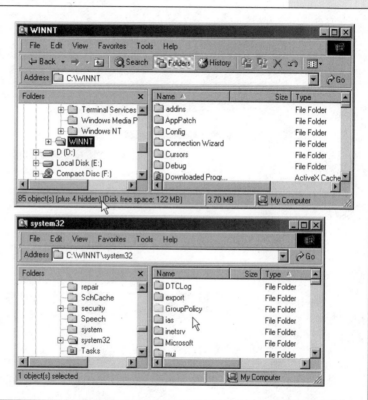

Figure 10-2:
Top: Even when Windows is hiding certain files, the status bar (as shown by the cursor here) lets you know that they're there.

Bottom: Though shown, the icons of ordinarily hidden files and folders (such as the Group Policy folder here) are dimmed to indicate that they aren't ordinary run-of-the-mill files.

Other Files in the WINNT Folder

By default, the installer for Windows 2000 puts Windows 2000 itself in the WINNT folder on your C: drive. This folder and its subfolders contain the thousands of files necessary for the normal operation of Windows 2000. Ignore them. Don't delete or change them unless you know what you're doing (and why you're doing it).

Program files

Program files are the files your applications need. They're generally in the C: \Program Files folder.

These files aren't protected or hidden, but you should leave them alone. If you no longer want a program, remove it as directed on page 129; don't just drag its folder to the Recycle Bin.

Speeding Up Virtual Memory

Virtual memory lets you keep more programs open than your actual installed RAM could technically handle. So why don't we all buy PCs with just one megabyte of RAM, and use virtual memory to give ourselves 500 MB of simulated RAM on the hard drive?

Because actual memory delivers data hundreds of times faster than a hard drive can. Virtual memory, when used in excess, slows things down. (When used at Microsoft's settings, however, you won't notice any slowdown. Indeed, the Windows 2000 virtual memory scheme constantly adjusts the amount of data stored in the pagefile so that it's no larger than necessary.

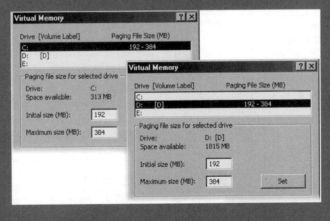

If you have administrative rights on your computer, and if your PC has more than one hard drive, you can optimize virtual memory (which may improve your PC's speed) by dividing the pagefile over as many hard drives as possible. Remove the pagefile from slower or heavily accessed drives—especially the drive with the system files. However, don't put pagefiles on more than one *partition* of the same physical disk drive.

To modify the amount or placement of your virtual memory, start by double-clicking the System applet in the Control Panel. Click the Advanced tab, then the Performance Options button.

In the Performance Options dialog box, you can see the total amount of virtual memory currently allocated. (Generally, the default size of the pagefile is the best one. In any case, don't make the pagefile *smaller* than the recommended size—1.5 times RAM.) Click the Change button to alter the pagefile configuration. Then, in the Virtual Memory dialog box, make the changes you want. Click OK when finished.

In the example pictured here, the initial configuration (top left) shows that the entire pagefile is on the already crowded C: drive, which is also where Windows 2000 Pro is installed. At lower right, a pagefile has been created on the separate D: drive, and the pagefile on C: has been deleted. You'll have to restart your PC for the change to take effect.

Pagefiles

No matter how much memory (RAM, or Random Access Memory) your computer has, Windows 2000 still wants more. Windows uses a scheme called *virtual memory*, a trick that lets it use hard disk space as simulated memory, to give itself more elbow room when you're running a lot of programs at once. Virtual memory works by swapping chunks of software code into and out of real memory into a file on your hard drive called a *pagefile* (or *swap file*).

At the time of installation, Windows 2000 creates a pagefile, usually called pagefile.sys, equal to one-and-a-half times the amount of *physical* (real) memory your PC has. (There may be more than one pagefile on your computer.)

Temp files

Temp files are, as you might guess, temporary files created by programs and by the system itself. (These files may store what your document looked like at each stage of your work, for example, so that an application will be ready in case you use the Undo command.) Each user has a Temp folder in his user profile folder (which is in the Documents and Settings folder). Another Temp folder is inside the WINNT folder. Many temporary files have the .tmp extension, though other file types can show up in Temp folders.

Most of the time, an application deletes its own temp files when you choose File→Exit. But if the system crashes or freezes before it has a chance to do this cleanup, you may find orphaned temp files littering your hard drive.

You can manually delete temp files that are no longer in use, but it's a tedious chore. A more efficient approach is to use Disk Cleanup periodically (see below). It seeks out and shows you temporary files, compressible old files (see Figure 10-3), temporary Internet files, and any other files cluttering your disks. You can then direct the program to delete some or all of those files.

Getting Rid of Unneeded Files

Windows 2000 and the applications you run eventually create a dreadful jumble of files on your hard drive. Over time, the ratio of useless files to useful ones grows higher and higher. The following sections cover the files that you can delete with impunity and files you can delete with some caution.

The Disk Cleanup Solution

Before attempting anything tricky in the war against unnecessary files, start by running Disk Cleanup. You can find this program at Start→Programs→ Accessories→System Tools. When you start Disk Cleanup, you select the drive you want examined; then the program reports on the files that can be deleted from that disk. Depending on your configuration, these files may include:

- **Downloaded program files.** Some Web pages send program files (such as Java applets and Active X controls) to your PC for temporary storage on your hard drive. These files aren't always deleted when you close your browser.

• **Temporary setup files.** When you install a program, its installer often creates setup files in the WINNT→Temp folder or in a folder it creates, but may forget to clean them out when it's done.

• **Temporary Internet files.** To reduce loading time for Web documents, Internet Explorer stores copies of previously visited pages in a Temp folder. (See page 239 for more on these *cache* files.) Each file is small, but you can quickly accumulate hundreds or thousands of them over time.

• **Recycle Bin.** If you turn on this option, Disk Cleanup will permanently delete all the files in the Recycle Bin. If this idea makes you nervous, leave the option unchecked, and do a manual clearing of the Recycle Bin, as described on page 96.

• **Temporary files.** As noted earlier, many programs deposit temporary files in the Temp folder; if the system crashes, the files remain. Disk Cleanup can delete them.

• **Temporary offline files.** Recently used network files are automatically *cached* for you (stored on your own hard drive) to use when you're disconnected from the network. Because they're only copies of the "real" files out on the network, it's safe to delete them.

• **Offline files.** These are files you've specifically *requested* to be cached for use when you're disconnected from the network.

• **Catalog files for the Content Indexer.** If the Indexing Service (see page 41) is running on one of your network servers, you can safely delete old catalogs.

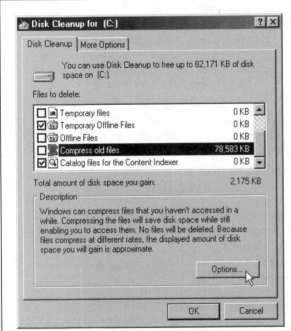

Figure 10-3:
If you click the Options button for "Compress old files," you can choose to compress all files that haven't been used for a particular length of time—from 1 day to 500 days. You'll still be able to access these files without even being aware that they've been compressed.

• **Compress old files.** This option doesn't delete anything; instead, it *compresses* files you haven't used lately to save disk space (Figure 10-3).

Tip: If you're nervous about what might be deleted, click the View Files button and take a look at the files scheduled for demolition.

Files You Can Delete

When you look over the files Disk Cleanup has targeted for extinction, you may find files with the filename extensions shown in the following table. You can decide how to treat these files based on the table description and your needs for space.

File Extension	What It Is
.avi, .mpg, .mov	A video file. Usually very large.
.bak	A backup file (created by Microsoft Word, among others). Delete the older ones.
.bk!, .wbk, .xlk	WordPerfect, Word, and Excel backup documents.
.bmp, .gif, .jpg, .tif	Graphics files, which can take up a lot of space. Some graphics formats (such as GIF and JPG) are compressed already and can't shrink any further, while others (such as BMPs) can be compressed to as little as one tenth their former size.
.cab	A type of compressed file used for software distribution. (For example, your Windows 2000 installation CD comes packed with CAB files.) Delete these if you've already installed the application and you have a backup of the program (in case you have to install it again).
.cbt	Video training files. Huge. If you've seen them once, that's usually more than enough.
.chk	File fragments saved by Disk Defragmenter; can also be a WordPerfect temporary file. Every now and then, you may be able to recover some text you lost in a crash by opening one of these files.
.gid	A Help index file. It's safe to delete this index, although Windows 2000 will rebuild the file when you next open Help.
.lnk	A shortcut.
.mid, .mp3, .wav, .wma	Sound files. Delete the ones you don't use.
.tmp	A temporary file. It's safe to delete any that don't bear today's date.
.zip	An archive file, such as a compressed file that you've downloaded from the Web or received by email. If you've already extracted the files, you can delete the archive.

Clear Your Documents List

As noted on page 47, Windows 2000 keeps track of the documents you use. It automatically creates a shortcut of each file you work on and stores it in the Start→Documents menu, on the premise that you'd like quick access to them in the future. The shortcut files in this folder are small, but hundreds of them may accumulate.

If you'd like to clear the shortcuts from the Start→Documents menu, the official Microsoft method is to choose Start→Settings→Taskbar & Start Menu. In the resulting dialog box, click the Advanced tab, and then click Clear.

If you'd like to delete only *some* of the Start→Documents items, open Windows Explorer (page 86) and navigate to Documents and Settings→[Your Name]→Recent folder. Delete the shortcuts of documents you'd like to eliminate.

Neither method deletes any actual documents; you're just getting rid of the Start→Document menu's *shortcuts*.

What You Mustn't Delete

As mentioned earlier in this chapter, it's important not to delete system files. But don't delete files beginning with the $ sign (such as $MFT), either, or those with the .dll extension. (A DLL, or *dynamic link library,* is a software module for a specific function [say, printing] that a program—or several programs at once—can access as necessary.)

When you have thousands of files, you eventually end up in the unenviable state known as DLL Hell. This condition arises when you have many, many DLL files—some useful, some worthless, and you can't tell which are which. The torture becomes even more exquisite when you suspect that you don't have the particular DLL file you need, despite having several DLL files (identically named) but with different sizes and dates.

The solution to DLL Hell is available at the DLL Help Web site *(http://support. microsoft.com/servicedesks/fileversion/dllinfo.asp),* a searchable database of information about file versions that ship with particular Microsoft products.

POWER USERS' CLINIC

Automating the Search for Deletion Candidates

Certain types of files are always candidates for deletion, but you don't want to get rid of them without examination. For example, a file with a *tilde* (~) as part of the name is probably suspect. Some LOG files are worth keeping (such as the ones in WINNT\System 32\Config folder). However, some applications (such as backup programs) generate many LOG files and may not clean them all up. Every now

and then, you can use the Windows 2000 Search program (page 36) with a search string like this one to search for files you can examine and delete if necessary:

*.log   *.??_   *.~*   ~*.*   *.bak   *.old   *.tmp
Once the search is complete, you can examine the file names found, or the files themselves, and delete them directly from the results window.

But instead of trying to learn the purpose of every file on your hard drive, you'll be safe following two rules of file deletion.

1. If you don't know what a file is, don't delete it.

2. If you think you know what a file is but have even a little bit of a reservation about whether you need it, make a new folder called Delete Pending. Move the file into that folder. Live life as usual. If nothing untoward happens (to your PC) for a reasonable period, go ahead and delete the file.

WINDOWS 2000 PRO: THE MISSING MANUAL

Part Three:
Windows Online

3

Getting to the Web

For millions of people, using the Internet is one of the most important functions of a PC. Few computer features have the potential to change your life as profoundly as the World Wide Web and email.

To join the Internet party already in progress, you need three components: a *connection*, such as a modem, cable modem, DSL, or corporate network; an Internet *account*; and Internet *software*, such as a Web browser or email program. This chapter guides you through setting up your computer for Internet access, and then shows you how to use Internet Explorer to find your way around the Web.

Note: Microsoft constantly improves and updates Internet Explorer. Windows 2000 comes with version 5.01, but that version has been succeeded by Internet Explorer 5.5 (or an even later version). Use the Windows Update tool (see page 58) to upgrade your version to the latest available.

While you're at it, you may want to install the free software component called Windows 2000 High Encryption Update. Doing so not only adds a few features to your browser, but also improves the security and stability of your system.

Getting an Account

Most people in big corporations connect to the Internet through the office network. The company sets up a high-speed Internet connection and attaches it to the network using a device called a *router*; if that's your situation, you've been spared the process of setting up and configuring an Internet account.

Most people at home, however, connect to the Internet using a standard dial-up modem, although a growing minority pays higher monthly fees for a higher-speed connection, such as a *cable modem* or *Digital Subscriber Line* (DSL).

Dial-Up Modems, Cable Modems, and DSL

For a dial-up connection, you connect a modem to a standard telephone line. Some people install phone line just for the computer; others let the modem share the regular voice line.

Tip: If you use a single phone line for both phone calls and modem calls, you can buy software (if you sign up for call waiting and caller ID features) to make this line-sharing more efficient. If you're surfing the Web when a voice call comes through, this kind of program makes a window pop up that tells you who's calling, so that you can decide whether or not it's worth signing off the Net to take the call. (You can read more about these programs, and download trial versions, by visiting *www.pagoo.com/cc.asp, www.angelfire.com/biz/cfscredit/icm.html,* or *www.callwave.com.*)

Once you've installed your modem (if it didn't come preinstalled), you can sign up for an account with an *Internet Service Provider* (ISP). The ISP supplies the telephone number that your modem will dial, along with the account name and password you use to connect. Most of the world connects to the Internet using this modem/ISP arrangement, thanks to its low cost, easy setup, and flexibility (you can easily switch ISPs whenever a better deal comes along).

The increasingly popular cable modems and DSL give you Internet connections that can be 5 to 50 times the speed of a traditional dial-up modem. For example, to download a 2 MB file with a standard modem, you have to wait at least 5 minutes. A cable modem, on the other hand, transfers the same file in about 10 *seconds.* Even complex Web pages pop up almost immediately.

Note, however, that these connections aren't as flexible as dial-up modems. Your local cable TV company provides your cable modem, so you can't very well switch

---

POWER USERS' CLINIC

Asymmetrical Internet Connections

Although it doesn't make much difference to most people, cable and DSL connections are usually *asymmetrical.* In other words, unlike standard dial-up modems, the data going to and from your PC run at different speeds—in these cases, information coming from the Internet *to* your computer runs many times faster than that data going *to* the Internet.

For activities like Web browsing and downloading files, this quirk doesn't present a problem. (When you download a file, your computer sends a tiny request to an Internet server, which sends a big file in response.) However, the relatively slow upstream connection makes cable and DSL connections unsuitable for running your own Web or other Internet servers. (On the other hand, the upstream speed of cable and DSL is still as fast as a dial-up modem, or faster.)

---

to another cable provider if you don't like the service. And you may find that the service slows down during peak hours.

A DSL connection is similar in many regards: Once again, the DSL box connects to an networking card in your computer; a technician from the DSL provider (often the phone company) does the installation and setup for you; and when the installation is complete, your computer remains online around the clock. You can even make phone calls and surf the Net simultaneously.

The biggest limitation of DSL is that your PC must be within a certain distance (about three miles) of the phone company's nearest central office. The faster the connection, the shorter the distance it can span.

Online Service vs. ISP

Once you've chosen a method of connecting to the Net, you need an Internet *account.* You can get one in either of two ways: by signing up for an *online service,* such as America Online (AOL) or Microsoft Network (MSN), or by getting a direct Internet account with an Internet service provider (ISP), such as EarthLink, IDT, AT&T, MCI WorldCom, or any of hundreds of smaller, local companies.

Tip: The Internet is filled with Web sites that list, describe, and recommend ISPs. One of the best such listings is at *www.boardwatch.com.* (Of course, until you've actually got your Internet account working, you'll have to do such research on a PC that *is* online, such as the free terminals available at most public libraries.)

Online services and ISPs present both significant pros and cons. For example:

- Most ISPs cost $20 a month for unlimited Internet use; America Online and MSN cost $22 per month.

Tip: You can also get *free* Internet access if you're willing to put up with an ad window that sits on your desktop. Search the Web for *free Internet access* to find listings and reviews.

- Online services strike many people as easier to use, because you can use a single program for all Internet functions, including email and Web surfing. When you sign up for an ISP, on the other hand, you use a different application for each function, such as Internet Explorer for surfing the Web and Outlook Express for email.

- Because online services are slightly easier to use than ISP accounts, and because they attract many first-timers, people who consider themselves Internet experts may look down their noses at MSN and America Online members.

Signing up for an online-service company is easy; you simply insert one of the ubiquitous starter CDs you find in your mailbox every week or so, or call the company to request one. When you run the installer, you type in your name, address, and credit-card number when requested, and begin surfing.

Signing Up with an ISP

If you'd prefer to sign up for a standard Internet (ISP) account, you'll probably follow one of these avenues:

- If you've signed up for DSL or cable modem service, a technician from the phone or cable company will visit you and set up your hardware and software.

- If you've signed up for one of the national ISPs, such as AT&T WorldNet or EarthLink, special setup software comes with your startup kit.

- If you're signing up for any other ISP, such as a regional one that doesn't provide setup software or a national one whose setup kit won't be arriving for days, you can use the Internet Connection Wizard to setup your Internet connection. That's the topic of the next section.

Getting a New Dial-Up Account

To get your ISP account going, make sure that your computer's modem is plugged into a phone jack. Double-click the Connect to the Internet icon on the desktop, or select Programs→Accessories→Communications→Internet Connection Wizard, and then follow these steps:

UP TO SPEED

Internet 101

What you see of the Internet are the features it provides, such as the Web and email. But physically, the Internet is a collection of networks connected by high-speed communications links known as the *backbone*. The major Internet Service Providers (ISPs) have large computers that are connected directly to the backbone. In turn, you connect to the ISP's computers and thus have a path to the Internet. When you deal with a smaller, local ISP, you're connecting to its network, which is in turn connected to a larger ISP's network. These connections might go through several generations of middlemen before the traffic gets to the backbone.

Information gets passed around the Internet using a set of common protocols known as *TCP/IP* (Transmission Control Protocol/Internet Protocol). *Protocols* are the languages that computers use to communicate with each other; TCP/IP is the most common networking protocol today. These protocols break the information generated by your Internet programs into chunks of data called *packets,* each of which contains the address of its destination computer. The pack-

ets are passed from one *router* (which connects the various Internet networks) on the Internet to another until they reach their destination, where they're reassembled into a news bulletin or an email from your mom.

The routers on the Internet exchange information about their networks with each other, so that if a packet encounters a roadblock (such as a crashed server) during its journey, the routers send it on using an alternate route. (You can thank the Internet's original designers in the U.S. Department of Defense for this capability; they wanted to build a communications network that had no central hub, making it impossible for an enemy to destroy the entire system in one attack.)

Your connection to the Internet can be through an ISP, online service, company or university network, cable modem or DSL phone connection, or even a wireless cellular connection—but in the end, you connect to someone who's connected to the Internet, and from there you can access everything that anyone has made available.

---

1. **Choose the first option on the Welcome screen (Figure 11-1).**

   You've just opted to use Microsoft's referral service to pick an ISP—an easy way to locate a dial-up Internet provider quickly.

   (If you have multiple dial-up settings, you're now asked to confirm where you're calling from. See page 161 for information on setting up multiple dialing locations.)

2. **Click Next.**

   Now the system dials a toll-free number; after a moment, a list of ISPs appears. Click each logo on the left side of the screen to read about the terms of the service, which usually is $20 per month for unlimited service.

3. **Click the name of an ISP that sounds attractive, and then click Next. Fill in your name, address, phone number, and of course, the most important bit of information—a credit card number.**

   Now the wizard dials a second time; this time, it's contacting the Internet company you've selected. The details of the service plan now appear on your screen.

   Pay careful attention, not only to what you tell the ISP but also to what the ISP tells *you*. In particular, take note of all numbers or procedures for *closing* your account. These companies don't stay in business by making it simple for you to disconnect from them (think health clubs). Nevertheless, they do give you all that information up front.

Figure 11-1:
If you don't have an account with an Internet Service Provider (ISP) yet, choose "I want to sign up for a new Internet account" to find an ISP using Microsoft's referral service.

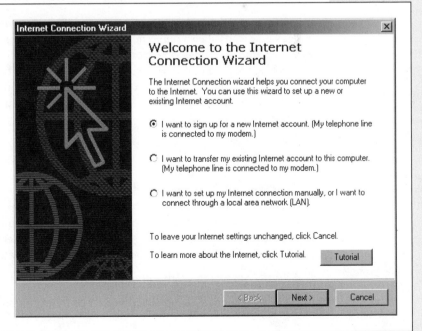

4. **Click Next. If you agree with the ISP's rules, click Accept, and then click Next.**

Now you're asked to invent an email address for yourself. The ending part of it is determined by your choice of ISP—*@earthlink.net,* for example, or *@juno.com.* The first part is up to you, but keep in mind that names like *Bob* and *Seinfeld* were snapped up long ago. If the name you type in isn't original, you'll be asked to try again with a different email name.

After successfully choosing a unique email address, you're shown a list of phone numbers. From this drop-down menu, choose a phone number that's local. If there are no local numbers listed here, and you'd rather not pay long distance charges every time you connect to the Internet, consider canceling this entire sign up operation and spending some time researching smaller, regional ISPs.

5. **Finish up with the Wizard.**

This may entail clicking your way through a few final welcome screens.

Note: As you compare ISPs, note that "unlimited access" rarely really means *unlimited*; you can't remain connected 24 hours a day. ISPs make their money by signing up many more subscribers that they have facilities to serve. They count on only a fraction of their users being connected at any one time (once again, think health clubs).

In some cases, the ISP automatically disconnects you after a certain amount of time, or after a period of inactivity. If you want a dial-up connection that really is connected around the clock, you'll have to pay for a dedicated port that's reserved for your use—at a substantially higher subscription rate.

Windows stores the information about your ISP, your name, password, and so on, into a single icon called a *connection icon.* You can see the one you've just created by choosing Start→Settings→Network and Dial-up Connections, as shown in Figure 11-2. There are dozens of ways to get online, but one way is to double-click this icon. Doing so produces the dialog box shown in Figure 11-2 at right—a box that will soon become extremely familiar. You encounter it every time you connect to the Internet.

Having set up your connection, you can skip ahead to "Navigating Internet Explorer." You're ready to explore the Net.

Transferring an Existing Dial-Up Account

If you have an existing dial-up account with an ISP (that you've been using on another computer, for example), choose the third option on the Welcome screen of the Internet Connection wizard ("I want to set up my Internet connection manually," as shown in Figure 11-1). Then click Next and follow these steps:

1. **Select "I connect through a phone line and a modem."**

Be sure the modem is connected to your computer and turned on.

2. **Click Next. Supply the phone number you dial to connect to the ISP.**

   There is an Advanced button on this page, but few ISPs require any changes to these settings.

3. **Click Next. Enter your account name (user name) and password for connecting to the ISP.**

4. **Click Next. Provide a name for the connection.**

   This is the name for the icon that you'll see in the Network and Dial-Up Connections folder (Figure 11-2).

5. **Click Next. Specify whether you want to set up an email account.**

   Because an email program (Outlook Express) is part of Windows 2000, you can set up your email to use it at this point. You must already know your email address (such as *yourname@earthlink.net*), the type of mail server your ISP uses, and the names of the incoming and outgoing mail servers. This is all information that your ISP provides to you.

6. **Follow the instructions on the screen.**

   On the final screen, the wizard offers to connect to the Internet immediately, so you can test that your setup is correct.

Figure 11-2:
Left top: The Earthlink and Juno icons represent Internet accounts created by the Internet Connection Wizard or the Make New Connection Wizard. One way to go online is to double-click this icon. You get the dialog box shown at lower right, where you can click Dial to go online. (If you turn on "Save password," you won't have to type your password in each time you go online.)

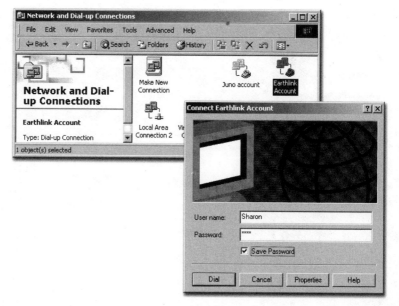

Reconfiguring a LAN (Network) Account

If you connect to the Internet through an office network (*local area network*, or LAN) at work or school, you're usually provided the information you need to connect to the Internet—at least at the beginning. But then suppose you get a different computer, or through a computing experiment gone horribly wrong, you manage to mangle the connection's settings beyond recall.

Here's how to set that connection up again (if you have the required information):

1. **Choose Start→Programs→Accessories→Communications→Internet Connection Wizard.**

   The wizard appears.

2. **Click Next. Select "I connect through a local area network (LAN)." Click Next.**

   Now you're asked how your network's *proxy settings* are configured. A *proxy server* is one way your network administrators may provide you with Internet access. The proxy server is a computer at your company that sits between your PC and the Internet, relaying Internet data traffic and, in some cases, filtering your browser's requests for Web pages. If your network uses a proxy server, you use this page to enable your computer to locate it.

   In general, the default option—"Automatic discover of proxy server"—is what you want. Windows 2000 will find out and fill in the proxy-server settings for you automatically.

FREQUENTLY ASKED QUESTION

Why Can't I Pick Door Number Two?

What's the deal with the middle option in the Internet Connection Wizard?

That's the "I want to transfer my existing Internet account to this computer" button. In theory, it's a terrific feature. It's designed to consult the actual membership database of your ISP, and then to fill in the settings on your new PC automatically.

If you select it—and why not, if you have some time to waste?—the system will connect to the toll-free referral service number and display

a list of Internet Service Providers that work with Microsoft's "fill in my settings for me" feature.

Internet Connection Wizard

Step 1 of 3: Selecting your Internet service provider

Click your ISP, and then click Next.

Internet service providers:

Prodigy Internet
My Internet service provider is not listed

< Back   Next >   Cancel

Unfortunately, at this writing, very few ISPs work with this feature, as you can see here. If your ISP *is* listed, just keep going; you'll be connected to the provider and asked to supply your user name and password. Once you're logged on to the ISP's system, you can locate a local telephone number and other information your PC will need to make the connection the next time.

---

3. **Click Next. Indicate whether you want to create an email account.**

   If you click Yes, you'll be asked for the email account settings. If you need help setting up your email account, see page 248. Click Next.

4. **Click Next. Turn on the "To connect to the Internet immediately" checkbox and then click Finish.**

   Your PC now tries to connect to the Internet via your network.

In addition to these settings, your computer must also have the correct TCP/IP configuration settings (as described on page 336) to access the Internet through the network. If you run into trouble, you can get help from the administrator of your network.

Connecting to the Internet

If you have a full-time Internet connection such as a cable modem, DSL, or company network, you don't have to do anything special to connect the Internet; you're connected constantly (although you may be required to enter a password each time you go online).

If you have a dial-up modem, however, you should now have a Connection icon in your Start→Settings→Network and Dial-up Connections folder. When you want to go online, you can double-click this icon (Figure 11-2, left). The Connect To dialog box appears, as shown in Figure 11-2, right. Just press Enter, or click Dial, to go online.

Connecting Automatically or Manually

It's often more convenient, however, if your PC dials automatically, on cue, whenever you connect to a Web page (with Internet Explorer) or send/receive email (with Outlook Express). You can turn on this feature when you use a dial-up connection the first time; an option to connect automatically appears on the sign-in screen.

If you chose an automatic connection and want to go back to a manual connection (where you're prompted for a phone number of password before connecting), or vice versa, follow these steps:

1. **Right-click the connection icon you want to modify; choose Properties from the shortcut menu.**

   The Connection Properties dialog box appears.

2. **Click the Options tab.**

   If you turn on "Display progress while connecting," "Prompt for phone number," or "Prompt for name and password, certificate, etc.," you'll be presented with the Dial-up Connection dialog box each time one of your Internet programs tries to go online. If you turn off all three checkboxes, your PC will dial automatically in those situations, without making a dialog box appear.

3. Click OK.

You can return to the automatic-connection routine by turning on any of the three boxes described in Step 2.

Disconnecting

While you're connected to your ISP, Windows puts an icon in the Taskbar tray, next to the clock (Figure 11-3). Its pop-up balloon tells you the speed of your connection (Figure 11-3, lower left); for a pop-up box bearing even more statistics, point to this Tray icon without clicking. You can watch the Tray icon's tiny dual monitors light up as data is transmitted across the connection.

Windows 2000 doesn't hang up the phone line unless you tell it to. If you want the connection to drop after a specified interval, open the Properties for the connection and select Options. In the Redialing Options section, change the "Idle time before hanging up" setting. If you set it for 20 minutes, for example, Windows will automatically break the connection when your system has been idle for 20 minutes—a handy arrangement if you have a tendency to wander off and get distracted while your PC connected.

You can also disconnect manually; just right click the "online" Tray icon and select Disconnect from the shortcut menu, or click Disconnect in the status box that appears when you first connect (Figure 11-3, top).

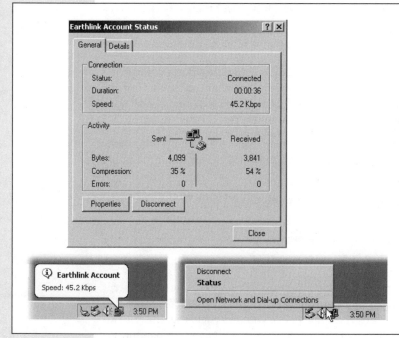

Figure 11-3:
Top: This status box appears when you're online.

Bottom: So does this balloon, which tells you the speed of your connection. To disconnect, click Disconnect in the status box, or right-click the Tray icon and choose Disconnect from the shortcut menu that appears (bottom right).

Internet Explorer

Internet Explorer is the Web browser that comes with Windows 2000. Despite all the hoopla, headlines, and lawsuits that surrounded it for several years, it's an excellent program. You can launch it in a number of ways:

- Double-click its desktop icon.

- Click its icon on the Quick Launch toolbar.

- Choose a Web site's name from your Start→Favorites menu.

- Type a Web address—its *URL* (Uniform Resource Locator)—into the Address bar of a window. A Web-page URL usually begins with the prefix *http://,* but you can leave that part off.

No matter which technique you use, the program now opens, your PC dials the Internet if necessary, and the Internet Explorer window fills with the starting page, called the *home page.* When you click a button or an underlined phrase, called a link or hyperlink, you're transported from one "page" (screen) to another. Several *billion* Web pages await you. (See Figure 11-4.)

Figure 11-4:
The main toolbar in Internet Explorer holds most of the basic navigational tools including buttons to move you forward and back, refresh the page, and go to your Home page. If the mouse pointer turns into a hand, you're pointing to a hyperlink. Click to follow where it leads.

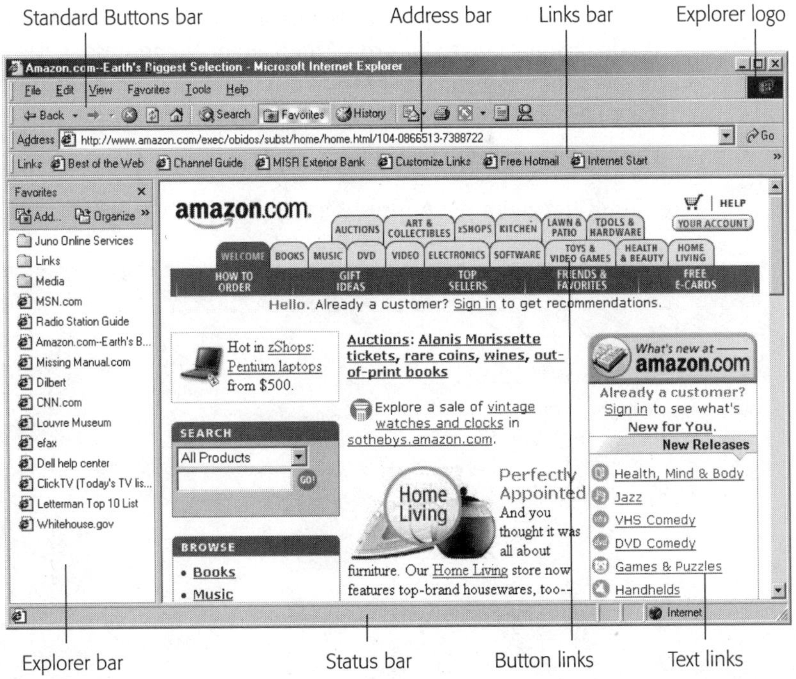

Tip: You can choose any Web page you like as your home page. To do so, navigate to the page you want to make your home page, choose Tools→Internet Options, and then click the Use Current button at the top of the General tab (or enter a different Web address in the Address box).

Or, if you prefer an empty "home page," choose Tools→Internet Options and click Use Blank. Some people prefer this setup, which makes Internet Explorer load very quickly when you first launch it, and doesn't waste any time loading some home page you've specified; instead, only an empty window appears. Once this window opens, *then* you can tell the browser where you want to go today.

The toolbar (Figure 11-4) offers navigational icons that help you on your way. The Back button, of course, takes you to the last page you viewed; to go to the page you were viewing *before* clicking Back, click Forward. Click the small triangle next to the Back or Forward button to display a list of pages you've viewed. To jump to one of them, click its name, or press the down arrow to highlight one and then press Enter.

Tip: You can press the Backspace key to go to the previous Web page. You can also press Alt+left arrow (for Back) or Alt+Right arrow (for Forward).

Entering Web Addresses

The fastest way to get to a Web site is often to type its address in the Address bar. To do this, click there (or press Alt+D), type the address (URL) of the page you want to visit, then click the Go button next to the Address box (or press Enter). After a moment, the Web page you requested appears on the screen.

You can use a few tips to make entering addresses easier and faster:

- Clicking in the Address box or pressing Alt+D automatically highlights the ad-

---

TROUBLESHOOTING MOMENT

Slow Pages and Reloading Pages

A Web page usually takes a moment to "load"—to arrive on your screen from the Internet. You can view the current progress of a Web page by glancing at the animated logo in the top right corner of the Internet Explorer window. If the page is still downloading, the logo moves (and a progress message appears in the Status bar at the bottom of the Internet Explorer window). If the logo isn't doing anything, neither is Internet Explorer. (There are exceptions; when visiting certain special types of Web pages, neither the logo nor the status bar shows anything.)

The time will come when a page appears to hang, or takes a very long time to download. When this happens, click

the Stop button on the toolbar. You've just halted any further Internet Explorer efforts to download the page, and sometimes this step even makes the rest of a half-missing Web page appear.

If the full page doesn't appear, click the Refresh toolbar button to make Internet Explorer download the page again. If a page takes an inordinately long time to download, sometimes hitting Stop and then Refresh can hasten things up a bit. Note that you can also reload a page or part of a page by right-clicking a blank area and choosing Refresh from the shortcut menu—a good trick for reloading only one *frame* (one rectangular region) of the page.

dress of the current Web page. You can then simply start typing a new address without having to first delete the previous address.

- You don't need to enter the *http://* portion of a Web address—Internet Explorer adds that for you.

- The standard corporate Web address is simply the company's name preceded by *www* and followed by *.com* (for example, *www.cnn.com* or *www.sony.com*). A quick way of entering this kind of address is to enter only the company name and then press Ctrl+Enter; doing so automatically fills in the *http://www* and *.com for* you.

Tip: Although most addresses end with *.com,* other extensions are common. Non-profit organizations' addresses often end with *.org,* government agencies with *.gov,* military sites with *.mil,* ISPs and other Internet organizations with *.net,* and schools with *.edu.* You may encounter two-letter country suffixes, too, including *.uk* (for Web sites based in the United Kingdom), *.za* (South Africa), and so on. (The country codes are usually derived from country's name in its own language. That's why the code for Germany is *de*–for Deutschland–instead of, say, *ge*.)

- You can press the F4 key (or use the drop-down menu at the right end of the Address bar) to view a list of URLs you've visited during this browsing session. You can press the up or down arrow keys to highlight them, and the Enter key to select one.

- When you begin to type into the Address bar, the AutoComplete feature compares what you're typing against the list of Web sites you've recently visited. Internet Explorer displays a pop-up list of Web addresses that seem to match what you're typing. So that you're spared the tedium of typing out the whole thing, you can click the correct complete address with your mouse (or use the down arrow key to highlight the one you want). The complete address you selected pops into the Address bar.

Tip: Internet Explorer can also remember user names, passwords, and other information you type into text boxes (*forms*) you encounter on Web pages. You can turn on this feature by choosing Tools→Internet Options, clicking the Content tab, clicking AutoComplete and turning on the appropriate checkboxes. Having your browser remember the names and passwords for your various Web sites is a great time and memory saver, even though it doesn't work on all Web sites. But consider turning this feature off if other people share your computer and you use the Internet to perform confidential transactions, such as online banking.

The Links Toolbar

The Favorites menu described on page 233 is one way to maintain a list of Web sites you visit frequently. However, opening a Web page listed in the Favorites menu requires a minimum of *two mouse clicks*—an exorbitant expenditure of energy. The Links toolbar offers enough room for a few Web-page icons. They let you summon a few, *very* favorite Web pages with only one click.

Figure 11-5 shows how you add buttons to this toolbar. (To remove a button, right-click it and choose Delete from the shortcut menu.) It's also worth noting that you can rearrange these buttons simply by dragging them horizontally.

Tip: As shown in Figure 11-5, you can drag a link from a Web page onto your Links toolbar. But you can also drag it directly to the desktop, where it turns into a special Internet shortcut icon. You can double-click this icon whenever you like to launch your browser and visit the associated Web page. Better yet, stash a few of these icons in your Start menu or Quick Launch toolbar for even easier access. (If you open your My Computer→C: drive→WINNT→Documents and Settings→[Your Name]→Favorites folder, moreover, you'll see these shortcut icons for *all* your Favorites. You can drag them to the desktop, Quick Launch toolbar, Links toolbar, or wherever you like.)

Figure 11-5:
Add a Web page to the Links bar by dragging its tiny page icon, as shown here. (You can also drag any link, such as a blue underlined phrase, from a Web page onto the toolbar.)

Status Bar

The Status bar at the bottom of the window tells you what Internet Explorer is doing (such as "Opening page…" or "Done"); when you point to a link without clicking, the Status bar also tells you what URL will open *if* you click.

If you consult this information only rarely, you may prefer to hide this bar, thus increasing the amount of space actually devoted to showing Web pages. To do so, choose View→Status Bar.

Explorer Bar

When you click the Search toolbar button or use the View→Explorer Bar menu, the *Explorer bar* appears at the left side of your browser window. Helpful lists appear in this special pane when you choose commands from the View→Explorer Bar menu:

- **Search.** Offers a compact search feature, like the one described in the next section.

- **Favorites.** A duplicate of the pages listed in the Favorites menu.

- **History.** A list of Web sites you've visited recently, arranged chronologically.

- **Folders.** Shows you the contents of your hard drive. (This function isn't particularly relevant to Web browsing, but it keeps the Explorer bar consistent with the one described on page 61.)

• **Tip of the Day.** This command takes away a *second* chunk of screen space from your Web-browsing activities, the better to display a hint or tip about Internet Explorer.

Searching on the Web

As noted above, finding major companies on the Web is usually easy—just enter the company's name in the Address bar and then press Enter.

Finding *specific* things on the Web is not so easy. This is where search services (also called search engines) come in. A search service is a Web site devoted to cataloging the entire Web and providing a way for you to search this catalog. You can use a search service to find Web pages of interest to you, either by searching for keywords or by using a so-called *directory style* search service to find Web pages by browsing a category list.

You can search in three different ways with Internet Explorer: using the Address bar, the Search toolbar button, or a search-engine Web page; the following discussion covers all three techniques.

Tip: If you find a Web page that's particularly useful, you can choose Tools→Show Related Links to open a list of pages that, according to a software robot, contain information that's similar to what's on the currently open Web page.

A Quick Guide to Search Services

There's no tidy card catalog of every Web page. Because Web pages appear and disappear hourly by the hundreds of thousands, such an exercise would be futile.

Fortunately, two types of search services await to help you find the pages you want—subject directories and search engines. A subject directory is like the subject catalog in a library: It groups Web sites by topic (such as sports, government, or astronomy).

GEM IN THE ROUGH

The Complete Guide to Web-Page Scrolling

If a Web page doesn't fit entirely in your browser window, you can, of course, use the vertical scroll bar to move up and down the page. But to save mousing, press the Space bar each time you want to see more. Press Shift+Space to scroll *up*. (The Space bar has its traditional, space-making function only when your insertion point is blinking in a text box or the Address bar.)

You can also press your up- and down-arrow keys to scroll. Page Up and Page Down scroll in full-screen increments;

and Home and End take you to the top or bottom of the current Web page.

Finally, if your mouse has a roller wheel, you can turn it with your finger to scroll the page, or click the wheel and move the mouse up or down to activate the AutoScroll feature. If you have a Microsoft Intellimouse Explorer mouse, you can also use the two special buttons located by your thumb (if you're right-handed) as Back and Forward buttons.

Unlike a library's subject catalog, though, subject directories contain only a tiny portion of the total number of documents on the Web; the sites are added to their listings manually, by human editors. Some of the best directory services are Yahoo.com and LookSmart.com. (The Search functions of MSN Search, Excite, and many other partners rely on the LookSmart directory.)

Search engines, on the other hand, use automated software to detect and index Web sites. These programs, called robots or spiders, roam the Web hunting for new pages. When the robot finds a new page, it reports the address, retrieves all or part of the page's text, and adds the information to a database. Even the best search engines cover only 10 or 20 percent of the Web (though that includes about 90 percent of the *useful* pages), so finding what you're looking for can be tricky. (Google.com is one of the best search engines; it's uncannily accurate in finding the information you want.)

Tip: You don't have to go to a search-engine Web page to begin your search; instead, you can simply type a word or phrase (such as *electric drapes,* for example) into the Address bar and then press Enter. (If Internet Explorer doesn't interpret your phrase as a search request, add the word *find* in front of it.)

Internet Explorer assumes that you mean, "*Find* electric drapes." The search results appear in the Search bar on the left; click a hyperlink to go to that Web page.

To control which search engines Internet Explorer uses when you perform this kind of search, see page 43.

Using the Search Bar

The Search bar (View→Explorer Bar→Search, or click the Search toolbar button) lets you search using multiple search engines at once. This left-side window panel works, in Internet Explorer, exactly as it does in desktop windows; see page 42 for a tutorial.

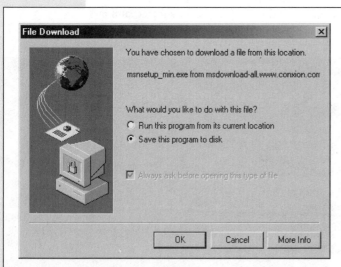

Figure 11-6:
In the File Download dialog box, select the Save This Program To Disk option and click OK. (Choose Run This Program From Its Current Location if you plan on installing the program immediately.) In the Save As dialog box, select a location to store the file (somewhere you can find it easily—perhaps the desktop or a Downloads folder you've created) and click Save. A dialog box displaying the download progress appears.

Downloading and Saving Files

To download a file from a Web page (such as a software update or add-on), just click the link for it (which may say, for example, Download Now). The File Download dialog box appears, as shown in Figure 11-6.

Tip: Suppose you're viewing a news-headlines Web page, and you spot a headline that interests you. By right-clicking the link and choosing Save Target As from the shortcut menu, you can download the actual Web page (text, graphics, or file) to your hard drive—without even going to that page first. Use the Save As dialog box to choose where to store the file and then click Save.

To save an image that you find on the Internet, right-click it and choose Save Picture As from the shortcut menu. In the Save As dialog box, specify the filename and location you want to use, and then click Save.

Tip: To turn a picture you find on a Web page into desktop wallpaper (see page 138), right-click the image and choose Set As Wallpaper from the shortcut menu.

Keeping Track of Useful Sites

Internet Explorer provides several ways to flag or preserve a Web page that's worth remembering.

The Favorites Menu

When you find a Web page you might like to visit again, choose Favorites→Add to Favorites (or press Ctrl+D). The Web page's name appears instantly at the bottom of your Favorites menu. The next time you want to visit that page, just choose its name from your menu.

Note: The Favorites menu, like the Windows 2000 Start Menu, can use the Personalized Menus feature described on page 51 to hide shortcuts you infrequently use. To turn this feature on or off, choose Tools→Internet Options, click the Advanced tab, and then select or clear the Enable Personalized Favorites Menu checkbox under the Browsing section.

Unless you're creating folders and organizing your favorites as you create them, you'll quickly find the Favorites menu becoming enormous and unwieldy. Organizing your Favorites (Figure 11-7) helps you deal with the disorder; nothing but ruthless pruning will help with the size.

Tip: Instead of organizing your Favorites using the method shown in Figure 11-7, you can open your Favorites menu in Windows Explorer, right-click a subfolder on the Favorites menu, and choose Explore from the shortcut menu. The Favorites folder opens in Windows Explorer; now you can move your shortcuts around, create folders, and delete shortcuts, just as you would other files in Windows Explorer (see page 86).

Importing and exporting a list of favorites

To import favorites or a bookmark file from another browser, choose File→Import and Export to launch the Import/Export Wizard, which lets you transfer collections of favorites into, or out of, other Web browsers. The wizard prompts you to indicate which browser has the bookmarks you want to import.

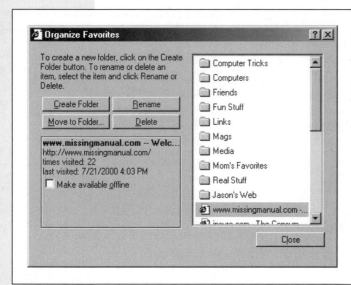

Figure 11-7:
To edit the Favorites menu, choose Favorites→Open Favorites. When the Open Favorites window opens, you can drag names up or down to rearrange the list, as shown, or click one and then use the buttons at left to rename, delete, or file it in a folder.

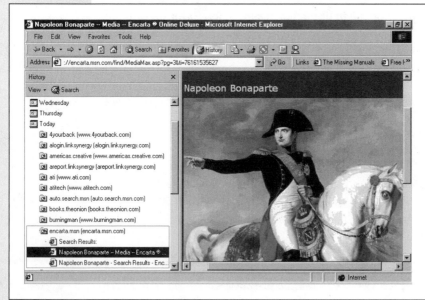

Figure 11-8:
To use the History folder, click a Web site to see a listing of the pages you visited at that site. Click a page to return to it. To view a different day, click on the day's listing. Click the View button at the top of the History bar to view pages by Site, Most Visited, or By Order Visited Today.

Making History Repeat Itself

This *history* is a list of the Web sites you've visited in the last 20 days (a number you can adjust). It's the heart of three Internet Explorer features: AutoComplete, described at the beginning of this chapter; the drop-down menu at the right side of the Address bar; and the History list in the Explorer bar. All of these are great features for those times when you remember having found an interesting page, but forgot to add it to your Favorites and no longer remember how you got there.

Tip: To change the number of days the History folder tracks, choose Tools→Internet Options, and then change the number in the "Days to keep pages in history" box at the bottom of the General tab.

To see the History bar, click the History toolbar button, or choose View→Explorer Bar→History. By default, you see a list of the Web sites you've visited today, as shown in Figure 11-8.

Emailing Web Pages

If you find a Web page that you'd like to share with a friend, you can easily send the link by email. Just choose one of these two commands:

- **File→Send→Page By E-mail.** Sends the entire Web page as the body of an HTML formatted email. This tactic isn't recommended unless you're sending the file to a *really* good friend—or one who has a cable modem—because the file may be huge.

- **File→Send→Link By E-mail.** Sends only the hyperlink. Your recipients can click the link to go directly to the page you want them to see.

Figure 11-9:
To save a Web page, choose File→Save As. Internet Explorer saves a Web page as a single HTML file, accompanied by a folder of image files. To save the page and graphics as a single file, choose the "Web Archive, single file" option from the "Save as type" drop-down menu. You can also choose "Web Page, HTML only" to save the Web page without any images, or "Text File" to save only the text on the Web page (without any HTML formatting codes or images).

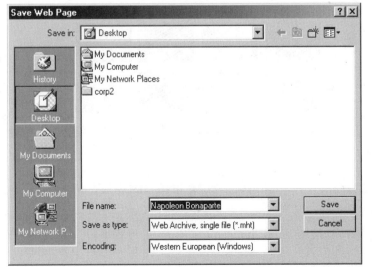

Saving Web Pages

The Web is a dynamic place; what's here today may well be gone tomorrow. To ensure that you'll always have a certain Web page that's valuable to you, save the page to your hard drive, as shown in Figure 11-9.

Printing Web Pages

Web pages sometimes have information that you need in printed form—a map and directions, a recipe, or a record of an online purchase, for example. The quickest way to print a page is to choose File→Print. To print only some of the text on a Web page, drag through it to highlight it, and then select File→Print; choose the Selection option in the Print dialog box to print only what you've selected.

Tip: Click the Print toolbar button to print using the default settings. Because you're not prompted for any additional information, such as how many copies you want, you save a step.

If you've upgraded to Internet Explorer 5.5 or newer, you can also make use of the new Print Preview feature (Figure 11-10).

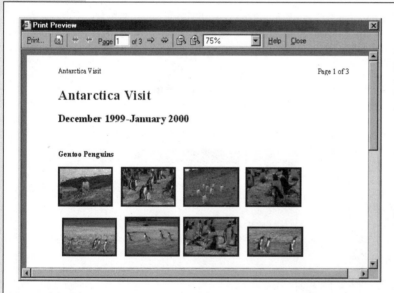

Figure 11-10:
Choose File→Print Preview to see how a Web page will appear when printed out. Use the Page box at the top of the window to enter a different page number to view, or use the arrow buttons next to this box to move to a different page. Use the percentage box, the Zoom In, and Zoom Out buttons to view the page in greater detail. When you click Print or choose File→Print, the Print dialog box appears.

Customizing and Security

To tweak your Internet Explorer setup by adding or removing buttons, tightening up its security settings, or keeping the Web sites you've visited private, use the following tips.

Customizing Your View

You can change several aspects of Internet Explorer's interface to suit your preferences, as shown in the next sections.

View Web pages full screen

To view a Web page in a full-screen view, maximizing the amount of the page you can see, choose View→Full Screen, or press the F11 key. Full Screen mode hides everything except your Web page and the Standard toolbar. Even the Windows Taskbar is temporarily hidden. (To pull it back into view, move the cursor over the bottom edge of the screen). You can still scroll the page, using the tricks described on page 231; meanwhile, you get to see much more of each Web page on each screenful.

To turn off Full Screen mode, click the Restore button at the top right of the window, or press F11. To make even the toolbar hidden (except when you move the cursor over the top edge of the screen), right-click the toolbar and choose Auto Hide from the shortcut menu.

Changing the text size of Web pages

If you find the text on a Web page too small or too big, change the text size using the View→Text Size submenu.

Note: Changing the text size with the View menu doesn't always make any visual difference; the effect depends on how the Web page was written.

Rearranging Internet Explorer's interface

When you first open it, Internet Explorer displays the Standard Buttons toolbar, Address bar, Links toolbar, and (at the bottom of the window) the Status bar. All of these toolbars and other screen doodads give you plenty of surfing control, but also occupy huge chunks of your screen space. The Web is supposed to be a *visual* experience; this encroachment of your monitor's real estate isn't necessarily a good thing.

To add or remove toolbars, choose their names from the View→Toolbars submenu. To rearrange toolbars, drag the small vertical line to the left of the toolbar you want to move to a new location (horizontally, vertically, or both). You can hide the Status bar, too, by choosing View→Status Bar; likewise, use the View→Explorer Bar submenu to hide the Explorer bars, if they're open.

Tip: If you really want to mess with Internet Explorer's interface, try dragging the Standard Buttons toolbar up *onto* the menu bar—just to the right of the Help menu. (You can combine other toolbars in this way, too.) This arrangement frees up a whole extra line, allowing you to view even more of your Web pages.

Customizing toolbars

Adding buttons to the toolbar for features you frequently use streamlines your Web browsing. On the other hand, getting rid of unwanted buttons reduces clutter and opens screen real estate, allowing you to put more than one toolbar on the same line or add some shortcuts to the Links toolbar.

To customize Internet Explorer's Standard Buttons toolbar, right-click it and choose Customize from the shortcut menu. The Customize Toolbar dialog box appears; Figure 11-11 shows you how to proceed from there. (Click Reset to undo your changes, or click Close to save them.)

Tip: To remove the Go button from the Address bar, right-click it and choose Go Button from the shortcut menu. (Pressing Enter performs the same function as clicking the Go button.)

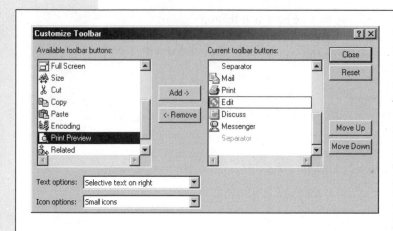

Figure 11-11:
In the Available Toolbar Buttons list on the left, select a button you want to include on the toolbar, and then click Add. To reposition a highlighted button in the right-side list, click Move Up or Move Down. To insert a separator line between buttons, organizing them into groups, add a Separator from the left-side list. Use the two drop-down list boxes below the list to control how toolbar text and icons appear.

Turning off graphics to speed up pages

Graphics are part of what makes the Web so compelling. But they're also responsible for making Web pages take so long to arrive on the screen. If you do serious reading and research on the Web, you can get frustrated by the amount of time it takes for a page to open.

You can greatly speed up the process by turning *off* the graphics, so that only text is downloaded. You still get fully laid-out Web pages; you still see all the text and headlines. But wherever a picture would normally be, you see an empty rectangle containing a generic "graphic goes here" logo, often with a caption that tells you what that graphic would have been.

To bring about this arrangement, choose Tools→Internet Options, click the Advanced tab, and scroll down to the Multimedia heading. Clear the Show Pictures checkbox. (You can also clear the Play Animations, Play Sounds, and Play Videos checkboxes to block these enemies of downloading speed as well.) Click OK when you're done. Now try visiting a few Web pages; you'll feel a substantial speed boost.

And if you wind up on a Web page that's nothing without its pictures, you can choose to summon an individual picture. Just right-click its box and choose Show Picture from the shortcut menu.

Covering Your Tracks and Conserving Disk Space

Several of Internet Explorer's features are designed to make browsing the Web faster and more convenient—but they also consume disk space and leave a record of the Web pages you've viewed. If you have a gigantic hard drive and a clear conscience about the sites you've been trolling, you can skip this section.

But if you want to change how much disk space Internet Explorer uses or wipe out your tracks, look at three things: the Temporary Internet Files folder, the History folder, and your cookies. Each of these is discussed in the following sections.

Caution: Even if you clear your Temporary Internet Files folder, the History folder, and delete any unwanted cookies, don't assume that you've covered your tracks completely. At many corporate workplaces, a proxy server (see page 224) or some other form of firewall makes it very easy for a network administrator to track who is viewing what Web sites. So don't stray any place you wouldn't want your boss to know about.

Temporary Internet files

To help speed the process of loading pages you've already seen, Internet Explorer saves the contents of *every* page you visit onto your hard drive. When you revisit a site, the saved file is opened—fast—thus eliminating the time-consuming process of downloading the contents again.

These saved-up Web-page files are called *cache* files. Internet Explorer stashes its cache in the C:→WINNT→Documents and Settings→[Your Name]→Local Settings→Temporary Internet Files folder. This folder has a limited capacity, which you can adjust (see Figure 11-12); Windows deletes older files automatically to make room for new files.

There are a couple downsides to the Temporary Internet Files scheme. First, caching Web pages and files on your hard drive reduces the space available for other programs and files; second, it leaves a record of what files and pages you've viewed.

If you want to delete all the files in the Temporary Internet Files folder, thereby temporarily freeing up some hard drive space (until the cache fills up again) and removing local traces of the files you've viewed, choose Tools→Internet Options, and then click the Delete Files button near the middle of the dialog box. The Delete Files dialog box appears; if you want to also delete any *offline content* you have stored (pages or files you've made available for viewing when you're not connected to the Net), select the Delete Offline Content checkbox. Click OK.

To change the amount of disk space that's allotted to the Temporary Internet Files folder, or how often Internet Explorer checks the Internet for new versions of files and pages stored in the cache, choose Tools→Internet Options, and then click the

Settings button in the Temporary Internet Files section to display the dialog box shown in Figure 11-12.

Tip: To force Internet Explorer to download a new copy of a Web page (instead of showing you the cached copy, which may be out of date), open the Web page and click the Refresh toolbar button.

Figure 11-12:
If it's important that pages be as up-to-date as possible (at the expense of browsing speed), select "Every visit to the page." If you have a very bad Internet connection, you may want to select Never, so that Internet Explorer always loads pages from the cache, if possible. Use the slider to change the maximum size of the folder, or use the View Files or View Objects button to view the pages or programs stored in the folder.

History folder

The History folder, while extremely valuable for finding Web pages you've previously visited, can also be incriminating. If you don't want your spouse to know about those models you've been drooling over (Maseratis and Jaguars, for example), clear the History folder as well as the record of addresses you've entered in the Address Bar. Choose Tools→Internet Options, and then click the Clear History button.

All about managing cookies

Cookies are small text file files that some Web sites store on your computer. A cookie might help the Web page remember, for example, your name, password, or credit card number, to spare you the retyping every time you visit a certain Web page. It can't do anything else—it can't give you a virus or take any information that you don't provide willingly.

If you ever switch computers, you can transfer all your old cookies so that the Web sites you visit will still remember you. To do this, choose File→Import and Export, click Next, choose either Import Cookies or Export Cookies, and click Next. Choose the browser or file you want to import from or export to, click Next, and then click Finish.

If you want to view the cookies stored on your computer, choose Tools→Internet Options, and then click the Settings button in the Temporary Internet Files section to display the box shown in Figure 11-12. Click the View Files button to open your Temporary Internet Files folder. Inside this folder, you'll see a list of files; at the top of the list are your cookies. You can delete cookies just as you'd delete any file.

Tip: If you're deleting cookies, don't forget to empty the Recycle Bin, too. Otherwise, all the cookies you've deleted will still be around—no longer functional, but still evidence of where you've been.

Security and Internet Explorer

If you pay any attention to the press, you may have a bad impression of Internet Explorer's security. Almost every day, it seems, Microsoft is admitting some new vulnerability of Internet Explorer and releasing a patch to fix it.

But Explorer isn't an insecure Web browser, ripe for hackers to pluck. Quite the contrary: Internet Explorer is very secure. But because of its immense popularity, it gets a lot of scrutiny from hackers who want their 15 minutes of fame. (After all, how famous can you get by hacking a browser than nobody uses?)

The odds of some hacker reaching out and touching your files—through the Internet, through your company's firewall—are infinitesimal. Still, if you're concerned, you can use the Windows Update tool frequently (see page 58) to keep your version of Internet Explorer (and Windows 2000 itself) up-to-date with the latest security patches. Also make sure that you have the High Encryption Pack installed, which provides *128-bit encryption*; this free software update makes secure transactions (such as transmitting your credit card information) much more secure.

GEM IN THE ROUGH

Limiting Access to Unsavory Sites

If there are children, or people who act like children, using your computer, you can employ Internet Explorer's Content Advisor feature to limit access to Web sites containing offensive material.

However, Internet Explorer's built-in tools are quite limited, permitting or rejecting only sites that have voluntarily given themselves ratings on the scale devised by a group called the Internet Content Rating Association.

As you can well imagine, the Ratings feature is, therefore, far from foolproof. The overwhelming majority of sites aren't rated at all (and most don't need to be). Still, if you want to use the feature, choose Tools→Internet Options,

click the Content tab, and then click Enable in the Content Advisor section.

Other programs, including CYBERSitter and McAfee's Internet Guard Dog, are more flexible in screening out Web pages, though they, too, have limitations. Some scan for "forbidden" words and will block legitimate medical sites that, for example, use the actual names of actual body parts. Others use criteria that they don't disclose.

Of course, the *real* solution to unsavory Web sites is parental supervision, plus frank discussions between parents and children.

Depending on whether you're concerned about invasions from the outside (hackers over the net) or the inside (mischievous children, prying relatives), you may want to look at a couple of other IE security features.

Security zones

Internet Explorer and Windows 2000 let you and your company place every Web site on earth into four categories, called *security zones:*

- **Restricted Sites.** Off-limits sites that have been determined to be dangerous to your computer.

- **Trusted sites.** These are Web sites you're confident won't send anything fishy to your PC.

- **Local Intranet.** Web sites in this category aren't on the Internet at all; instead, they're on your own office network, and are therefore likely to contain only 100 percent safe files.

- **Internet.** This category means "all other Web sites"—those you haven't put into one of the other categories.

Each zone, or category, can have its own security settings that control what Web sites and network locations belonging to the zone can and can't do.

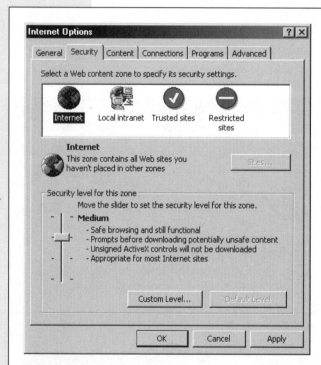

Figure 11-13:
Highlight a zone to view the security settings for that zone. To change the security settings, move the slider to the desired security level, or to change individual security settings, click the Custom Level button and use the Security Settings dialog box to configure individual settings. To add sites to the Trusted Sites or Restricted Sites zones, select the zone, click the Add Sites button, enter the Web address for the site in the provided box, and click Add.

For example, sites in the Restricted Sites zone can't run ActiveX programs (mini-programs that your computer downloads from Web sites), download files, or store cookies on your computer. To adjust the security settings, choose Tools→Internet Options and then click the Security tab (Figure 11-13).

Erasing the AutoComplete trail

As noted earlier in this chapter, Internet Explorer's AutoComplete feature memorizes the information you enter in Web-page forms (such as your name, address, credit card number, and so on). The next time you begin typing one of these information tidbits, AutoComplete kicks in, automatically filling in the remaining letters. This feature can make filling out order forms and logging onto password-protected Web sites faster and easier (because you won't have to memorize your passwords or how to spell your name).

AutoComplete entries are encrypted on your hard drive, so other network citizens can't gain access to, say, your bank account Web site—*unless* somebody sits down at your PC when you're away and have forgotten to log off.

To change AutoComplete settings, see Figure 11-14. You can delete a specific Auto-Complete entry in a Web form, too: When the list of AutoComplete entries appears (when you're entering data in the form, or when you press the down arrow key in a form field with an AutoComplete entry), select the entry you want to delete and press the Delete key on your keyboard.

Figure 11-14:
Choose Tools→Internet Options, click the Content tab, and then click the AutoComplete button. In the AutoComplete Settings dialog box, select what you'd like to use AutoComplete for—addresses in the Address bar, Web page forms, or user names and passwords on Web page forms. To clear all stored form entries, click the Clear Forms button; to clear stored passwords only, click Clear Passwords.

Microsoft Profile Assistant

The Microsoft Profile Assistant can store all your personal information (name, address, and so on). Microsoft's engineers imagined that one day, specially programmed

Web sites could "ask" Internet Explorer for information from your profile, in an effort to save you some typing. Internet Explorer would respond by telling you what information is being requested, and asking your permission to share it with the Web page. (To change the information in your profile, choose Tools→Internet Options, click the Content tab, and then click My Profile.)

Unfortunately, the Profile Assistant feature hasn't caught on; very few Web sites have been made "Profile Assistant-aware."

Getting Information about Internet Explorer

If you need information about Internet Explorer, perhaps for troubleshooting purposes when working with a help desk technician, there are two things to do. The first is to choose Help→About Internet Explorer, which shows you the current version number, lists any Service Packs (update kits released by Microsoft) you've installed, and reveals the encryption strength of your copy.

For more in-depth information about Internet Explorer's settings, you can use the System Information tool. Right-click My Computer and select Manage from the shortcut menu. Double-click System Information, and then the Internet Explorer 5 folder. The "folders" that appear show you the version numbers, browser settings, security levels, and other technical parameters.

UP TO SPEED

What You Need to Know about Plug-ins

Most Web pages contain text and pictures. A few, however, offer sound, movies, or animation. By itself, Internet Explorer doesn't know how to play this kind of onscreen show. It needs assistance from a software add-on called a *plug-in.* Once installed on your PC, a plug-in lets Explorer play a specific kind of sound, movie, or animation. Plug-ins are free; most are available at *www.plugins.com.* (The ones you'll need most often are Flash, Shockwave, and RealPlayer.) When you visit a site that requires a new plug-in, an Internet Explorer dialog box asks you if you'd like to download the plug-in.

Outlook Express: Email and Newsgroups

E mail is one of the most important communication forms in business. Email provides an easy and inexpensive way to share information and carry on conversations with people anywhere in the world.

This chapter covers using Outlook Express, the email program that comes with Windows 2000. However, the techniques in this chapter also work reasonably well on many other mail programs, including Netscape Messenger, Qualcomm Eudora, and Microsoft Outlook 2000.

Note: Don't confuse Outlook, a component of Microsoft Office, with its slimmer sibling Outlook Express. In addition to its email features, Outlook also offers a calendar, to-do list, and compatibility with Microsoft Exchange Server. Outlook Express has charms of its own, however, that aren't in Outlook 2000, including support for using Hotmail accounts, integration with MSN Instant Messenger, and a topnotch program for reading newsgroups (Internet bulletin boards).

Starting Out with Outlook Express

To start Outlook Express, either click the Outlook Express button on the Quick Launch toolbar, or choose Start→Programs→Outlook Express.

Choosing an Email Provider

If your PC is attached to a big network, you probably already have an email account. But if you're setting up a new peer-to-peer network (see Chapter 15) or you're running Windows 2000 Pro on a non-networked PC, you may still be faced with the chore of choosing an email provider.

It's not an easy choice. First, you must choose between free accounts and accounts provided by your ISP (see Chapter 11).

When you sign up for a free email account, such as Hotmail *(www.hotmail.com)* and Juno *(www.juno.com)*, you read and send email using a Web browser. These accounts require almost no setup, and let you get your email from any computer that can access the Web; on the other hand, processing email using a Web browser is generally slower and more cumbersome than using a real mail program such as Outlook Express.

There are exceptions: For example, you can configure Outlook Express to check your Hotmail account as if it were a normal email account. Most Web-based email services let you check your "regular" (POP or IMAP) email accounts via Web browser, too (sometimes for an additional fee). And some free accounts actually work as a "regular" email account, allowing Outlook Express to easily check your email.

Tip: If you're not crazy about the email address that your company, school, or ISP assigned to you, you can sign up for a fee-based *vanity email* service (at *www.vanitymail.com,* for example). It gives you an email address of your own choosing (such as *jerrym@Show-Me-The-Money.com* or some other catchy address); messages sent to that address get automatically forwarded to your "real," much less memorable address.

UP TO SPEED

What are POP, IMAP, and Web Mail Servers?

Mail servers (the computers that process email on the Internet) come in three popular flavors—*POP3*, *IMAP4*, and Web-based mail. Certain Outlook Express features work differently depending on which kind of account you have, so these terms are worth getting to know.

POP servers (most people drop the "3") are the oldest type, and the kind that works with the most email programs and ISPs. A POP server transfers your email to your computer's hard drive—a system that works fine as long as you always use the same computer for email.

IMAP servers are newer and more capable than POP systems, but not as universally supported by ISPs and mail programs. With an IMAP mail account, all messages are stored on the mail server somewhere on the Internet, so that you can access your messages from any computer. The mail-server computer remembers which messages you've read, filed, sent, and so on. Outlook Express (ver-

sion 5.5 and later) can retrieve mail from IMAP servers, but with a limitation: It can't apply *message rules* (see page 268) to mail from IMAP (or Web-based) email accounts. If you want to use the message-rules feature on IMAP mail, use Microsoft Outlook instead.

Web-based mail servers provide some of the advantages of IMAP by storing all mail out on the Internet, but take that convenience a step further by letting you check your email from any Web browser—a great feature if you need to check mail from someone else's computer or a public terminal. The downsides are that the Web site is often slow, the mail interface is awkward and less powerful than a dedicated email program, and you have to put up with ads. Even though Outlook Express can retrieve your email from Hotmail, doing so is still slower and less reliable than using a POP or IMAP account. (That's the price you pay for free email.)

If you pay for your ISP service, you get one or more email accounts. The accounts they provide are typically POP-based, and are usually faster and more reliable than free email accounts. However, not all ISPs give you Web access to your email, and if you decide to change ISPs, you lose your email address.

Tip: Services like Bigfoot *(www.bigfoot.com)* provide free email forwarding for life. All email sent to the address Bigfoot assigns to you is forwarded automatically to your "real" email address. If you change ISPs, you don't have to change your email address; you just update your forwarding address to reflect your new email account. Your correspondents will never know the difference. (The vanity email services described in the previous tip offer this benefit, too.) The downside to using forwarding is that it can delay your email anywhere from a minute to a couple days if the company's servers are overloaded.

Opening Outlook Express

To launch Outlook Express, either click its icon on the Quick Launch toolbar or choose Start→Programs→Outlook Express.

If you haven't used any other email software on the computer before, the first thing Outlook Express does is invite you to make it the default mail program. (If you *have* previously used other email software, Outlook Express asks this question later.) Click Yes if you've decided to use Outlook Express as your primary email program; otherwise, click No.

Tip: If you chose not use Outlook Express as your preferred mail program, clear the "Always perform this check when starting Outlook Express" checkbox to prevent it from asking this question every time you use the program.

Next, you see the Internet Connection Wizard, prompting you to setup a mail account (see "Setting Up Email Accounts" on the next page).

Importing Settings and Data from Another Program

If you've ever used another email program on this computer, Outlook Express now asks if you'd like to import the settings, messages, and address books from the other program(s). (It can import this information from most popular email programs. In the unlikely event that it doesn't recognize yours, choose File→Import to import them manually.) A wizard walks you through the steps: choosing the older program, specifying which accounts you want to import, indicating which elements (addresses, messages) you want imported, and so on.

When you click Finish, Outlook Express completes the importing process, so that you can begin your life with Outlook Express accompanied by the familiar surroundings of your old messages and addresses.

Setting Up Email Accounts

If you used the Internet Connection Wizard (see Chapter 11), or if a network administrator has configured Outlook Express for you, you can skip this section; Out-

---

look Express already knows your email account settings.

Otherwise, to set up or view these settings, choose Tools→Accounts. Click the Mail tab, then the Add→Mail to start the Connection Wizard.

1. **In the Display Name box, type the name you want to use when sending email.**

    You're supposed to enter your real name here, but you *can* enter some other name, like HotStuff or Your Royal Highness. (Just remember not to email your boss using this account.)

2. **Click Next. Enter the email address for the account.**

    If you don't actually have an account, and you've just been bluffing it up to this point, you may select "I'd like to sign up for a new account from Hotmail" to remedy the situation. (Although you might want to shop around for a bit first to get the best kind of email account for you.)

3. **Click Next. Enter your mail server information.**

    If you chose the Hotmail option, you're taken directly to the Setup Hotmail Account Wizard. You're asked to provide your name, some information about yourself, a sign-in name, password, and other information. When you finish, your new Hotmail account will be listed on the Mail tab of the Internet Accounts dialog box. You can view or change the settings for this account by clicking the Properties button.

    Otherwise, select the type of mail server your account uses from the "My incoming mail server is" drop-down list box. (*Hint:* It's probably a POP3 server.) Enter the incoming mail server's address in the Incoming Mail box. In the Outgoing Mail box, enter your SMTP server address. Click Next.

    If you don't know your incoming or outgoing mail server names, ask someone who would know: your ISP (for your personal or home account) or network administrator (for your work or business account).

4. **Enter your account name and password.**

    Your account name is usually the first part of your email address—the part that comes before the *@mydomain.com* part. To make Outlook Express remember your password, turn on the "Remember password" checkbox.

Tip: The "Remember password" option saves you a step when you check your mail, but remember that a passing spy who sits down at your PC can theoretically check your email without entering a password.

    If your Web server requires secure password authentication (most don't), turn on "Log on using Secure Password Authentication."

5. **Click Next, and then click Finish. Click Close in the Accounts dialog box.**

    If the mail account is an IMAP account (see page 246), you're now asked if you want to download a list of folders. Click Yes, then use the Show/Hide IMAP Folders dialog box to choose the folders you want to display, as shown in Figure 12-1.

If you're *not* using an IMAP account, you won't be asked any such thing; in fact, you're now ready to start using email.

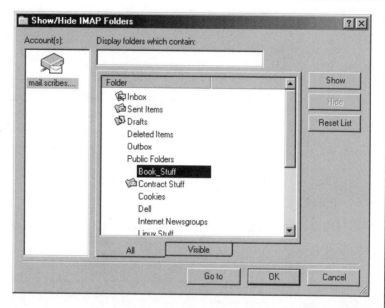

Figure 12-1:
The Show/Hide IMAP Folders dialog box lets you choose which folders you want to see on your mail server. The Inbox, Sent Items, and Drafts folders are selected by default. To add other folders to the list, select the desired folder and click Show. To see what folders you've selected at a glance, click the Visible tab.

UP TO SPEED

The Outlook Express Starting Page

Outlook Express displays a summary page when you launch the program. This page provides quick links to some of the most common tasks in Outlook Express, such as reading unread messages, writing a new message, reading newsgroups, or looking up people in the Address Book.

At first, you may find this page a handy way to start using Outlook Express. However, as you use the program more, you may discover that you'd rather

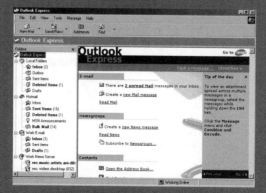

go directly to your Inbox when Outlook Express starts. In that case, turn on the "When Outlook Express starts, go directly to my Inbox" checkbox at the bottom of the page. You can also turn off the "Tip of the day" feature on this starting page by clicking the X to the right of the "Tip of the day" heading. (To turn the tips back on, click the Tips hyperlink that appears near the top right of the page.)

An Outlook Express Tour

Outlook Express displays information in several *panes*, or sections of the window, as shown in Figure 12-2. They include:

- **The Folders pane** (on the left), which lists such email "folders" as the Inbox, Outbox, and Sent Items. You see a separate folder for each of your email and newsgroup accounts, including Hotmail, IMAP-based email accounts, or news servers.

Tip: The bold number in parentheses after a folder name lets you know how many of its messages you haven't yet read.

- The **Inbox** holds mail you've received, and the **Outbox** holds mail you've written but haven't yet sent. **Sent Items** holds copies of messages you've sent **Deleted Items** holds mail you've deleted, as described later in this chapter. Finally, **Drafts** holds messages you've started but don't want to send just yet.

- **Message list.** When you click a folder in the Folders pane, you see, in the upper-right quadrant of the window, a list of the messages inside.

- **Contacts pane.** Underneath the Folders pane, you may see the Contacts pane. As with the Folders pane, you can hide it by clicking the X in its upper-right corner. It shows a list of contacts in your address book.

- **Preview pane.** Below the message list, you can read the currently selected message's contents. This arrangement is an extremely useful way to quickly read messages; once you've highlighted a message in the message list, you can scan your mail just

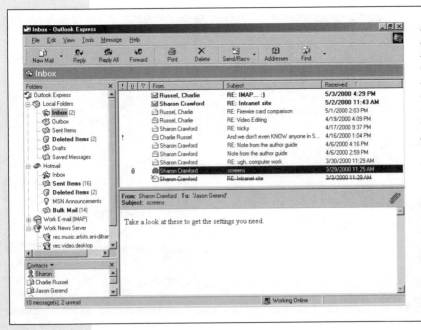

Figure 12-2:
In the Folders pane, select the folder that contains the new message (usually the Inbox). This displays the contents of the selected folder in the pane on the right. Unread messages show up with bold text. To read a message, click it once to see its contents in the Preview pane at the lower-right corner of the window. Double-click a message to view the message in its own window.

by pressing the down-arrow key, watching the text of the messages flash by in the Preview pane.

- **Toolbar.** Above all of these panes is the toolbar, whose buttons you can use for the most commonly performed tasks in Outlook Express.

Reading and Managing Email

While Outlook Express doesn't match a paper and pencil in terms of intuitiveness, once you get familiar with the program, you'll find it faster and more efficient than letter-writing ever was.

Checking Email

The first thing you probably do when you get to work (or wake up, if you tend to sleep under your desk) is check your email. For many, email has become the single most important form of communication. If Outlook Express doesn't automatically check your email when you start it, click the Send/Recv button on the Outlook Express toolbar to check for new messages.

Tip: You can also check for new messages by pressing F5.

Outlook Express also checks for new messages every 30 minutes. You can change this setting by choosing Tools→Options; change the number of minutes in the "Check for new messages every" number box, or turn this feature off entirely.

Reading Mail

When you get a new mail message, it appears in your message list with bold text and a closed envelope icon next to it, indicating that you haven't read it yet. To read it, click the Inbox icon if necessary, and then click the message's name once in the message list (Figure 12-2).

GEM IN THE ROUGH

Working Offline

For those not fortunate enough to have a full-time Internet connection (such as cable modem or corporate network), Windows 2000 offers a special Offline mode. When this mode is turned on, Internet Explorer, Outlook Express, Outlook, and any other compatible programs recognize the fact that you're not online; instead, they show you whatever *cached files* are available (messages and Web pages stored on your hard drive). This mode is especially handy when you're confronted with limited connection time, long distance charges, or other people wanting to use the phone line. You can con-

nect to the Internet, download the messages you want to view, and then switch to Offline mode while you read, reply, and compose new messages.

To switch to Offline mode, chose File→Work Offline. Later, when you're once again hooked up to an available phone line, you can then send the mail messages you wrote or check for new mail by clicking the Send/Recv button. Outlook Express asks if you want to go Online; click Yes. Now your PC connects to the Internet (or, depending on your settings, prompts you to make the connection).

Tip: Outlook Express doesn't usually show you the email address of the person who sent you a message—just the plain-English name. Usually, this arrangement is what you want. But if you want to see the email address of the sender, double-click the message to open it in its own window, right-click the sender's name in the "From:" field, and choose Properties from the shortcut menu.

If you then want to copy the email address, choose Copy from the shortcut menu (or choose Add To Address Book to create a contact for the sender, as described on page 263).

Opening File Attachments

Typed messages aren't the only communiqués you'll get by email; people may also attach files to the messages they send you, such as Word documents, graphic images, or *Zip files*. (A Zip file is a file, or group of files, that's been compressed into a smaller, single, easily emailed file. You must "unzip" such a file using a program like WinZip, available at *www.winzip.com.*) Sometimes people don't even bother to type a message; you wind up receiving an empty email message with a file attached. You know when a message has an attachment because a paper-clip icon appears next to its name in the Inbox (see Figure 12-3).

Opening attachments in the Preview pane

If you're reading a message in the Preview pane, click the paper-clip icon in the upper-right corner of the message. From the list of files that appears, select the attachment you want to open, or select Save Attachments to save the attachments to your hard drive.

Opening attachments in the message window

If you double-click a message's name in the list, so that it opens into its own window, you have more flexibility:

POWER USERS' CLINIC

Checking Messages on a Specific Email Account

By default, Outlook Express gets the email for all of your accounts (if you have more than one) whenever it checks for new messages.

You can exclude specific accounts from this normal message-checking process, as described on page 276. But you can also manually send and receive messages from a specific account. To do this, choose that account's name from the Tools→Send and Receive submenu, or the drop-down menu next to the Send/Recv button on the toolbar. These submenus also offer commands called Send All (which only sends messages, but doesn't check for new

ones) and Receive All (fetches new messages, leaving any unsent messages unsent).

These commands can be handy, for example, if you use a POP mail server and you want to send yourself a message that you plan to download when you're at another computer. If you try that trick using the normal Send/Recv button, chances are good that Outlook Express will send your message and download it again in one fell swoop, foiling your plan. But if you use the Send All command, you'll send the message without receiving it until you're ready.

- Right-click the attachment icon, select Save As from the shortcut menu, and then specify the folder in which you want to save the file.

- Drag its icon out of the message window and onto any visible portion of your desktop, as shown in Figure 12-3.

- Double-click the attachment's icon in the message. If you were sent a document (such as a photo, Word file, Excel file, and so on), it now opens in the corresponding program (Photoshop, Word, Excel, or whatever). After the attachment is open, use the File→Save As command to save the file into a folder of your choice; otherwise, you won't be able to open the file again except from within Outlook Express.

Caution: Email attachments are the most common source of viruses. *Never* open an attachment from someone you don't know. For strictest safety, don't open an attachment from someone you *do* know, either, unless you were expecting it. An up-to-date antivirus program can help, but still be wary of attachments.

One giveaway that an attachment may be a virus is an .exe or .vbs extension. However, even innocuous-appearing attachments such as files with a .doc extension (Microsoft Word files) can contains viruses. See page 396 for more information on protecting yourself from viruses.

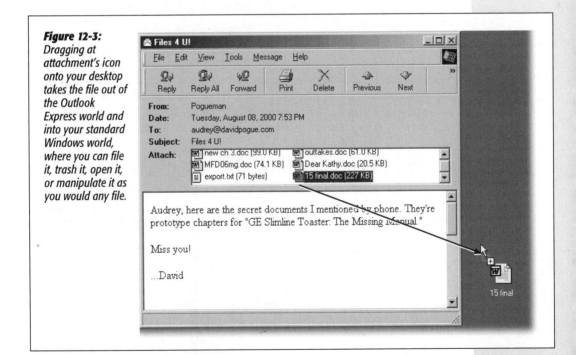

Figure 12-3:
Dragging at attachment's icon onto your desktop takes the file out of the Outlook Express world and into your standard Windows world, where you can file it, trash it, open it, or manipulate it as you would any file.

Replying and Forwarding Messages

After reading a message, you may want to reply to it or forward it to a third person. Doing so is easy: While viewing the message either in the Preview Pane or in a separate window, click the Reply or Forward button on the toolbar. If you click Reply, you get a new message that's addressed to the person who sent the email. (If the message was originally addressed to multiple recipients, you can send your reply to everyone simultaneously by clicking the Reply All button instead.) As a courtesy to your correspondent, Outlook Express places the original message at the bottom of the window, denoted by brackets; just type your message, click Send, and the deed is done.

Clicking the Forward toolbar button creates a new message containing the contents of the message you were viewing. In the "To:" box, enter the name of the person you want to send the message to and click Send.

Note: If the original message came with an attached file, Outlook Express doesn't fasten the attachment to a reply; it *does* include the attachment when you *forward* a message, however.

Deleting Messages

Few people keep all incoming email. That's why Outlook Express makes it easy to delete messages, and even provides an easy way to recover deleted messages if you change your mind.

To delete a message, select or open the message you want to delete, and then click the Delete toolbar button (or press Ctrl+D). The message moves to the Deleted Items folder. If you change your mind, just click the Deleted Items folder, find the message, and drag it into any other folder. (If you have an IMAP mail account, the message stays where it is, but appears crossed out, as shown by the bottom message in Figure 12-2. To restore it, right-click it and choose Undelete from the shortcut menu.)

To empty the Deleted Items folder, right-click it in the Folders list and choose Empty 'Deleted Items' Folder from the shortcut menu.

Tip: To make the folder empty itself every time you exit Outlook Express, choose Tools→Options, click the Maintenance tab, and turn on "Empty messages from the 'Deleted Items' folder on exit."

To get rid of deleted messages on an IMAP server, click the Purge toolbar button. (If you find it annoying to see a long list of the deleted messages on your IMAP server, you can hide—but not permanently remove—deleted messages by choosing View→Current View, and then turning off the Show Deleted Messages option on the submenu.)

Printing Messages

While most people rarely print out email messages, doing so is occasionally useful (when the email contains directions, for example). To print a message that's on the screen, click the Print button on the toolbar. Use the Print dialog box to specify any options such as number of copies, and then click the Print button.

WORKAROUND WORKSHOP

Printing Unsent Messages

Outlook Express has a strange little limitation in its printing function: it doesn't let you print an outgoing message until after you've sent it.

Here's a sneaky workaround: Close the message you're writing, and then click Yes to save the message in the Drafts folder. Select the Drafts folder in the Folders list, select the message you want to print, and then click the Print toolbar button. That's a convoluted way to print a message, but it gets the job done.

Composing and Sending Messages

Writing messages is the other half of the email equation; if you don't write messages, you won't receive any. (None you *want*, anyway.)

Fortunately, writing message in Outlook Express is easy:

1. **Click the New Mail toolbar icon (or press Ctrl+N).**

   An empty email window appears.

2. **Type the email address of the recipient into the "To:" field.**

   If you want to send this message to more than one person, separate their email addresses using semicolons, like this: *bob@earthlink.net; billg@microsoft.com; steve@apple.com.*

   As in most Windows dialog boxes, you can jump from blank to blank in this window by pressing the Tab key (to proceed from the "To:" field to the "Cc:" field, for example).

   You don't have to remember and type out all those email addresses, either. As you type, Outlook Express compares what you're typing with the names in your Address Book. If it finds a match—that is, if you've typed *zar* and your Address Book contains a name *Ed Zarynski*—Outlook Express completes the typing for you. (If it guesses wrong, just keep typing; Outlook Express politely removes its suggestion.)

   Alternatively, you can open your Address Book, if it's not already visible in the lower-left corner of your screen. Just click the tiny book to the left of the word "To:" or "Cc:" in the mail message window to display the Select Recipient dialog box. Find the recipient in the list (either by scrolling or by typing the first few letters of the name.) Then add this person's name to the "To:" list by double-

---

clicking the name, clicking the "To:" button, or pressing Alt+T. (The "Cc:" and "Bcc:" buttons let you send carbon-copy or blind carbon-copy messages.) You can repeat this process to add other names. If you can't find the person in any of your address books, click the Find button to search the Internet or company network for the person.

If you have multiple address books (or multiple folders in your Address Book), use the drop-down list just above the list of names to indicate which one you want to search.

3. **To send a copy of the message to other recipients, enter the email address(es) in the "Cc:" field.**

   Cc stands for *carbon copy*. There's very little difference between putting all your addressees on the "To:" line (separated by semicolons) and putting them on the "Cc:" line; the only difference is that the Cc people will know that they've been Cc'ed. Getting an email message where your name is in the "Cc:" line implies: "I sent you a copy because I thought you'd want to know about this correspondence, but I'm not expecting you to reply."

   Once again, you can use the address book to speed up typing in these names, and you can separate email addresses with semicolons. Press Tab when you're finished.

4. **Type the topic of the message in the "Subject:" field.**

   Some people, especially in the business world, get bombarded with email. That's why it's courteous to put some thought into the Subject line (use "Change in plans for next week" instead of "Hi," for example).

   Press the Tab key to make your cursor jump into the large message-body area.

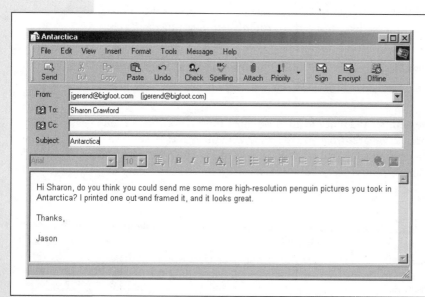

Figure 12-4:
When you're finished composing your message, click the Spelling toolbar button to check your spelling (an option available only if you have Microsoft Office on your machine). Caution: The spell-checker in Outlook Express doesn't check the spelling of the subject line, so type carefully.

5. **Enter the message in the message box (the bottom half of the message window, Figure 12-4).**

   You can use all the standard editing techniques, including using the Cut, Copy, and Paste commands to rearrange the text as you write it.

6. **Click Send (or press Alt+S).**

   If you're connected to the Internet (online) when you click Send, the message is sent immediately; otherwise it goes into the Outbox, to be delivered the next time you connect and check your email.

Tip: If you'd rather have Outlook Express dial the Internet and send a newly composed message every time you click Send, see page 281.

UP TO SPEED

Blind Carbon Copies

A *blind carbon copy* is a secret copy. This feature lets you send a copy of a message to somebody secretly, without any of the other recipients knowing that you did so. The names in the "To:" and "Cc:" fields appear at the top of the message for all recipients to see, but nobody can see the names you typed into the Bcc: box. To view this box, choose View→All Headers.

You can use the "Bcc:" field to quietly signal a third party that a message has been sent. For example, if you send your co-worker a message that says, "Chris, it bothers me that you've been cheating the customers," you could Bcc your boss or supervisor to clue her in without getting into trouble with Chris. (Note, however, that email is never completely "safe." A good rule to live by is never to say any-

thing in email that you want to remain a secret from someone else. It's *so* easy for your recipient to hit the Forward button and send the message on to someone you might not want it to go to.)

The Bcc box is useful in other ways, too. Perhaps you want to send email messages (containing jokes, for example) to a long list of recipients. Your recipients will have to scroll through a very long list of names if you've placed them in the "To:" or "Cc:" field.

But if you use the "Bcc:" field to hold all the recipients' email addresses, your recipients won't see any names but your own at the top of the email. (Unfortunately, spammers, those awful people who send you junk mail, have also learned this trick.)

The Drafts folder

Outlook Express lets you save an incomplete message as a *draft*, to be finished later. To do this, just close the message you've started composing. Outlook Express asks if you'd like to save changes to the message; click Yes. The message winds up in the Drafts folder.

To resume writing the message, go to the Drafts folder, open the message and continue writing. When you're finished, click the Send button.

Sending Mail Attachments

Sending text messages is fine, but it's not much help when you want to send some-body a photograph, a Word or Excel document, and so on. Fortunately, attaching such files to email messages is one of the world's most popular email features.

To attach a file to a message, click the Attach button on the message toolbar. When the Insert Attachment dialog box opens, navigate through the folders on your drive to locate the file and select it. The name of the attached file appears in the message in the Attach field. (You can repeat this process to send several attached files with the same message.) When you send the message, the file tags along.

If you have a high-speed connection like a cable modem, by the way, have pity on your recipient. A big picture or movie file might take you only seconds to send, but tie up your correspondent's modem for hours.

POWER USERS' CLINIC

Attaching Your Business Card to a Message

Besides attaching files, you can also attach an electronic business card to messages, giving the recipients a quick way of adding *all* of your contact information to their Address Books. Outlook Express sends business cards in the vCard format, which modern email programs (including Outlook Express, Outlook, Netscape Messenger, and Eudora) can read.

To set up the Business Card feature, display the Inbox, and then choose Tools→Options. Click the Compose tab. In the Business Cards section at the bottom of the dialog box, turn on the Mail checkbox, and then select your own name from the list box. (If you don't have a contact entry for

yourself, create one first.) After selecting your contact entry, clear the Mail checkbox unless you want to attach your business card to *all* outgoing mail messages (which you probably don't). Click OK.

To attach the business card to an individual message, in the message window, choose Insert→My Business Card. A small address card icon appears in the top right of the window, next to the "To:" or "From:" box (depending on your system).

When your message arrives in your colleagues' Inboxes, they can add it to their Address Books with only a couple of clicks (see Figure 12-8).

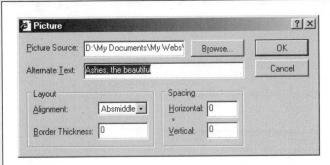

Figure 12-5:
Click the Insert Picture toolbar button to insert a picture in your message. Click Browse to locate the image file. Enter a text description of the image in the Alternate Text box; if recipient doesn't want to or can't download the image, she'll see this Alternate Text. The other text boxes specifies how text wraps around the image, the space and border you want, and so on.

Tip: If you can see the icon of the file you want to attach in its folder window behind the Outlook Express window, you can also attach it by *dragging* the icon directly into the message window.

Inserting Text and Images in a Message

Sometimes it's easier to insert some text or graphics directly into the body of a message than to attach a separate file. For example, you can insert text directly into a message from any text file or HTML file by choosing Insert→Text From File. As shown in Figure 12-5, you can even insert a picture into the body of your message.

Formatting Text

The vast majority of email messages sent today are still plain-text messages with no formatting, images, or color. Perhaps that's because people want to maintain compatibility with those less fortunate individuals with older email programs or palmtops, which may not be able to read HTML (formatted) messages. Or maybe it's because people appreciate the simple elegance of plain text. Of course, the real reason is probably that people don't know *how* to add formatting, or simply don't bother sprucing up their messages.

Figure 12-6:
Using the Formatting toolbar (in the middle of this window), you can change the font, size, and character formatting (bold, italics, or underlining) of highlighted text. You can also change the text color, add a numbered or bulleted list, or change indentation and alignment. To add a hyperlink, select the text you want to serve as the link, then click the Create a Hyperlink button (rightmost on the toolbar). To insert a horizontal line, click the toolbar button that's second from right.

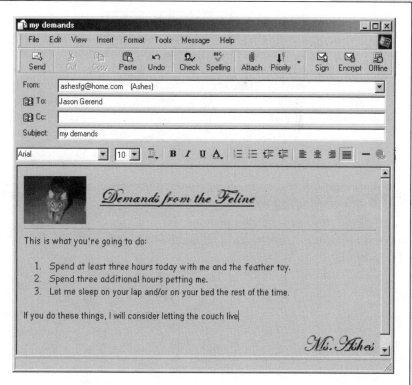

Whatever the reason, the bottom line is that formatted text in email is usually unnecessary, and occasionally annoying. However, when you think it's appropriate, text formatting can be a fun way to add a little creativity to your correspondence.

Using the formatting toolbar

If the Rich Text toolbar shown in Figure 12-6 isn't already visible, choose Format→Rich Text (HTML). Then, after highlighting some text in your message, use the formatting buttons and drop-down menus on the formatting strip, much as you would in a word processor.

Tip: Think twice before formatting your text with an obscure font; if your recipient doesn't have the font installed on their system a different font will be substituted.

You can even add a background image, sound, or colored backdrop for your message. To do so, use the submenu of the Format→Background command.

Turning off HTML formatting codes

If your recipient uses a very simple or very old email program, or a palmtop, you may get complaints about the HTML formatting codes that Outlook Express, by default, embeds in your outgoing messages.

Fortunately, Outlook Express lets you change the message format for an individual message, for all messages to a particular person, or for all outgoing messages. To change a message's format to plain text, in the message window, choose Format→Plain Text. To specify that a certain contact in your Address Book should always receive plain text messages, click the Addresses toolbar button in the main Outlook Express window, double-click the person's name, click the Name tab, and then select the "Send Email using plain text only" checkbox at the bottom of the tab.

And to change the default message format for *all* outgoing messages, see page 281.

POWER USERS' CLINIC

HTML Code in Email

If you know how to write HTML code, you can manually change the HTML markup for a message. Choose View→Source Edit. Voilà! You've just added three tabs at the bottom of the window—Edit, Source, and Preview.

The Edit tab is like a normal message window; the Source tab provides a color-coded display of the actual HTML markup, which you can edit; and the Preview tab shows what the message will look like to the recipient, and reflects changes to the code that you may have made that don't appear properly in the Edit tab, such as Dynamic HTML effects (if you're handy with *DHTML*, an HTML variant that gives greater control over the layout of page elements).

Using Stationery

Outlook Express's *stationery* provides another quick way to make messages a little more visually interesting (unfortunately, it can't do anything for the *content* of your messages). Much like the stationery you might buy at an office-supply store, Outlook Express's stationery can provide a pretty background or special fonts for your messages.

To choose the stationery you want to use for a new message, click the triangle next to the New Mail toolbar button and pick stationery from the list, or choose Select Stationery to view all stationery. In the Select Stationery dialog box, click a stationery icon to preview it, then click OK. (You can also use this dialog box to create or edit stationery.)

You can also apply stationery to a message you've already started writing. In the message window, use the submenu of the Format→Apply Stationery command to select the stationery you want. To create new stationery using the background of an existing message, select or open the message and then choose File→Save As Stationery.

Caution: Because stationery can make an email message much larger than a text-only message, it's considered impolite to use it in messages for mailing lists or news groups.

Note, too, that stationery relies on the HTML formatting feature described in the previous section; so certain email programs may display stationery codes as garbage symbols.

Using the Address Book

Unless you make a living counting cards at Vegas (and even if you do), you probably can't remember all the email addresses, phone numbers, and addresses in your social and business circles. Fortunately, Outlook Express comes with an Address Book that can store just about every bit of information about a person.

Figure 12-7:
On the left is the Folders and Groups pane, which shows your contacts (located in the Main Identity's Contacts folder), along with any groups or subfolders you've created. The right pane lists the contacts in the currently selected folder. Double-click a contact to view or edit the contact's information.

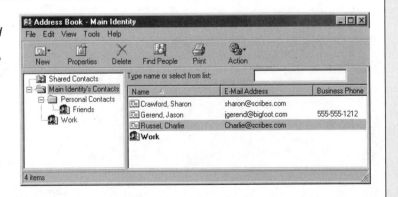

The easiest way to open the Address Book is to click the "To:" or "Cc:" button while composing a message. Doing so opens the Select Recipients dialog box, a stream-lined window, onto your Address Book.

The Select Recipients dialog box is useful when sending an email message; but to create new contacts, organize contacts, or look up information other than email addresses, you should use the full Address Book window. To open it, click the Addresses toolbar button in the main Outlook Express window, as shown in Figure 12-7, or choose Tools→Address Book, or press Ctrl+Shift+B.

Unfortunately, this feature doesn't always work as well as advertised; it often displays a map showing only the *city* of your contact. There's hope, however: Outlook 2000 exhibited this problem when it was first released, and Microsoft later fixed it, so the problem may disappear in subsequent revisions of Expedia Maps or Outlook Express.

You can sort the list either by clicking the appropriate list heading (such as Name or E-mail Address) or by using the View→Sort By submenu. (This submenu is where you'll find the much sought-after Sort By First Name and Sort By Last Name options.) The View menu also lets you change the contact display from detailed list form to a simple list, large icon, or small icon view.

Tip: You can make the Business Phone and Home Phone columns display other information, such as Company, Job Title, or Pager. Just right-click the heading itself (Business Phone or Home Phone) and choose the field you'd rather see from the shortcut menu.

Creating Contacts

By far the easiest way to create a contact is by receiving an electronic business card from the contact. All you have to do is click the address card icon in the upper right corner of the message window, choose Open from the pop-up menu, review the contact, and then close it.

The *next* easiest way to create a new contact is to grab the sender's email address from a message you've received, as shown in Figure 12-8.

GEM IN THE ROUGH

Mapping Street Addresses With Outlook Express

The version of Outlook Express that ships with Windows 2000 includes a feature that was once available only in Outlook 2000: a View Map button. When you click it, your PC connects to the Internet, opens Internet Explorer, and shows you an actual color map (courtesy of Expedia.com) that pinpoints your colleague's actual location. A "Get driv-

ing directions to this location" link appears just below the map, for added usefulness.

To use this feature, open your Address Book, open a contact, click the Home or Business tab (depending on which address you want to view), and then click the View Map button.

Tip: You can right-click on any message in your mail folders and choose Add To Address book to create a new contact for the sender without opening the message.

Of course, you can always create a contact from scratch, too. To do this, click the Addresses toolbar button in the main Outlook Express window, click the New toolbar

Figure 12-8:
Open a message from the person you want to add to the Address Book, right-click his name in the "From:" field of the message header, and choose Add To Address Book from the shortcut menu. Review the new contact, using the various tabs to enter any additional contact information, and click OK to save the contact.

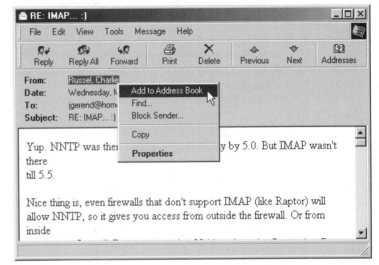

Figure 12-9:
In the E-Mail Addresses box, enter the email addresses for the contact, making sure to click the Add button after entering each address. Use the Edit and Remove buttons to modify or delete addresses you've already entered. Don't forget to indicate which one is the main email address by clicking it and then clicking the Set As Default button.

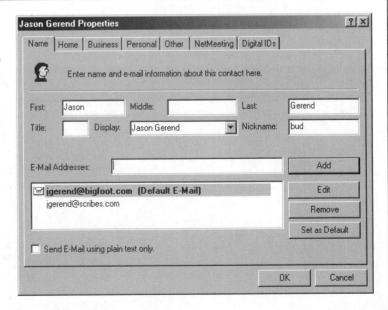

button in the Address Book window, and choose New Contact from the menu that appears. On the Name tab of the new contact (Figure 12-9), enter the contact's name as you want it to appear in your Address Book.

Use the Display box to control how the contact's name appears in the Address Book contact list; you can use one of Outlook Express's proposed variants (first/last, last/first, and so on), or you can type in whatever form you like. (The Display format you choose here overrides the Sort By First Name or Last Name setting of your master Address Book list.)

Tip: The Nickname box is a handy little feature that isn't included in Outlook 2000 (take that, Outlook!). Whenever you address a new message to the contact, you can simply type her nickname in the "To:" field; Outlook Express will fill in the rest.

The other tabs of this massive Contact Properties dialog box are straightforward. They include:

- **Home** and **Business**. Among other things, these tabs contain Web Page fields that you can use to enter the contact's personal and business Web site addresses.

- **NetMeeting.** On this tab, you can enter the person's online conferencing address, if they use Microsoft NetMeeting for Internet phone calls and video teleconferencing (see page 180). (You'll probably have to ask your contact for this information, or search for it using NetMeeting.)

- The **Digital IDs** tab is where you *could* associate a digital ID with the contact. Digital IDs let a sender place a digital signature on a message, to help you confirm that it wasn't sent by an imposter. However, you can only associate a digital ID with a contact if the contact already sent you an exported version of her digital ID. You could then highlight the associated email address, click Import, and se-

---

FREQUENTLY ASKED QUESTION

Identities and Shared Contacts

In my Address Book, I see a drop-down menu that lists something called Main Identity's Contacts. To the best of my knowledge, I have only one identity; what's that all about?

The Identities feature is designed to allow several people to use Outlook Express, each with his own Address Book and set of message folders. (You can create new Identities, and switch Identities, only if you open the Address Book by choosing Start→Programs→Accessories→Address Book; the feature is missing if you open the Address Book from within Outlook Express.)

You may also have noticed an Address Book category called Shared Contacts; that's where you can file names and addresses that you want to make available to all Outlook Express Identities in the current Windows 2000 user profile.

But on a Windows 2000 machine, all of this is almost entirely pointless; if you intend to share your Windows 2000 PC with someone else, you'll probably want to create a full user *account* for each person, as described on page 371. Doing so provides a more secure, simpler, and much more thorough system of keeping each person's PC settings (and Outlook Express environment) separate.

---

lect the digital ID file that the contact sent you and that you saved to your hard drive.

But why bother with this kind of hassle? To share her digital ID, all your colleague has to do is send you a signed message—much simpler. Her ID is then automatically added to her contact information when you open the message.

Creating Groups of Contacts

If you find yourself often sending to a certain group of people—your family or your friends, for example—you can create a *group*. Thereafter, you can send a message to all members of the group by choosing the group's name from the Address Book.

To create a group, open the Address Book, click the New toolbar button, and choose New Group from the menu that appears. Type a name for the group in the Group Name box, and then click Select Members to add existing contacts to the Group.

In most respects, groups work just like a single contact. To send an email to a group, simply enter the group's name in the "To:" box of an outgoing message, or choose it from the Select Recipients dialog box. To view a group's properties, double-click its name in the Address Book. Groups differentiate themselves visually, however: In the Address Book, you don't see an email address for a group, and its name appears in bold with a slightly different contact icon.

Finding People

Sometimes you can't find the contacts you're looking for. Maybe you have a giant Address Book; maybe they just aren't in your Address Book. In any case, Outlook Express provides a Find People tool designed explicitly for this situation.

WORKAROUND WORKSHOP

Excluding Group Members from a Message

While Groups are great, they can present an awkward problem: Suppose you want to send a message to everyone in a group *except* one or two people.

You could make a new group with only the people you want in it, but if you intend to send only a single message with these addressees, that would be overkill. You could skip using the group address altogether, and manually add each person to the recipient list, but that's hardly efficient (especially if you don't remember everybody who's in the group or if it contains a large number of contacts).

If you find yourself in this predicament often, consider creating a separate *folder* in your Address Book for the members of a group. (To do so, open your Address Book and

choose File→New Folder; give the new folder a name. Then drag names from your Main Identity list onto the new folder icon—or, if you'd like these names to appear *both* in the folder and in the main list, right-click each name and use the Copy command in the shortcut menu. Click the folder, right-click the empty list, and choose Paste from the shortcut menu. Repeat as necessary.)

In addition to placing the contacts in the Group, place the members of the group in this new folder. Then, when you want to send a message only to some of the people in the group, you can click the "To:" button in your mail message, select the group's folder from the Main Identity's Contacts box, and then choose only the names of people you want to receive the message.

To open the Find People tool, use the Find drop-down menu on the toolbar in the main Outlook Express window, then choose People from the menu that appears (or click the Find People button on the toolbar in the Address Book window). For details on using these dialog box to find an email address or other contact information, see page 43.

Deleting and Organizing Contacts

Your Address Book may eventually get cluttered, especially if you don't turn off the slightly-to-extremely annoying Outlook Express feature that adds everyone you write to your Address Book. (To learn how to disable this feature, see page 281.) There are two ways to deal with this clutter: delete contacts, or organize them into folders.

To delete a contact, group, or folder from the Address Book, click its name and click the Delete toolbar button; click Yes in the confirmation box. (It doesn't go to the Deleted Items folder; it's gone for good.)

FREQUENTLY ASKED QUESTION

Canning Spam

Help! I'm awash in junk email! How do I get out of this mess?

Spam, besides being a convenient and tasty meat-like product, is a much-derided form of advertising that involves sending unsolicited emails to thousands, even millions of people. While there's no pleasant or instant cure for spam, you can take certain steps to protect yourself from it.

1. If you have more than one email account, consider using one just for online shopping, Website and software registration, and newsgroup posting. Spammers have automated software robots that scour every *public* Internet message and Web page, automatically locating and recording email addresses they find. These are the primary sources of spam, so at least you're now restricting the junk mail to one, secondary mail account.

2. When filling out forms or registering products online, always look for checkboxes requesting permission for the company to send you email or share your email address with its "partners." Just say no.

3. When posting messages in a newsgroup, insert the letters NOSPAM somewhere in your email address in the News Account Properties dialog box (page 272). Anyone replying to you via email must manually remove the NOSPAM from your email address, which is a slight hassle; but meanwhile, the spammers' software robots (which aren't very bright) will lift a bogus email address from newsgroup posts.

4. Create *message rules* filtering out messages containing typical advertising words such as *casino, guaranteed, loan,* and so forth. (You'll find instructions in this chapter.)

5. Turn on any junk mail filters available with your email account. For example, Hotmail provides an Inbox Protector that screens a large amount of spam into a separate Bulk Mail folder.

6. If you really have a spam problem, get a new mail address. Give it to people you trust; use the old address only for junk mail, and check it for messages only infrequently.

If you have a lot of contacts, or if you'd like to maintain separate groups of contacts (such as work contacts and personal contacts), consider creating *folders* inside the Address Book. To do so, open the Address Book, choose New→Folder, type a name for the folder, click OK, and then drag names from the main Address Book list onto the newly created folder icon.

Be aware, however, that each folder appears to Outlook Express as a separate Address Book. For example, when using the Select Recipients dialog box to look in the Address Book for someone, you may not find the name of someone you *know* you've entered; in that case, you probably need to select a different folder from the drop-down list box at the top of the dialog box.

Handling Large Amounts of Email

As email has become a more important means of communication, the messages many people receive have escalated greatly. Some of it is junk mail, also known as *spam*.

Outlook Express provides useful weapons in the fight against email overload—message rules, multiple mail folders, customized folder views that show only key messages, and the ability to search for messages in your mail folders.

Organizing Messages

There may come a time when you realize that there are more messages in your inbox than dollars in your checking account. This is usually a good time to create some additional folders to store your messages (or get a better job).

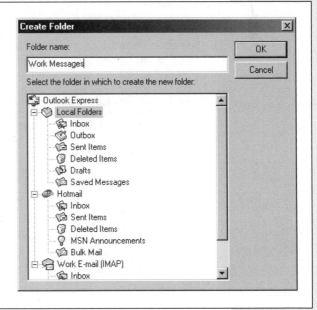

Figure 12-10:
To create an email folder, right-click an existing folder and then choose New Folder from the shortcut menu. In the Create Folder dialog box, type a name for your new folder, and then click OK. To move a folder into another folder, drag it from its current location in the Folders pane on top of any other folder.

Many people create individual folders for work mail, friends and family messages, junk mail, and sometimes forwarded jokes. (Depending on your friends, you may receive a lot of these.) Figure 12-10 shows the procedure for creating new folders. The most powerful way to use these folders that you create is in combination with Message Rules, discussed next.

To move messages out of the Inbox into one of your homemade folders, just drag them onto the folder's icon. To *copy* the message(s) to another folder, right-click them, choose Copy To Folder from the shortcut menu, select the folder you want to copy the messages to, and then click OK.

Tip: You can place folders inside other folders to further subdivide messages. For example, in the Work folder you might have a separate folder for each of your current projects.

Processing Email with Message Rules

You can configure Outlook Express to process your email automatically, sorting messages into different folders, replying or forwarding messages, or deleting messages, among other things. This ability is extremely useful for people who have to process a lot of email.

Creating a message rule

To create an email message-processing rule, while viewing your Inbox (Figure 12-11, top), choose Tools→Message Rules→Mail. Then:

1. **Use the top options to specify how Outlook Express should select messages to process.**

   For example, you may want to use the "Where the From line contains people" option to process only messages from a certain group of people, such as your co-workers. To flag messages containing *loan, $$$$, XXXX, !!!!,* and so on, use the "Where the Subject line contains specific words" option.

2. **Specify *which* words or people you want the message rule to watch out for.**

   In Box #3 of this dialog box, you see a summary of the rule you're building. Click on a hyperlink (such as "Where the From line <u>contains people</u>") to fill in additional information, such as the addresses or Subject-line words to watch out for. Enter the name for your rule in the last box and then click OK.

3. **In the second list box, choose the actions you want to perform on messages that match the criteria.**

   If, in Steps 1 and 2, you've told your rule to watch for junk mail containing *$$$$* in the Subject line, here's where you can tell Outlook Express to "Delete it" or "Move it to the specified folder" (a Possible Spam folder, for example).

4. In the bottom box, name your mail rule. Click OK.

Now the Message Rules dialog box appears (Figure 12-11, bottom). Here, you can manage the rules you've created, choose a sequence for them (those at the top get applied first), and apply them to existing messages.

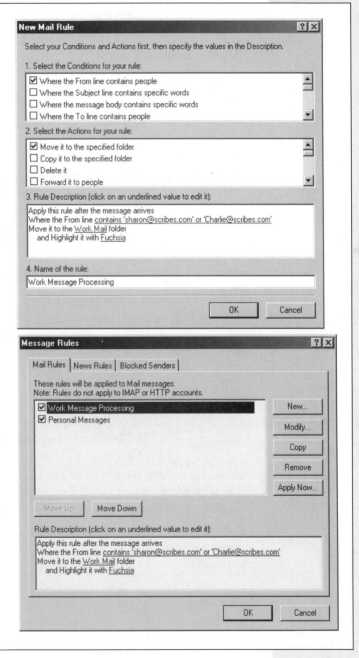

Figure 12-11:
Top: Mail rules can screen out junk mail, serve as an email answering machine, and call important messages to your attention.

Bottom: All mail rules you've created appear on the Mail Rules tab. Select a rule to see what it does, and use the Move Up and Move Down buttons to specify the order in which rules should be run. Click New to create additional rules. Click Modify to change the currently selected rule, or use the Copy button to create a copy of the rule, which you can then adjust. Select a rule and click Remove to delete the rule, or clear the checkbox next to the rule to simply disable it.

To run a rule on messages you've already received, click the Apply Now button, select the rules you want to run, click the Browse button to choose what folder to run the rule(s) on, and then click Apply Now.

Two sneaky message-rule tricks

You can use message rules for many different purposes. But here are two of the best:

- **Create a spam filter.** When a spammer sends out junk email, he usually puts your address on the "Bcc:" (blind carbon copy) line, so that you can't see who else got the message. This characteristic makes it easy for you to screen out such mail; create a message rule that looks for messages "Where the To or CC line contains people [*your* address]"—and files them into the Inbox as usual.

  But then create another message rule "For all messages" that puts messages into a folder called Possible Spam. Because the second rule doesn't kick in until *after* the first one has done its duty, the second rule affects only messages in which your name appeared on the "Bcc:" line (which is almost always spam). Once a week, you can look through the Possible Spam folder in case a legitimate message found its way there.

- **The email answering machine.** If you're going to be on vacation, turn on "For all messages" in Step 1, and then "Reply with message" in Step 3. In other words, you can turn Outlook Express into an email answering machine that automatically sends a canned "I'm away until the 15th" message to everyone who writes you.

Tip: Be sure to unsubscribe from any email lists before you do this; otherwise, you'll incur the wrath of the other Internet citizens by littering their email discussion groups with copies of your auto-reply message.

Blocking Messages from Specific People

Besides creating message rules, you can also block messages from individual senders. To do this, select a message from the person you want to block in the message list; then choose Message→Block Sender command. Outlook Express asks if you want to remove all messages you've already received from this person; click Yes, if you like.

To view the list of blocked senders, choose Tools→Message Rules→Blocked Senders. In the Blocked Senders tab of the Message Rules dialog box, you can turn on individual checkboxes that block mail and news messages from each person.

Note: Message rules and blocked senders in Outlook Express don't work with IMAP folders or Web-based mail accounts (such as Hotmail). Consider switching to Outlook if these features are important to you (although even Outlook doesn't work with Web-based mail accounts).

If you're using Hotmail, be aware of the fact that Hotmail has a blocked senders feature that is available from its Web site, as well as a handy Bulk Mail folder that intercept all mass-mailings—which are almost always junk mail.

Using Views

Another way of dealing with a large amount of email is to customize your *view* of the messages—a drastically underused Outlook Express feature. Views help you deal with large amounts of email by hiding some messages from view. For example, Outlook Express is happy to show you *only* messages that you haven't yet read, or that the sender marked Priority 1, or that came from people at work. See Figure 12-12 for an example of views in action.

Tip: The View→Current View→Group Messages By Conversation command is extremely useful—an excellent way to help organize your messages. It collapses each stream of back-and-forth email discussion on particular topic ("Re: Design suggestions") into a single "message" in your Inbox. A + button appears beside it; click that button to "expand" the heading into an indented list of all messages in that "thread."

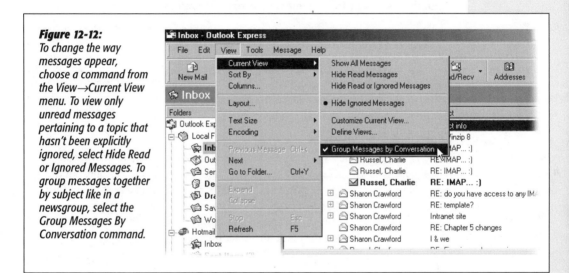

Figure 12-12:
To change the way messages appear, choose a command from the View→Current View menu. To view only unread messages pertaining to a topic that hasn't been explicitly ignored, select Hide Read or Ignored Messages. To group messages together by subject like in a newsgroup, select the Group Messages By Conversation command.

Defining custom views

As shown in Figure 12-12, Outlook Express comes with several useful canned views. But in times of email overflow, you can create your own custom filters, too. Here's how it goes:

1. **Choose View→Current View→Define Views.**

   The Define Views dialog box appears; if you've worked with message rules, as described in the previous section, these options should look distinctly familiar. Here's where you create new views, modify existing views, or delete unneeded views.

2. **In the first box, select the conditions messages must meet to be displayed or hidden.**

   For example, if you want your view to show only messages that are older than three days old (and therefore deserve your attention first), select "Where the message was sent more than days ago."

3. **In the second box, click any underlined words to fill in the necessary information.**

   For example, to hide messages about a specific subject, select "Where the Subject line contains specific words" in the first section, click <u>contains specific words</u> in the second section, and enter words you want Outlook Express to watch for.

4. **In the second box, specify whether you want the messages you've described to be hidden or shown.**

   Do so by clicking the <u>Show/Hide</u> link.

5. **In the last box, enter a name for the new view, and then click OK.**

   Your new view is ready to use; just choose its name from the View→Current View submenu.

Tip: The Views toolbar lets you quickly switch views. To make this toolbar appear, right-click the Outlook Express toolbar and choose Views Bar from the shortcut menu.

Searching for Messages

Finding a specific message in an overcrowded Inbox can be tricky. You can always sort the messages by sender, subject, or date to help find a key message, but this can only help so much. A more powerful way to locate a key message is to use Outlook Express's built-in Find Message capability. You can search for messages according to several criteria: who sent them, text in the "Subject:" line, when they were sent or received, whether or not they had file attachments, and so on.

Tip: One of the most useful elements of the Find Message feature is the Message box. If you can't remember a message's subject or sender's email address, but you *do* remember what it was about, you can search for words *inside the message* by typing them into the Message box.

This kind of search takes a long time, especially if you're searching your entire message collection. But in a pinch, it can pluck an important needle out of your correspondence haystack.

Reading Newsgroups

Newsgroups are Internet bulletin boards. There are over 30,000 of them, on every conceivable topic: pop culture, computers, politics, and every other special (and *very* special) interest. You can use Outlook Express to read and reply to these messages almost exactly as though they're email messages.

Setting Up a News Account

To set up Outlook Express for reading newsgroups, choose Tools→Accounts, then click the News tab. When you click Add→News, you'll be launched into a newsgroup-specific version of the Internet Connection Wizard. You'll be asked for the name you want to use when posting messages (usually your real name), the email address you want stamped on your newsgroup postings (see page 266 for some antispam techniques), and your *news server* information—an address (provided by your ISP or network administrator) that tells Outlook Express how to connect to the Internet's newsgroups.

When you click Close, Outlook Express offers to download the entire list of newsgroups (Figure 12-13, top). If you click Yes, your PC connects to the Internet and downloads the complete list of newsgroup names—all 30,000 of them. (If you connect by modem, this process takes a minute or two, as you can imagine.) As shown in Figure 12-13 (bottom), you wind up in the Newsgroup Subscriptions dialog box, where the complete list awaits your perusal.

Finding Newsgroups and Messages

If you know the name of a particular newsgroup, you can use the "Display newsgroups" search box at the top of the Newsgroup Subscriptions dialog box to located it by name, as shown in Figure 12-13.

Tip: A better way to locate newsgroups and messages is to use the *deja.com* newsgroup search engine. Use Internet Explorer to visit *www.deja.com/usenet,* where the searching tools are far superior to those in Outlook Express.

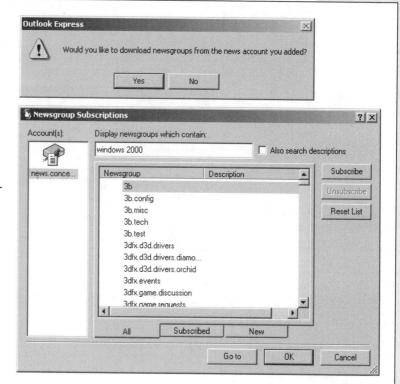

Figure 12-13:
Top: After you create a newsgroup account, Outlook Express offers to fetch the list of every newsgroup on the Internet.

Bottom: In the box, enter the text you want to look for in the newsgroup's title (such as windows 2000, *as shown here). If you turn up an appealing-sounding topic in the gigantic list beneath, double-click its name to subscribe to it, so that Outlook Express will download the latest messages on that topic each time you connect.*

Reading and Downloading Messages

When you click OK, you return to the main Outlook Express screen. At the left side of the window, under the heading bearing the name of your newsgroup server, you'll see the names of the newsgroups you double-clicked in the previous step.

The next time you connect to the Internet, Outlook Express downloads all of the messages in the discussions to which you've subscribed. (There may be just a few messages, or several hundred; they may go back only a few days or a couple of weeks, depending on how much "traffic" there is in each discussion.)

To read the messages on one of these topics, click its name, as shown in Figure 12-14. At this point, you can read them exactly as though they're email messages.

Tip: If there's a *thread* (series of messages on the same subject) that you want to monitor, click in the eyeglasses column (Figure 12-14). An eyeglasses icon appears next to the name of the thread. When Internet citizens post new messages in the thread, its name (and the newsgroup name in the Folders list) turns red. To *ignore* a thread, on the other hand, click in the eyeglasses column twice to display a red circle next to the topic. Now Outlook Express won't waste time downloading messages on that topic each time you connect.

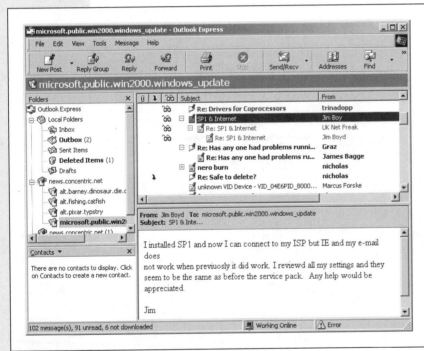

Figure 12-14:
Select the news-group you want to view from your list of subscribed news-groups in the Folders list (you may need to click on the + sign next to your news server first). Reading newsgroup mes-sages is just like reading email in Outlook Express: Select a message to display it in the Preview pane, or double-click a message to open it in a separate window.

Working Offline

If you connect to the Internet using a standard modem, you can download all of the latest newsgroup messages in one fell swoop, disconnect, and then read the messages at your leisure without tying up the phone line.

To do this, click a newsgroup's name in your Folder list. Once Outlook Express is finished downloading the *headers* (subject lines) for all the messages, choose File→Work Offline to disconnect from the Internet. Then take your time reviewing the message headers. Whenever you find one that looks interesting, click in the column labeled with an arrow; a downward-facing arrow appears next to the message's name (see Figure 12-14). You've just marked it for downloading later. Mark all the messages you want to read in this way.

When you're ready to download them, choose Tools→Synchronize Newsgroup, select "Get messages marked for download," click OK, and then click Yes when asked if you'd like to go online. Outlook Express connects to the Internet and downloads the messages you selected.

Tip: Marking messages for downloading is useful even if you stay online. Some messages take a long time to download, and you may find it handy to download the messages all at once, so you don't have to wait while each message you want to read downloads.

Replying, Composing, and Forwarding Messages

Working with newsgroup messages is very similar to working with email messages. For example:

- To reply to a message, select or open it. Then click either the Reply Group toolbar button (to post a reply on the newsgroup for all the Internet to see), or the Reply toolbar button (to send a private email message to the author of the post). Compose the message and click Send when you're finished.

- To forward a message, select or open it. Then click the Forward toolbar button. Compose the message; click Send.

- To compose a new message, click the New Post toolbar button. You can include file attachments, too (use the Attach toolbar button). Compose the message; click Send.

Tip: The best way to irritate everyone on a newsgroup (other than spamming the newsgroup with advertisements) is to ask a question that has already been answered recently on the newsgroup. Before asking a question, spend five minutes reading the recent newsgroup messages to see if someone has already answered the question. Also consider visiting *www.deja.com,* a Web site that lets you search all newsgroups for particular topics.

Customizing Outlook Express

Fooling around with email is a time-honored time-waster. However, some of Outlook Express's options can actually be time-*savers*, including custom signatures, junk mail filters, and so on. This section covers a few of the ways you can bend the program to your will.

Managing Mail Accounts

As noted at the beginning of this chapter, Outlook Express can handle multiple email accounts. You might have one email address provided by your company, another by your ISP, and a third by Hotmail. To manage settings for your various mail accounts, choose Tools→Accounts, and then click the Mail tab (Figure 12-15).

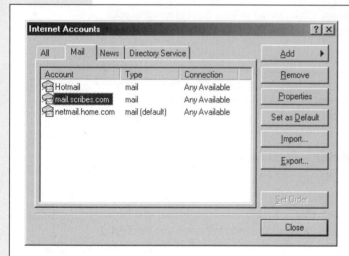

Figure 12-15:
To change the default account used when sending email, click the account you want and then click Set as Default. To export the settings for a mail account, making it quick and easy to setup the mail account again on a different computer, select the account, click the Export button, and then use the Export Internet Account dialog box to save the account settings to disk. Use the Import button to import previously exported settings.

The gateway to the account-fiddling screen is the Properties button. It summons a dialog box that offers five screens full of settings, which are described in the following sections.

General tab

The General tab, shown in Figure 12-16, is where you modify the name and email address used with the account.

If you don't want Outlook Express to check this account's mail every time you check your email, clear the "Include this account when receiving mail or synchronizing" checkbox. You can still check the email for this account manually whenever you like, just by using the Send/Recv toolbar button's drop-down menu. In the meantime, however, you save yourself some time by omitting accounts you don't need checked every day.

Servers tab

Use the boxes provided here to verify or change your mail server settings (see page 248).

Tip: If your outgoing mail server requires you to log on, use the Outgoing Mail Server section of the Server tab to configure the logon process. This requirement is not common, however.

Figure 12-16:
On the General tab, you can edit the name that Outlook Express gives this email account. (It can be anything you like.) The Name box stores the name you used to set up the account (usually your real name). The email address you enter on the General tab is the address that recipients will see; if they decide to add you to their address books, this is the email address they'll get.

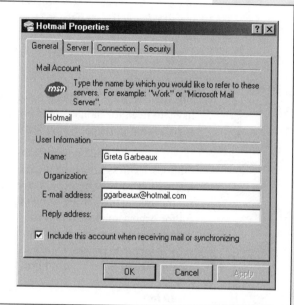

Connection tab

Use this tab to specify how the account should connect to the Internet (if, indeed, you have more than one method available). Your choices might be your ISP, your corporate network, and so on. If you need to always use a specific method of connecting to the Internet—perhaps because your work email is only available when you're connected to your company's network—select this checkbox and then choose that connection method from the drop-down menu.

To allow the account to connect using any available connection, on the other hand, clear the "Always connect to this account using" checkbox.

Security tab

Email isn't the most secure way of corresponding. Anyone can pretend to be someone else simply by changing the mail software's Name and Email address settings; and determined hackers can easily intercept and read email messages.

For most people, this theoretical vulnerability really isn't a problem. Deviant individuals usually have better things to do than pretend to be your mother on email or to intercept and read sappy love letters and boring work mail. However, there are times when security is important. Maybe you want to send someone your credit-card information by email (which, by the way, is not a good idea) or sensitive work information. Or perhaps you need to assure to your recipient that you are indeed who you claim to be. In these situations, you should consider using Outlook Express's *message encryption* and *digital signatures* features. (The rest of the time, don't bother.)

This advanced tab lets you configure how this email account sends digitally signed or encrypted email. Before you can configure these settings, you need to acquire and install a *digital ID* (see page 367); then click the Select button in the Signing Certificate section to choose that ID when sending digitally signed messages with this account. Use the Algorithm box to select the encryption algorithm to use, if necessary.

Advanced tab

The Advanced tab (not present for a Hotmail account) includes settings you're un-likely to need to change; for example, the Outgoing Mail and Incoming Mail boxes specify what ports your mail server uses.

If you encounter bad connections or slow servers, the Server Timeouts slider tells Outlook Express how long it should wait before giving up when checking or send-ing mail. If you frequently get error messages reporting that the server "timed out," try increasing this setting to two minutes or more. Another setting that can be use-ful for ornery mail servers is the "Break apart messages larger," which breaks large messages into smaller chunks, to accommodate mail servers that refuse to send or receive larger messages. (Such servers typically choke at 64 KB or 1 MB, but you might have to experiment to find the optimal setting.)

IMAP tab

If your mail server is an IMAP server, you'll find this additional tab in the mail account's Properties dialog box. Use it to change how Outlook Express deals with special IMAP folders. For example:

- **Root Folder Path** specifies the folder on the server that contains all your mail folders. You generally leave it blank, but if you can't find your mail folders, ask your administrator or ISP what the correct setting should be.

- **Check for new messages in all folders.** Remember that if you have an IMAP ac-count, a distant computer on the Internet actually stores your messages, in fold-ers that you've created there. If you receive new mail only in your Inbox folder and don't need Outlook Express to check your other folders, you can clear this checkbox to reduce the amount of time it takes to check your mail.

- **Store special folders on IMAP server.** Outlook Express generally stores the Sent Items and Drafts folders on the IMAP server, too, so that you can look up previ-ously sent messages and message drafts from anywhere you can access your ac-count. If you don't want to store these folders on the server (to save disk space there, for example), clear this checkbox. Or, if you prefer, you can specify different folders to hold these messages by editing the Sent Items Path and Drafts Path boxes.

Customizing Outlook Express's Interface

Outlook Express's interface is well designed; but on the grounds that it-takes-all-kinds, Microsoft offers you the flexibility to make a few modifications. You can customize Outlook Express's toolbar, change which panes of the Outlook Express window show up, or modify the Preview pane.

Editing toolbars and panes

While Outlook Express's toolbars are well designed for most people, you may find that with a little customization, you can make them work even better for yourself. To customize Outlook Express's toolbar, right-click it and choose Customize from the shortcut menu; as you'll quickly discover, the dialog box that lets you add or remove Outlook Express toolbar buttons is the same one you use to edit toolbars in desktop folder windows. See page 237 for details.

To show or hide Outlook Express's various windowpanes, or to change how the Preview pane works, choose View→Layout (Figure 12-17).

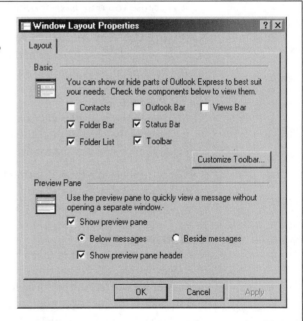

Figure 12-17:
In the first part of the Window Layout Properties dialog box, select which panes of the interface you want to display. To change how the Preview pane is displayed, use the checkboxes and option buttons in the Preview pane section; click OK when you're done.

Changing General Options

Most of the options in the Tools→Options dialog box are self-explanatory, but here are a few that are tricky and/or especially useful:

- **When starting, go directly to my 'Inbox' folder.** Skips the Outlook Express summary view when opening the program.

- **Notify me if there are any new newsgroups.** Whenever you check for new newsgroup messages, you'll be notified if there are any new newsgroups. (There almost always are.)

- **Send and receive messages at startup.** Makes Outlook Express check for new mail as soon as you open the program. If you have a dialup connection, you may well want to turn this option off, so that you can read and write some messages before connecting to the Internet.

- **Check for new messages every __.** Controls whether or not Outlook Express intermittently checks for new messages automatically, and if so, how often. If you're online all the time (you lucky cable modem, DSL, or corporate network member), by all means, let Outlook Express keep your Inbox frequently updated. Otherwise, use the drop-down list box to control how often, if ever, Outlook Express should connect to the Internet unbidden.

- **Make default.** To make Outlook Express the default mail or news program, use the Make Default buttons at the bottom of the General tab. (If they're dimmed, it's because you only *have* one mail or newsreading program.)

Changing the Way Messages Are Read and Sent

The following list presents some of the noteworthy options you may want to change on the Read, Send, Receipts, and Connection tabs of the Tools→Options dialog box.

On the Read tab

- **Mark message read after displaying for __.** This option marks a message as having been read—changing its typeface from bold to not bold—if you leave it highlighted in the message list for five seconds or more, even without opening it.

- **Get __ headers at a time.** Controls how many newsgroup message headers Outlook Express downloads at each connection. If you have a high-speed Internet connection, you may want to increase this setting to, for example, 1000.

Receipts tab

Use these options to request that a receipt be emailed to you when your outbound messages are read. Note that this is somewhat of an imposition on your recipients' privacy; most will feel uncomfortable sending back such a receipt if they don't plan to respond to the message promptly. (Furthermore, this feature works only if the recipient's email program offers a similar feature; Outlook Express, Outlook, and Eudora all do.)

You can also control how Outlook Express responds to receipts requested of *you* on this tab.

Send tab

- **Save copy of sent messages in the 'Sent Items' folder.** Keeps a copy of each message you send.

- **Send messages immediately.** If this checkbox is on, Outlook Express connects to the Internet and sends each new message the instant you click the Send button. That's fine if you have a high-speed, full-time Internet connection. But if you have a standard modem, you might wish you didn't have to wait while your PC dials and connects each time you finish writing a message.

  If you clear this checkbox, clicking the Send button places a new outgoing message into your Outbox. There it will sit until you click the Send/Recv button, whereupon Outlook Express will send *all* waiting messages.

- **Automatically put people I reply to in my Address Book.** Every time you send a reply to someone, Outlook Express adds that person's name and email address to your Address Book. This feature can fill up your Address Book with superfluous email addresses; you may want to turn off this option.

- **Include message in reply.** When you click the Reply button, Outlook Express generally pastes the original message at the bottom of your reply, to help your correspondent remember what she'd said originally. If you're trying to keep your messages small, you can turn off this option.

- **Mail Sending Format and News Sending Format.** These sections control the default message format you use for email and newsgroup posts, as described on page 259. Plain Text is best for News messages; HTML message format is a safe choice for email correspondence. (As noted on page 259, you can always switch to the other format on a message-by-message basis.)

Connection tab

- **Hang up after sending and receiving.** Makes Outlook Express disconnect from the Internet after checking messages. This feature ensures that you won't accidentally leave the phone line tied up all day, but also means that you can't continue to browse the Web on the same call.

- **Ask before switching dial-up connections.** This option is for people who have set up several different dial-up connections (see page 311). It ensures that Outlook Express won't disconnect one call, just so it can dial another to check email.

Creating Signatures

Adding an automatic signature to your mail can save you considerable time. For business messages, you can include your name, title, company, telephone number, and so forth. You can have a different signature for personal mail. In fact, you can have as many signatures as you like, and switch among them as necessary.

To create and manage signatures, select Tools→Options, and then click the Signatures tab. To create the signature, see Figure 12-18.

Then, if you'd like the signature stamped at the bottom of every outgoing message automatically, turn on "Add signatures to all outgoing messages"; if you like, clear the "Don't add signatures to replies and forwards" checkbox.

You can even set up a different default signature for each of your mail accounts. To do so, select a signature, click the Advanced button, and then select the appropriate email accounts.

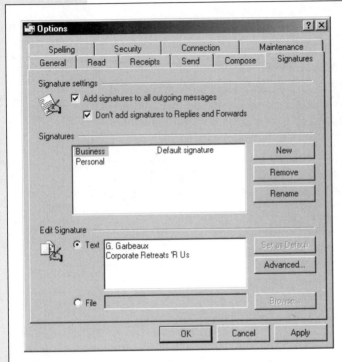

Figure 12-18:
Click the New button in the Signatures section to create a new signature. In the Text box at the bottom of the dialog box, enter the text you want to use as a signature, or choose the File option to use an HTML or text file as your signature. Use the Rename and Remove buttons to manage your signatures. To choose a default signature, select it from the list of signatures and then click Set as Default.

Tip: You can also attach an electronic business card with outgoing messages. To do this, use the Business Cards section of the Compose tab to include your contact information (attached as a industry-standard vCard file) with email. By the way: It's not polite to include a business card with newsgroup posts.

Cleaning Up Outlook Express Files

If a lot of mail or newsgroup messages pass through your copy of Outlook Express, you'll occasionally need to pay attention to maintenance chores such as emptying the Deleted Items folder, compacting your messages, or deleting downloaded messages.

To perform these tasks, choose Tools→Option from the Tools; click the Maintenance tab. This tab lets you configure how Outlook Express maintains itself by deleting old email and newsgroup messages, for example.

Backing Up Messages

While it's important to regularly back up all files on your computer (see Chapter 18), it's *very* important to back up the files that you really care about—such as your documents and email messages.

You can back up your Outlook Express messages and Address Book either by using a backup program such as the one described in Chapter 18 or by manually copying Outlook Express folders onto a Zip disk or CD.

To perform the latter kind of backup, follow these steps

1. **Choose Tools→Options from the Tools menu, click the Maintenance tab, and then click the Store Folder button.**

   The Store Location dialog box appears, showing you (in the form of a Windows *path)* where your messages are stored.

2. **Highlight the entire folder path.**

   Do that by clicking at the very left of the path and dragging the cursor carefully all the way to the right end of the text.

3. **Press Ctrl+C to copy the path to the Clipboard. Click OK, and then open Windows Explorer.**

   See page 86 for more on opening Explorer.

4. **Click in the Address box to select the current address, press Ctrl+V, and then press Enter.**

   You've just pasted the path of, and then jumped to, the folder containing all of your mail and news data.

5. **To backup your data, drag this folder to your backup location (such as a Zip disk or network drive).**

   Alternatively, open your backup program and use it to backup this folder.

Tip: You don't have to keep your Outlook Express messages in the folder suggested by the program. You can choose any folder to hold them. In Outlook Express, choose Options→Tools, click the Store Folder button on the Maintenance tab, click the Change button, and then select a different folder. Click each OK button to resurface.

Part Four:
Network Survival

4

Working on the Network

S ooner or later, almost everyone who uses Windows 2000 Professional is con-nected to a network. It may be a giant corporate network with hundreds or thousands of computers, a smaller "workgroup" network in a small business, or an even smaller network that connects two or three computers in your home so that they can share your Internet connection and printer. In each case, Windows 2000 is an excellent choice for networking, thanks to its reliability (you rarely have to run around the office to restart a crashed PC) and security features.

The biggest advantage of a network is that it can improve efficiency by letting you share files, folders, printers, and other resources. Networking also helps to prevent lost data, because it's so easy to back up your files onto different computers.

The biggest *dis*advantage of networking is the risk of security problems: Once files and folders become available to any computer on the network, you have to take care to ensure that only appropriate individuals can access them; see Chapter 17 for more on security options. The other unfortunate aspect of networking is that its configu-ration, terminology, and troubleshooting can be extremely complex.

Note: This chapter is called *Working* on the Network, not *Building* a Network. Corporate Windows 2000 networks generally rely on Windows 2000 *Server,* installed by networking professionals. This chapter cov-ers using a network that somebody else has designed and installed.

There is a kind of network you can create on your own, however—a smaller one that doesn't require Windows 2000 Server. Chapter 15 offers step-by-step instructions.

Navigating Your Network

The primary purpose of a network is the sharing of files, folders, disks, and printers. Before the invention of Local Area Networks (LANs), you had to move files from computer to computer using floppy disks (a method called a *sneakernet* due to its reliance on good footwear). A LAN lets network citizens share several different components of its computers, including files and folders, disks, and printers.

So that computer professionals won't go quietly insane repeatedly saying "files, folders, disks, and printers" when discussing networking, they use the collective term *resources*. And once they've made one of these resources available to the network, they call it a *shared resource*—or just *share* for short.

Figure 13-1:
Double-click My Network Places to open this window. At the very least, you'll find the Add Network Place and Entire Network icons. If you're a member of a workgroup, you'll also see Computers Near Me. You (or your network administrator) may have added shortcuts to other computers to this window, too.

UP TO SPEED

Networking Terminology

As you learn more about networks, you'll hear certain technical terms with increasing frequency. For example:

Client/Server Network (Domain). This is the biggest and, in the business world, most common kind of network. It requires at least one central server (called a domain controller) that maintains the master list of accounts, passwords, and access privileges (who's allowed to use which resources on the network). The other computers on the network (the clients) look to the domain controller for information on passwords, group memberships, and other security information. From your own PC, you can still control who on the network is allowed to see your various files and folders, as described later in this chapter.

Peer-to-Peer Network (Workgroup). In this arrangement, there's no server machine on the network; or, to be more precise, every computer is both a client and a server. Each computer manages its own security and user list. This kind of network is popular in small businesses and homes, both because it's less complicated to set up and because it's less expensive (you don't have to buy a server computer that nobody can actually use to run applications). Setting up a peer-to-peer network is covered in Chapter 15.

Remote Network. In this scheme, you connect to a network from a distant location, whether it's the Internet, a local area network (LAN) at your office, or any other network that you use intermittently. Getting and using access to a remote network is described in Chapter 14.

My Network Places

The icon on your desktop called My Network Places (Figure 13-1) is the gateway to the other computers and devices on the network. Double-click it to browse, search, and bookmark shared drives, folders, Web pages, and printers.

FREQUENTLY ASKED QUESTION

Computers Near Me

What are the "computers near me"? An icon by that name shows up in my Network Places window.

When you're part of a workgroup (as opposed to a domain), Windows 2000 Pro adds an icon to My Network Places called Computers Near Me. (If your PC is part of a domain, you don't see this icon.)

The Computers Near Me icon is a convenient time-saver.

When you open Computers Near Me, you see icons only for the computers in your own workgroup. You don't see any other computers on your network, including PCs in other domains or workgroups. Microsoft assumes that you'll do most of your collaborating with people whose computers are in your workgroup, and that they're physically closer to you than other computers on the network. That second assumption is questionable, but generally true.

Getting to the shared resource you want involves several double-clicks, as you work your way through the network hierarchy. Here's how you'd get to a particular shared folder on a typical corporate domain:

1. **Double-click the My Network Places icon on the desktop.**

   The My Network Places window opens, shown in Figure 13-2. The very first time you double-click the My Network Places icon on your desktop, you see two icons: Add Network Place and Entire Network (see Figure 13-2). (You may also see a Computers Near Me icon, as described in the sidebar box above.) The Add Network Place icon is described on page 290; for now, proceed like this:

2. **Double-click Entire Network.**

   Now you see a window containing two more icons: Microsoft Windows Network and Directory. You use these icons to access the various other machines on the network, just as you navigate through the drive hierarchy in the My Computer window.

   The Directory icon enables you to access resources that have been published in the Active Directory (see page 22). On large networks, administrators do this "publishing" to spare you from having to browse through hundreds or thousands of computers, looking for a particular shared resource.

3. **Double-click Microsoft Windows Network.**

   A list of the domains and workgroups on the network appears.

4. **Double-click the icon of the domain or workgroup you want.**

   Now you see icons for the computers in that domain or workgroup.

5. **Double-click a computer icon.**

The window now shows all of the shares on that computer: drives, folders, or printers.

6. **Double-click one of the shared drive or folder icons to display the files and subfolders inside.**

Now you see the list of shared folders, disks, files, and printers on that computer. You can use them as though they were right there on your own computer.

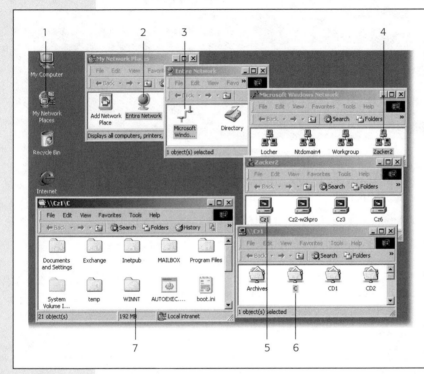

Figure 13-2:
Finding a certain shared folder, disk, or printer involves a series of double-clicks in successive windows. Start with the My Network Places icon on the desktop (1), then Entire Network (2), Microsoft Windows Network (3), the domain or workgroup you want (4), the computer's icon (5), and finally, the icon of the disk, folder, or printer you want (6). In this example, you wind up looking at the contents of the shared folder (7).

Add Network Places icons

Double-clicking icon after icon as shown in Figure 13-2 is one way to find a certain disk, folder, or file. But if you find yourself using a certain shared folder or disk often, you may find it more convenient to create a shortcut for it right in the My Network Places window.

The Add Network Place Wizard lets you do just that. Double-click its icon in the My Network Places window. On the first screen (Figure 13-3), you can click the Browse button to select a shared drive or folder; a subsequent wizard screen invites you to assign an alternate name to the shared resource as it will appear in your My Network Places window.

Tip: You can also make a shortcut to a shared folder or drive by dragging the folder or drive to the desktop and selecting Make Shortcut Here from the pop-up menu.

Instead of clicking Browse, however, you may sometimes find it more efficient to type the path to the drive or folder you want. Into the wizard's first text box, you can type a network address in this form:

\\ComputerName\ShareName\Filename

This special path format (called the *Universal Naming Convention,* or UNC*)* can pinpoint a shared folder or file on the network without requiring a long series of double-clicks from the My Network Places icon.

For example, suppose a particular picture file is on somebody's computer at c:\Graphics\Photographs\Antarctic\Alert Adelie Penguin. (See page 32 for details on this Windows path notation.) If the Antarctic folder has been *shared* (see page 295), you can open the file from across the network using its UNC path:

\\WS1\Photos\Alert Adelie Penguin

The double backslash means that WS1 is the name of a computer on the network (a single backslash would mean it's a folder at the top level of the local hard drive—that is, not in any other folder); *\Photos* is the share name for the Antarctic folder. (As noted later in this chapter, a folder's real name may not match its *shared* name—the name you see over the network.)

Tip: In UNC paths, capitalization doesn't matter.

Now the wizard proposes a name for it (which you're welcome to change).

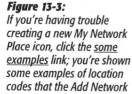

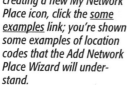

Figure 13-3:
If you're having trouble creating a new My Network Place icon, click the some examples *link; you're shown some examples of location codes that the Add Network Place Wizard will understand.*

After you click Finish, you'll be connected to the shared folder or drive. The next time you open My Network Places, you'll see the new Network Place icon. Double-click it to open the corresponding folder or drive in a window on your desktop. You can use the contents of the window as if it were on your own computer.

Using Windows Explorer

Instead of using the Network Places icon on the desktop, you can also survey the network landscape using Windows Explorer.

The left pane of the Windows Explorer window lists an icon for My Network Places. As shown in Figure 13-4, you can click the + button to see a list of the computers and shared resources on them. The hierarchy is exactly the same as that in My Network Places, and nearly all of the Explorer tricks you've learned when working with local drives (see page 86) also work on network shares.

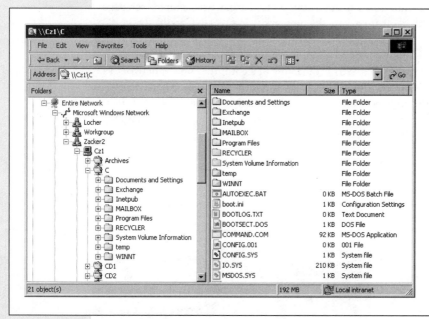

Figure 13-4:
The advantage of using Windows Explorer to look over your network is that you can simultaneously access folders and files on your local computer from this window, making it easier to copy files between the computers.

Mapping a Network Drive

Suppose there's a folder or drive that you use all the time—but it's on another computer. For that circumstance, the best solution is to *map* the frequently visited place so that it appears as a local drive on your computer.

Using this trick, you can assign a *letter* to a particular shared drive or folder on the network, just as your local hard drive is called C: and your floppy drive A:.

Doing so provides two benefits. First, these disks and folders now appear directly in the My Computer window. Getting to them is much faster, because you're saved several layers of double-clicking required by the My Network Places window. Second, when you choose File→Open from within one of your applications, you'll be able to jump directly to a particular shared folder by typing its letter, instead of having to double-click, ever deeper, through the icons in the Open File dialog box.

Tip: Your network administrator may have already set up a few of these mapped drives in your My Computer window. Plenty of people use these "hard drives" every day, not even aware that they "point" to drives elsewhere on the network.

Mapping Drive Letters to Shares

To map a drive letter to a shared network folder or drive, follow these steps:

1. **Double-click My Network Places, then Entire Network, then Microsoft Windows Network.**

   Continue expanding disks and folders until you find the shared folder or drive that you want to have mapped.

Tip: Windows 2000 Professional lets you map drive letters to shared *sub*folders (folders within a share) on the network. For example, in previous versions of Windows, you mapped drives to *\\servername\sharename*. In Windows 2000, you can also map drives to *\\servername\sharename\ foldername*.

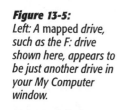

Figure 13-5:
Left: A mapped drive, such as the F: drive shown here, appears to be just another drive in your My Computer window.

Right: By default, mapped drives are persistent, meaning that the system automatically remaps them every time you log on. If you want the drive mapping to appear only in your current Windows session, turn off the "Reconnect at Logon" checkbox. When you log on next, the mapped drive will be gone.

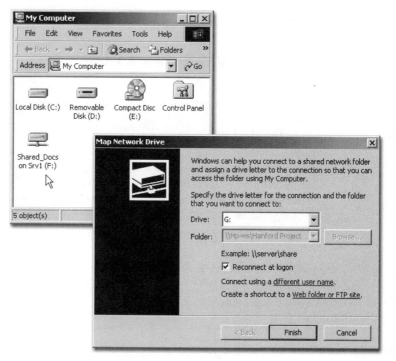

2. **Right-click the share you want to access and select Map Network Drive from the shortcut menu.**

   The Map Network Drive dialog box appears (Figure 13-5, right). Windows proposes the next available drive letter, but you can choose any other unused letter except B.

3. **Click Next to finish the mapping.**

   Your My Computer window now displays a new "disk" icon (Figure 13-5, left), representing the shared drive or folder that's actually elsewhere on the network.

Tip: By default, Windows 2000 Pro connects to the network share you've selected using the name and password you supplied when logging on to the computer. The "Connect using a different user name" option in the Map Network Drive dialog box lets you specify a different name and password for the connection to this share. For example, if you're working at a colleague's computer, and you want to access a private file on your machine, you can map a drive to it using your own name and password, without having to log off and log in again as yourself.

Disconnecting a Mapped Drive

To remove a mapped drive's icon from your My Computer window, open My Computer, right-click the drive, and select Disconnect from the shortcut menu.

When you disconnect a mapped drive, you're just removing it from the list of drives shown on your computer. It has no effect on the actual folder or drive. You can always remap it, if necessary.

Working With Network Files

Now that you know how to open shared drives and folders from across the network, you can start using the files you find there. Fortunately, there's nothing much to it:

At the Desktop

When you're working at the desktop, you can double-click icons representing the files and folders in a network share to open them, drag them to the Recycle Bin, make copies of them, and otherwise manipulate them exactly as though they were icons on your own hard drive (depending on the permissions you've been given, as described on page 298). Chapter 5 contains much more detail on manipulating files.

Caution: There's one significant difference between working with "local" files and those that sit elsewhere on the network: When you delete a file from another computer on the network, the file doesn't go to the Recycle Bin. Instead, it's deleted immediately and permanently; you can't undo the action or recover the file from the Recycle Bin.

Inside Applications

When you're working in a program, opening files that sit elsewhere on the network requires only a couple of extra steps:

1. **From within the program, choose File→Open.**

   The Open File dialog box appears.

2. **From the "Look in:" drop-down menu, choose My Network Places.**

   You see a display of the same icons that would normally appear in the My Network Places window.

3. **Double-click your way to the folder containing the file you want to use.**

   In other words, open the Entire Network icon, then the Microsoft Windows Network icon, a domain or workgroup icon, a computer icon, a share icon, and so on, until you arrive at the file that you want to open.

4. **Double-click the file you want to use.**

   The file opens. You can work on the document just as if it were sitting on your own computer.

At this point, using the File→Save command saves your changes to the original file, wherever it was on the network (if you've been given permission to make changes). You can also choose File→Save As to store a copy of the file on your own computer.

Sharing Files, Disks, and Printers

So far in this chapter, you've been reading from the point of view of the person accessing other computers on the network. This section details how to make the components of *your* computer available to other people on the network.

You share something the same way whether it's a drive, a folder, or printer: You highlight its icon, turn on sharing, type a name for the share, and adjust its settings. Thereafter, anyone else on the network can see icons for the resources you've shared by double-clicking My Network Places on their own desktops.

Step 1: Finding the Icon to Share

The first step in making a resource available to the network is to locate its icon. For example:

- **Disk drives.** To locate the icon of the disk you want to share, double-click the My Computer icon on your desktop. You'll see icons for all the drives on your system. (When you make a drive available to the network, you also make every folder *on* it available.)

- **Folders.** Sharing folders has distinct advantages over sharing an entire drive. By sharing only a folder or two, you can keep *most* of the files on your hard drive out of view from curious network comrades. Furthermore, sharing only a folder or two makes it easier for them to find files you've made available, because they don't have to root through your drive looking for the appropriate folder.

To specify the folder you want to share, locate its icon using either Windows Explorer or the My Computer icon (page 86).

- **Printer Shares.** Choose Start→Settings→Printers to open the Printers window, which has an icon for each printer your computer knows about. (See Chapter 16 for more on these printer icons.)

Step 2: Turning on Sharing

After you've located the icon of the drive, folder, or printer you want to share, proceed like this:

1. **Right-click the resource's icon; from the shortcut menu, choose Sharing.**

   If you don't see a Sharing command, choose Properties instead, and then click the Sharing tab. Either way, you're now facing the Sharing tab of the Properties dialog box.

2. **Click "Share this folder" or "Shared as" (see Figure 13-6).**

   The other options on the dialog box spring to life.

Tip: When sharing an entire drive, you'll find that the "Share this folder" option is already selected, and the drive already has a share name (its drive letter plus a dollar sign, such as C$). Windows 2000 creates this kind of *administrative share* for every hard drive on the computer. To allow other users (including nonadministrators) on the network access to the drive, you must click the New Share button and supply another share name in the New Share dialog box. You can then go on to click the Permissions button to configure user access to the new share, as described later in this chapter.

---

3. **Type a new name for the share, if you like.**

   As shown in Figure 13-6, you can choose a name for the resource you're sharing that's different from its folder name or drive letter. This technique prevents network users from knowing exactly where the shared folder is on your drive.

Tip: If you append a dollar sign ("$") to a share name, the system creates the share, but makes it invisible. Users browsing the network can't see the share in their Windows Explorer or My Network Places windows. They can, however, map a drive letter to it by manually typing the path to the share in the Map Network Drive dialog box—if they know about your secret share.

You can also use the Comment field to type additional information that further clarifies what's in the shared folder or disk. But remember that other people on the network won't see your comments unless they switch their My Network Places window into Details View (by choosing View→Details).

Tip: If you're sharing a printer on a network where some machines are running different versions of Windows, click the Additional Drivers button. (Those other machines need appropriate printer-driver software, even if the printer is elsewhere on the network.) A list of drivers appears; turn on the checkboxes for the versions of Windows that will be sharing the printer, and then click OK. (You may be asked to insert the to Windows 2000 Pro installation CD.)

Figure 13-6:
The Sharing tab for a disk or folder. The Share name *is what other people will see when they open their My Network Places desktop icons. Make this name as helpful as possible within the 12-letter length limit.*

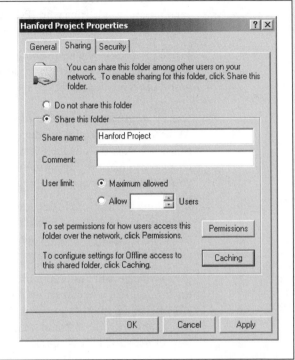

WORKAROUND WORKSHOP

Problems with Share Names

If you have machines on your network that run MS-DOS (or Windows versions through 3.11) that will be accessing a shared folder, you must follow the 8.3 naming convention (such as *filename.doc* or *myfolder)* in the share name. Otherwise, the DOS or Windows 3.x machines won't be able to "see" the shared resources over the network. Similarly, Windows 95 or 98 machines won't see a shared *printer* that doesn't conform to the 8.3 naming standard.

The *actual* names of files or folders (as opposed to their

share names) can be up to 255 characters long, as described in Chapter 5. DOS users connecting over the network will see the names in the 8.3 format. (Windows 2000 maintains 8.3 equivalents for the long file and folder names, which a DOS machine can recognize, but it doesn't do the same for share names.)

To make matters even stranger, some applications don't recognize printer names longer than 31 characters, no matter what operating system is on the computer.

If you were to simply click OK at this point, you would make this resource available to everyone on the network. But before leaving the dialog box, take a moment to survey the identification and security options.

Step 3: Limiting Network Access

When you make a folder or drive available to the network, you don't necessarily want to give your co-workers permission to run wild, trashing your files, renaming things at random, and vandalizing your JPG photos. In fact, you can limit people's access on an individual basis, thanks to the Permissions button shown in Figure 13-6.

When you click it, you get the dialog box shown on the left in Figure 13-7. Setting up permissions involves two steps: identifying the person (or group) to whom you're granting permission, and then specifying how much access you want to grant them.

Specify whose freedom you're about to limit

At the top of the Permissions dialog box, you'll see a list of users and possibly groups of users. If you see only the Everyone icon there (the default), then any permission changes you make will apply to everyone on your network. You'll make the resource you're sharing fully or partially accessible to everyone at once, to the same degree.

That's fine for very public documents. But in many cases, you may prefer to share a folder or drive *selectively*. If you're in Accounting, for example, you might want to make the company salary spreadsheet accessible by the other accountants in your workgroup, but off-limits to everyone else in the company.

That's why the Add button (Figure 13-7, left) lets you add users or groups of users to the list—so that you can set up different levels of access for different people. Page 371 offers help in setting up accounts for individuals or groups—a task generally left to network administrators, except when you *are* the administrator (on a peer-to-peer network, for example).

Here's how you'd go about setting up permission to access a folder you've just shared, starting with the dialog box shown on the left in Figure 13-7:

1. **Click Add.**

   Now the Select Users, Computers, or Groups dialog box appears (right in Figure 13-7). If you scroll down far enough into the list, you'll see the names of the other people on your network, and any groups you or your network administrator have created.

Note: If your computer is logged on to a domain, the list of users and groups you see here is being supplied by the domain controller. The list shows the accounts that have been created in the Active Directory by a network administrator.

If you're part of a workgroup, on the other hand, the list of users and groups is stored on your own computer. You may have to create new accounts for specific people (page 371) in order to grant them access to your shares.

---

2. **Double-click the name of the person or group for whom you're setting permissions.**

   The name appears in the bottom box. Repeat until the box lists everyone who's entitled to access the shared folder.

3. **Click OK.**

   After a moment, you return to the Permissions dialog box.

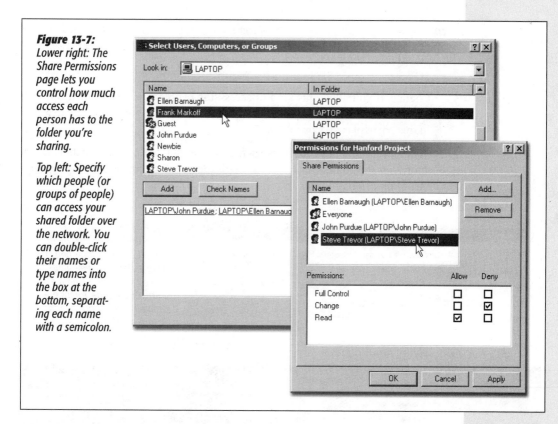

Figure 13-7:
Lower right: The Share Permissions page lets you control how much access each person has to the folder you're sharing.

Top left: Specify which people (or groups of people) can access your shared folder over the network. You can double-click their names or type names into the box at the bottom, separating each name with a semicolon.

4. **Highlight Everyone and click Remove.**

   You've just ensured that *only* the users and groups you've specified can access your shared folder.

Specify how much access

In the Permissions dialog box, the names of the people you've authorized appear at the top. Highlight the first name, and then use the Allow or Deny checkboxes at the bottom of the dialog box to restrict his vandalistic impulses like this:

- **No access.** If you don't turn on any checkboxes, the person or group whose name you've selected can't access this shared resource at all. They won't even know it exists.

- **Read.** Click the Allow checkbox for the Read line (and no other lines) for a "look, don't touch" policy. Other people on the network will be allowed to open and read what's inside this disk or folder, but won't be able to save changes, rename anything, delete anything, or deposit any new files.

Note: Other people on the network can *copy* folders and files from a Read-Only folder or disk onto their own computers. From there, they can do whatever they like. But they can't copy the changed files back to your shared folder or disk.

- **Change.** If you allow this kind of access, the people you've identified can open *and edit* the shared documents. They just can't delete the files or create new ones in this particular disk or folder.

- **Full.** *Full* access gives your network friends the right to do whatever they want to your files and folders, exactly as though they were sitting at your computer— including deleting them.

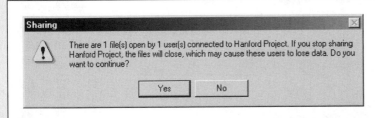

Figure 13-8:
It's poor manners to turn off sharing while another person is using it. Better to wait until nobody's actually using the share. Clicking Yes forces the removal of the share and the closure of any open files.

FREQUENTLY ASKED QUESTIONS

Allow vs. Deny

Why does Windows 2000 provide both Allow and Deny checkboxes in the Permissions dialog box? Isn't not allowing permission the same as denying it?

In this case, no. "Deny" permissions always take precedence over "Allow" permissions.

For example, if somebody has been granted access to a share because he's a member of a group, you can explicitly revoke his permission by using the Deny checkboxes

for his account. You've just overridden the group permission, just for him, leaving the rest of the group's permissions intact.

You can also use the Deny checkboxes to override permissions granted by *inheritance* from a parent folder. For example, you can grant a user access to the C: drive by sharing it and assigning her Allow permissions to it, but then prevent her from accessing the C:\Program Files folder by sharing that and *denying* her permission.

When you've assigned the appropriate permissions to each person, click OK, then OK again. You'll see that the icon for the resource you just shared has changed; a hand now cradles the icon to help you remember what you've made available to your network colleagues.

Stopping Sharing

Removing sharing from a folder, drive, or printer is simply a matter of opening the Sharing dialog box for the icon in question. Click "Do not share" and then OK. If someone on the network is actively using the share, you'll see the advisory box shown in Figure 13-8.

Network Printing

When you're on a network, it's likely that no printer is plugged directly into your computer—but somewhere in the building, connected to your machine by cables, sits a shared printer (or several). To find out what printers you can use, choose Start→Settings→Printers; the Printers window opens, showing the icons for any printers whose software you've installed, along with an Add Printer icon.

If the printer icons all have cryptic names, right-click each in turn, selecting Properties from each shortcut menu. The resulting dialog box usually provides more information (see Figure 13-11) about the type of printer and where it is.

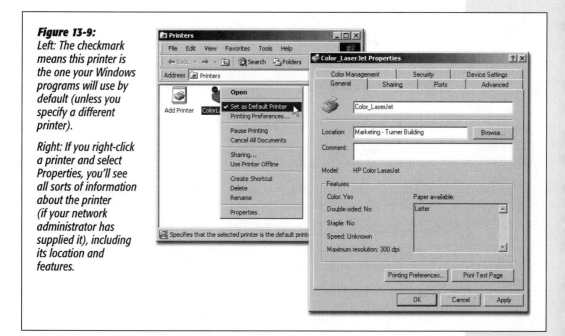

Figure 13-9:
Left: The checkmark means this printer is the one your Windows programs will use by default (unless you specify a different printer).

Right: If you right-click a printer and select Properties, you'll see all sorts of information about the printer (if your network administrator has supplied it), including its location and features.

Selecting an Everyday Printer

If you're lucky enough to have several printers you can use, you need to set one as your default printer—the one your Windows printouts will go to unless you change the setting.

To specify your favorite printer, right-click its icon in the Printers window; choose Set As Default Printer from the shortcut menu (Figure 13-9, left).

Adding a Network Printer

When your generous manager buys a new printer for the network (and turns on Sharing for it), you'll be able to use it—but first you need to find it on the network and then tell your computer about it.

Locating a printer using Active Directory

As noted on page 22, *Active Directory* is a feature of Windows 2000 Server, the corporate-network version of Windows 2000. It's a central directory that lists (and lets administrators manage) applications, files, people—and printers.

If you work on an Active Directory-based network, you add a network printer to your Printers folder like this:

1. **Choose Start→Settings→Printers. In the Printers window, double-click Add Printer.**

   The Add Printer wizard opens.

2. **Click Next. Select Network Printer; click Next again.**

   Now you arrive at the Locate Your Printer screen.

3. **If the "Find a printer in the Directory" option is available, select it and click Next.**

   If not, see the next section, "Locating a Printer by Browsing."

4. **In the Find Printers dialog box, specify a printer name, location, or the features you need to use, if you like.**

   These options will help narrow the choices if you're in a big company. (Leave these fields blank if you want the search to list all of the printers in the directory.)

5. **Click Find Now.**

   Windows 2000 contacts a domain controller on the network, which supplies a list of the printers that meet your criteria.

6. **Highlight the name of the printer you want to add and click OK.**

7. **Indicate if this printer is to be your default printer. Click Next.**

8. **Review the choices you've made and click Finish.**

Note: Selecting a network printer this way doesn't guarantee that the printer is turned on, functioning, filled with paper, or even physically there—only that it exists in the Active Directory. Check with your network administrator if you're unsure of which printer you should use.

Removing a printer from the Printers window is easy. Right-click the printer in the Printers folder and select Delete from the shortcut menu. After you confirm that you want to delete the printer's icon, it disappears.

Locating a Printer by Browsing

If Active Directory isn't used on your network, you'll need to browse around to find the network printer you want. To do so, follow these steps.

1. **Choose Start→Settings→Printers. In the Printers window, double-click Add Printer.**

   The Add Printer wizard opens.

2. **Click Next. Select the Network Printer option and click Next again.**

   Now you arrive at the Locate Your Printer screen.

3. **Select "Type the printer name." If you know the exact name that the printer has been given, type it in.**

   If not, click Next to browse for the printer. A list of shared printers on your network appears; highlight the one you want to add to your Printers window.

4. **Click Next. Indicate if you want this printer to be your default printer. Click Next. Review the choices you've made and click Finish.**

Printing

Once you've set up your machine to use the printers on your network, sending printouts to them isn't any more difficult than the everyday printing: With a document on the screen, choose File→Print, and proceed as described on page 353.

POWER USERS' CLINIC

NTFS Permissions

Using the Permissions controls described on the previous pages gives certain people access to your shared folder *over the network*. However, anyone who sits down at *your* desk and logs into your computer can still see and use what's in the folder, because the Share Permissions feature only controls access *over a network*.

In addition to share permissions, Windows 2000 provides another, completely independent mechanism for controlling access to the drives, folders, and files on your computer. This mechanism, known as *NTFS permissions,* works only for drives that have been formatted using the NTFS drive-formatting scheme described on page 413.

Using NTFS permissions is most decidedly a power-user technique, however, because of the added complexity it introduces; entire books have been written on the topic of Windows 2000 security alone. For now, a pair of warnings is in order. First, note that, by default, Windows 2000 grants the *continued on next page*

NTFS Permissions *continued*

Everyone group Full Control over all NTFS files and folders. When you modify the NTFS permissions for your files and folders, make sure that everyone who needs to access them has the appropriate permissions. For example, in order for a network user to access a shared folder, she must have both share permission *and* NTFS permission for that folder.

Furthermore, if you're not careful, it's entirely possible to "orphan" a file or folder (or even your entire drive) by revoking everyone's permission to it, even your own, making it *completely* inaccessible by anyone. Before you start working with NTFS permissions, it's a good idea to create an extra user account on your system (see page 371) and grant it Full Control for all of your drives, just in case something goes wrong.

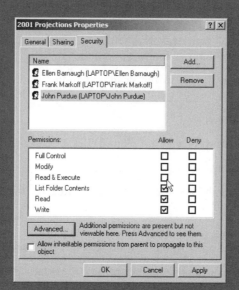

If you decide to proceed, here's how you restrict access to a shared folder so that only certain users and groups can access it , even when visiting your machine. Start by right-clicking the shared folder; choose Properties from the shortcut menu. (Note: NTFS permissions aren't just for shared *folders*. You can also use them to restrict access to individual files.)

In the Properties dialog box, click the Security tab. Click Add; double-click the names of the people to whom you want to grant access; click OK.

You return to the Security tab, where their names appear. So far, all of this should feel familiar. But look at the bottom of the dialog box, shown here: Now you have far greater control over who can do what—even when they're sitting at your machine.

By clicking the Allow and Deny checkboxes, you can specify exactly how much permission these group members will have.

Turn on **Read** if you want them to be able to examine the contents of the folder, but not make changes. **Read & Execute** is primarily useful for applications; it means your selected colleagues can actually run the programs in question. **Write** means that people can make changes to the files or folders, and create new ones in the shared folder; **Modify** is the same as Write, but adds permission to *delete* the shared folder or file; **Full Control** even lets someone *change* the permissions you've just spent so much time setting up. If you're sharing a folder (instead of a file), you'll also see a **List Folder Contents** option, which, of course, lets your visitors see what's *in* the folder.

Finally, for best sanity preservation, turn off the "Allow inheritable permissions" checkbox at the bottom of the window. In the warning box, click Remove. ("Inheritable permissions" means that the user or group can inherit permissions to the selected file or folder from the folder that encloses it. For example, assigning somebody permission to access the C: drive also grants him the same permission to all of the folders *on* that drive, unless you select one of those subfolders, clear this checkbox, and assign him new permissions.)

Remove all other users and groups from the Security tab by clicking each name and then clicking Remove. (Leave an administrator account in place, however, if none of the group members are administrators; see page 369 for details on Administrator accounts.)

Finally, click OK. You return to the desktop; now your file or folder is secure, both over the network and in person.

Dialing In to a Network

For most people, *remote access* means practically nothing. After all, to most people, "remote" means someplace like Nepal or Antarctica, and "access" doesn't help.

But for anyone who telecommutes from home or travels with a laptop, remote access can be an important concept indeed. It means *temporarily connecting to another computer,* usually by dialing in. Once you're connected to the network at work (or your desktop computer at home), you can perform a number of useful work-related functions:

- **Use documents.** Open, or grab copies of, important documents that you may have left behind, or that have been updated at the office while you've been away.

- **Run programs.** You probably won't need to access the network's copy of Word or Excel; they're probably on your laptop already. But many companies have specialized applications, such as databases, that are constantly updated and not easily transferred to other machines. Thanks to remote access, you can run such programs no matter where you are.

- **Check your email.** By checking your *work* email account while you're out of the office, you can stay in touch while traveling. You won't have to spend your first two days back in the office snowed under by accumulated messages.

You can connect to a distant network either directly or indirectly:

- **Dial-up access.** Your modem dials the phone number of a remote-access *server,* a program on the remote network that's designed to accept incoming calls of this kind.

• **Virtual Private Network.** This glamorous name refers to a simple idea: connecting to your office network via the Internet. Virtual Private Networks (VPNs) are becoming more popular, because they allow you to use your existing Internet connection to connect to your office network, avoiding the hassle and long-distance charges you'd incur if you directly dialed the remote access server.

This chapter covers both kinds of connections.

Making Dial-Up Connections

Dialing into a corporate network is fairly easy; your system administrator sets up everything on the receiving end and gives you the information you need. But connecting to your own computer at home, or a *peer-to-peer* network that you administer (see Chapter 15), is quite different. This section covers each of these connections—to a corporate network and to a standalone PC or peer-to-peer network.

Connection to a Corporate Network

You can dial into your office network only if (a) its network administrator has prepared the network to accept incoming calls (by installing *remote access server* software), and (b) he's configured your account to permit dial-in access.

If all is well with these conditions, here's the additional information you'll need from your administrator to dial into your company's network (or *any* secure, client/server network):

• **Telephone number.** The receiving modem's phone number.

• **Protocols used.** Your network's *protocol* is the communications language it uses. Your remote network may "speak" TCP/IP, NetBEUI, IPX/SPX, or a combination. Fortunately, you don't need to know anything about these protocols—only which one your network uses. (It's usually TCP/IP.)

• **TCP/IP configuration.** The *Dynamic Host Configuration Protocol* (DHCP) is a service that automatically configures all of the TCP/IP parameters a computer needs to communicate with a network. Most medium-sized and large networks run DHCP on their Windows servers, to prevent administrators from having to manually configure each workstation.

Ask your network administrator: Does the office network's remote server assign IP addresses using DHCP? If not, you'll need to know several number codes: the *IP address, subnet mask, domain name,* and *DNS servers.* (Actually, if your network doesn't use DHCP, your administrator will probably want to configure your laptop *for* you.) See "Configuring TCP/IP" on page 336 for more about TCP/IP and its settings.

• **Username and password.** If you're connecting to a Windows 2000 or Windows NT remote server, you can use the same username and password you use when you're on that network. If it's another type of remote server, you'll need to know the name and password to connect.

Once you have this information in hand, you can create a dial-up connection with these steps:

1. **Right-click My Network Places; choose Properties from the shortcut menu.**

   Or choose Start→Settings→Network and Dial-up Connections. Either way, the Network and Dial-up Connections window appears.

2. **Open Make New Connection.**

   The Network Connection Wizard opens.

3. **Click Next. Select "Dial-up to private network"; click Next.**

   Now you're asked for the phone number of your company's remote-access server (the computer that accepts incoming calls).

4. **Enter the telephone number of the remote server.**

   You can enter the entire number, including any prefixes or area codes. If you dial up from more than one location, or if there are multiple area codes for local numbers in your area, turn on "Use dialing rules," so that Windows 2000 can dial the correct prefixes for your current location. (Dialing rules are especially handy if you frequently need to switch between dialing a 9 for an outside line—as is common in offices—and an 8, which is common in hotels.)

5. **Click Next. Indicate whether or not this connection should be available to everyone, or only you.**

   If you're the only one who'll be dialing with the computer you're setting up, turn on "Only for myself." If it's conceivable that somebody else with an account on your computer might want to borrow your laptop to connect to his own files back at work, turn on "For all users."

6. **Supply a name for the connection, turn on the desktop-icon option if you like, and click Finish.**

   If you let Windows 2000 put an icon for this connection onto your desktop, then you've got an easy way to dial the office: Just double-click this icon, which bears the name you typed in the final step.

Windows may try to make this connection immediately. If so, click Cancel; it's worth taking a moment to fine-tune your settings before connecting, as described next.

Configuring the Connection Properties

When you've completed the Network Connection Wizard, you wind up with a new connection icon in your Network and Dial-up Connections window. To adjust its settings, right-click it and select Properties from the shortcut menu (Figure 14-1).

The most important properties in the Properties dialog box include:

General tab

The General tab shows the modem being used for the connection and the phone number(s) for the connection. In many corporate environments, you won't need alternate phone numbers; the receiving end probably uses a modem *pool* or some other method of handling several simultaneous incoming calls. However, if your administrator provides alternate numbers, click the Alternates button to add them.

Options tab

On the Options tab, you'll find more settings for dialing and redialing that apply to this connection. Here's what they mean:

- **Display progress while connecting.** When this box is checked, starting a connection causes a box to appear that describes the call's status as it dials, connects, and so on.

- **Prompt for name and password.** A security precaution that requires you to type in your username and password each time you dial in (instead of letting Windows remember your password).

- **Include Windows logon domain.** If you're using a laptop that you also use at work (connected to the office network, for example), it may already be configured to logon to the office's Windows 2000 *domain* (see page 21). In that case, you can skip this checkbox.

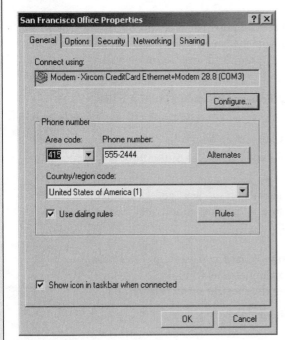

Figure 14-1:
The presence of so many adjustable properties for a connection stems from the fact that telephone lines were never designed to carry data. Early modems were slow and persnickety; you had to tweak your settings just to get a decent connection. Fortunately, these days, you rarely (if ever) have to change most of these settings.

But if you're calling a Windows 2000 domain from a computer that *isn't* ordinarily a member of it, check this box. (This option—and the "Prompt for name and password" option described above—are unavailable if your computer *is* a member of the domain you're calling and you've turned on the security options on the Security tab, described below.)

- **Redialing Options.** Most of these options specify what happens when your call encounters busy signals or a dropped connection. The "Idle time before hanging up," on the other hand, sets the period of inactivity before your PC disconnects the call to free up the line. Bear in mind that the server you're dialing may *also* have an automatic-disconnect timer that will override any setting you have here.

Security tab

If you're connecting to a Windows 2000 or Windows NT remote server, select Typical and (from the drop-down menu) "Require secured password." If the remote network is your company network, the username and password you use to dial in are probably the same ones you use in the office. If so, turn on "Automatically use my Windows logon name and password."

If you're connecting to another type of remote server, select "Advanced (custom settings)" and then click the Settings button to set the correct security protocols. This is not a job for the unwary; you'll need detailed information from the administrator who runs the remote server.

GEM IN THE ROUGH

The Mysteries of Roaming Profiles

Windows 2000's *roaming profiles* feature offers you a remarkable degree of flexibility: You can sit down in front of any computer on the network (or even connect from the road), log on, and view the desktop and settings of your *own* computer—desktop icons, wallpaper, Start menu configuration, network connection icons, and all—wherever it happens to be. No matter where you log on, your desktop and other settings follow. Behind the scenes, a roaming profile is essentially a copy of your user profile (as found in the Documents and Settings folder on your machine) that's stored on a shared network server.

Roaming profiles are intended for use on networks where all of the workstations have been set up exactly the same way. In a university computer lab, for example, you may use a different PC each day; but thanks to your roaming profile, you'll find your familiar desktop and Start-menu shortcuts

exactly where you left them. (And they always open the same files and programs, which are stored on a server.)

You *can* use your roaming profile when you dial into the network from the road, but you may not always get the results you expect. For example, when you double-click your connection icon, you can access the files, disks, printers, and other resources of the network you've reached, but you don't see your roaming profile; the desktop on your laptop remains the way it was before you connected. (Connect this way, in other words, if a roaming profile is set up for you on the network, but you don't want to use it.)

But if you log off Windows and then log on again, you're offered (at the Log On to Windows screen) an option called "Log on using dial-up connection." That option gives you your roaming profile after your laptop has dialed and connected to the network.

Data encryption is another in the long list of Windows 2000 security features; it ensures that any data sent to or from your computer is first scrambled so that an Internet-dwelling spy can't possibly intercept your transmission. That's an unlikely scenario; but if it concerns you (or your network administrator), turn on "Require data encryption." Now your computer will connect only to a server that has *also* been set up to use data encryption. (If the checkbox is cleared, your computer will *try* to encrypt its data; but it won't refuse to connect if the server on the other end doesn't also use encryption.) The bottom line: Check this box only if the network administrator advises you to do so.

Note: If you're connecting to a non-Microsoft remote server, select Advanced→Settings for the encryption options. If the administrator tells you that the remote server is set up to handle data encryption, she'll also tell you how to adjust the encryption settings here.

Networking tab
On the Networking tab, the only change you conceivably want to make is to turn on File and Printer Sharing for Microsoft Networks. Doing so lets users on the remote network access the shared drives and folders on *your* PC while you're connected. (See Chapter 13 for details on making your folders available to others.) If that's not necessary or desirable (and it's usually not), leave it unchecked.

Your network administrator will tell you how to fill in the remaining settings here (TCP/IP address, DNS server address, and so on) if they're required.

Logging On Using Dial-Up Connection
To dial into your network, just turn on your computer as usual; when the Log On to Windows screen appears, choose "Log on using dial-up connection." If your username and password are the same for logging on remotely as they are on the domain, that's all there is to it; you'll be simultaneously authenticated to connect to the network and use its resources. In other words, you'll then have the same access to the network that you'd have if you logged on directly to the domain. You can open the My Network Places window or Windows Explorer and start working exactly as you would at the office. (*Almost* exactly; if you've dialed into the office using a modem, you'll find that your network access is fairly slow.)

Tip: While you're connected to the dial-up server, you can make a shortcut of a file or folder you plan to use again. (You can also *map* a folder to a drive letter, as described on page 292.) The next time you want to connect, just double-click that shortcut (or drive icon in My Computer); if you accept Windows 2000's offer to dial the remote network, you go right to the file or folder you double-clicked, saving you several steps.

You don't have to dial into the remote network at startup time, however; you can also choose Start→Network and Dial-up Connections→[your connection name]. In this case, however, you may not have as much access to the network as usual (because no *domain logon script* is run and *domain policies* are not applied).

Connecting to Email

Checking office email while away from the office is one of the most popular uses of remote-access technology. If the company you work for maintains its own mail servers, you probably use Outlook, Microsoft Exchange, Lotus Notes, or some other email program that handles both internal corporate email and Internet email. These programs have their own remote-access features; your network administrator can help you configure them so that you can keep in touch with office mail even when you're away.

If you just want to check your own email during your travels, however, you can use Outlook Express. Dialing the Internet from outside your regularly scheduled local calling area involves two steps:

1. **Create a new connection icon for your ISP in whatever new city you're in.**

   One easy way to do that is to choose Start→Settings→Network and Dial-Up Connections; in the resulting window, right-click the connection icon for your ISP and choose Create Copy from the shortcut menu.

   Now you have a second icon, which you can rename (to, say, "Earthlink in Chicago"). If you right-click it and then choose Properties from the shortcut menu, you'll be able to change the phone number and other dialing settings, including the dialing rules (see page 160).

2. **Tell Outlook Express to use the new connection.**

   In Outlook Express, choose Tools→Accounts, click the Mail tab, select the email account you want to check, and then click the Properties button (Figure 14-2).

Figure 14-2:
Use this drop-down menu in Outlook Express to switch from one ISP phone number to another. You can also use it to switch from using your dial-up modem to using a network connection to the Internet, too. That is, when your laptop is in the office, choose Local Area Network from this drop-down menu; when you're on the road, choose the appropriate ISP connection.

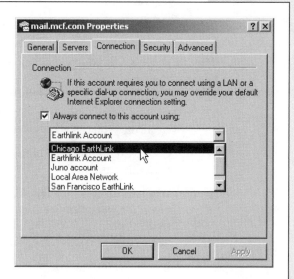

Now, to tell Outlook Express that you'd like it to switch to your new "out-of-town" connection setup, click the Connection tab, and then select the Internet connection you're currently using from the drop-down list box. Click OK, then Close.

Tip: To change the default connection for *all* Internet activity, double-click the Internet Options Control Panel applet, and use the Connections tab.

Connecting to a Single Windows 2000 Pro Computer

A network isn't the only thing you can reach by dialing in from the road. You can also dial directly into a single Windows 2000 Pro computer—a useful feature if, for example, you travel with your laptop and would like to dial up the Windows 2000 Pro desktop machine in your home office. All you need is a modem in each computer and the software built into Windows 2000.

Preparing the home-base PC

Before you can dial in, you need to prepare your Windows 2000 Pro machine to accept a remote call. First, log in as an administrator (see page 369), and then follow these steps:

1. Choose Start→Settings→Network and Dial-Up Connections. Double-click Make New Connection.

   The Network Connection Wizard appears.

2. Click Next. In the Network Connection Type dialog box, select "Accept incoming connections."

3. Click Next again. Select the device that will be accepting the incoming connection.

   It's probably your modem, and there's probably only one.

4. Click Next. Choose "Do not allow virtual private connections."

   (Virtual Private Networks are described later in this chapter. If you decide to create one, you can always run this wizard again.)

5. Click Next. In Allowed Users, check the names of users who will be able to dial in to this computer.

   Windows 2000 is showing you a list of everyone with an account on this computer; for maximum security, permit as few people as possible to connect. For security reasons, don't turn on the Guest Account or any account with a system name (such as IWAM and IUSR) under any circumstances.

   If you like, you can also click a username, then Properties, then the Callback tab to specify a *callback number*. This option makes your PC immediately hang up on anyone who calls in (after identifying the calling computer), and then dial the number you provide here.

This option is yet another security measure; in other words, if you're being visited by some hacker in Germany who's masquerading as a telecommuting co-worker, he'll be deprived of a connection. The PC will call the genuine telecommuting co-worker at home.

(If you turn on "Allow the caller to set the callback number," your machine can prompt the caller to *provide* a callback number. In this case, the callback feature isn't for security—it's to centralize the long-distance phone charges.)

Tip: If you set a callback number, include all necessary prefixes; Windows 2000 Pro doesn't use its usual Dialing Rules system (see page 160) for callbacks.

6. **Click Next. In the Networking Components dialog box, leave all the protocols and services checked.**

   If the computer you're setting up is on a network, your callers will have access to the network. If that's not what you want, highlight each protocol in turn and select Properties. Then turn off "Allow callers access to my local area network."

7. **Click Next. In the final dialog box, you're asked to give a name to the connection. Type a name, and then click Finish.**

   A new icon appears in the Network and Dial-Up Connections folder, along with all the other connections you've configured, bearing the name you just typed.

UP TO SPEED

Security Considerations When Your PC Can Receive Calls

Enabling your work PC to accept remote connections opens it up to some security risk. The biggest risk, however, is making this setup without getting permission from your company. In some corporations, an unauthorized connection could get you fired.

Even if you're connecting to your solo computer in your home office, however, take reasonable security precautions. First, keep the number of authorized callers to a minimum (preferably one) and change your password to something

as complex as possible.

Second, temporarily disable the incoming connection whenever it's not being used. To do so, choose Start→Settings→Network and Dial-Up Connections; double-click the icon you created for incoming connections. On the General tab, clear the checkbox next to the modem. Click OK. (When you want to enable the connection again, turn that modem checkbox back on again.)

Virtual Private Networks

Virtual Private Networking is dial-up networking with a twist. Instead of dialing the number of your distant network's modem, you connect to the Internet (by modem or any other means), and then use the Internet to link you to the remote network.

This arrangement is not only cheaper (long-distance connections to the home office in Abu Dhabi can really add up), but also more reliable: When you connect via regular phone connection, many things can go wrong. But when one computer on the Internet goes down, your data is instantly and automatically rerouted to its destination.

In short, VPNs lets you make connections quickly and cheaply almost anywhere in the world. You don't need dedicated, end-to-end private lines, and you can configure extremely tight security.

POWER USERS' CLINIC

How a VPN Works

In a VPN, both ends of the connection make a link to the Internet. (Technically, any private network can serve as the link between the two computers, but almost everyone uses the Internet.) Instead of sending a packet of information as generated by the originating computer, the VPN encapsulates the packet in an additional header. The header provides routing information that lets the encapsulated data pass through the intermediate network. The data is encrypted, so that even if some rebel spy intercepts the packet, he can't read it without the encryption keys.

At the other end of the connection, your PC strips off the encapsulation and decrypts the data. To you, the data appears as though it's been sent over an unremarkable private link.

A VPN in Windows 2000 consists of a *VPN server*, a *VPN client*, a *VPN connection* (the portion of the connection in which the data is encrypted), and the *tunnel* (the portion in which the data is encapsulated). The tunneling is done through one of the two tunneling protocols included with Windows 2000, the Point-to-Point Tunneling Protocol (known by the charming acronym PPTP) or the Layer Two Tunneling Protocol (L2TP).

Setting up the *receiving* end of virtual private networking is the province of the network administrator or, in even larger enterprises, the person who manages the remote access servers.

But once a remote access server at work has been set up to accept VPN connections, connecting from your computer at home or on the road is actually easier than connecting through a regular dial-up connection. Here's how it's done.

1. **Choose Start→Settings→Network and Dial-Up Connections. Double-click Make New Connection.**

   The Network Connection Wizard appears.

2. **Click Next. On the Network Connection Type screen, select "Connect to a private network through the Internet." Click Next.**

   Now you're asked whether or not you want Windows to connect to the Internet whenever you try to connect to the VPN. Since you can't very well connect to a VPN *without* an Internet connection, the second choice is generally what you want.

3. **Click "Automatically dial this connection."**

   Use the drop-down menu to specify the Internet account you want to use.

4. **Click Next. Supply the hostname or IP address of the server or network you're connecting to.**

As usual, ask your network administrator for this information.

5. **Click Next. Specify whether the connection is for you alone or for all users of the computer.**

In other words, will anyone else with a user account on your computer want to connect to the office network? If not, click "Only for myself."

6. **Click Next. Supply a name for the connection and click Finish.**

Another icon will appear in the Network and Dial-Up Connections folder, labeled with the name you just typed.

Now the Initial Connection dialog box appears, offering you the opportunity to connect to the virtual network right now. Click Yes or No, as suits your schedule.

Thereafter, whenever you want to make the connection, double-click the VPN's icon in the Network and Dial-Up Connections folder. First, the modem dials and connects you to the ISP (if you're connecting by dialing in). Next, you're prompted for your username and password for the remote access server's network; finally, the connection is made.

At this point, you can use the distant network exactly as though you're connected to it in person. (The giant exception, of course, is speed: Some moves you make over the phone lines, such as opening applications on the remote network, may seem glacially slow.)

Offline Files (Synchronization Manager)

Microsoft and other companies have been wrestling with the problem of offline files for a very long time. In a nutshell, the problem is this: When you take a file *offline* (off the network and onto your laptop, for example) and then edit it, two versions of the file exist. But suppose that, in the meantime, someone else modifies that same file on the network. Now there are two *different* versions of the document, neither of which is the same as the original.

Now suppose that *several* people took the same file offline on their laptops and made changes to it. How can the various versions be reconciled?

One very limited solution is the Briefcase, described on page 325. Another, more successful attempt at a solution—new to Windows 2000—is called Offline Files (or Synchronization Manager). Although using it may appear to be convoluted at first (and second) glance, it actually works to solve the seemingly intractable problem of "document-version hell."

How Offline Files Work

The Offline Files function is primarily designed for portable computers that are only intermittently connected to the network. It can also be useful, however, if your connection to the network is in place only part of the time, or if the connection is unreliable. Files in any shared folder on a Microsoft Windows network can be made available offline.

In short, the Offline Files feature works like this: Files that you mark for offline use get copied, or *cached,* to your local hard drive. When the network is unavailable, a notification balloon appears in the Taskbar to let you know. Now that you're un-plugged, you can edit the files that have been cached on your machine; make whatever changes you like.

When you return to the office (or dial in), the Synchronization Manager compares the files you've worked on with the originals on the network. Then it automatically updates the files in both directions, so that you and the network wind up with exactly the same, up-to-date files. (If the network copies have been edited in the meantime, Windows asks you how to handle the conflict: Whether one copy of the other should take precedence, or whether you want to keep both copies.)

Note: The cached copies of offline files are in a hidden system folder called CSC in your WINNT folder. Under no circumstances should you move or delete files directly from the CSC database. It's hidden for a reason. Open the files only from the Offline Files folder on the desktop, the My Network Places window, or Windows Explorer, as described later in this chapter.

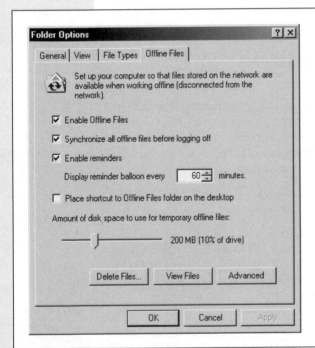

Figure 14-3:
It's an excellent idea to leave "Synchronize all offline files before logging off" turned on; otherwise, you may head off on a business trip with a set of out-of-date files.

Step 1: Turn On the Master Switch

Before you can make files available offline, you need to make sure that the feature itself is turned on. To do so, open My Computer or another desktop folder, and choose Tools→Folder Options. Click the Offline Files tab, and make sure that "Enable Offline Files" is turned on, as shown in Figure 14-3.

While you're at it, you might want to adjust some of the other settings here. For example:

- **Synchronize all offline files before logging off.** This option ensures that you'll have the most recent versions of the files and folders you need whenever you log off the office network. It would be hard to imagine a situation when this *isn't* what you want.

  (This feature isn't available when you connect by dialing in, however.)

- **Enable reminders.** A Taskbar balloon will remind you, once an hour, that you're not connected to the network. These reminder balloons can help you keep your thinking straight if you're on and off the network many times a day.

- **Place shortcut to Offline Files folder on the desktop.** When you open this Offline Files shortcut on your desktop, you see a handy list view of every file that came from the network, with special information columns that indicate its synchronization status, availability, original location on the network, and so on. This shortcut is certainly a convenience, although it destroys the illusion that offline files are still *on* the network (see Figure 14-3).

POWER USERS' CLINIC

Advanced Options

If you click the Advanced button in the dialog box shown in Figure 14-3, you can change what the computer does when it goes offline. The default setting is simply to notify you (with a Taskbar balloon saying that the connection has been lost).

"Never allow my computer to go offline" does not, of course, actually prevent your computer from going offline. Instead, it means that if the network connection is lost,

the network files won't be available (no offline files) *except* the ones you've added to the exception list by clicking Add, as shown here.

You can use the Exception list with either of the two options in this dialog box. For example, this computer will begin using offline files if the network connection is dropped, *except* if the connection to Srv1 is lost. In that case, no offline files will be available.

Tip: If you choose not to create an Offline Files shortcut on your desktop, you can click the View Files button shown in Figure 14-3 to open the same window.

- **Amount of disk space to use for temporary offline files.** The offline-files cache is set to max out at 10 percent of a hard drive's capacity. (At that point, Windows 2000 purges older offline files to make room for new ones.) This may be too much or too little, depending on how heavily you use offline files. This slider lets you adjust that limit.

Note: This limit applies only to *automatically* cached files, as described on the next page; files you've selected manually don't count toward the total.

Step 2: Choose the Files You Want

Selecting the files you want to use offline is quite simple. Once you're connected to the network (directly or remotely), proceed like this:

Grabbing files

To make individual *files* available offline, open Windows Explorer or My Network Places to find the shared files or folder, exactly as described on pages 289-291. When you locate the files you want, right-click each and select Make Available Offline from the shortcut menu (Figure 14-4). (Alternatively, highlight the file icon and then choose File→Make Available Offline.)

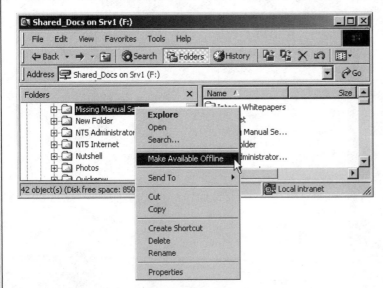

Figure 14-4:
Select only the files you really need. Marking an entire drive or a large folder may seem like a good idea, because you'll have everything you need while on the road—but you'll quickly fill up your hard drive's Offline Files folder, and when you return to the office, you'll suffer very long synchronization times.

Tip: If you right-click a *shortcut* to a file and choose Make Available Offline, Windows finds the file and makes it available. This trick doesn't work with a shortcut to a *folder*, however.

Grabbing folders

You can make entire folders available offline, too, but do so with caution (see Figure 14-4). Find its icon in Windows Explorer or My Network Places; right-click the folder and choose Make Available Offline from the shortcut menu.

If you choose a folder that has subfolders, Windows asks if you want only the folder and the files immediately inside it, or to include the subfolders as well. In any case, Windows now copies the selected files from the network to your hard drive.

Automatic file grabbing

You can also set up a shared folder so that whenever somebody on the network opens the files inside, the files are cached automatically (onto that person's computer). Your fellow network members can keep working on the files they've opened from your PC, even if the network suffers a temporary outage, without even being aware that the files are now "offline." See "Making Shared Folders Available," later in this chapter, for more information.

The Offline Files wizard

The *first time* you use the Make Available Offline command, the Offline Files wizard appears; it offers some of the same options shown in Figure 14-3. After you've answered a few questions and clicked Finish, Windows copies the selected files from the network to your hard drive. (A progress bar lets you know how it's going.)

Note: The *second* time you make a file or folder available—and thereafter—no wizard appears. Once you've chosen the offline files you want, the copying begins immediately.

Step 3: Work with the Offline Files

Even after you've marked files for offline availability, double-clicking their icons still opens the original, network copies—*as long as you're still connected* to the network.

But when you log off from the network, Windows 2000 checks to make sure your laptop has the most recent copies of the files; it may do some additional copying, if necessary. (If you didn't turn on "Synchronize all offline files before logging off," as shown in Figure 14-3, you must synchronize manually before logging off, as described below.)

Once you're disconnected, you can open your My Computer or My Network Places icon; even though you're untethered, you'll see icons for the shared disks and folders, exactly as though you're still plugged into the network. A red X appears on the drive icons, however, to remind you that all of this is only an illusion; Figure 14-5 shows the effect.

Those drives may appear unusually empty, however; in fact, they appear to contain *only* the files and folders you marked for offline use. You can open up and use these files and folders just as you would when you're at the office; you can even save or copy new documents "onto" those drives, or "into" those folders. You even have the same permissions (page 291) that you had when connected to the network.

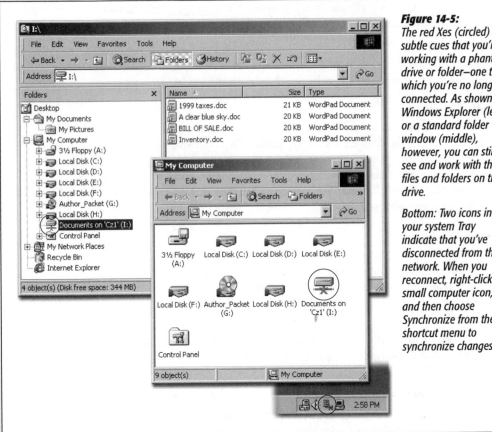

Figure 14-5:
The red Xes (circled) are subtle cues that you're working with a phantom drive or folder—one to which you're no longer connected. As shown in Windows Explorer (left) or a standard folder window (middle), however, you can still see and work with the files and folders on this drive.

Bottom: Two icons in your system Tray indicate that you've disconnected from the network. When you reconnect, right-click the small computer icon, and then choose Synchronize from the shortcut menu to synchronize changes.

Two things help you identify files that originated on the network: First, a double-arrow "badge" appears on the lower-left corner of an offline file's icon. Second, if you highlight an offline file and then open the File menu, you'll see a checkmark next to the Make Available Offline command.

Tip: If you opted for the Offline Files shortcut icon on your desktop (see page 317), you don't have to open My Computer or My Network Places to see the offline files and folders. Instead, just double-click that shortcut.

Step 4: Reconnect and Synchronize

When you return to the office and plug your laptop into the network, Windows automatically synchronizes the folders or files you marked for offline use with the network copies (unless you've turned off this option). When it synchronizes, Windows compares the files and folders on the network server with the copies on your machine, and handles any discrepancies as intelligently as it can. For example, suppose that:

- **Your copy of a document, or the network copy, has been edited since the last synchronization.** Windows copies the newer version so that both "sides" have the same updated version of the file.

- **Your copy *and* the network copy of a file have both been edited.** Windows asks you which copy to keep, and offers you the option of keeping both copies under different names. (See Figure 14-6.)

- **You deleted your copy of the file.** If the network copy hasn't changed, Windows deletes it, too. (If the network copy *has* changed, Windows asks if you want to pick up another copy from the network or delete the file from the server.)

- **Someone deleted the network copy.** Windows deletes your copy, too, if it hasn't changed. If you edited your copy while you were away from the network, Windows 2000 Pro offers you a choice of copying *your* copy of the file to the network or deleting your copy.

- **Someone added a new file to a folder you'd marked for offline use.** Windows automatically copies the new file into your Offline Files folder.

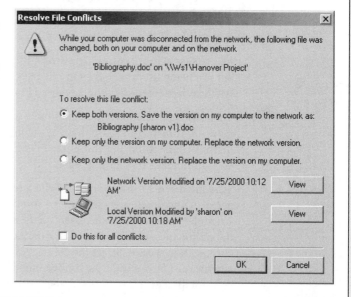

Figure 14-6:
The Resolve Conflicts dialog box lets you view either version of the file and decide to keep either one or both. Generally, you'll want to make this decision a case-by-case basis. But if it's clear that all your conflicts will be resolved in the same way, you can turn on "Do this for all conflicts."

Synchronizing manually

If your computer is set to synchronize automatically, it will do so as soon as you reconnect to your LAN. You have to trigger this synchronization manually, however, under these circumstances:

- One of the offline files is *open* on your local machine.
- You're connecting over a "slow link" (a dial-up connection).

Note: Knowing when to synchronize manually is very important. If you fail to synchronize upon your return to the network, you may open the shared files and folders that *appear* to be on the network–but *the changes you make will be saved locally* (only on your laptop). Furthermore, you may not have access to the rest of the network until you synchronize your changes.

In these cases, start a manual synchronization by opening the Offline Files folder, Windows Explorer, or My Computer; choose Tools→Synchronize. Select the folders to be synchronized, and then click the Synchronize button. (You can also right-click the Offline Files icon in the system Tray, which is pictured in Figure 14-5; choose Synchronize from the shortcut menu.)

Other ways to synchronize

To no one's surprise, Windows 2000 Pro offers a zillion ways to synchronize files. To change your synchronization settings, open Windows Explorer, My Computer, or Offline Files, and choose select Tools→Synchronize. Click Setup; on the Logon/Logoff tab, specify the connection and the offline files you'd like to synchronize automatically when you log onto, or off of, your computer. If you'd rather have Windows 2000 ask you before synchronizing, turn on the "Ask me" checkbox at the bottom of the dialog box.

The other tabs of this dialog box offers some specialized syncing features:

- **Idle-time synchronization.** To synchronize files while your computer is connected but not being used, click the On Idle tab (Figure 14-7). Select the files you want synchronized, then click the Advanced button.

  This setting is useful if your computer spends a lot of time connected to the network; it helps to ensure that your laptop's files are always up to date. (For a dial-up connection, the computer is unlikely to remain idle for periods long enough to make this setting practical.)

- **Scheduled synchronization.** The Scheduled tab lets you set up your machine to perform updates at specified times. (You might set up a regular synchronization schedule to ensure that other users on the network have to most recent version of the offline files, for example.) Click the Add button to start the Scheduled Synchronization wizard. Select the connection and the files to be synchronized, and whether or not you want the connection to be made automatically (by dialing) if your computer isn't connected to the network at the scheduled time. Set the schedule for updates.

Provide a name for this particular synchronized schedule. After you click Finish, your scheduled sync's name appears among the Current Synchronization tasks on the Scheduled tab. You can always modify any of the scheduled tasks on this page by highlighting the one you want to change and clicking Edit.

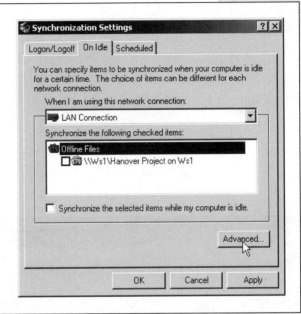

Figure 14-7:
By default, Windows waits for 15 minutes of inactivity before starting synchronization, and then updates every 60 minutes as long as the connection remains active. Click the Advanced button to change these settings.

Quick vs. Full Synchronization

The synchronization process doesn't always leave you with a set of files that are identical to those on the network. In some circumstances, the files are only copied one way (from your laptop to the network, for example). For example, sometimes Windows gives you a Full synchronization, and sometimes only a Quick one:

- **Full synchronization.** The latest versions of all offline files are copied both to and from your laptop. Your machine is now completely up to date with the network.

- **Quick synchronization.** Unlike a Full sync, this one-way, much faster process checks to make sure that you have a copy of every network file you've flagged for offline use. If a new document was dropped into one of the network folders since your last sync, for example, you'll get a copy of it.

  But a Quick sync doesn't compare the file *versions* on your laptop and on the network server to make sure that your copies are the most *current* copies. It just makes sure that you have *a* copy of every file.

Clearly, it's important to do a Full synchronization periodically. This table lets you know when Windows 2000 gives you a Quick sync, and when a Full one:

Type of Synchronization	Offline Changes Sent to the Network?	Network sends files offline?
Automatic synchronization when logging on	Yes	No
Synchronize while idle	Yes	Quick
Scheduled Synchronization	Yes	Full
Right-click the offline files icon on the Taskbar and select Synchronize	Yes	No
Select Tools→Synchronize	Yes	Full
"Synchronize all offline files before logging off" is on	Yes	Full
"Synchronize all offline files before logging off" is off	No	Quick
Right-click file and select Make Available Offline	No	Quick

TROUBLESHOOTING MOMENT

Clearing the Offline Files Cache

Suppose you've become completely confused about which files are which, or you're finished with your traveling and would like to reclaim the disk space being used by your laptop's offline files. To completely clear the offline files database, you can *reinitialize the cache*.

Doing so deletes all the offline files from your offline files folder (including any changes you've made). Note, too, that you'll have to restart the machine, and that you can't undo a reinitialization. (You can always go back to the network and make the files available offline once again, however.)

To reinitialize the cache, open Windows Explorer or your Offline Files folder. Choose Tools→Folder Options→ Offline Files. While pressing the Ctrl and Shift keys, click Delete Files. Read the warning dialog box and confirm that you know what you're doing.

Making Shared Folders Available

On a network, the network administrator generally decides which files and folders can be made available for offline use. However, if you're on a stand-alone computer or a peer-to-peer network (see Chapter 15), *you* will be specifying which folders you want to share in this way.

To do so, right-click the folder in Windows Explorer or My Computer and select Properties from the shortcut menu. Click the Sharing tab. Turn on Sharing, as described on page 296; finally, click Caching to open the setting dialog box shown in Figure 14-8.

If the "Allow caching of the files in this shared folder" box is checked, use the drop-down menu to indicate how you want the files to be handled:

- **Manual Caching for Documents.** Files are available for offline use; the people connecting to your machine are responsible for synchronization.

- **Automatic Caching for Documents.** Any files your colleagues open (from the network) will be automatically made available offline on their machines (subject to the hard drive limit shown in Figure 14-3).

This setting is useful when you're accessing important files across an unreliable or temporary network connection.

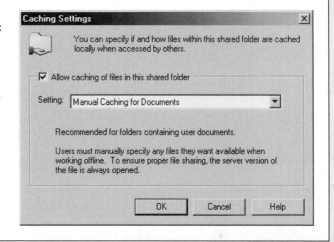

Figure 14-8:
This dialog box determines how Windows will handle the files you share when a network user selects them for offline use. The uppermost checkbox is the on/off switch for making this shared folder available offline. If you remove the check, the files in the folder won't be available for offline use at all.

The Briefcase

The Briefcase (which appears when you right-click the desktop and choose New→Briefcase form the shortcut menu) was an earlier Microsoft attempt to help you keep your files straight when you transport them from desktop to laptop, or from home to work.

The Offline Files feature described in this chapter is a far superior means of keeping your document versions straight. But if you're intrigued by the Briefcase, here's how it works.

Start by finding the icons of the documents you'll want to work on when away from your main PC. Drag them onto the My Briefcase icon. Now connect your laptop to the desktop PC, if it isn't already. Or, if you plan to take your files with you on a disk (such as a floppy or Zip disk), insert it. Drag the My Briefcase icon onto the laptop or the disk.

You're ready to leave your office. When you get wherever you're going, feel free to open and edit the documents in the copied Briefcase "folder" icon; just be sure to leave them there.

When you return to your main PC, reconnect the laptop or reinsert the travel disk. Open the disk or laptop window, and double-click its My Briefcase icon. In the Briefcase window, click Update All. Windows copies the edited files back to their original folders on your desktop-PC hard drive, automatically replacing the older, original copies. (If you highlight only some of the icons in the Briefcase window, you can instead click Update Selection; Windows copies only the highlighted icons back to the main PC.)

- **Automatic Caching for Applications.** Use this setting only for programs or files that can't be modified while offline.

Tip: Automatic caching for programs can be a little tricky. For example, suppose you open Microsoft PowerPoint but don't use the design templates. Later, when offline, you'll be able to run PowerPoint–but you won't be able to use any design templates, because they never got copied to your hard drive. Only program files that actually *run* get automatically cached.

Building a Peer-to-Peer Network

As noted in Chapter 13, Windows 2000 is all about networking; most of the world's Windows 2000 Pro computers are connected to a network in some way. Big corporate networks require the purchase of Windows 2000 Server, a computer or two that do nothing but run the network, and the services of a professional network guru.

If you're running a small business—or even a household—on Windows 2000, however, you're still invited to the network party. Without having to buy extra computers, operating systems, or staff, you can create a smaller, less complex kind of network called a *peer-to-peer* network. It's ideal for setting up several PCs to perform the convenience tricks that make networks so attractive:

- Opening drives and folders on one computer while seated at another.

- Sharing a single printer among all of your computers.

- Installing programs from shared CD-ROMs.

- Communicating with other users on the network using email, chat, and even (with the proper hardware) audio and video. (NetMeeting, described on page 180, makes many of these features possible.)

- Sharing a single Internet connection.

- Running your own personal *intranet* Web server (that is, create a "Web site" that only the other machines on your network can visit).

- Backing up your files to a single network tape or disk drive.

- Venting your aggressions on your family and co-workers with multiplayer games.

Once you get used to having a network in your home or office, you'll wonder how you ever lived without one. Gone will be the days when you had to use the "sneakernet" to print out a file by copying it to a floppy disk and carrying it to another machine.

Peer-to-Peer Networking

In a peer-to-peer network, the computers function as equals. Unlike a Windows 2000 Server network, where a central computer maintains the list of passwords for everyone on the network, each peer-to-peer network PC maintains its own security settings, list of authorized users, and so on.

When only a handful of computers are involved, the maintenance tasks aren't overwhelming. But when the network grows larger than about ten computers, peer-to-peer networking becomes unwieldy, because each user must have an account on each computer that he wants to access over the network. At that point, it's a good idea to start thinking about adding a Windows 2000 Server system.

On a peer-to-peer network, each person decides which files and folders to share, and who should be able to use them. This method of networking is simpler but less secure than a Windows 2000 Server network, where all of the security data (such as who can access what) is stored in a central location.

In other words, you won't find peer-to peer networks at the Pentagon, but they're fine for your home or a small office.

Hardware Requirements for Networking

Generally speaking, PCs are sold with all of the networking *software* included in the operating system, but none of the networking *hardware*.

You can connect the computers using any one of several different methods. Some networking kits save you the trouble of wiring your home by sending networking signals along the wiring that's already *in* your house—telephone or electrical wiring. Other kits provide *wireless* networking, which works by transmitting radio waves from PC to PC. You can even get fiber-optic cable kits for networks.

But these networking methods are more expensive and usually much slower than the world's most popular networking system: Ethernet. Tens of millions of Ethernet systems have been installed around the world. Ethernet hardware is readily available at almost any computer store, although you'll find a better selection of products and better prices by shopping online or from catalogs. Ethernet is the easiest and least expensive kind of network to configure and maintain—and it's fast. This section shows you how to create an Ethernet network.

An Ethernet network requires three components: *network interface adapters,* Ethernet cables, and an Ethernet hub.

Network Interface Adapters

You may hear this kind of circuit board called a networking card, a network interface card, or a NIC ("nick"). Either way, it looks like a standard expansion card; one goes into an expansion slot (PCI or ISA) in each PC, as described in Chapter 16.

When shopping for networking cards, consider these features:

- **Bus (slot) type.** If you have a desktop system, a PCI card is the fastest and cheapest kind of network card. Alternatively, you can use a USB network card that you simply plug into a USB port on a desktop or portable computer. If you're using a laptop that doesn't have a built-in NIC, you'll probably want to get a network card that adheres to the *CardBus PC Card* standard (which is faster than the standard PCMCIA PC Card standard).

- **Network Speed.** You can buy Ethernet gear that runs at three speeds: 10 Mbps (megabits per second), called *standard* Ethernet; 100 Mbps, called *Fast* Ethernet; and 1,000 Mbps, called Gigabit Ethernet. On a Fast Ethernet network, you can copy files from one PC to another in a tenth the time it would take on a standard Ethernet setup. (Gigabit Ethernet, a relatively new and expensive development, is overkill for most peer-to-peer networks.)

Fortunately, Fast Ethernet equipment costs almost the same as standard Ethernet gear. Furthermore, all Fast Ethernet cards these days are actually dual-speed cards, meaning that they can run at *either* 10 or 100 Mbps.

To run at the faster speed, your network's NICs, hub (described next), and cables must *all* be Fast Ethernet-capable. When a computer with a dual-speed NIC powers up, the card communicates with the hub at the fastest speed offered by both. It's a good idea, therefore, to buy dual-speed networking cards for your computers now, even if you plan to run them at 10 Mbps using a standard Ethernet hub. Later, you can simply replace the hub with a Fast Ethernet model and increase the speed of your entire network to 100 Mbps.

UP TO SPEED

What's a Megabit?

The speed of a local area network (LAN) is measured in *megabits per second* (Mbps). In this context, a megabit is one million bits, with each bit representing a 0 or a 1.

Bits per second is the same measuring system as that used to quantify modem speeds, except that networks run much faster. A 33.6 Kbps modem, for example, runs at about 33,600 bits per second, while a standard 10 Mbps Ethernet network runs at about 10 million bits per second, and Fast Ethernet at about 100 million bits per second. As you can

imagine, the speed of even a standard Ethernet network connection runs rings around the fastest modem. File transfers that would take minutes, hours, or days using a modem are completed in seconds on a LAN.

In fact, even the *fastest* Internet connections pale in comparison to Ethernet speeds. The T1 connections that corporations and service providers use to connect to the Internet run at only 1.44 Mbps—many times faster than your dial-up modem, but much slower than even a modest LAN.

The only penalty for running your network at the faster speed is in its expandability. With standard Ethernet, you can expand the network by connecting up to four hubs together, while Fast Ethernet limits you to two.

Network Hubs

A hub—an inexpensive box with five, eight, or more jacks (ports) for Ethernet cables—is the central point of an Ethernet network. It physically connects all the cables and, therefore, all the computers. To build the network, you connect the networking card in each computer to the hub with a cable.

Ethernet hubs are available with different numbers of ports. Large corporate networks use elaborate rack-mounted affairs, but you can buy a reliable, brand-name Ethernet hub no larger than a paperback book, designed to accommodate five or eight computers, for less than $75 (see Figure 15-1).

Tip: It's a good idea to buy a hub with an extra port or two for future expansion.

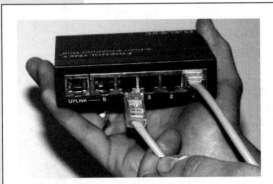

Figure 15-1:
Ethernet hubs have RJ-45 ports, often in multiples of four, plus a special port called an **uplink** *or* crossover *port, which you can use to connect one hub to another. When you connect hubs in this manner, the computers all become part of the same LAN. Just be sure not to connect more than four standard Ethernet hubs together or more than two (Class II) Fast Ethernet hubs.*

Like networking cards, hubs come in regular or Fast Ethernet versions. However, unlike networking cards, which are nearly all dual-speed, many hubs support regular *or* Fast Ethernet, but not both. If all computers on your network have Fast Ethernet cards, you may be tempted to buy a single-speed Fast Ethernet hub. But remember that someday, you may want to add a 10 Mbps Ethernet device, such as a cable modem, network appliance, or a computer with an older USB Ethernet adapter. In that case, you'd be better off with a dual-speed hub, one that supports both Fast Ethernet and standard Ethernet. Dual-speed hubs are only slightly more expensive than single-speed hubs.

Tip: When buying network cards and hubs, be sure that you're buying gear whose packaging specifically states that it's Windows 2000 compatible.

Network Cables

Ethernet wiring looks like telephone wire, but the two aren't the same; both the wire (called *10BaseT, 100BaseT* or *Cat 5* cable) and the little clip at each end (called a *RJ-45* connector) are slightly fatter on network cables than on a phone cable.

Professional installers buy their network cable in bulk, run it through walls and ceilings, and then attach the connectors to the ends. When you're building a small network for your home or office, however, you can buy prefabricated cables of various lengths, with the connectors already attached.

Any computer store or mail-order outfit will know what you want if you simply request "Ethernet cable." Most cables today are labeled Category 5, which is fine for both standard and Fast Ethernet networks. (Category 3 cable works for standard Ethernet, but not Fast Ethernet; Category 5 *Enhanced,* or Category *5E* cables, are intended for use with Gigabit Ethernet.)

Installing Network Hardware

Once you've purchased the right hardware, installing it is easy:

1. **Install a NIC into each computer that you want to connect to the network.**

   Installing a network card is just like installing an audio adapter, internal modem, or other expansion card. You open the computer case (usually the hardest part), remove the slot cover from an open expansion slot, insert the NIC into the slot, and secure it with the screw that held the slot cover in place.

   If your network card is a PC Card, insert it into your laptop.

2. **Find a central location for the hub and plug it into a power socket.**

   Once everything is connected, you won't need to access the hub unless there's a problem, so you can put it somewhere out of sight, such as behind a piece of furniture. (In corporate offices, it's often hidden away in a wiring closet.) Your best bet is to find a location central to your computers, so that you can keep cable lengths to a minimum.

3. **Insert one end of a cable into the NIC on each computer, run it to the hub, and plug the other end into a hub port.**

   You can run the cables from the computers to the hub in almost any way you wish: behind furniture, through walls, or inside drop ceilings.

   Note, however, that two things can threaten the health of your cables: pinching and electromagnetic interference. Don't walk on your cables, rest furniture on them, or secure them to baseboards with standard square staples. You should also avoid running cables near fluorescent light fixtures, electric motors, nuclear reactors, and the like.

Finally, when you connect the computer cable to the hub, don't use the port marked Uplink or Crossover. It's for connecting hubs together or sharing a cable modem or DSL router among all the computers on your network.

Installing Networking Software

Fortunately, once you've purchased the hardware for your network, there's nothing else to buy; Windows 2000 Professional contains all the software you need to get your computers communicating.

GEM IN THE ROUGH

Two-Computer Ethernet—and Direct Connections

If you want to network only two computers, you can do so without having to buy and set up a hub.

All you need is a special cable called a *crossover cable,* which can connect two computers directly. It costs about $10 at your local computer store or online shop; just run the cable directly from one networking card to the other. Everything else in this chapter works exactly as though you had purchased a hub and were using a "real" Ethernet network.

There's another way to connect two machines, too—one that doesn't even require Ethernet cards: *direct connections.* You can create this kind of miniature homemade network only if (a) the computers are close to each other, and (b) they both have parallel ports, serial (COM) ports, or infrared ports.

If both machines have parallel ports, you need a Basic or Fast parallel cable from Parallel Technology (*www.lpt.com*); if both have serial ports, you need a *null modem cable* (and lower expectations; serial connections aren't as fast as parallel for this purpose).

To begin, log onto the first PC with an account that has administrative privileges, as described on page 369. Now run the Network Connection Wizard (choose Start→ Settings→Network and Dial-Up Connections, then double-click the Make New Connection icon). Click Next. Choose "Connect directly to another computer"; click Next again.

Now you're asked if the computer you're using will be the

host (the machine whose files will be shared) or the *guest* (the one that will be accessing shared resources on the other machine). Choose Host, and then click Next.

On the remaining wizard screens, you're asked to specify the port you're using to connect the machines (you see a list of all unused serial, parallel, or infrared ports); which users are allowed to use this connection; and a name for the connection icon.

Windows responds by creating an Incoming Connections icon in the Network and Dial-Up Connections window. You can adjust its properties to change the settings you've just made. (It also lets you change the settings for other kinds of incoming connections, such as the Virtual Private Networks and dial-in connections described in the previous chapter.)

Repeat all of this on the other machine, this time designating it the Guest. An icon called Direct Connection appears in *its* Network and Dial-Up Connections window.

At this point, you're ready to connect. On the guest machine, double-click the Direct Connection icon, enter your name and password (you must have an account on the host machine), and click Connect. An icon on your Taskbar tray appears that lets you know you're connected; if you point to it without clicking, a popup window appears that shows you the connection speed and other statistics. You can open the My Network Places icon on the guest machine; you'll see the shared folders, disks, and printers, just as though they were connected via "real" network.

The building blocks of the Windows 2000 networking architecture may sound technical, but there's no avoiding them; as you set up your network, you'll need to install at least one of each software component:

- **Network adapter drivers** are the drivers for your networking card. Windows 2000 Professional includes drivers for most of the popular networking cards manufactured today. (Most cards come with a driver disk, as well.)

- **Clients** are software modules that redirect your computer's requests for access to network file and printer resources. For example, when you use an application's File→Open menu and select a file on a network drive, the client redirects the request for access to the file from the local file system to the network share.

- **Protocols** are the languages spoken by the computers on the network. For two systems to communicate, they must have at least one protocol in common.

- **Services** are programs that load automatically whenever the PC starts up—in this context, modules that let Windows 2000 Professional share its own resources and provide other network services.

The following sections examine the installation of each of these modules in turn.

Installing the Adapter Driver

Most network cards today support the Plug-and-Play standard (see the next chapter). After installing the card, all you have to do to install its driver is turn on the computer; Plug and Play detects the new card and installs the appropriate driver.

In fact, if you perform a fresh installation of Windows 2000 Professional with the networking card already installed, the setup program installs the driver *and* all the software modules you need for basic network communications (as described in the following sections). If you add the networking card *after* installing Windows 2000, Plug and Play detects the card and installs its driver, but you must then install the other networking modules yourself.

If Windows 2000 detects your card, but doesn't have a driver for it, the system prompts you for the location of a driver. Virtually all NICs come with drivers on a floppy disk or CD-ROM; simply direct the program to the location of the driver files. The system does the rest. (See Chapter 16 for help with installing NICs that Plug and Play doesn't recognize.)

Installing a Client

Once you've installed your network adapter and its driver, you're ready to install the other networking software components—including the *client* software. Here's how to go about it:

1. **Choose Start→Settings→Control Panel. Open the Network and Dial-up Connections folder shortcut.**

   The Network and Dial-up Connections window appears.

2. **Right-click the Local Area Connection icon; choose Properties from the shortcut menu.**

If the Local Area Connection icon doesn't appear, then you haven't successfully installed your networking card and its software.

3. **Click Install.**

If you've just installed your card, the Local Area Connection Properties dialog box displays the adapter driver in the Connect Using box, and the Components box starts out blank (Figure 15-2, left.) The Install button lets you begin adding components.

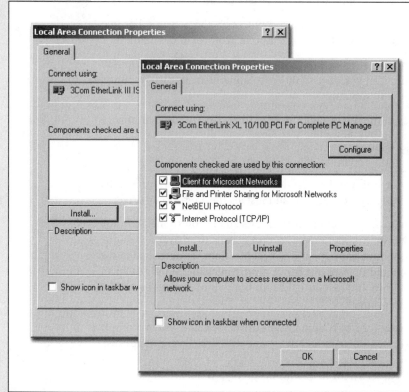

Figure 15-2:
Creating a small network involves adding at least three software components to this list, shown before (left) and after the installations are complete: a client, a protocol, and a service. If you turn on "Show icon in taskbar when connected," an icon appears in the Taskbar tray that indicates when you're connected to the network.

4. **Highlight the Client component type and click Add.**

The Select Network Component Type dialog box appears.

5. **Highlight Client; click Add.**

A list appears, showing the available clients in Windows 2000 Professional.

6. **Select Client for Microsoft Networks and click OK.**

The other option here, Client for NetWare Networks, is exclusively for Novell NetWare servers—something you probably don't have on your homemade, peer-to-peer network.

After a moment of thought, your PC shows the client module's name (Client for Microsoft Networks) in the Components list. Be sure that its checkbox is turned on.

At this point, you could click the Close button to complete the client installation. But if you leave the Local Area Connection Properties dialog box open, you can proceed with the next part of the networking software installation.

Installing Protocols

Your next step involves installing a *protocol*—a networking language. Windows 2000 Professional includes three protocol modules that you can use on your peer-to-peer network, but the computers on your network can't communicate unless you've installed at least one common protocol on each one.

If you've just followed the preceding steps to install the client module, continue as described here. (If not, follow the previous Steps 1 and 2 before proceeding with these steps.)

1. **Click Install.**

   The Select Network Component Type dialog box appears.

2. **Click Protocol, then Add.**

   Now the Select Network Protocol dialog box appears (see Figure 15-3), listing the protocols available in Windows 2000.

   Choose **Internet Protocol (TCP/IP)** if you'd like the various PCs on your network to be able to use a single Internet connection simultaneously (such as a phone line or cable modem), as described on page 339. TCP/IP has other advantages, too: It's the networking language spoken by the Internet and the majority of the world's LANs, and it's almost infinitely expandable. Its disadvantage is that it requires a trek through some technical turf—you must configure each computer with its own unique *IP address,* as described on page 336.)

   On the other hand, if sharing a single Internet connection *isn't* one of the goals of your networking experiment, choose **NetBEUI Protocol**. It's much easier to set up than TCP/IP and provides the same basic network features.

   NetBEUI (NetBIOS Extended User Interface) is used almost exclusively on small Microsoft Windows networks. Its primary advantage is that it requires no configuration. All you have to do is install the protocol module; your network is ready to go. The drawbacks of NetBEUI are that it doesn't work through a *router* (you can't connect several NetBEUI networks together to form a larger network), and you can't use it to access the Internet. (You can still use TCP/IP for *individual* dial-up connections to the Internet, while running NetBEUI on your internal network; you just can't share a single Internet connection among the networked PCs.)

Choose **NWLink IPX/SPX/NetBIOS Compatible Transport Protocol** only if you have a NetWare server on your network. (You'd know it if you did.)

3. **Highlight one of the listed protocols and click OK.**

After a moment, you return to the Local Area Connection Properties dialog box, where the name of the protocol you chose now appears in the list. You can close the dialog box now (or leave it open if you'd like to install another module). Make sure that the checkbox next to the protocol is filled before you close the dialog box.

At this point, as before, you could click the Close button to complete the protocol installation. But to finish up the networking software installation, leave the box open.

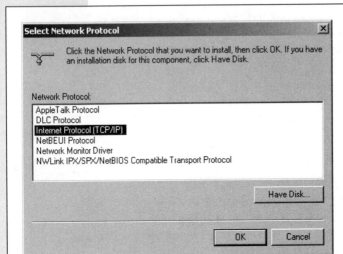

Figure 15-3:
Windows 2000 Professional offers six protocol modules, but only the Internet Protocol (TCP/IP), NetBEUI Protocol, and NWLink IPX/SPX/ NetBIOS Compatible Protocol modules are suitable for general networking. AppleTalk Protocol lets your PC talk to Macintosh computers, DLC Protocol module is for printing, and the Network Monitor Driver supports the Network Monitor application included with Windows 2000 Server.

Configuring TCP/IP

If you chose the TCP/IP protocol, as described in the preceding section, you must now configure each workstation with its own *IP address* that's unique on the network. (If you chose one of the other protocols, skip down to "Installing Services.") As noted above, TCP/IP's primary disadvantage is this configuration step, which isn't necessary for any of the other protocols.

Here's how to go about it. (If the Local Area Connection Properties dialog box isn't already open, open it using steps 1 and 2 on pages 333–334.)

1. **Highlight "Internet Protocol (TCP/IP)" in the Components list and click the Properties button.**

The Internet Protocol (TCP/IP) Properties dialog box appears, as shown in Figure 15-4.

2. **Click "Use the following IP address."**

Unless you have a device acting as a DHCP server on your network (such as a DSL/cable modem router or a Windows computer running Internet Connection Sharing), select "Use the following IP address."

Figure 15-4:
The Internet Protocol (TCP/IP) Properties dialog box is where you configure the IP address for a network interface, as well as the other TCP/IP settings. If you have a second NIC in the system, the Network and Dial-up Connections control panel has a second Local Area Connection icon with its own Properties dialog box. You must assign the second NIC its own IP address and other settings. In the same way, if you have a dial-up connection to the Internet, it has its own IP address, assigned by your ISP.

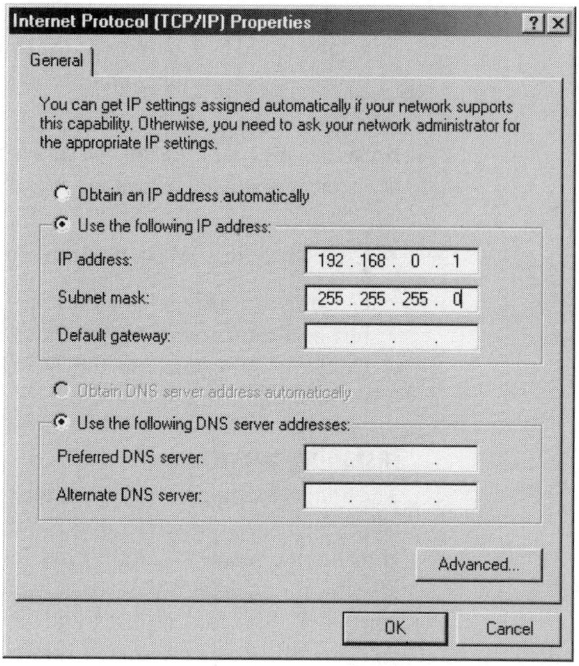

3. **Enter an IP address in the field provided.**

An IP address consists of four integers between 0 and 255, separated by periods (such as 192.168.22.7). Part of the IP address identifies the network, and the other part identifies the computer itself (which is called the *host* in TCP/IP lingo).

Every Internet-connected computer in the world has its own, exclusive IP address that's been registered (usually by an ISP) with a body called the Internet Assigned Numbers Authority (IANA). You could conceivably obtain registered addresses for your networked PCs from an ISP; your machines could then connect to the Internet using one computer as a router. But there are several reasons why that's not a good idea. First, ISPs nearly always charge extra for registered IP addresses; second, connecting your computers to the Internet this way makes them vulnerable to attack from the insidious forces prowling cyberspace.

Instead, you can configure your workstations with a special sequence of IP addresses that have been set aside expressly for use on private networks. Because these addresses aren't accessible from the Internet, your systems are safe from outside intrusion, and it doesn't matter that other computers in the world may be using the same numbers.

These special addresses all begin with *192.168*. The third number can be any integer, as long as it's the same on every computer on your network. For the fourth number, give each machine a different integer between 1 and 254.

For example, the IP addresses for your first computer might be 192.168.1.1; the second could be 192.168.1.2; the third could be 192.168.1.3, and so on (although there's no reason the final numbers have to be consecutive).

Tip: As you type in the IP address, you can advance from one chunk of the address to the next either by clicking the corresponding fields or by typing a period after each integer.

---

4. **Click the Subnet Mask field and enter the value 255.255.255.0. Then click OK.**

Clicking the OK button closes the Internet Protocol (TCP/IP) Properties dialog box and returns you to the Local Area Connection Properties dialog box. The changes you've made to the TCP/IP configuration won't take effect until you reboot the system.

Installing Services

The final networking component type is the *service*, a program that loads automatically when the computer boots. In this context, it means *networking* services included with Windows 2000 Professional—namely, the one called File and Printer Sharing for Microsoft Networks, which lets you grant other users access to your computer's files, folders, disks, and printers over the network. (Without this service, you can still access the shared resources on *other* machines, but other users can't access yours.)

POWER USERS' CLINIC

Other TCP/IP Settings

When you share an Internet connection with your network using a DSL router or cable modem or a Windows computer running Internet Connection Sharing, you won't need to configure TCP/IP. If the systems are configured to obtain IP addresses automatically, the device or computer sharing the connection provides the proper TCP/IP settings to all computers.

However, in some instances, you may need to manually specify the Default Gateway (router) that you want your computers to use to access the Internet.

You also must supply the IP address of one or more *DNS servers*, running either on your network or on your ISP's. You make both of these settings on the same page of the box shown in Figure 15-4.

To install the File and Printer Sharing for Microsoft Networks service, use the following procedure. (If the Local Area Connection Properties dialog box isn't already open, open it using steps 1 and 2 on pages 333–334.)

1. **Click the Install button.**

   The Select Network Component Type dialog box appears.

2. **Click Service, then Add.**

   Now you're in the Select Network Service dialog box.

3. **Highlight File and Printer Sharing for Microsoft Networks; click OK.**

   You're back at the Local Area Connection Properties dialog box one last time.

4. **Click the Close button.**

If you've installed a number of networking components one after the other, having progressed steadily through this chapter, clicking the Close button completes the installations. Windows may now ask you to insert the Windows 2000 Professional CD-ROM; finally, when the installation procedure finishes, you'll be prompted to restart the computer.

Once the system restarts—and after you've repeated all of the steps described in this chapter on *every* PC on your network—your network is ready for action. You should be able to log on to the network, open My Network Places or Windows Explorer, and see icons representing the other computers on the network, exactly as described on page 289. By double-clicking those computer icons, you can see and open the folders on the other PCs of the network—at least those that have been *shared*, a procedure described on page 295.

Sharing an Internet Connection

Once your network is running, your computers can share disks, folders, files, and so on, using the techniques described in Chapter 13. However, the small-network function that's rising the fastest in popularity is Internet connection sharing.

Many homes have two or more computers these days, and even small offices usually have more than that. But connecting their users to the Internet has always been a problem. Individual dial-up connections require a modem, a phone line, and an ISP account for *each* computer, which adds up to a considerable expense and inconvenience. The other traditional method, which involves the installation of a router and a high-speed connection to an ISP, is fine if your multinational corporation is showing a profit this month.

Fortunately, Windows 2000 Pro offers a built-in feature called Internet Connection Sharing, which offers a clever alternative. It lets you share one Internet connection, using a modem, cable modem, or DSL hook-up, with the other computers on the network. If one of your PCs is blessed with a cable modem or DSL, this arrangement can save you a lot of money—the other computers on your network can enjoy the same always-online, high-speed access without your having to pay another $40 a month for each. And if you use a standard dial-up modem, everybody in the house can be surfing the Internet at the same time, over the same phone-line connection. (When you launch your Web browser or email program on the PC downstairs, for example, the *upstairs,* router PC dials or connects; you surf in the kitchen *via* the upstairs PC. If the upstairs PC is turned off, nobody else in the house can go online.)

Tip: As a bonus, Windows 2000's Internet Connection Sharing feature also provides your computers extra safety from hackers.

To use Internet Connection Sharing, the *gateway* computer—the one that will actually connect to the Internet—needs both a connection to the Internet (via modem, DSL, or cable modem) *and* a connection to your local network. If you're using a DSL connection or cable modem, you may therefore have to install *two* network cards in your computer, one for your DSL router or cable modem, the other for your network.

Before you begin, test the gateway PC's Internet connection by browsing the Web, and its network connection by connecting to another PC. Then proceed like this:

1. **On the gateway PC, choose Start→Settings→Network and Dial-up Connections.**

   The Network and Dial-up Connections folder opens, revealing an icon for your connection to the Internet.

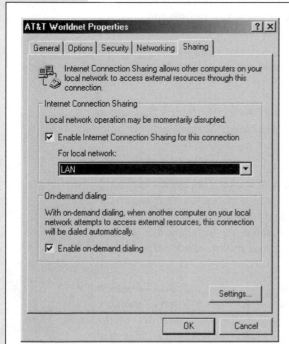

Figure 15-5:
If you're sharing a dial-up connection, make sure that the Enable On-Demand Dialing checkbox is turned on; if you have multiple network cards, select the network connection to which you want to provide Internet access.

2. **Right-click your connection to the Internet; choose Properties from the short-cut menu.**

   The Properties dialog box appears.

3. **Click the Sharing tab, then turn on Internet Connection Sharing (Figure 15-5).**

   If you'd like the gateway machine to connect to the Internet automatically whenever another computer on your network tries to connect—an excellent idea—make sure that "Enable on-demand dialing" is also turned on.

4. **Click OK. Configure all other computers to configure their IP addresses automatically.**

   That is, on each machine, choose Start→Settings→Network and Dial-up Connections. Double-click the network-connection icon; double-click "Internet Protocol (TCP/IP)"; select "Obtain an IP address automatically"; click OK, then OK again; and then reboot the computer. (If the Internet protocol [TCP/IP] isn't listed, install it as described on page 335.)

5. **Configure each computer to connect to the Internet via the local network.**

   To do so, choose Start→Programs→Accessories→Communication→Internet Connection Wizard. Select "I want to set up my Internet connection manually," and then click Next. On the subsequent wizard screens, you'll be asked if you'd like Windows to detect your proxy settings automatically (you probably do, unless you know the correct settings) and whether or not you want an Internet mail account (probably not, for this purpose). Click Finish; the deed is done.

Part Five:
Managing Your Computer

5

Adding and
Removing Hardware

When it comes to adding new components to your PC, the bad old days of Windows NT were pretty dreadful. Installing a printer was difficult—but installing a sound card or modem was an exercise in masochism. A CNN (Certified Network Nerd) credential was essential.

That's because, when you attach a new component to your PC (modem, scanner, printer, networking card, digital camera, and so on), it won't work unless it has its own communication channels to your PC's brain—technical resources with such helpful names as interrupt request (IRQ) lines, direct memory access (DMA) channels, I/O addresses, and memory addresses. Your PC has a limited number of these resources; in the days before Plug and Play, the computer's components may have competed for the same channels or memory addresses, resulting in *resource conflicts* that could take hours to solve, if a solution was even possible.

Microsoft's Plug-and-Play technology is designed to eliminate much of this hassle. When you connect a Plug-and-Play device to your PC, Windows 2000 automatically and instantly configures its resource settings, and even installs its driver software, with very little effort on your part. Changing hardware components hasn't become completely effortless, but the pain is less severe and certainly less widespread, thanks to the Plug-and-Play standard.

This chapter covers Plug and Play; what to do when Plug and Play doesn't work; troubleshooting add-on equipment; and other aspects of adding new equipment to your machine.

Hardware and Windows 2000

Windows 2000 Pro works with a very wide range of hardware, but it's happiest with the components you'll find on the Hardware Compatibility List (HCL). In fact, you probably shouldn't even consider buying new equipment for your Windows 2000 Pro PC that *isn't* on the HCL (visit *www.microsoft.com/hcl*, then search for the product you're considering buying). On the other hand, if you already have hardware that you don't want to replace and that isn't on the list, try it. Plenty of hardware that isn't on the HCL works under Windows 2000 anyway. Some will work just fine. Some will be flaky; that's the stuff you end up having to replace.

But if reliability is important to you, you can reduce the reboots, crashes, and system lockups to almost zero by using only hardware from the HCL and only Windows 2000 logo software. Microsoft guarantees that items on the HCL will work with Windows 2000. If you run into a hardware problem with a non-HCL part, the manufacturer may send you to Microsoft, and Microsoft will send you to the HCL.

UP TO SPEED

Hardware Jargon

Driver and *port* are terms that you need to understand in order not to be driven mad by hardware talk. A driver (also called a device driver) is a piece of software that introduces your computer to a particular piece of hardware (modem, printer, scanner, keyboard, or whatever). This software includes all the information Windows needs to communicate with that hardware.

Ports are the conduits through which information is transferred in and out of your computer. In general, ports are physical plugs on the back of your computer, such as ports for a printer (parallel or USB port), modem (serial or USB port), monitor (VGA port), and so on. Ports also have a software component in Windows, so it's possible to disable a port through Windows or even change some of the port properties to accommodate special hardware.

Adding Hardware

When adding hardware to the inside of your computer, or to its serial or SCSI ports, the basic rules are:

1. Turn off the computer.

2. Plug in the hardware.

3. Turn on the computer.

For most modern hardware components, that's all there is to it. When you turn the computer on, a window announces that Windows 2000 has detected new hardware and is installing its software. You can use the new device immediately thereafter.

For external devices that plug into a USB port, FireWire port, or PC Card slot, the process is even simpler: Just connect the gadget. If it's a Plug-and-Play compatible device, Windows 2000 recognizes, configures, and installs the driver software for it automatically, without your having to turn off or restart the computer.

Tip: If your device isn't recognized when you plug it in, restart your computer.

Adding Hardware

The Add/Remove Hardware Wizard

Unfortunately, the Plug-and-Play system isn't foolproof. To install the drivers for older, *non*-Plug-and-Play hardware, or Plug-and-Play hardware that Windows 2000 doesn't recognize for some reason, run the Add/Remove Hardware Wizard like this:

1. **Plug the new equipment into the computer, and turn the computer back on.**

2. **Choose Start→Settings→Control Panel. In the Control Panel window, double click Add/Remove Hardware.**

   The Add/Remove Hardware Wizard begins.

3. **Click Next.**

   On the "Choose a Hardware Task" screen, the option you want ("Add/Troubleshoot a device") is already selected.

4. **Click Next again.**

   Now Windows 2000 searches for new hardware.

   If the wizard can't find any new hardware, it opens a window showing the hardware it knows about and asking which device is troubling you (Figure 16-1).

   If your new hardware is listed, click its name and then click Next. If Windows now reports that it's working properly (which it obviously isn't), click Finish to

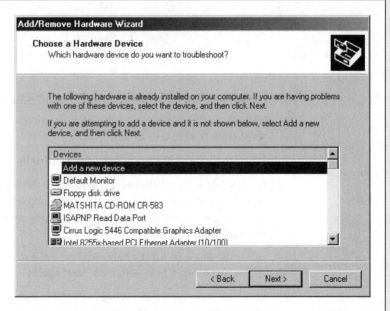

Figure 16-1:
Windows reports on the devices it finds. If your new hardware is listed, highlight it and click Next. If it's not shown, highlight Add a New Device and click Next.

launch a Troubleshooter (a troubleshooting wizard). If the Troubleshooter doesn't solve your problem, see page 359.

If your hardware *isn't* listed, proceed like this:

5. **Highlight the "Add a new device" option at the top of the list; click Next.**

   Windows offers a choice: "Yes, search for network hardware" and "No, I want to select the hardware from a list." There's no harm in letting Windows search; in fact, you may save time. If Windows can't find the hardware, you'll get to choose the device from a list anyway (Figure 16-2).

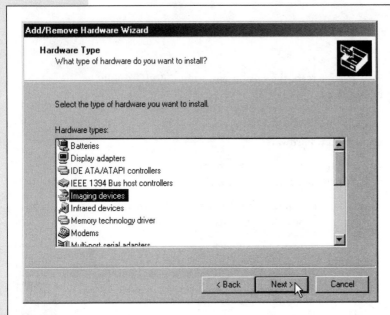

Figure 16-2:
Highlight the type of hardware and click Next. If the hardware doesn't fall into any of the categories listed, scroll to and select Other Devices to choose from the complete list of manufacturers and equipment.

6. **Click Next. If the Windows search comes up empty-handed, click Next again.**

   If the wizard finds no new hardware, it shows you a list of device types (Modems, Network adapters, and so on).

7. **Select the type of hardware you want to install; click Next.**

   Now Windows opens the two-paned Select a Device Driver window, listing manufacturers' names on the left, and the model names and numbers of their products on the right. If you don't see your device listed here, click Have Disk (see the sidebar box below).

8. **Select the manufacturer's name and model name and number of the hardware you're installing. Click Next, then Next again.**

   Windows may ask for the Windows 2000 installation disk; in any case, it generally finds the required drivers and installs them.

Note: Even users who don't have administrator privileges can install most Plug-and-Play devices. That's a handy feature for remote or mobile users, but it does reduce security.

TROUBLESHOOTING MOMENT

Hardware Exactitude

If your hardware isn't on the list of equipment in the Add/Remove Hardware Wizard, it's either because the hardware is newer than Windows 2000 or so old that Microsoft decided not to include it on the list.

If the hardware is very new, there may be a disk with drivers included with the device. If so, put the disk in the drive and click the Have Disk button in the Select a Device Driver window shown here.

No disk? For old or new hardware, look on the manufacturer's Web site for the appropriate driver.

No driver on the Web site? Call the manufacturer and insist that they send you the driver.

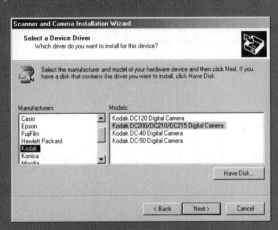

If all else fails, you can try this long-shot remedy: Select the manufacturer's name in the Select a Device Driver window and look for a *similar* model to yours. For example, suppose you're trying to install a Kodak DC290 digital camera, as shown here.

Now suppose you know that Kodak has no Windows 2000 drivers for this model—but you know that the camera is part of the DC200/DC21/DC215 series. As a last-ditch effort, you could try the DC200 driver, which may well work. (However, don't try this trick for some essential bit of hardware, such as a display card or hard-disk controller. You may end up with a computer that refuses to boot.)

Installing a Printer

If you're on a corporate network, you probably already have access to an office printer (or several) on the network; the setting-up duties have been left to a network guru. This section covers installing and setting up a *local* printer (one that's plugged directly into your computer).

Tip: When Windows people talk about *installing a printer,* they're generally not talking about hooking up the actual printer to the PC. Instead, they refer to installing and setting up the printer's *software and settings.* Once you've installed a printer, a printer icon for it appears in your Start→Settings→Printers window.

If your printer is newish (roughly 1999 or later vintage), it's probably Plug-and-Play compatible. Windows 2000 will detect and install it without much help from you. All you have to do is reboot your computer after installation. An even more recent

---

printer model, one that uses a USB or FireWire connection to your PC, is *hot-pluggable:* that is, you don't need to turn off the computer before plugging it in. This time, Windows 2000 will automatically detect the printer's presence and then perform the entire driver installation—no reboot required.

Tip: No special user rights are necessary to install a Plug-and-Play printer connected to your machine. Non-Plug-and-Play printers, on the other hand, require a user account with administrative privileges (see page 369).

Once you've connected the printer to the computer according to the manufacturer's directions, plugged it in, and turned it on, the next steps depend on which kind of connection the printer uses:

- **Parallel port (also called the printer or LPT1 port).** Turn on your computer. Select Start→Settings→Printers. Double click Add Printer. In the Add Printer Wizard, select "Local printer," and turn on "Automatically detect my Plug and Play printer." Follow the screen directions to complete the installation.

- **USB or FireWire (IEEE-1394).** No need to even turn off your computer. As soon as you connect the printer to the computer, Windows 2000 announces that it has detected new hardware and proceeds to install and configure the printer's driver.

- **Infrared.** Turn the printer on and position it so the infrared connectors on the printer and computer are no more than about three feet apart. After a few seconds, the computer will recognize the printer and install its driver without further fuss. If the infrared doesn't appear to be working, check in Device Manager (page 357) to see if it is installed correctly.

In each case, an icon representing the printer now appears in your Printers window, bearing the name you gave it during the installation. You can double-click this icon to see the printouts in line to print (see page 353).

The Add Printer Wizard

If the installation process doesn't go smoothly, Windows 2000 offers a wizard that lets you perform the installation manually: the Add Printer Wizard.

Installing a printer that isn't detected

Occasionally, Windows 2000 doesn't manage to detect a printer—even a very common printer. In that case, the Add Printer Wizard can bail you out.

To open the wizard, choose Start→Settings→Printers. The Printers window opens, where icons for any correctly installed printers appear—along with the Add Printer icon. Double-click it to start the wizard.

As you click through its screens, the wizard asks you to specify the printer's manufacturer and model, to provide a name for the printer, to specify if the printer is to be your default printer in Windows, whether or not you want to share the printer, and if you want to print a test page.

Windows 2000 will configure the printer and install the necessary driver (you may be asked for the Windows 2000 Pro installation disk). When it's all over, you'll find an icon for the printer in your Printers folder.

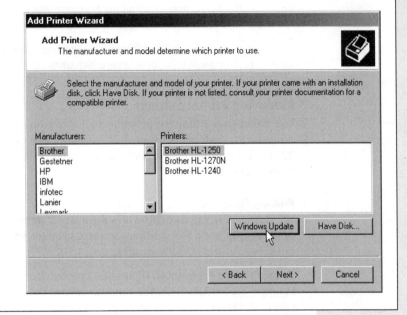

Figure 16-3:
If the printer isn't on the first list (left) and you're connected to the Internet, click the Windows Update button to download the latest models (right).

Installing an unlisted printer

If your printer isn't even listed in the "Printers:" list (Figure 16-3), you may still be able to get it to work with Windows 2000. If the printer is new, check to see if it's on the Hardware Compatibility List. If so, get the driver from the manufacturer, or check the Microsoft site for drivers at *www.microsoft.com/windows2000/upgrade/compat.*

Tip: If your printer isn't on the Hardware Compatibility List and no driver is available, check to see if the printer has a *compatibility* or *emulation mode,* in which it appears to the computer as a better known brand such as a Hewlett Packard LaserJet or Epson Stylus. Then you just need to install the printer exactly as if it were the model it emulates.

To install a printer for which you've obtained a driver, use the Add Printer Wizard, exactly as described on the previous section. But when you see the list of printer manufacturers and printer models, click the Have Disk button.

Windows prompts you to insert the manufacturer's installation disk. If the driver is on a floppy or CD, insert it; otherwise, click Browse to find the driver (one you downloaded, for example) on a local or network drive. (The file will have an .inf extension.) If the wizard finds more than one driver, or finds a driver that supports multiple printers, you may have to choose the correct one from a list.

Continue through the wizard's dialog boxes as described earlier; when it's all over, an icon for your printer appears in the Printers window.

Tip: To remove a printer from your computer, right-click the printer icon in the Printers window and select Delete from the shortcut menu. You'll be asked to confirm that you want to delete the printer or, in the case of a network printer, that you want to remove your connection to the printer.

Before deleting a printer, check to make sure the *printer queue* (see page 353) is empty. Windows 2000 will try to clear the queue before deleting the printer, which can cause a print job to be lost.

Modifying Printer Settings

You can change a long list of settings for any kind of printer; these properties are different for each printer model. In addition, you can edit the settings Windows 2000 calls Printing Preferences for each printer (called Document Defaults in Windows 98 and Windows NT).

Printing Preferences

Printing Preferences configures how documents are printed—within the limitations of the printer itself. For example, on some printers, you can specify quality settings or the type of paper you're printing on.

To see Printing Preferences, right-click a printer icon in the Printers window; select Printing Preferences from the shortcut menu. Or select Layout or Paper/Quality tabs in the Print dialog box of the program you're using (Figure 16-4).

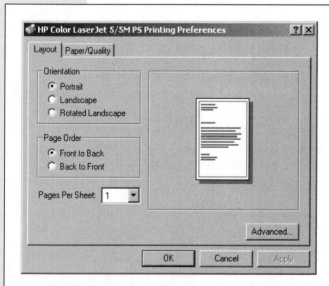

Figure 16-4:
Depending on the printer, choices under Printing Preferences can include print orientation, duplexing, page order, pages per sheet, paper size, and paper source.

Printer Properties

Even more settings are available in each printer's Properties dialog box, which appears when you right-click a printer icon and select Properties from the shortcut menu. This dialog box may have as many as eight tabs, filled with options. Some examples:

- **General tab.** Describes the printer, shows its name, and lets you note its physical location (a handy tidbit if you work in a big corporation).

- **Sharing tab.** Lets you share this printer so that other computers on the network can use it. (See page 295 for more on printer sharing.)

- **Ports tab.** Lets you specify and configure which ports your PC uses for printing, and contains the on/off switches for *bidirectional support* (which lets you printer report errors such as paper jams) and *printer pooling* (which lets several identical printers, connected to a single server, appear to Windows 2000 as though they're a single printer).

- **Advanced tab.** Offers assorted options having to do with when the printer is available, which driver to use, whether or not to insert a blank page between printouts, and so on.

- **Color Management tab.** For color printers only; lets you use the optional *color profiles* feature, which helps maintain color fidelity from screen to paper.

- **Security tab.** Governs how much access a network user or group has to use this printer (see Chapter 17).

- **Device Settings tab.** When available, shows you the printer's paper size, memory total, and other statistics.

- **Utilities tab.** When available, offers options for head alignment, nozzle cleaning, and so on.

Tip: In general, print settings in an application override any settings made in a printer's Properties dialog box.

Managing the Printer Queue

When you or others on the network send printouts (known as print *jobs*) to a printer, the jobs line up in a nice orderly queue, waiting for their turn to be printed. Unless you're on a network where access to the printer queue is controlled by a security policy, you can view and manage the queue by double-clicking a printer icon in the Printers folder (Figure 16-5).

While you're printing, a small icon of a printer appears in the system Tray. Double-click the icon to open the printer queue. Once the queue window is open, you can perform several useful printout-management tricks:

Tip: In an effort to minimize network traffic, the printer queue doesn't update the list of waiting printouts constantly. Press F5 often while you're viewing a network printer's queue to keep it updated.

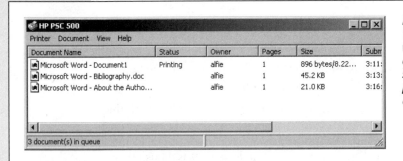

Figure 16-5:
The print queue shows what documents are queued up, their current status, owner, number of pages, size in bytes, and date submitted.

Reordering the queue

The usual order in a print queue is first in, first out, but there may be times when you want to rearrange the order of the waiting print jobs. Perhaps you've sent a very long print job to the printer and don't want to cancel it, but you have a one-page job that you must have *now*.

To reorder the print jobs, just drag the name of the print job up or down the queue list.

Tip: You can only reorder print jobs that haven't begun printing yet.

Deleting a job from the queue

If you have second thoughts about a print job that hasn't started printing yet, you can delete it from the queue easily enough; just right-click the document name and select Cancel from the shortcut menu.

If the document is already printing, the process is a bit iffier. Your printer has its own memory (the *buffer*) which stores the printout as it's sent from your PC. If you pause or cancel printing, you're only stopping the PC from sending *more* data to the printer. That's why a page or two may still print after you've paused or canceled a printout. If it's important to cancel the printout instantly, your best bet is to cancel the print job and then press the printer's reset button, if there is one, to clear its memory buffers. (To clear the buffers of some laser printers, you may have to turn them off and then on again.)

Pausing, resuming, and restarting the queue

As long a print job is in the queue and hasn't started printing yet, you can pause it temporarily, permitting other jobs in the queue to continue printing, in effect moving ahead in line; just right-click the document and select Pause. To let the printout continue, right-click its name again and this time choose Resume.

You can also make a certain print job start over from the beginning—a useful practice if you discover that the first 14 pages of your white paper have been inadvertently printed on pink paper. To do so, right-click the document in the print queue and select Restart from the shortcut menu.

Stopping and restarting a printer

To pause all the print jobs on a printer, right-click the printer icon in the Printers folder and select Pause Printing from the shortcut menu. Choose Pause again to resume printing. To clear the entire print queue, right-click the printer icon and select Cancel All Documents from the shortcut menu (Figure 16-6).

Tip: You can't empty the print queue by simply powering down your computer. Print jobs are saved (spooled) to your hard drive, so even if the system goes down, the jobs will reappear in the queue when you start the computer again.

Figure 16-6:
Right-click a printer icon to pause and restart printing. Select Cancel All Documents to empty the printer's queue.

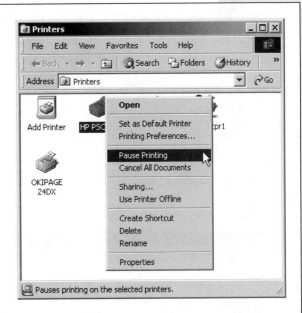

Installing Scanners and Cameras

Fortunately, most scanners and cameras these days are Plug-and-Play devices. Usually, all you need to do is turn the computer off (and even that's not necessary for USB connections), plug in the device, and turn the computer back on.

But if your device isn't Plug-and-Play compatible, or it is but Windows 2000 Pro doesn't recognize it, you can fall back on the Scanner and Camera Installation Wizard to get its drivers in place.

It works much like the other wizards described in this chapter. Choose Start→Settings→Control Panel. Double click Scanners and Cameras. In the resulting dialog box, click Add to start the installation wizard. You'll be asked to select the manufacturer and model names for your gadget; if you don't see them listed, click the Have Disk button to install the drivers that came with the scanner or camera (or that you've downloaded from the maker's Web site).

Tip: Even if Windows 2000 has a driver for your scanner or camera, check the manufacturer's Web site for the most current drivers. Camera drivers in particular are frequently revised and improved.

To configure your scanner or camera, double click the Scanners and Cameras tool in the Control Panel. Highlight the device name, and then click the Properties button.

PC Cards

If you want to add a networking card or modem to your notebook computer, you'll have to buy a *PC card* for it—a metal, credit-card-sized adapter that slips into a slot on the computer's side.

A PC card installation won't work unless both the card and the PC-card *socket* are compatible with Windows 2000. Fortunately, Windows 2000 Pro is compatible with just about all the PC cards and PC card sockets that you're likely to encounter.

Most PC cards are Plug and Play: you insert the card into the PC slot on your computer, and Windows 2000 detects it and installs its driver.

Tip: If your PC Card is a network adapter, both the PC Card socket and the network driver must be Plug-and-Play–compatible.

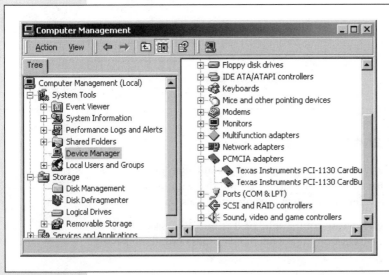

Figure 16-7:
This laptop's Device Manager lists two PC Card sockets (PCMCIA is the old name for PC Cards) showing that Windows 2000 Pro recognizes the hardware.

To verify that Windows 2000 Pro has recognized your PC Card socket, right-click My Computer; choose Manage from the shortcut menu. In the Computer Management window, click Device Manager; on the right side of the window, look for an entry for PC Card Socket or PCMCIA Adapter (Figure 16-7).

Adding and Removing PC Cards

When you insert a PC Card, Windows 2000 Pro recognizes the card and places an icon in the system tray at the end of the Taskbar (Figure 16-8).

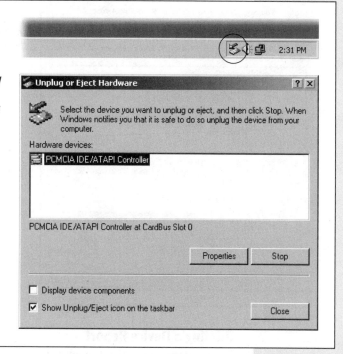

Figure 16-8:
Top: Right-click the Tray icon representing your PC card.

Bottom: The Unplug or Eject Hardware dialog box opens. Highlight the PC Card you want to remove and then click the Stop button. In a few seconds, Windows 2000 Pro will notify you that it's safe to remove the card.

Use the Tray icon to *stop* a PC Card before you remove it, as shown in Figure 16-8. If you don't, a dialog box (Figure 16-9) chastises you for an "unsafe removal." Fortunately, in most cases, there's no reason to remove the card at all between uses—and tucked away in the PC Card socket, the card can't get lost or damaged.

The Device Manager

The Device Manager is your link to all things hardware. As shown in Figure 16-7, it lists every component of your PC, and lets you install, uninstall, update, or troubleshoot your device drivers.

To open Device Manager, right-click My Computer and select Manage from the shortcut menu. Double click Device Manager in the left pane to open the device "tree" in the right pane (Figure 16-7). Click a plus sign to see the actual model names for these components that are installed in your PC.

Tip: Device Manager lists most of your PC's components, but not all; it may hide non-Plug-and-Play devices, among others. On rare occasions, you may need to see these devices to troubleshoot a problem.

To view hidden devices in Device Manager, choose View→Show Hidden Devices. Repeat the selection to hide them again.

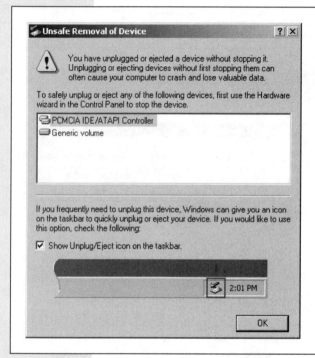

Figure 16-9:
This is the notification you get if you remove a PC Card without stopping it. It's not an idle threat, either—many a laptop owner has crashed the computer by doing that very thing.

Printing a Device Report

Device Manager can print reports about your system, including a system summary and reports about a particular device or class of device—if you're familiar with IRQs and other resources (see page 344), such a list can be a useful troubleshooting tool. To produce a report, follow these steps:

1. **Open Device Manager.**

   For a report on a particular device or class of devices, highlight the device in the right pane.

2. **Choose View→Print.**

   The Print dialog box appears.

3. **Select the type of report you want, then click Print.**

Troubleshooting Hardware Problems

To troubleshoot components of your PC that aren't working, it helps to know what's going on behind the scenes.

Resources and Conflicts

As noted at the beginning of this chapter, your PC's components require unique communication channels called *IRQs* (Interrupt Request Levels), reserved areas of memory called *I/O addresses,* and other assignments that reserve the components' places in your system. These technical settings are collectively called *resources.*

If your sound card occupies IRQ 11 and has an I/O address that starts at 6100, then Windows knows how to contact the card when, for example, your email software wants to play a "You've got mail" sound. If your printer also occupies these same resources, the operating system could send a sound code to printer, confusing it thoroughly and probably producing no reaction from the sound card. And it's not enough to set just a hardware component to the right channels; their drivers must be independently tuned to the same channels if they're to communicate.

Plug-and-Play technology identifies your devices and their requests for resources and referees among them. When two devices request the same resource—the same memory space, for example—Windows 2000 shifts settings in order to accommodate every element of your system. Sometimes Windows allocates a resource to more than one device, and then shuffles the resource around like an apartment shared by two people working different shifts.

Troubleshooting with Device Manager

When you have a hardware problem, your first stop should be Device Manager, which can teach you a lot about the nature of the problem.

If the device is marked by an exclamation point, it has some degree of malfunction. (On the other hand, the lack of an exclamation point doesn't necessarily mean that the device is working properly.)

To solve the problem, right-click the device's name in the list and select Properties from the shortcut menu. The Properties dialog box has two to five tabs, depending on the device. Start by clicking the Troubleshooter button and following the instructions.

If the troubleshooting wizard doesn't solve the problem you're having, consider alternatives. For example, the device may need a different driver, or the driver may be installed incorrectly (in which case you should reinstall the driver, carefully following the installation instructions).

Changing a driver

To change the device driver in Device Manager, follow these steps:

1. **Right-click the device's name on the right side of the Device Manager window; choose Properties from the shortcut menu.**

The Properties dialog box appears.

2. **Click the Driver tab, then click the Update Driver button.**

The Upgrade Device Driver Wizard opens.

3. **Click Next.**

The wizard asks if you want to search your computer for a better driver (among the drivers in the Plug-and-Play database) or choose a driver from a list. Let the system search; if it doesn't find a suitable driver, you can always run the wizard again and select the second option.

4. **Click Next.**

On the Locate Driver Files window, you're offered the opportunity to insert a floppy or CD that contains more recent drivers for your balky component—and a "Specify a location" checkbox that lets you select a driver you've downloaded to your PC. You can also instruct the wizard to check the windows Update web site for a new driver.

5. **Click Next.**

The wizard leads you through the process of selecting a driver from the disk or folder location you've specified.

Driver Signatures

As security and quality precaution, Microsoft now stamps a *digital signature* on every driver included with Windows 2000. "Signed" drivers have been tested and should work reliably.

Using the System applet in the Control Panel, you can tell Windows what you want to happen when a device driver's installer attempts to place an *un*signed driver on your machine:

- **Ignore.** Windows will permit all drivers to be installed, whether signed or not.

- **Warn.** Windows will tell you that the driver is unsigned, and give you the option not to install it. This is the default setting.

- **Block.** Windows won't let any unsigned driver be installed.

In general, Warn is the best option; it lets you choose to accept or decline drivers on a case-by-case basis. Besides, unsigned drivers often work perfectly well, and you may not have an alternative.

However, to ensure the highest level of system reliability, you can change this setting to only permit signed device drivers:

1. **Choose Start→Settings→Control Panel. Double click the System tool.**

The System Properties dialog box appears.

2. **Click the Hardware tab and then the Driver Signing button; click Ignore or Block** (Figure 16-10), **and then click OK.**

Simply blocking unsigned drivers means that an installation just terminates without explanation; of course, on some networks, that may be exactly what the network administrator wants.

Figure 16-10:
Only an administrator can change the Administrator option. When this option is checked, the selected file signature verification applies to all users, not just whoever is currently logged on.

Troubleshooting Unknown Devices

In Device Manager, an unknown device is indicated by a yellow question mark. Determining why Windows doesn't recognize it can be difficult, because you have few clues to go on; but the problems often lie with a missing or badly written device driver.

Tip: An unknown device isn't necessarily something you need to waste time diagnosing. If the devices you use are all functioning properly, and the unknown device doesn't seem to be slowing down your PC (which happens if your hard disk controller is unrecognized), you can generally leave the unknown device alone.

Here are a few reasons you may find a piece of your machine described as *unknown:*

- **The device doesn't have a device driver.** When a device doesn't have a driver available, Device Manager displays the device as unknown, and places it in the Other Devices folder—a common phenomenon with USB and FireWire composite devices. In addition, a status of "Error Code 1" or "Error Code 10" may appear when you view the properties of the device.

• **The driver is a Windows 95/98 driver.** You can't use *virtual device drivers* (.vxd files, common among Windows 98/95 drivers) with Windows 2000, and installing them on your Windows 2000-based computer may cause the device to be listed as unknown.

Tip: Windows 98 or Windows Me drivers (which Windows 2000 displays as WDM, or Windows Driver Model, file) may work in Windows 2000, but use a certified Windows 2000 if one's available.

• **Unrecognized Device ID.** Windows 2000 doesn't recognize a piece of hardware as a Plug-and-Play device unless it comes tagged, behind the scenes, with a particular *identifier*, such as vendor ID, device ID, subsystem ID, subsystem vendor ID, or revision ID. If such an ID is missing, or if your computer doesn't recognize the ID, Device Manager may list the device as unknown.

In all of these cases, the solution is the same: Remove the device from Device Manager by selecting it and clicking the Uninstall toolbar button. Then reinstall the device, providing a Windows 2000-specific driver during the installation process. (You may need to download updated drivers from the manufacturer's Web site for this purpose.)

If the device isn't detected at all, you may have a problem with the port the device is plugged into, or the device might be faulty. Try plugging a different device into the port or plug your device into a different computer to see if it will function properly. If you can't remedy the situation, contact your hardware manufacturer.

Tip: Devices that bridge bus types, such as a device driver that permits a parallel port device to look like a SCSI bus, are frequent culprits when you find an unknown device in Device Manager.

If reinstalling the driver doesn't do the trick, disconnect or remove your PC's hardware components one at a time, beginning with the most recently installed, until the unknown device no longer shows up in Device Manager. You've just figured out which one was causing the problem.

Check to see if the device's driver is digitally signed (see page 360). If, during the device driver installation, Windows 2000 detects that a device driver is not digitally signed, you see a message: "Not Digitally Signed." If you're using an unsigned device driver, try replacing the driver with a signed Windows 2000 driver. (Even a digitally signed device driver can appear as unknown in Device Manager, however.)

Checking Hardware with System Information

System Information is a handy tool for detecting and correcting all kinds of PC problems. The technical information it reveals may not all be meaningful to you, but may help a technician solve your problem over the phone, for example.

To open System Information, right-click My Computer; choose Manage from the shortcut menu. Under the System Tools heading, expand System Information (Figure 16-11).

When trying to solve hardware troubles, three System Information components are relevant: System Summary, Hardware Resources, and Components.

- **System Summary** shows a basic profile of the computer, including the version number of the operating system, the amount of physical and virtual memory, the manufacturer's name, and the model number.

- **Hardware Resources** displays hardware settings such as input/output addresses, memory addresses, and interrupt requests.

- **Components** displays information about peripheral devices, ports, printers, and storage, among other things. This table summarizes the contents of the Components folders.

Highlight any of the folders to print out its contents or save the contents to a text (.txt) file, which the program places in the My Documents folder.

Caution: Printing out the entire System Information folder (which includes all the information in all the subfolders) can easily total 50 pages. A complicated system can take a hundred pages. So it's best to be selective about printing.

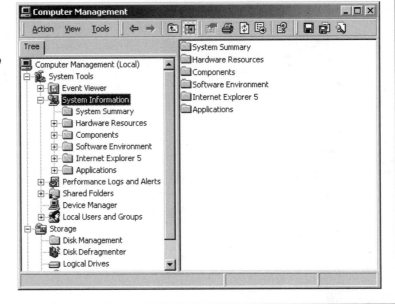

Figure 16-11:
System Information can help you gather information about your system— either to use yourself or to turn over to a Help Desk or technical support person.

Security, Accounts, and Administration

On a large network, virtually all administrative chores are centralized; you probably have little or no control over the configuration of Windows 2000. Truth be told, most people who aren't professional computer nerds don't *want* to have to deal with technical matters. However, if you're using Windows 2000 Pro as a stand-alone machine (or on a peer-to-peer network), you can't call the administrator when something goes wrong—you *are* the administrator.

This chapter describes the Windows 2000 tools that fall under the category of "administration."

Security Basics

If there's one thing Windows 2000 is good at, it's security. In fact, there are so many ways to make your computer and data secure, you can easily tie yourself into knots.

How much security is enough? The decisions are much like the ones you have to make about your home. Yes, you can install a burglar alarm, locks, bars on windows, and a guard dog. You'll increase security, but also increase the chances of setting off false alarms, losing keys, getting trapped in a fire, and getting bitten. Computer security offers the same tradeoffs: You want enough security to discourage invaders, but not so much that you're constantly running into roadblocks of your own making.

Here are a few of the steps you can take to keep your data private:

- **Keep your computer and data *physically* secure.** If people wander into your workspace all the time, always log off before leaving your computer, or use a password-protected screen saver. Save your data to a secure server (if there is one) on the network.

- **Install antivirus software.** Install an antivirus program designed for Windows 2000. Make sure it's set to scan every floppy disk and downloaded file. Check the software company's Web site for downloadable updates to the antivirus software at least once every two weeks.

- **Use a firewall if you have a persistent Internet connection.** For a dial-up connection, the security settings of Internet Explorer offer adequate protection; you can set them to be quite strict.

  However, if your connection to the Internet is "up" all the time—that is, if you have a DSL or cable connection—you need something more. Consider buying *firewall* or *proxy server* software to rule out the possibility of Internet hackers.

- **If your data needs protection, consider encryption.** The Encrypting File System (EFS) in Windows 2000 can *encrypt* files or folders (on NTFS partitions; see page 413). Once you've protected a file in this way, you can use it normally. But if someone with another user account tries to open the file, he'll see only an Access Denied message.

  To encrypt a file or folder, right-click its icon; choose Properties from the shortcut menu. Click the Advanced button to bring up the Advanced Attributes dialog box (Figure 17-1), and turn on "Encrypt contents to secure data." (Turning off this same checkbox decrypts the file.)

Tip: You don't have to decrypt a file before emailing it; Windows 2000 does that for you automatically.

Figure 17-1:
If you encrypt an individual file, your word processor (and other programs) may save a new copy of the file when you edit it, deleting the encrypted copy in the process. Unless you remember to encrypt the new version every time, you could end up saving an unencrypted version. That's why it's a good idea to encrypt folders, not individual files, so that new files added to the folder will also be encrypted.

- **If your email is sensitive, consider encryption *and* digital identification.** The usual advice is to put nothing in your email that you wouldn't want posted on the bulletin board of your local supermarket. If your company owns the computer and network that you're using for the email, that's very good advice.

Outside of work, think of your email like regular postal mail: Your letters pass through many hands, and yet you entrust your mortgage payment, tax returns, and valentines to snail mail with every expectation that they'll arrive unopened. Nevertheless, it would be foolish to put your plans to commit tax fraud, embezzlement, or adultery in any kind of mail.

If your mail and data are of a kind that a business rival, disgruntled hacker, or divorce lawyer would love to get their hands on, get the Microsoft Windows 2000 High Encryption Pack—but not before reading *www.microsoft.com/security/new.asp* and getting up to speed.

If email security is important to you, consider getting a *digital ID*—a software certificate that verifies that you are who you say you are and lets you encrypt your outgoing email. To get a digital ID, open Outlook or Outlook Express, choose Tools→Options, and then click the Security tab. If you click the Get a Digital ID button, Windows connects you to information about digital IDs, how they work, and how to get one.

Setting Local Security Policy

In Windows 2000, the security *policy* is a collection of settings that governs how tightly secured your particular computer is.

To look over your own computer's security policy, choose Start→Settings→Control Panel, then double-click the Administrative Tools folder. (It's available only if you have administrative privileges, as described on page 369.) Double-click Local Security Policy. The broad categories of security settings you can change here appear on the left side of the window (Figure 17-2). As you click these folders, the right side of the window show these subgroups of policies:

- **Password Policy** establishes the guidelines the users of this machine must follow when choosing a password, such as password length and how often they're required to *change* their passwords as a security precaution.

- **Account Lockout Policy** configures Windows 2000 to *lock out* user accounts after a certain number of invalid logon attempts (an indication that somebody is trying to guess a password).

- **Audit Policy** sets up Windows 2000 to record (audit) certain events, such as logon attempts and account management activities.

- **IP Security Policies on Local Machine** configure Windows 2000 to use a special form of IP (Internet Protocol, the cornerstone of the TCP/IP protocol suite) that transmits data over the network in encrypted form.

- **User Rights Assignment** determines what your various user groups are allowed to do in Windows 2000, such as whether or not they're allowed to shut down the system, back up files, and so on.

- **Security Options** includes options to allow full access to all drives when using the Recovery Console, to shut down the system without logging on, and to hide the name of the last person who logged on (in the Welcome to Windows dialog box described on page 20).

To see the list of individual settings (policies) in one of these categories, click its + button. In the right pane, you see the plain-English descriptions of the policies, the current setting for your (local) machine, and the *effective* setting. (If your computer is part of a network domain whose administrator has set up a security policy, the domain settings override your local machine's settings. That's why the *effective* setting may not match the local setting.)

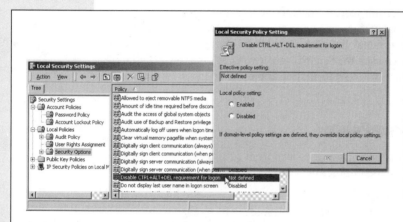

Figure 17-2:
Local Security Policy is simply a long list of individual security-related settings; double-click one to open a dialog box where you can adjust the options. For example, you might decide to disable the Ctrl+Alt+Delete requirement for logging on (see page 20), as shown by the inset.

To change a setting, double-click its name in the right pane. As shown in Figure 17-2, a dialog box appears to let you change the corresponding setting for your machine.

POWER USERS' CLINIC

Configuring Multiple Computers

If you're part of a peer-to-peer workgroup and have several computers to configure, you can set up one machine and create a template to use on the other computers, saving you the trouble of adjusting the same sets of Security checkboxes over and over again.

To do so, set up the security settings on the first computer, then highlight Security Settings in the left pane. Choose Action→Export Policy→Local Policy. Give the template a descriptive name with the filename extension *.inf—security policy.inf*, for example—in a shared folder. Then log on to each computer in turn (as an administrator) and open Local Security Settings. Select Action→Import Policy. Locate the template in the shared folder and select Open.

Users, Groups, and Administrators

As you know from Chapter 2, you can't use a Windows 2000 computer without first logging on; and for that, you need a username and password. They're your keys to your Windows 2000 *account*.

If you work in a company where somebody else maintains all the computers, understanding accounts (and the related concepts, groups and administrative rights) isn't essential to your everyday work. But if you maintain your own small network, or if you'd like a better understanding of the "Access denied" messages that may sometimes appear when you use your PC, an understanding of these notions may prove very valuable.

User Accounts

User accounts are extremely important in Windows 2000. Your user account determines your *privileges*—that is, exactly what you're allowed to do on the network and even on your own PC, including which files and folders you can open, which printers you can use, and which Control Panel settings you can change. Your user account also tells Windows which user *profile* to use when you log on, as described on page 374.

Administrator Accounts

Every Windows 2000 Pro computer comes with a special account called Administrator. If you log onto your PC as the Administrator, you can change any of its Control Panel settings, use the Computer Management tool (page 371), install non-Plug-and-Play hardware—and, more important, you can add, delete, or change *other* people's accounts on this machine.

Tip: You don't necessarily have to have *the* Administrator account to make these kinds of changes; you can also have an account that's been added to the Administrator *group,* described below.

When you install Windows 2000, the setup program creates the Administrator account automatically; whoever performs the installation specifies the password. If you installed Windows 2000 yourself, you therefore know the password; you can access the Administrator account whenever you like.

But if you work in an office where someone else is responsible for installing, configuring, and maintaining your computer, whether or not you're given administrative access to the machine is up to them. The system administrator might give you the Administrator password, set up a local account for you under a different name with limited administration privileges, add your domain account to one of the local groups with administrative privileges (using the Users and Passwords control panel), or grant you no administrative access at all. It all depends on the policies of your company.

Groups

In a corporation with hundreds or thousands of employees, the network administrators would go quietly mad if they had to configure every user account's privileges individually—Read-Only access to this folder, Full access to that folder, no rights to back up the system, permission to log on, and so on. Fortunately, Windows 2000 lets administrators create *groups* with canned sets of identical privileges. When the company hires a new worker, all the network administrator has to do is add her user account to the appropriate existing group (such as Accounting or Creative).

Groups are especially handy when you're sharing a folder on your PC with other people on the network. You can simply tell Windows 2000 which *group* is allowed to see what's inside (as described on page 295), and your security task is complete.

Note: If you belong to several groups, your privileges are cumulative; you get the maximum rights of both groups. For example, if the General group isn't allowed access to the Secret Projects folder, but you're also in an R&D group that *is* allowed to see it, you'll have access to it.

To save the network administrator's time, Windows 2000 Pro comes with several predefined groups, each with certain privileges already set up. Some of the most useful ready-made groups are:

- **Administrators.** The Administrator account described above is part of this group, of course. But an administrator can add any other account to this group, giving *them* the full range of privileges on your machine (including managing users and groups like this one).

- **Power Users.** People in this group can do many of the things administrators can do, including editing user accounts and groups, sharing and managing printers, and sharing and managing shared files. But they aren't allowed to perform some administrative tasks like backing up files, changing device drivers, or managing security and audit logs.

- **Users.** Most people, on most Windows 2000 networks, belong to this group; in fact, *every* account (except Administrator and Guest accounts) belongs to this group. It offers basic access to the computer, with none of the administrative privileges described in the previous paragraphs, and without the right to share folders (page 295) or create local printers (page 349).

- **Guests.** People who connect to the network only occasionally may be members of this group. (The built-in Guest account belongs to this group, too.) You don't need a password to log onto the network as a member of the Guest group, but you can't do much on the network, either (as determined by the administrator).

Note: The Guest account is turned off by default, primarily for security reasons; if the Guest account is enabled on your machine, anyone on your network can see the folders you've shared (unless you've restricted access to them as described on page 298). And if the shared folders are on a FAT drive (page 413), these anonymous users can even *change or delete* your files. Use the Guest account with caution.

- **Everyone.** You'll see this group listed when you share a folder or printer; it refers, sure enough, to *anyone* who uses this computer, whether on the network or when seated in front of it.

- **Authenticated Users.** This group is the same as Everyone, except that it omits the Guest account (and any other anonymous user).

Adding a User Account

As noted earlier, you can add, delete, and edit user accounts only if your account has Administrator or Power User privileges. If you fit that description, then you can use the Computer Management tool to perform almost every administrative task, including setting up user accounts.

To begin, choose Start→Programs→Administrative Tools→Computer Management, or right-click My Computer on the desktop and select Manage from the shortcut menu.

UP TO SPEED

Domain Accounts and Groups

The accounts and groups described on the previous pages all apply to *your* computer; they're *local* users and groups, and govern who can log onto your particular computer. You generally use local accounts and groups only when you've set up a peer-to-peer network, as described in Chapter 15. On a peer network, each user logs on to her local machine. If you want to give a network user access to your drives, you have to create an account on your machine with the same name that she uses to log on to hers. Similarly, if you want to access every computer on the network, you need a separate account on every computer.

If your network has been set up with domains running Windows 2000 Server (see page 21), however, there's another set of user accounts and groups at work–*domain* accounts and groups, which govern users' access to all of the machines on the network. (Some of the predefined groups include Domain Admins, Domain Guests, and Domain Users.) In this environment, you log on to the domain, not the local machine, and that one domain account can grant you access to any resource on the network. The only time you might have to log on locally is to perform

administrative tasks on your PC that require special access.

When you participate in a domain, shared resources (such as folders) are usually stored on servers, not on individual workstations like yours. However, you can share your computer's resources by granting domain users access to them (see page 295). This way, you don't have to create a local account for everyone who might need to access your machine. To simplify the process of granting domain users this kind of access, you can create a local group with permission to access your drives; then you can add domain users and groups to the local group as described in this chapter.

The interaction between local and domain accounts can sometimes be confusing, which is why in many cases, domain administrators don't give individual users the administrative privileges needed to create their own local users and groups. By using only domain accounts and maintaining shared resources on servers instead of workstations, network administrators can exercise complete control without running around creating local users and groups on individual machines.

Note: *The Administrative Tools folder only appears in the Start menu if you activate it by choosing Settings→Taskbar & Start Menu, clicking the Advanced tab, and turning on Display Administrative Tools.*

To add a new user account to your computer, click the System Tools icon, then Local Users and Groups. On the right side of the window, right-click Users and select New User from the shortcut menu.

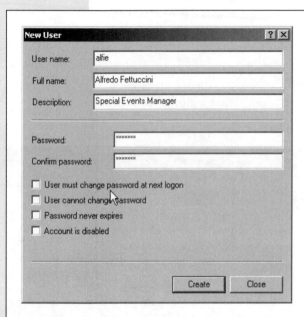

Figure 17-3:
"User must change password at next logon" addresses the fact that, as the creator of this new user's account, you know his password. The next time the user logs on, he'll have to change his password.

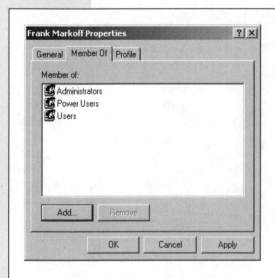

Figure 17-4:
The Member Of dialog box shows you which groups this person belongs to. To add him to another group, click Add; in the resulting dialog box, double-click the group name (or several of them), and then click OK.

Supply a user name, full name, a password, and password rules (Figure 17-3). Click Create, then Close, to wrap up the task.

Editing, Deleting, and Disabling User Accounts

To make changes to an account you've created, open Computer Management, exactly as described above. Click the Local Users and Groups folder; on the right side of the window, double-click Users, then double-click the account's name. Finally, in the Properties dialog box, click the Member Of tab (see Figure 17-4). It shows you a list of the groups that include this user. If you'd like this person to become part of another group too, click Add, also shown in Figure 17-4.

To rename or delete an account, just right-click it and choose Rename or Delete from the shortcut menu.

Tip: When you delete an account, you lose all of its settings, even if you later create another account with the same name. If somebody in your group is just going on sabbatical, disable her account instead of deleting it, so that you'll save yourself the trouble of re-creating all of her privileges and settings.

To do so, double-click her name in the Computer Management window, and then turn on "Account is disabled" (as shown in Figure 17-3). Click OK.

Creating a Group

On a peer-to-peer network, there's no central server that maintains a list of users and groups. As a result, you have to re-create your groups on each computer. As you can imagine, this is a lot of work, and changing group membership is a real pain, because you have to make the change on every machine.

Fortunately, you don't *have* to set up a group on every machine. The group feature can still be useful just on one computer: when you want to limit access to a folder on your machine to certain people, for example.

See page 295 for a step-by-step description of sharing a folder and making it available only to a certain group of people. Those instructions don't cover creating the group to begin with, however; here's how to do it:

1. **Open the Computer Management window.**

   To do so, right-click My Computer on the desktop and select Manage from the shortcut menu.

2. **Click System Tools, then Local Users and Groups.**

   The right side of the screen shows two folders: Users and Groups.

3. **Right-click Groups; choose New Group from the shortcut menu.**

   The New Group dialog box appears.

4. **Type a name for your new group, and then click Add.**

The Select Users or Groups window appears, listing every user you've set up (and several existing groups).

5. **Add the members of your network to the new group, as shown in Figure 17-5.**

   Check the "Look in:" drop-down list at the top of the Select Users or Groups dialog box to make sure you're adding user accounts from your local machine, and not from your domain (unless that's what you intend).

6. **When you've added every name you want to add, click OK, then Close.**

   You return to the Computer Management window, which you can close, if you like. From now on, your newly created group will appear in the list that appears when you share a folder (see the illustration on page 299).

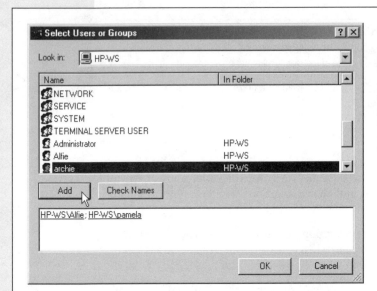

Figure 17-5:
To add users to a group, double-click a name in the list (or click it once, then click Add). Repeat until the bottom box shows the name of everyone who's permitted to see your files. Remember to add yourself to the group if you plan on being able to access the group's files.

User Profiles

Your *user profile* stores everything your computer knows about the environment for your user *account:* your desktop icons and wallpaper, Start menu configuration, My Network Places shortcuts, and so on. Windows 2000 has four types of profiles:

Local User Profile

The local user profile is the default profile type. It sits on your computer; unlike some other kinds of profiles, it doesn't follow you when you use another computer. In other words, you have a separate user profile on every computer at which you log on locally (as opposed to over the network).

Roaming Profiles

As described on page 309, a *roaming profile* is a user profile that's stored on a network server, which lets you sit down at any computer on the network—or even dial in from the road—and be treated to the same profile settings (desktop, Start menu, and so on) you'd see if you were actually sitting in front of your regularly scheduled PC.

Mandatory Profiles

A *mandatory profile* is essentially a read-only roaming profile. When the administrator gives you a mandatory profile, you're allowed to make changes to your desktop environment, but they're not saved. The next time you log on to the network, the server again downloads the mandatory profile's settings to your computer.

Default User Profiles

When a new user logs on, Windows 2000 creates a new user profile, which inherits its settings from the *default user profile*. In other words, the default profile is like a template that serves as a starting point for a new user's environment.

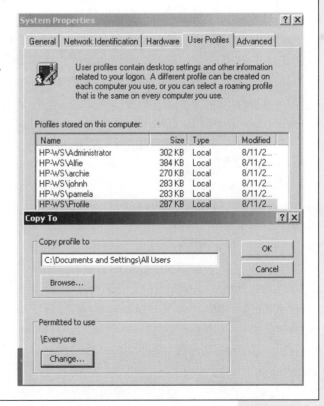

Figure 17-6:
Browse to the Default User folder under Documents and Settings. Change the "Permitted to use" setting to Everyone. You'll be warned that Default Users already exists, but don't let that put you off. Click Yes.

If several people use the same computer and you want to create identical profiles for each user, you'll save time by modifying the default user profile. Users will be able to change their individual profiles, but you'll avoid having to set up the basic settings over and over again.

To customize the default user profile, follow these steps:

1. **Set up a new user on your computer with a name like** *Profile*.

   See page 371 for guidance in making a new account.

2. **Log on as Profile, and set up the computer the way you want it to appear.**

   Create necessary shortcuts, dial-up settings, and network places; map drives, set wallpaper, and so forth.

3. **When you're finished, log off. Log on again using an account with Administrator privileges.**

4. **Right-click My Computer and select Properties.**

   The System Properties dialog box appears.

5. **Click the User Profiles tab.**

POWER USERS' CLINIC

Using Multiple Accounts for Security

If you're the administrator on your computer, it's a good idea to use the Administrator account only when performing administrative tasks; spend *most* of your time on the computer logged on with a normal user account.

The reason is that administrative accounts are the favorite target of hackers; if you're constantly logged on as an administrator, you provide a bigger target. If you should walk away from your machine without logging off, for example, anyone who sits down at your computer has full power over your system.

Fortunately, you don't have to log off your normal account

and log on again as an administrator every time you need to perform an administrative task. Instead, you can capitalize on a clever time-saver called the Run As feature.

It works like this: While pressing the Shift key, right-click the program you want to run (its icon or even its name in the Start menu); then choose Run As from the shortcut menu. The dialog box shown here appears, offering you the chance to run the program with the security credentials of a different user account—such as an account

that as Administrator privileges.

You've just saved yourself a time-consuming log off/log on.

> **Run As Other User**
>
> You may not have the necessary permissions to use all the features of the program you are about to run. You may run this program as a different user or continue to run the program as SCRIBES\sharon.
>
> ○ Run the program as SCRIBES\sharon
> ● Run the program as the following user:
>
> User name: Administrator
> Password: ******
> Domain: SHARON-LAPTOP
>
> [OK] [Cancel]

Find the profile called Profile and click Copy To. Click Browse, and save the profile into the Documents and Settings→Default User folder, as shown in Figure 17-6.

Tip: Inside the Documents and Settings folder, you'll find another very useful folder called All Users. This folder doesn't contain a complete user profile, but it does contain certain key subfolders that you can use to configure the environment for every user of the system, even after their user profiles have been created. For example, if you copy a folder full of shortcuts to the Documents and Settings→All Users→Start Menu→Programs folder, for example, those shortcuts will appear in every user's Start menu.

Event Viewer

The Event Viewer lets you read three logs maintained by Windows 2000:

- **Application Log,** which tracks events in connection with programs.

- **Security Log,** which is a list of security events.

- **System Log,** which records events generated by the operating system.

None of these logs are of any interest whatsoever—unless you're trying to troubleshoot mysterious problems. These logs track extremely long lists of "events," usually without significance to the average person. Figure 17-7 shows the Event Viewer displaying a System Log with many errors and warnings that may sound dire, but often have no discernible effect on your computer.

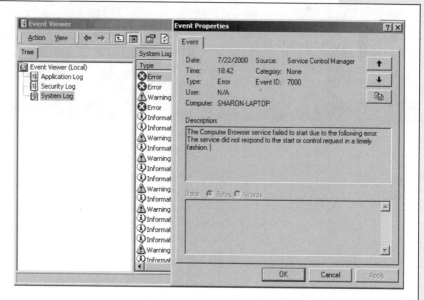

Figure 17-7:
You can double-click any entry in a log to see the event's properties. Most of the errors recorded here are transitory conditions that would otherwise be forgotten. But this would be one place to research a chronic and mysterious problem with a program or a printer, for example.

If you find an error or warning, double-click it and read its description, which may include suggestions for resolving the error. If the description isn't very helpful (and they often aren't), connect to the Internet and search Microsoft's Knowledge Base (at *http://search.support.microsoft.com*), using the event number listed.

Tip: You can also get to Event Viewer through Computer Management, which appears when you right-click My Computer and choose Manage from the shortcut menu.

Administrative Extras

Windows 2000 comes with a wide-ranging collection of tools that are the province of network administrators—they're not designed for everyday use. You'll find them in your Start→Programs→Administrative Tools folder: programs like Performance, Services, Data Sources (ODBC), Component Services, and Telnet Server Administration.

The **Performance** tool collects and displays real-time data about memory, disk, processor, network, and other activity in a graph, report, or histogram.

Services are programs that usually run on your system all the time in the background. You can use this console to control when, if, and how the services load.

Data Sources (ODBC) (Open Database Connectivity) is a programming interface that lets your programs access data in database management systems that use Structured Query Language (SQL) data access standard.

An administrator can use **Component Services** to deploy and administer COM+ programs (that is, customized applications composed of modular components) from a graphical user interface, or to automate administrative tasks using a scripting or programming language. Software developers use component services to configure routine component and program behavior, such as security and participation in transactions, and to integrate components into COM+ programs.

Telnet Server Administration is a link to a command window from which you can run Telnet to perform remote access and administration in a mixed operating-system environment.

If all of this sounds like deep technical territory to you, then just be glad you're not a network administrator. But if all this sounds like Christmas in July, get your own copy of Windows 2000 Server and start playing around with it.

Backup

W hen your hard drive fails, a virus attacks, or another disaster befalls you, you can lose everything—your bank records, your work files, even your saved Quake games. To protect yourself and your data, you must back up (make safety copies of) your data regularly.

If you're on a typical corporate network, you won't have to worry much about backing up; a highly paid network administrator has probably set up a network-wide backup system that works automatically. But if you've created a peer-to-peer net-

Figure 18-1:
When you launch Windows 2000 Pro's Backup program, the Welcome screen's buttons let you launch the Backup and Restore Wizards, as well as create an Emergency Repair Disk (ERD). An ERD contains a file called Setup.log that specifies the locations of files used to repair your system in the event that your system or boot files are damaged.

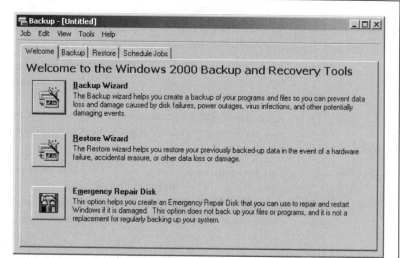

work, or if you're using Windows 2000 Pro on a stand-alone computer, you can use Windows 2000 Pro's Backup program precisely for this purpose.

Microsoft licensed this powerful backup program from Veritas Software. It lets you back up entire disk drives or selected files and folders, at times and under the conditions you specify.

It's a simple matter to use the wizards included with Backup to perform basic backups (known as *backup jobs*), as shown in Figure 18-1. But a bit of planning is in order if you want to create a reliable and efficient backup strategy. This chapter guides you through using Backup and devising a backup strategy.

Backup Media

Selecting a backup medium requires a tradeoff between speed, capacity, cost, and convenience. For example, you *could* back up your files onto floppy disks, but the process would be slow, expensive, and inconvenient—backing up an 8 GB drive would require over 5,000 disks. That's why, depending on the amount of data you have to back up and the amount of time you have to perform the backups, you may want to purchase a dedicated backup device, such as:

- **A tape drive.** Magnetic tape is the traditional backup medium in the corporate world; it's reasonably economical, reliable, and fast. The drawback is that the drive is useless for anything else. You can't see what's on a tape drive through Windows Explorer or My Computer, for example, as you would a hard disk, floppy, or CD-ROM drive. Furthermore, you can't access a file at, for example, the end of the tape without winding through all of the files preceding it first. As a result, magnetic tape drives can back up data at high speeds, but restoring individual files can be time-consuming; the drive has to run the tape forward to locate each one. It can't simply drop the heads on the right spot, as a disk drive can.

  Fortunately, unless you're particularly inept or disaster-prone, you'll be doing a lot more backing up (which is fast and easy with a tape drive) than restoring individual files from the tape.

- **A cartridge drive.** Cartridge drives, such as the popular Zip and Jaz drives, work like hard drives—except that you can remove the cartridges. You can access them just as you would any other drive on your system; in fact, you can even back up your data to them without using a backup program. Just drag or copy your files as described on page 94. These drives are slower than hard drives, but much faster than tape.

  The two drawbacks to the use of cartridge drives for backup are their limited capacities and their high disk prices. The Iomega Jaz drive is available in a 2 GB version; to back up a 10 or 20 GB drive, you'd need five or ten disks—at $100 each! The 100 MB Zip drive would require dozens.

- **A writable CD-ROM drive.** Writable CD-ROM technologies (drives that let you "burn" your own CD-ROMs) have become very popular add-ons; some new computers even offer them built-in. You can buy either CD-R (recordable) drives, whose discs you can record only once, or CD-RW (rewritable) drives, whose discs you can erase and re-record as many times as you like.

CDs hold only about 660 MB, but the blanks are dirt-cheap—usually under a dollar each, making the cost per megabyte only 15 cents or less (the lowest of any popular backup medium). Even if you back up to CD-Rs and throw them away when they're outdated, the costs remain low.

Comparing Storage Costs

When assessing the cost of a backup drive, don't forget to factor in the cost of the tapes or disks, too. To compare storage costs of different drive types, which may seem to be apples and oranges, compute the *cost per megabyte* of storage.

To do this, divide the cost of one cartridge or disk by its capacity in megabytes. For example, a 4 mm magnetic tape might cost as much as $20, while a Zip cartridge is only $15. But the tape can hold as much as 8 GB of data, for a cost of approximately 1/4 cent per megabyte; the Zip disk, which holds only 100 MB, is far more expensive at 15 cents per megabyte.

Creating a Backup Strategy

Backing up is a chore; if the process is too inconvenient, it's a chore that you'll tend to neglect. Therefore, a big part of creating a backup strategy is simplifying the process and automating as much of it as you can.

To create a backup strategy, you have to know the following information:

- **How much data is there to back up?** The amount of data is a big factor in choosing a backup drive; you want to change the tape or disk as few times as possible during the process. If most of your backup jobs require only one tape or disk, you can schedule them to run unattended—a great feature.

- **How much time to you have to back it up?** For a home computer, time is usually not a factor in backing up. You can simply start the process and go about doing other things. In an office environment, however, you may have a limited amount time to back up your data. If you have a lot of data to back up, and a short time to do it in, then you'd better get a faster backup drive.

- **How often do you have to back it up?** The frequency of your backups should depend on how often you change or create new files and how important they are. For some people, a weekly full backup is sufficient. Others may have new data that they want to back up every night; in some cases, you may want to back up sensitive data every *hour*.

There are several different types of backup jobs, which you can combine to form your backup strategy.

Full Backups

A *full* backup (which Backup calls a *Normal* backup) is a complete backup of every file on your PC, including special operating system elements such as the Windows 2000 registry. If your hard drive ever fails completely, you'll be able to restore every shred of software from your backup—even if it's onto a new hard drive—and wind up with an exact duplicate your old system at the time of the last backup.

Every backup strategy should begin with a full backup; but fortunately, you don't have to do one every day. Most of the files on the average PC, such as application and operating system files, never change; after the first full backup, subsequent backups can protect only the files that have changed. If a full restore of the system becomes necessary, you first restore the system from the full backup, and then restore the files that have changed since then, overwriting the older copies from the full backup.

Partial Backups

A *partial* backup protects only some of your files—for example, only those that have changed since a certain date.

One popular backup strategy, then, goes like this. At the beginning of the week (or even the month), you perform a full backup, no matter how many disks or tapes it takes. On the other days of the week (or weeks of the month), you perform partial backups. Because partial backups are so small, you may be able to leave one tape in the drive for a week or more while your scheduled partial-backup jobs run automatically. This "set and forget" arrangement is an excellent setup; it's so convenient that you're more likely to actually *do* your backing up.

When it comes time to run the Backup program, you'll be offered a choice of partial-backup options:

- **Incremental backup.** If you choose this option, Backup copies only files that are new or changed since the last *full* backup. *Incremental* backups go much faster (and use fewer disks) than full backups, since Windows has to copy only a few files each time. But they're less convenient if the worst should happen, and you need to restore all your files from the backup disks; you'll have to restore each backup job in chronological order, beginning with the full-backup disks. (You may want to consider doing a full backup once a week or once a month, and incremental backups in between.)

- **Differential backup.** The first *differential* backup copies the files that have changed since the last full backup; so far, it's the same as an incremental backup. However, the second differential backup *also* backs up all changed files since the full backup, and so does the third. In other words, if you perform a full backup on Monday, the differential backups on Tuesday, Wednesday, and Thursday each back up *all* the files that have changed since Monday.

Of course, this system requires more backup disks, because you're actually making duplicate and triplicate copies of certain files. But the payoff comes when your hard drive dies and you have to restore the entire system. Instead of having to restore each day's backup job (as you would with an incremental backup), you have to restore only one full backup and *one* differential backup set (the most recent one)—a relatively fast and simple procedure.

This technical tradeoff between convenience at backup time and convenience in case of disaster should sound familiar to anyone who's ever had to choose between two insurance policies, one of which costs less but has a higher deductible.

Creating a Backup Job

To launch Backup, choose Start→Accessories→System Tools→Backup. The welcome screen lets you launch the Backup Wizard, the Restore Wizard, or create an Emergency Repair Disk.

Using the Backup Wizard

Here's a complex example that shows off the Backup Wizard's long list of options:

1. **Click the Backup Wizard button on the Backup program's Welcome screen.**

   A wizard Welcome window appears.

2. **Click Next. Specify what you want to back up.**

   On the What To Back Up page, use the radio buttons to specify whether you want to back up everything on the computer; selected files, drives, or network data; or only the *system-state data* (see the sidebar below).

   If you elect to back up the entire system or just the system state data, skip to Step 5.

UP TO SPEED

The System State

The *System State* option in Backup backs up special information that Windows 2000 needs in order to run. This information lurks in places that backup can't back up as it would any old file, either because this information is invisible or because it's in use when the Backup program is running.

On a Windows 2000 Professional system, the system state includes such advanced elements as the *boot files, the COM+ Class Registration Database,* and the *Registry.* If the unthinkable ever comes to pass, and you're forced to restore your backed-up files to a new hard drive, you must restore the System State along with the contents of all of your drives if you want your computer to look and work as it did before the disaster.

That's why you should select the System State item as part of all of your backup jobs; it doesn't add much to the length of the job and it provides you with the most protection. However, note that if you use your Windows 2000 Pro machine to back up other computers on the network, Backup program can't back up their system-state data—only the data from your own PC.

---

3. **Click Next. Select files and folders to back up.**

On the Items To Back Up page (see Figure 18-2), you see a Windows Explorer-like, expandable display of your system's My Computer and My Networks Places information. Select the drives, folders, and files that you want to back up by clicking the checkboxes next to each, whether on your own PC or on the network.

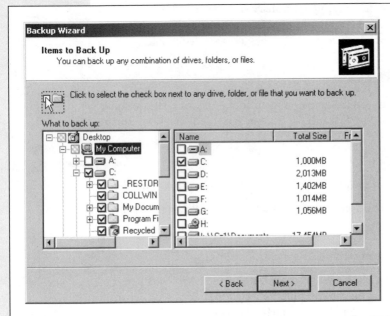

Figure 18-2:
The Items To Back Up page contains an expandable display much like that of Windows Explorer, except that each drive, folder, and file has a checkbox next to it that you use to select that object for inclusion in the backup.

4. **Click Next. Select the medium you want to use for the backup.**

The Backup Media Type selector lists the backup drives installed on your computer, plus an entry called File. The options you're offered depends on the kind of medium you chose; for example, if you select a tape drive, you can indicate whether you plan to back up onto a fresh tape or one you've already partially filled using Backup.

The File option lets you create a backup as a single, unified file on your hard drive, which you can save later by copying it to another PC on the network or to a backup disk. (Of course, your system isn't really protected until you copy this backup file to another drive or computer).

If you now click Next, the Completing the Backup Wizard page appears; you can click the Finish button to start the backup immediately. But suppose you want even more control over this backup job.

5. **Click Next. Click the Advanced button.**

A new screen of settings appears.

6. **Select a backup type.**

On the Type of Backup page, you specify what kind of backup you want to perform (see Figure 18-3).

Each kind affects what's backed up, and what happens to their *archive bits,* differently. The archive bit is a behind-the-scenes switch on every file, an invisible flag, that tells Backup whether or not the file needs backing up. In a **Normal** backup, for example, a file whose archive bit is On (needs backing up) gets copied to your backup disk—and then its archive bit gets reset to Off, so that Backup won't make another copy of it the next time it runs.

Your other options include Copy, Incremental, Differential, and Daily. **Copy** backs up the files, but doesn't turn off their archive bits; in this case, you're simply using Backup as a copying program. An **Incremental** backup copies only files whose archive bits are on, and then turns them off. A **Differential** backup grabs the files that need backing up, but doesn't turn off their archive bits; as described earlier in the chapter, they'll therefore be backed up again the next time you perform a Differential backup.

Finally, the **Daily** backup looks for the files you created or changed today; it doesn't mark them as backed up.

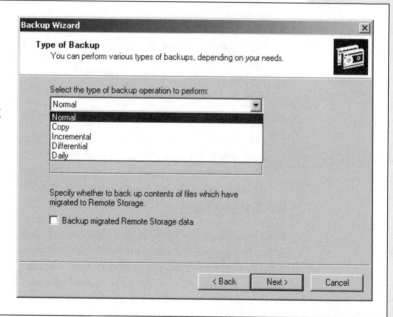

Figure 18-3:
The Type of Backup page simplifies the process of performing specific backup jobs such as incrementals and differentials without worrying about manipulating the archive bits yourself.

7. **Turn on verification and compression, if you like.**

On the How To Back Up page, you can specify whether you want the program to *verify* the backed up data by taking the extra time to compare the copy with the original to make sure that nothing went wrong during the backup process. You can also specify whether or not you want the use *hardware compression,* if your drive supports it. (Hardware compression is circuitry that makes the files take up less space on the backup drive to help you save on the cost of disks or tapes. If your drive offers compression, use it.)

8. **Click Next. Change the media options, if necessary.**

   On the Media Options page, you can specify whether you want to append the backup job to the tape you selected (if it already contains data) or record over it. You can also restrict access to this specific disk or tape to the owner and the system's Administrator user.

9. **Click Next. Set backup label options.**

   Backup can print a label for you that identifies the disk or tape. On this screen, you can view and edit what the label will say.

10. **Click Next. Set up a schedule.**

    On the When To Back Up page, you can specify whether you want to run the backup job right now, or schedule it to run at a later time. If you select Now and click the Next button, you go directly to the wizard's completion page (Step 11).

    If you click the Later radio button, a Set Account Information dialog box appears, in which you specify the user account that you want the backup job to use when it runs. The account you select must have permission to access the drives, folders, and files you intend to back up. On subsequent wizard screens, you'll be asked to name your backup job, to choose a schedule, whether or not you want Backup to wait for a time when the computer is idle and (if it's a laptop) running on AC power, and so on.

11. **Complete the wizard.**

    The Completing the Backup Wizard page summarizes all the settings you've just established. If they look good, click Finish to create the job. Now the program begins the backup (or adds it to the schedule, if that's what you requested).

Restoring Files

Restoring files is less complicated than backing them up. (That's fortunate, considering the emotional state of anyone who's just experienced a total hard-drive meltdown.) That's because, unless you're a spectacularly unlucky individual, you don't perform restores as often as you do backups, and you don't schedule them. The Backup program's Restore Wizard does all the work for you. (You can also restore your files manually, using the program's Restore page.)

Using the Restore Wizard

To restore files using the Restore Wizard, proceed like this:

1. **Click the Restore Wizard button on the Backup program's Welcome page.**

   Selecting the Restore Wizard launches a standard wizard Welcome window.

2. **Click Next. Select a backup device.**

   The What To Restore page contains the now-familiar expanding display that lists your PC's backup devices. The display lists a File icon, too, so that you can restore from a backup file you saved in step 4 of the preceding instructions.

   Click the plus sign next to one of the icons to display the backup media that you've created with it.

3. **Select the tape or disk that contains your backup. Select the data to restore.**

   When you select the backup disk or tape, the right pane in the What To Restore page contains an expandable list of its contents. Turn on the checkboxes of the files and folders you want to restore, as shown in Figure 18-7.

Note: Whenever Backup backs up your files, it remembers which files it put on which backup disks by creating, on the final disk or tape, a table of contents for itself.

That's why, as you browse the files listed on a backup disk, you may be asked to insert that final disk or tape. Only then can Backup show you what's on it.

---

4. **Click the Advanced button, if you like.**

   Ordinarily, Backup restores every backed-up file back onto your hard drive in exactly the same folder that it came from. And if the original file is still *in* that

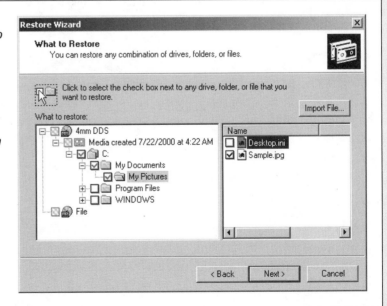

Figure 18-4:
The Restore Wizard's What To Restore page is similar in format to Windows Explorer, except that it displays only the contents of a particular backup tape or disk. You can select from the backup tapes, disks, or files you've created, or click the Import File button to read the contents of a backup file you created on another Windows 2000 system.

original folder, it doesn't wipe out the existing file with the copy on the backup disk. If that arrangement sounds good to you, skip to Step 9.

But suppose you'd like Backup to put the files in a *different* folder, or you want them to *replace* the duplicate files it encounters. In that case, continue like this:

5. **Click Advanced. Select a folder destination for the restored files.**

   On the Where To Restore page, you can specify where you want the restored files to go: into the folders they came from, or some other disk or folder.

   If you choose a different location, Backup restores the files and folders you've selected, doing its best to reconstruct the original folder hierarchy. Unless you turn on Single Folder, that is; in that case, Backup dumps all of the selected files directly into the folder you've chosen, loose (not in folders).

6. **Click Next. Indicate whether or not you want Backup to overwrite duplicate files.**

   What should Backup do if a file it's trying to restore already exists in the destination folder? You can choose from among three options: **Do not replace a file on my computer** (Backup won't restore any file that's already on the hard drive), **Replace the file on my computer only if the file is older** (Backup will replace a file on your hard drive if it's an *older version* than the backed-up copy); or **Always replace the file on my computer** (Backup will restore every file, replacing its equivalent on the hard drive, regardless of which is newer).

7. **Click Next. If the restore summary page looks good, click the Finish button.**

   Backup swings into action, asking you to insert backup disks or tapes as necessary, and restores your backed-up files safely back onto your hard drive.

Maintenance and Troubleshooting

M ost people don't begin life as technophobes, but dealing with a poorly functioning computer on a regular basis would drive anyone to want to throw the whole thing out a window. Although Windows 2000 is extremely stable and reliable, it's the product of very smart but imperfect humans, so it isn't perfect. Sometimes it needs the intervention of another very smart but imperfect human—*you*—to keep it in tip-top shape.

Analyzing Your Maintenance Needs

If you want to keep your system healthy, you need to regularly maintain it. If your company enjoys the attention of a full-service network administrator, you may be spared many of these tasks; but if you're in charge, here's a maintenance schedule suggestion (see Chapter 18 for more on the backup tasks described here):

Task	How Often?
Back up your data (differential backup)	Daily
Back up your data (full backup)	Weekly
Back up your computer (differential backup)	Weekly
Defragment your hard drive	Weekly
Update your virus definitions	Monthly
Back up your computer (full backup)	Monthly
Run a virus check on your computer	Weekly
Run Windows Update	Monthly
Run the Disk Cleanup Utility	Monthly
Check your hard drive	Monthly
Update your Emergency Repair Disk (page 414)	Anytime you change your system
Check for updates to other programs	As necessary, or every six months

You may want to perform some of these chores more or less often, depending on your needs. For example, if all your data is stored on a network server, you may never need to do a backup, because backing up the server is the network administrator's job. But if you're writing your dissertation, incorporating a decade of research, you'll want to back up frequently, make multiple copies, and keep them in multiple locations.

Tip: While you can manually perform these tasks, it's usually much easier to set the Scheduled Tasks tool to do most of them automatically, at a time when you're not using the computer. Scheduled Tasks is discussed on page 166.

Updating Your Software

Using the most up-to-date software can make a big difference in how well your system runs. Software manufacturers occasionally release software *patches* that improve the stability or features of their software; Microsoft releases Service Packs and Security Updates that improve Windows; hardware manufacturers release new drivers; and virus prevention programs periodically require updates that protect you from new viruses. Use the following sections to keep your software up-to-date.

Using Windows Update

Windows Update is the one-stop shop for updates to Windows 2000. Like the Windows Update feature in Windows 98, Windows Update is a Web site that offers updates to the Windows 2000 operating system and related programs, such as Internet Explorer and MSN Messenger. However, Windows Update for Windows 2000 goes a step farther: It also offers certified updated drivers for various hardware components.

FREQUENTLY ASKED QUESTION

Updated Drivers

I looked for updated drivers for my networking card on the Windows Update Web page, but I didn't find it listed—very fishy, especially because I know that the manufacturer has a newer driver than the one I've got. What's going on?

Microsoft only posts drivers on the Windows Update Web site that have passed the Windows 2000 certification process. This requirement ensures that the drivers are stable and mostly bug-free, and is a more stringent process than many hardware manufacturers use.

For the most stable and reliable system possible, use only

these certified drivers, even if newer drivers are available directly from the hardware manufacturer.

However, if you like to play games—especially 3D accelerated games—it can be a good idea to download the latest drivers directly from the hardware manufacturer, or even get so-called *reference drivers* from the maker of your hardware's chipset. For example, if you have a display card based on a popular nVidia chipset (such as the GeForce 2), go directly to nVidia's Web site *(www.nvidia.com)* and download the latest reference drivers. Reference drivers can speed up the machine, but be prepared to return to the certified driver if you run into trouble.

To check Windows Update for new postings, log on to the local machine using an account with administrative privileges (see page 369) and follow these steps:

1. Choose Start→Windows Update.

Your PC connects to the Internet, Internet Explorer opens, and the Windows Update page appears.

Tip: If you're not logged in as an Administrator, hold down the Shift key (after opening the Start menu), right-click Windows Update, and choose Run As from the shortcut menu. Use the Run As dialog box to run Windows Update using an account with Administrator privileges. (The Run As feature is covered on page 376).

---

2. Click the Product Updates link.

Windows Update scans your computer to see what updates you need and displays a list of updates (as shown in Figure 19-1).

3. Select the updates you want.

Select the checkbox next to any updates you want to download and install. At the very least, include all Critical Updates and any relevant Recommended Updates.

Tip: If you're on a dial-up Internet connection, you probably won't want to download *every* update listed on Windows Update. Aside from Critical Updates, you can probably wait for the next service pack (which includes all updates) and order it on CD-ROM—an especially handy option, considering that the Windows 2000 Service Pack 1, for example, is 82 MB, compressed.

Microsoft releases service packs two or three times per year.

Figure 19-1:
Updates are divided into several categories—Critical Updates (which you should probably install immediately), Picks Of the Month (which are optional, but recommended new features or program updates), Recommended Updates (which are optional, but recommended updates to your system), Additional Windows Features, and Device Drivers. To view the updates you've already installed, click the Show Installed Updates or Installation History buttons.

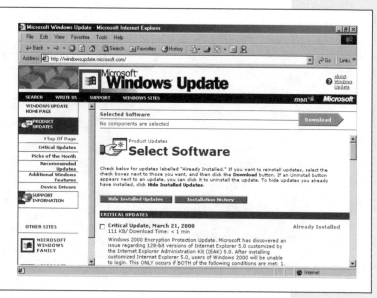

4. Click the Download button to download the updates you selected.

Now you see a list of updates you've selected to download. If you want to view more in-depth information about your selected updates, including instructions, click View Instructions.

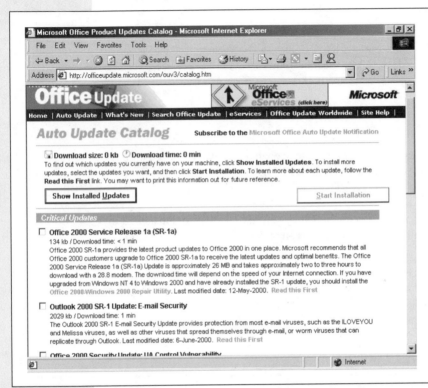

Figure 19-2:
Microsoft's Office Update Web site lists the updates that are available for your version of Office. Most other software manufacturers provide links to downloadable updates, too. Once downloaded, find the files you downloaded to your hard drive and double-click them to install the updates.

FREQUENTLY ASKED QUESTION

Service Packs

What are Service packs, and how do I install them?

For the price of a download or a nominally priced CD, a Service Pack gives you regular improvements and fixes for your system. In Windows NT, they were a mixed blessing; if you needed to reinstall something from the original Windows NT CD, you also needed to reapply the latest Service Pack.

Windows 2000 is designed to eliminate this repetitive ritual. You should be able to install each Service Pack only once.

Even reinstalling a component from the Windows 2000 Professional CD won't force you to reinstall the Service Pack.

To install the latest Service Pack, go to Microsoft's Windows 2000 Web site at *www.microsoft.com/windows2000*, and follow the links provided to download it. Service Packs are cumulative; each new release contains the updates in all of the previous Service Packs, so you don't have to worry if you miss one. (Before you install the Service Pack, you should update your Emergency Repair Disk, as described on page 415.)

---

5. Click Start Download to begin downloading the selected components. In the
   License Agreement dialog box that pops up, click Yes.

   After the updates download, they typically install themselves automatically. Some
   may launch their own setup programs—in these cases, walk through the setup
   program as you would with any other piece of software. If Windows prompts
   you to restart your computer when it's finished, you can either agree and restart
   your computer immediately, or click Cancel, and restart your computer later. (If
   a restart is required, the update will not take effect until the computer is rebooted.)

Updating Applications

If a program runs smoothly under Windows 2000, you don't need to check for updates to it more than once or twice a year. If you experience frequent problems with
your application, check more often—the software manufacturer may be hard at work
on a patch or update that will fix your problem.

To update a program, visit the software manufacturer's Web site and look for a Support or Download link. You may have to poke around a bit. Some manufacturers are
shy about advertising that their software might ever need to be fixed. Figure 19-2
shows Microsoft's Office Update Web site *(http://officeupdate.microsoft.com)*, which,
surprisingly enough, looks and functions much like Windows Update!

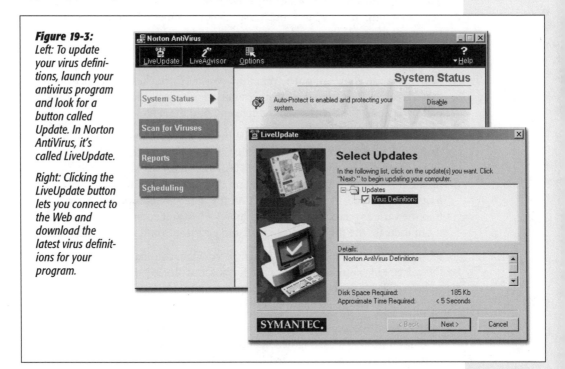

Figure 19-3:
*Left: To update
your virus defini-
tions, launch your
antivirus program
and look for a
button called
Update. In Norton
AntiVirus, it's
called LiveUpdate.*

*Right: Clicking the
LiveUpdate button
lets you connect to
the Web and
download the
latest virus definit-
ions for your
program.*

Virus protection programs are a special case, since they work well only if they are kept extremely up-to-date; virus protection programs don't work against viruses they don't know about. To update your virus *definitions*, as the part of the software with the virus knowledge is called, use the built-in update function of your virus protection program, as shown in Figure 19-3. Check for new definitions at least once a week.

Tip: Virus warnings you get via email are almost invariably hoaxes—a form of information vandalism (see page 297). Always check with a reputable source of virus information (such as Symantec's AntiVirus Research Center, *www.symantec.com/avcenter)* before passing on one of these messages.

Housecleaning Tips

If you want to keep your Windows 2000 system clean and with a lemon-fresh scent, you need to do a little housekeeping every now and then. While Windows 2000 Pro can run a long time without much maintenance, your computer will benefit from the use of the tools described in the next sections.

Defragment Your Hard Drive

When you use your computer, Windows constantly fetches and returns files from the hard drive. To a large extent, the overall perceived speed of your system depends on how quickly the PC can find, return, and find these files again.

Ideally, Windows would store every file in one piece, in one location on the hard drive surface, and always return it to that spot so that the file could be retrieved in one smooth operation. However, in this less-than-ideal world, Windows has to break up files into numerous fragments and on different parts of the hard drive. This *file fragmentation* doesn't have any effect on the data—Windows still knows where to find the various pieces, which it reassembles when you open a fragmented file—but it can increase the time it takes to load and access files and programs.

Files are most likely to get heavily fragmented when your hard drive gets so full that there aren't big chunks of open space for holding files in one piece—and especially when you delete or copy a lot of files. Running Disk Defragmenter reunites all those file fragments and makes hard drive access faster.

Microsoft once claimed that disks formatted with the NTFS file system (see page 413) never need to be defragmented; but in fact, for best speed, NTFS drives need to be defragmented just as often as FAT or FAT32 disks.

Tip: If you often move large files around on your hard drive, burn your own CDs, or edit digital video, you may want to defragment your hard drive fairly often.

To defragment your hard drive, use the following steps:

1. Launch Disk Defragmenter.

To open Disk Defragmenter, right-click My Computer; select Manage from the shortcut menu. In the Computer Management window, expand the Storage icon (if it isn't already expanded), and then click Disk Defragmenter. (Alternatively, right-click a local drive in Windows Explorer, choose Properties from the shortcut menu, click the Tools tab, and then click the Defragment Now button.)

On the right side of the window, you'll see a list of the *volumes* (disks or disk partitions) on your computer.

2. Click the volume you want to defragment, then click Analyze.

Disk Defragmenter examines the selected volume to see if it needs to be defragmented (Figure 19-4).

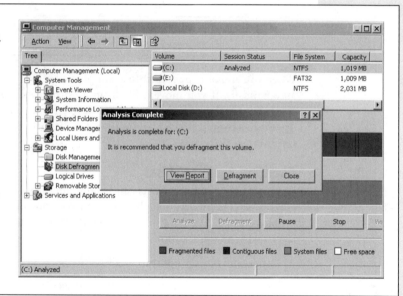

Figure 19-4:
After analyzing a volume, Disk Defragmenter gives a recommendation on whether or not you should defragment the drive, based on the severity of the fragmentation. Click the View Report button to see the full scoop, click Defragment to defragment the volume, or click Close to get back to the main Disk Defragmenter window.

3. Click Defragment.

Disk Defragmenter gets to work on your drive, juggling file segments, lifting some into memory and depositing them elsewhere on the drive, then moving other (smaller) files into the newly created free space. This shuffling process goes on for some time, as file fragments and whole files are moved around until every file lies on the drive in one piece.

You can keep working on your PC as the defragmenting proceeds, although the process will take longer. After defragmentation is complete, you can click the View Report button, or simply click Close.

Tip: If your drive is heavily fragmented, you may need to use Disk Defragmenter several times in order for it to be fully defragmented. And if your drive is almost full, run Disk Cleanup first.

Compressing Folders

If you're running short of disk space, you can use Windows 2000's disk *compression* feature to make your files take up less space on the hard drive. You can compress whole drives (volumes) as well as individual files and folders. Using compression doesn't noticeably slow down Windows 2000 Professional.

To compress a file or folder, choose Properties from its shortcut menu. Then, in the General tab, click the Advanced button to display the Advanced Attributes dialog box; turn on "Compress contents to save disk space." To compress an entire disk or disk partition, choose Properties from its icon's shortcut menu. Then, in the General tab of the Properties dialog box, turn on "Compress drive to save disk space."

Note: Encryption (described on page 366) and compression are mutually exclusive. Encrypted files can't be compressed, and compressed files can't be encrypted.

When you add or copy a file into a compressed folder, Windows 2000 compresses it automatically. If you move a file from a *different* NTFS drive into a compressed folder, the file also gets compressed. However, if you move a file from the *same* NTFS drive into a compressed folder, the file retains its original state, either compressed or uncompressed.

Guarding Against Viruses

Contracting a computer virus can be anything from a nuisance (your email program is used to forward naughty email to everyone in your address book) to a real problem (lost data). It's also something that you can easily prevent with simple—but consistent—precautions:

1. **Get an antivirus program.**

   Some examples are Norton AntiVirus *(www.symantec.com)*, McAfee VirusScan *(www.mcafee.com)*, or Norman Virus Control *(www.norman.com)*. Don't buy any antivirus program that you can't update over the Internet.

Tip: You might have to log on as an Administrator to install, update or perform scans using your antivirus program. Or, to save time, use the handy Run As feature described on page 376.

---

2. **Update your antivirus definitions.**

As soon as you install your new antivirus program, connect to its manufacturer's Web site to update your virus definitions, so that the program has the most up-to-date information about current viruses.

3. Scan your system.

Once your virus definitions are current, do a thorough virus scan of your computer.

4. Turn on autoprotection.

Enabling your antivirus program's autoprotect feature can prevent your system from acquiring viruses. Also, make sure to enable any email scanning features your program may have.

5. Update your email software.

Newer email program versions are almost always more secure than older ones, and in some cases, much more so. For example, if you use Microsoft Outlook 2000, download and install the latest Office Service Pack, which contains new security settings to help prevent email viruses.

6. Be careful with strange emails and all attachments.

While religiously using and updating an antivirus program is essential, it doesn't protect you 100 percent. Viruses tend to spread quickly at first, and you might just be on the unlucky, early end of a long chain of contagion.

UP TO SPEED

How to Identify a Hoax

The first known virus hoax on the Internet was circulated in 1988. Since then, there have been many, many others. Passing these hoaxes on to your friends and colleagues is not only a waste of time and bandwidth, it's also terribly embarrassing when you later find out the whole thing was a fake. Here's how to detect a hoax:

There are two factors that make a successful virus hoax: (1) technical sounding language, and (2) credibility by association. If the warning uses high-tech jargon, most people will tend to believe the warning is real. For example, the very first recorded virus hoax says: "The virus distributes itself on the modem subcarrier present in all 2400 baud and up modems.... The virus sets a bit pattern in one of the internal modem registers.... The virus then attaches itself to all binary incoming data and infects the host computer's hard disk."

Wow, pretty convincing stuff—even today. Of course, a little research will show that there is no such thing as a subcarrier, and that viruses can't be transmitted in the way described.

As for credibility by association: The virus hoax cited above includes the statement, "I do research and development for a local computer telecommunications company," which would lead you to think that the writer might know what he's talking about. The hoax usually cites someone's alleged expertise, or claim that the warning originated with IBM, CBS News, or some other reputable source.

You should also be *especially alert* if the warning urges you to pass it on to your friends—invariably the sign of a hoax. So is the indication that it is a Federal Communication Commission (FCC) warning. The FCC itself has said that it never has, and never will, disseminate warnings on viruses.

As in other areas of life, it pays to look before you leap. *Never* open an email attachment without thinking, even if it appears to be from someone you know. If the message doesn't quite make sense, or you don't know what the writer is talking about, email the sender and inquire about the message. Some viruses spread through email attachments that the sender doesn't even know were sent. In particular, view attachments with the filename extensions .exe, .com, or .vbs with great suspicion. Never open one unless you've verified who sent it and why.

Perform Disk Checks

You may be shocked to hear this, but computers are not perfect. Even an advanced, generally sturdy file system like NTFS can develop problems, especially if you've turned off your computer without using the Shut Down command or experienced a crash that forced you to reboot. Usually, Windows 2000 corrects any resulting problems immediately; but if your computer suddenly seems to be much slower, you should run a disk check.

While NTFS is pretty much self-correcting, FAT and FAT32 most certainly are not— you should check for disk errors once every month or so.

To perform a disk check, right-click the drive in Windows Explorer, and choose Properties from the shortcut menu. Click the Tools tab, and then click Check Now; see Figure 19-5.

Tip: If you turn on either of the checkboxes shown in Figure 19-5, you can't perform a disk check on your system drive (the drive containing Windows 2000) without rebooting your computer. In other words, you'll save time by scanning the disk first; if it turns up any problems, *then* turn on "Scan for and attempt recovery of bad sectors checkbox" and perform the scan.

Figure 19-5:
If you want the disk-checking program to fix any errors it finds automatically, turn on "Automatically fix file system errors checkbox"; to be more thorough, turn on "Scan for and attempt recovery of bad sectors."

Clean Up Your Hard Drive

With hard drive prices as low as they are, most people can afford to waste a bit of hard disk space. However, like that tiny closet in your bedroom that seemed so enormous before you moved in, there are times when even your multigigabyte drive isn't quite big enough.

When you find yourself running short of disk space, start by uninstalling any programs you no longer use, using the Add/Remove Programs tool in the Control Panel (discussed on page 127). If you need still more room, see "Getting Rid of Unneeded Files" on page 209.

Automate Your Maintenance

When there are routine maintenance tasks that you'd like to perform, it can be really handy to set up some or all of the tasks to be performed automatically—obviating the need for you to muck about with them yourself.

Windows 2000 provides the Scheduled Tasks utility for just this purpose. See page 166 for instructions on how to use this tool.

Tip: You can't schedule Windows 2000's Disk Defragmenter to run completely automatically. But using the Scheduled Tasks utility, you can schedule it to run at the end of the day, reminding you to start it going before you quit work or go to bed.

Basic Troubleshooting

Hardware problems typically show up in the form of a computer that won't boot or a piece of equipment that doesn't work (a modem or a sound card, for example). Software problems show themselves when a particular program locks up your system, a program stops working, or your computer slows to a crawl.

Many computer troubles can be solved using the Windows 2000 troubleshooting wizards known as Troubleshooters. To locate the appropriate troubleshooter for your problem, choose Start→Help, then click the Contents tab. Double-click Troubleshooting and Maintenance, then Windows 2000 Troubleshooters.

Of course, a troubleshooter is useless if your computer doesn't start, as described next.

Computers that Won't Start

Startup is generally a smooth and predictable process. When there's a problem with startup, it's always because *something* has changed. You may have added a new sound or video card, installed new memory, changed a hardware setting, or even acquired a virus. (A new video card is by far the most likely culprit when the operating system doesn't start.)

Until you determine the cause, you'll have a hard time fixing the effect. Start by returning to the instructions that came with the new hardware to see if there's an additional driver that must be installed, a jumper that must be set, or a mistake in installation.

"Non-system disk or disk error"

If, at boot up, the computer stops and displays an error message that says, "Non-System disk or disk error; Replace and strike any key when ready," you've probably left a (nonbootable) floppy disk in the drive.

Remove the floppy disk, and then press any key to start Windows.

If there is no floppy disk in the drive, you may have a serious problem with your hard drive. A virus may have infected the drive, in which case you should run an antivirus program. Or the drive may have gone on to that hard drive graveyard in the sky, which means that you'll have to install a new hard drive.

The computer boots, but the screen is blank

If your computer boots, but you don't see *anything* onscreen, check to see if your monitor is turned on and securely plugged in to the computer and to power.

If the computer starts but the screen in Windows isn't readable, reboot the computer. When it says "Starting Windows 2000—for troubleshooting and advanced startup options press F8," press F8; choose Enable VGA Mode from the list of options (by typing its number or pressing the arrow keys); and then press Enter. The problem is with your display settings: Either you specified a refresh rate or resolution that your monitor doesn't support, or you installed an incorrect display driver.

When your system boots, go into the Display Control Panel tool (see page 138) and change your resolution or monitor refresh rate to a lower setting, or uninstall the display driver you installed.

The computer boots, but Windows doesn't start

If the PC only *starts* to start up, but the familiar Windows desktop never appears, the culprit may be a recalcitrant device driver or recently installed hardware component.

Try booting in *Safe Mode,* which loads only those parts of the operating system necessary to start Windows, and nothing more.

To use Safe Mode, watch closely when your computer boots; when your computer says "Starting Windows 2000—for troubleshooting and advanced startup options press F8," do what it says: press F8. Select Safe Mode from the list (by typing its number or pressing the down-arrow key) and press Enter. Your system will then attempt to boot into Safe Mode.

You'll know it when you see it; not only do the words "Safe Mode" appear in the corners of your screen, but because Windows doesn't load the driver for your video card (on the assumption that it may be causing the very problem you're trying to troubleshoot), your desktop may look fuzzy, enlarged, and pale.

If Windows successfully loads in Safe Mode, you can try rebooting normally and see if it starts OK. If you have an idea why the system didn't boot properly (such as a new piece of hardware), you should take care of it before you reboot. For example, disable the device in Device Manager (page 357), or uninstall any new software drivers you might have installed.

If your problem is in the Windows 2000 Registry (see page 405), there's a chance you can easily fix it by booting with an older copy of the Registry—the Last Known Good Registry. To do this, reboot your computer. Once again, when the screen says "Starting Windows 2000—for troubleshooting and advanced startup options press F8," press F8. Select the Last Known Good Configuration option and press Enter. Your computer now starts up using a version of the Registry that it had saved the last time you successfully booted your system. You'll lose any changes you've made to the Registry since then (such as programs you've installed or system settings you've changed); but if your system boots, that's what counts.

When nothing else works: The emergency repair process

If you can't get your computer started using Windows 2000 Safe Mode or the Last Known Good Configuration, you should use the Emergency Repair Process. Grab your Emergency Repair Disk (ERD). (Steps for creating an ERD are on page 415.)

1. **Boot from the Windows 2000 CD or floppy disks.**

   To start up your PC from the Windows 2000 CD, try inserting the CD and then restarting the computer. If that doesn't work on your PC model, you may have to make changes to the boot procedure, as directed by the manufacturer. And if your system doesn't support booting from the CD-ROM at all, boot from the first of the four Windows 2000 startup floppy disks.

Tip: If you don't have a set of Windows 2000 boot floppies, you can make one on any computer running any version of Windows by running the Makeboot.exe program. You'll find it in the Bootdisk folder on the Windows 2000 CD-ROM.

---

2. **Press R to specify that you want to repair an existing installation of Windows 2000, then press R again to specify that you want to use the Emergency Repair Process.**

   Now a choice of manual or automatic repair appears.

3. **Press F to let Windows 2000 automatically repair your system, or M to manually specify which actions Windows 2000 should perform.**

   Using the Fast Repair option is the quickest and most assured way to get your system functioning; it's the best option for most people. If you want to proceed cautiously, press M and then select the options you want to perform.

Caution: Using the Fast Repair option restores a copy of the Windows 2000 Registry that was created when you first installed Windows 2000, *erasing* any customizations or changes you may have made since, such as installing Service Packs. If this repair is too drastic for you, try the Manual option first.

---

4. **Insert your up-to-date Emergency Repair Disk and press Enter to begin repairing your system.**

   If you don't have an ERD, press L to force Windows 2000 to try to locate where Windows 2000 is installed. If it locates your installation, press Enter to accept it. (Next time keep your ERD updated. Your luck won't always be this good.)

POWER USERS' CLINIC

Using The Emergency Recovery Console

A new feature for Windows 2000 is the Emergency Recovery Console—an enhanced version of the command prompt that you can use to boot your computer, even if your computer won't boot any other way. The Emergency Recovery Console lets you access NTFS, FAT, and FAT32 disks and partitions, which should make most veteran Windows NT users rejoice. (It's not unknown for NT veterans to install a separate copy of Windows NT just to gain access to a broken copy). However, the Console is only for serious users who know what they're doing. Furthermore, unless you use the Local Security Policy tool in the Start→Programs→ Administrative Tools folder to enable the Local Policies→Security Options→Recovery Console: "Allow floppy copy and access to all drives and folders" setting, you will only be able to access the root directory of your hard drive and the \WINNT folder.

Still, the Emergency Recovery Console is an incredibly handy tool for power users. To use it, boot from your Windows 2000 CD-ROM or boot disks, press R, and then press C. Specify which Windows 2000 installation you want to log on to (most likely 1), and then enter the *original* Administrator password (the one you entered when installing Windows 2000), if one was set. At the command prompt, type *HELP* to see a list of all the commands you can use from the Recovery Console.

System Instabilities

While a computer that won't start is horrifying, there are few things more frustrating than a computer that boots perfectly well but exhibits intermittent system crashes—the computer freezes, reboots, and/or displays a blue screen error message (unaffectionately known as the Blue Screen Of Death). Fortunately, Windows 2000 is *much* more resistant to system crashes than Windows 98 and Windows Me—but not completely immune.

As with a computer that refuses to boot, first ask yourself what's changed since the last time the computer worked well. If you can't be sure, then look for a pattern to the problem. Perhaps the computer hangs and then displays the Blue Screen Of Death when making a CD-ROM or when capturing video. Or you installed a new video driver to make a game run faster, and it's causing everything else to run slower! If you've changed anything, change it back and see if the stability problem goes away.

Tip: Poorly written device drivers are one of the most common causes for system instability, so if you've installed any drivers that aren't certified for Windows 2000 by Microsoft, consider them prime suspects. Try removing them and installing certified drivers such as the ones included with Windows 2000 or ones found on Microsoft's Hardware Compatibility List *(www.microsoft.com/hcl)*.

Next, go to Event Viewer (covered on page 377). Look for warnings or errors. If you find any, double-click them and read their descriptions (which often include suggestions for resolving the error). If the description isn't very helpful (and it often isn't), connect to the Internet and search Microsoft's Knowledge Base using the event number listed.

If you're getting the dreaded Blue Screen Of Death, write down the message that appears on the blue screen and check Event Viewer to see if it was recorded there. Search the Knowledge Base for the error message listed;—often you'll find a specific article that you can use to fix the problem. (Remember, considering the number of computers running Windows 2000 Pro, the odds are quite small that you are the very first person to have a particular trouble.)

If all else fails, one very reliable way of fixing what ails a computer is to reinstall Windows. This is not nearly as drastic as it sounds, though it is time-consuming. You can reinstall either as an "upgrade"—all your settings and programs are kept intact—or as a clean install, which means you start over from square one. (Neither reinstallation type harms your data, but the second method requires reinstallation of all programs.) Both kinds of reinstallation are described in Appendix A.

Try performing an upgrade install first; in many cases, this kind of installation fixes your system instability or corrects startup problems. (If you can start in Safe Mode, but can never manage to get Normal mode to work correctly, boot in Safe Mode and *then* perform an upgrade reinstallation of Windows 2000.)

Note: If you reinstall Windows 2000 as an upgrade, you'll have to reinstall any Service Packs you may have installed.

Freeing a Locked Up System

It's very rare for Windows 2000 Pro to *lock up* or *freeze,* as was common with previous versions of Windows (and other operating systems, as well). This stability is, after all, one of its biggest selling points in the business world.

If the action on the screen does come to a halt—and your keyboard and mouse clicks produce no response—the problem is almost always with one of the programs you're running. Often the system can sort these things out if you just allow a little time. Wait a minute or two to see if the problem resolves itself. (You'll know, because all at once, you'll see Windows react to all those mouse clicks and keystrokes that you entered before realizing the system had stopped.)

If allowing some time to pass doesn't do the trick, press Ctrl+Alt+Delete to display the Windows Security dialog box. Click Task Manager (see Figure 19-6).

Bear in mind that once a program shows in the Task Manager as "Not responding," you'll *have* to close it down and restart it if you want it to work again. There's no point in waiting around for it to cure itself; any unsaved work you have in the program may be lost. The newer the program, the less likely data will be lost. On the other hand, the newer the program, the less likely it is to lock up unexpectedly.

On the bright side, you can almost always force the program to close and reopen without having to restart the entire operating system. Windows 2000 Pro is very good about isolating various software processes from one another, and the failure of one is very unlikely to cause the failure of others.

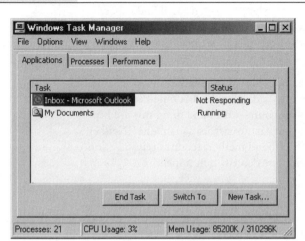

Figure 19-6:
If your system stops working, it's usually the fault of one program. Click the Application tab and look for the Task labeled "Not responding." Highlight that task and click End Task. After you click End Task, it may take as much as a minute for the non-responding program to close. You may even have to order it to End again.

Where Else to Get Help

The troubleshooting tips in this chapter cover the problems you're most likely to encounter. But as any PC veteran can tell you, there's an almost infinite list of other things that can go wrong. Here are some other places to turn when Windows 2000 glitches raise their ugly heads:

• **Microsoft Knowledge Base.** A wealth of information is in Microsoft's Knowledge Base, located at *http://search.support.microsoft.com.* Here you can search the same database of articles that Microsoft Tech Support uses when handling customer problems.

• **Microsoft Newsgroups.** If you don't know enough to find the problem in the Knowledge Base, try one of the online newsgroups at *www.microsoft.com/windows2000/support/newsgroups.* The newsgroups are an amazing resource; just post your question politely and succinctly (but with all necessary information), and check the newsgroups again; you'll probably find several intelligent responses in a matter of hours.

Note: The newsgroup links on this Web page work only if you've configured Outlook Express or another newsreader to access a news server. See page 272 for more information.

- **Free phone help.** If you bought Windows 2000 Pro in a box (that is, it didn't come on your computer), you can call Microsoft for free phone help at any hour—twice. Consult the Getting Started booklet for restrictions and phone numbers.

  If Windows 2000 came preinstalled in your machine, on the other hand, you're supposed to call the computer company with your Windows questions.

- **Expensive phone help.** Once you've used up your two free calls, you can still call Microsoft with your questions—but they'll charge you plenty per incident. Fortunately, each problem is a single incident even if it takes several calls to fix the situation. This service is available 24 hours a day.

Tip: If you're not in the United States, direct your help calls to the local Microsoft office in your country. You can look up a list of these subsidiaries at *www.microsoft.com/support.*

UP TO SPEED

The Registry

Here and there, in books, articles, and conversations, you'll hear references to the Windows *Registry*.

The Registry is your PC's master database of settings. It includes your preferences, the way Windows 2000 and other applications are set up to run on your computer, what hardware is installed, and what software drivers are used to run

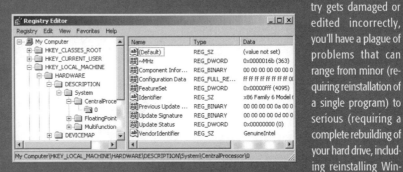

the hardware. This information isn't stored in a plain English format; it takes the form of a hierarchy of long, coded strings of text and numbers. (The applets in your Control Panel are little more than safe, easily understood "front ends" for various Registry settings.)

As you can well imagine, the Registry is an extremely important cog in a Windows machine. That's why Windows marks your Registry files as invisible and nondeletable. If the Registry gets damaged or edited incorrectly, you'll have a plague of problems that can range from minor (requiring reinstallation of a single program) to serious (requiring a complete rebuilding of your hard drive, including reinstalling Windows and all applications.)

Windows 2000 comes with a program called RegEdit, which you can use to make changes to the Registry. But don't use it unless you have no alternative. Registry editors bypass the standard safeguards provided by administrative tools, which prevent you from entering conflicting settings or settings that are likely to damage your system.

Part Six:
Appendixes

6

Installing
Windows 2000 Professional

I f you're on a corporate network, someone else probably handles Windows 2000 installations; you can skip this appendix (and the delightful experience of installing a new operating system). And if you've just bought a new computer with Windows 2000 computer preinstalled, you're similarly excused from reading the following pages.

But if you're upgrading your machine from an earlier version of Windows, read on to determine whether your computer is up to the Windows 2000 challenge and how to plan your installation. (And if you're *reinstalling* Windows 2000, skip straight to "Prepping Your System" on page 414.)

UP TO SPEED

Help with Upgrading and Compatibility

In addition to the Hardware Compatibility List (page 346), Microsoft maintains Web sites and white papers on meeting hardware requirements for Windows 2000.

Start with the Windows 2000 home page *(www.microsoft. com/windows2000/default.asp)*; you can branch out from there for product and technical information.

If you're wondering if your current system will work with Windows 2000, download and run the Readiness Analyzer at *www.microsoft.com/windows2000/upgrade/compat*. On

the same page are links to search for wholly compatible computers, software, and the latest device drivers.

See *www.microsoft.com/windows2000/library/planning/ client/deploy.asp* for a guide to deploying Windows 2000 Pro in a business environment.

For problem solving, search the Microsoft Knowledge Base *(http://search.support.microsoft.com/kb/)*. It's a veritable Encyclopedia of Microsoftiana.

Before Installing

Before proceeding, make sure that your computer can handle Windows 2000; plan your installation; and then prepare your machine for it. The following sections help you with each of these tasks.

Check the Hardware Requirements

To run Windows 2000, your computer should exceed Microsoft's minimum system requirements. Yes, Windows 2000 Pro will run on a minimally configured machine, but using your PC will be about as much fun as drag racing in a Geo Metro. The table below shows the minimum, realistic, and recommended equipment for best speed.

Component	Minimum	Realistic Minimum	Recommended
CPU	Pentium 133 MHz	Pentium 200 MHz	Pentium 300 MHz or better
RAM	32 MB	80 MB	128 MB
Hard Disk	2 GB with 650 MB free	2 GB with 1 GB free	4 GB with 2 GB free

Using the Readiness Analyzer

To determine if you have incompatible hardware or software on your computer, run the Windows 2000 Readiness Analyzer (a free program available at *www.microsoft.com/windows2000/downloads/deployment/readiness/default.asp*).

This tool analyzes your system and reports any hardware or software on your system that Microsoft knows to be incompatible with Windows 2000. To use it, run the Chckupgrd.exe file, click Yes in the License Agreement, and then view the results of the Readiness Check.

If the Readiness Analyzer reports that some of your hardware or software is incompatible with Windows 2000, check with the corresponding manufacturers. Often the manufacturer's Web site offers a new driver or software patch for downloading.

Tip: If you can't run the Readiness Analyzer for some reason, consult the Hardware Compatibility List (HCL), as described on page 346.

Planning Your Installation

You'll have to make three major decisions when installing Windows 2000. First, you have to decide whether to perform a *clean install* or a standard *upgrade;* second, you have to decide how to *partition* your hard drive; and third, you'll have to specify which *file system* you prefer—FAT32 or NTFS. This section covers all three decisions.

Upgrade or Clean Install?

Microsoft thinks it's doing you a favor by designing the Windows 2000 installer to upgrade your existing Windows installation, without disturbing any of your settings, fonts, drivers, and so on—and, more important, without requiring you to reinstall your programs. This kind of installation is simply called an *upgrade.*

But you can wind up with a fairly glitchy PC if you attempt to upgrade to Windows 2000 from Windows 95, 98, or Me in this way. That's why there's a second way to use the Windows 2000 installer: You can perform a *clean install,* described on page 417.

When you do a clean install, Setup makes no attempt to preserve your existing settings, applications, and so on. It installs a virginal, completely independent, perfect copy of Windows 2000 Pro into its own folder on your hard drive.

A clean install entails a lot of hassle, because when it's over, you must re-create all of your settings and reinstall all of your programs. But in general, a clean install is the best recipe for a trouble-free PC. Most people shrink from the idea of "starting all over," because they want to preserve their software configurations. However, an upgrade may bring out-of-date drivers, Windows 2000-incompatible programs, and other problems into your new Windows 2000 world.

Upgrading from Windows NT

Upgrading to Windows 2000 is extremely easy from Windows NT 4; just run the Windows 2000 installer as usual (see page 416).

Note: During the installation, if Windows 2000 can't find Windows 2000-specific drivers for a device on your system, it will use Windows NT drivers it finds already installed. While this approach usually works, using Windows NT drivers under Windows 2000 limits the power saving and Plug and Play features of your system. Upgrade the drivers to Windows 2000 drivers as soon as possible.

Upgrading from Windows 95 or Windows 98

The fact that it's even possible to upgrade from Window 95 or Windows 98 to Windows 2000 is incredible. The operating systems, their applications, and their drivers are completely different.

But just because you *can* perform such an upgrade doesn't mean it's a good idea. As noted earlier, upgrading from Windows 95 or Windows 98 can be fraught with difficulties. To install Windows 2000 on a computer running any operating system other than Windows NT Workstation 4, consider performing a clean install, as discussed later in this chapter. (And do so, furthermore, only if your PC is relatively new *and* all of its components are on the Windows 2000 Hardware Compatibility List.)

If you can't bear the idea of a clean install, try an upgrade. If the upgrade fails or produces unsatisfactory results, you can always do a clean install later.

Upgrading from Windows Me

You *can't* upgrade from Windows Me to Windows 2000, except by doing a clean installation.

Planning Partitions

If you're performing an upgrade installation, skip this section. If you're doing a clean install, however, pay attention—how you *partition* your hard drive has a big impact on what features you can use, the speed of your system, and the compatibility of your system in a dual-boot configuration.

When you partition a hard drive, you subdivide it into several chunks, each of which shows up in your My Computer window with a different icon, name, and drive letter.

The first thing to decide is how many partitions you need and how big they should be. If you're not creating a dual-boot configuration (see the sidebar above), a single partition will do; in fact, partitioning otherwise creates a good deal of administra-

---

POWER USERS' CLINIC

Running Multiple Operating Systems (Dual-Booting)

It's perfectly possible to keep more than one operating system on a single computer, which is known as a *dual-boot* configuration. This setup is ideal for many people making the transition from Windows 9X to Windows 2000; whenever you need a program or device that doesn't work in Windows 2000, you can simply reboot into the other version of Windows.

To set up a dual-boot, you perform a clean install of Windows 2000 alongside your existing operating system. Thereafter, each time you start up your PC, Windows 2000 pauses for 30 seconds so you can choose which operating system you want to launch. Press the up or down arrow key to highlight the name of the operating system you want, then press the Enter key. The Windows version you selected now launches and takes over your PC.

But dual-booting does present some complications. First, you must install each operating system onto its own disk *partition* (described above). Second, for smoothest sailing, you should install your applications onto each "side" of your computer. Third, you need a different computer name for each operating system. The computer will appear on the network as, say, *Dell 95* when it's booted into

Windows 95, and as (for example) *Dell 2K* when it's booted into Windows 2000.

Next—and this is where dual-booting gets complicated—the hard-drive formatting scheme you select comes into play here, too (see the facing page). If you format the Windows 2000 partition using the NTFS scheme, you won't be able to access any of the Windows 2000 partition's files when you've started up the computer with Windows 95, 98, or Me. (The only other operating system that can fully access Windows 2000 NTFS partitions is Windows NT 4 with Service Pack 4 or later.) For example, if you boot up from your C: drive partition, which contains Windows 98, the D: partition that contains Windows 2000 will apparently disappear, along with the all the files it contains. (The boot partition—the C: drive—must be formatted with the FAT or FAT32 scheme, so that Windows 9X can boot from it.)

Therefore, if you want to be able to access your Windows 2000 partition from another operating system, you'll need to use the FAT or FAT32 file system for all of the partitions—but then, of course, you lose the security and feature benefits of the NTFS system.

---

tive hassle (such as specifying the proper "drive" for every program you install) that you can probably do without.

If you're planning a dual-boot setup, you need a separate partition for each operating system. Each partition should have enough room for all programs you want to use in each operating system.

File Systems: NTFS vs. FAT

One critical decision you'll have to make as you install Windows 2000 is which *file system* to use. A file system is the structure your computer uses to organize, name, and track files on the hard drive. Over the years, Microsoft has developed several such systems, making improvements each time. Before Windows NT and 2000, the world's leading file systems were called FAT (also known as FAT16), and FAT32 (which stand for *file allocation table,* as though that's any help).

Windows 2000 can format your hard drive with the FAT file system, just as Windows 95, 98, and Me can. But it offers the option of using something much better: NTFS (for *NT file system).*

NTFS offers a long list of useful advantages over the older FAT file systems, some of which are described in the relevant chapters of this book. Here's a summary:

• **Better security.** When you share folders (see page 295) on a FAT drive, you can specify who on the network is allowed to access their contents. That's not such hot security; if an evildoer wants to root through your secret files, all he has to do is sit down at your PC when you're not around.

  NTFS, on the other hand, also lets you specify who can open those folders *in person*—that is, when sitting right down at your computer and logging in.

• **Better control over sharing.** As noted above, if your hard drive is formatted with FAT, you can control who on the network is allowed to access certain shared *folders.* But on an NTFS hard drive, you can limit your network comrades' access on a *file-by-file* basis (not just folder-by-folder).

• **File encryption.** As noted on page 366, NTFS lets you *encrypt* certain files so that nobody else can read them.

• **Bigger, faster, better.** NTFS can handle hard drive sizes of up to 2 TB. (That's not tablespoons—it's *terabytes;* 1,024 GB makes up a terabyte. Put another way, a TB holds about as much as one million floppy disks.) In theory, the FAT32 system can handle a 2 TB drive, too; but in practice, Microsoft recommends a maximum partition size of 32 GB to avoid slowdowns.

  Files generally open faster on NTFS drives, too, and are easier to recover in the event of disaster.

There's only one reason to consider formatting your drives with anything other than NTFS, and that's if you're setting up a dual-boot system, for reasons described on the facing page.

Tip: To find out which file system your hard drive uses, open My Computer, right-click drive icon, and choose Properties from the shortcut menu. You'll see the File System information near the top of the dialog box.

Prepping Your System

Just as surgeons don't start operating in the parking lot with whatever tools are handy, you should postpone upgrading until you've done the necessary preparatory work.

Back up your data

"Perform regular backups" is the oldest advice in the computer business, ranking right up there with your mom's admonition not to run with a pencil in your hand. But mom was right and so is this: back up your PC before playing with it. See Chapter 18 for details on backup strategies. (The program described there, Backup, was included with all recent versions of Windows.)

Make a boot disk or ERD

If Windows 2000 Setup runs into trouble and your system won't start up, you have a problem. Without a *boot disk* and/or *Emergency Repair Disk* (ERD), you have a much bigger problem. A boot disk allows you to start up your system and (if you're lucky) get it working again. An ERD (for Windows NT users only), stores vital information about your current Windows installation that can be used to repair your installation in the event that Setup fails and leaves your system inoperable.

To create an ERD in Windows NT 4, choose Start→Run, type in *rdisk,* then press Enter. The Repair Disk Utility dialog box opens.

If you're running Windows 98 or Me, the equivalent disk is called a Startup Disk. To make one, choose Start→Settings→Control Panel, and then double-click the Add/Remove Programs icon. In the Add/Remove Programs Properties dialog box, click the Startup Disk tab, and click the Create Disk button. Insert the Windows CD-ROM, if prompted, and insert a blank floppy disk. Click OK to create the disk. (You can create Windows 95 startup disks the same way; note, however, that Windows 95 disks don't have built-in support for CD-ROM drives.)

Tip: Besides the files Windows 98 puts on a startup disk, consider copying the following files from the C:\Windows\Command folder to the floppy disk: fdisk.exe, format.com, scandisk.exe, and edit.com. Doing so will allow you to partition and format disks, check them for errors, and edit configuration files without having to insert the Windows 98 CD-ROM.

Check for viruses

Viruses can really screw up an installation, so run a thorough virus check with an up-to-date virus-scanning program before you install Windows 2000. But after you've run the virus scan, *turn off* the virus-scanning program until you have Windows

2000 installed. Antivirus programs can wreak havoc when installing a new operating system.

Uninstall incompatible programs

If the Readiness Analyzer reported that you have a program that's incompatible with Windows 2000, uninstall it before running Setup. This step is especially important for disk utilities and antivirus programs.

Decompress your hard drive

If you're upgrading a Windows 95 or 98 drive that you'd compressed using DriveSpace, decompress it before proceeding; Windows 2000 is incompatible with DriveSpace.

Update your BIOS and download new drivers

Your *system BIOS* (basic input/output system) is the software that permits certain very basic functions of your PC to operate the instant you turn it on, even before Windows has started up.

The version of your computer's BIOS plays an important role in the success of your Windows 2000 installation. Although older BIOS versions generally work fine with Windows 2000, updating your BIOS to the latest version makes your machine more stable and may enable ACPI support (a power-saving feature) under Windows 2000. (Many computers built *after* Windows 2000 shipped still don't have BIOS versions recent enough to support ACPI under Windows 2000.) You can generally download the latest BIOS revision for your computer from the BIOS manufacturer's Web site (or its motherboard manufacturer's Web site).

Caution: Follow your computer manufacturer's instructions *very* carefully when updating your BIOS. If you do something wrong, such as turning off your computer in the middle of the process, you may render your computer inoperable.

Download the latest Windows 2000 drivers for any devices or peripherals you have, such as sound cards, display drivers, and network cards. Although you may not use them during Setup, you'll want to update the drivers immediately after installation, so it makes sense to download them beforehand.

Gather ye tools

You won't want to go hunting for a driver disk, CD, or manual when you're arm-deep into the Windows 2000 Setup process. Find them and have them handy *before* you need them. Besides the Windows 2000 CD-ROM and this book, locate your program disks, Windows 2000 device driver disks you might have (or have created after downloading drivers from the Internet), your system and data backups, your emergency boot disk, and, if you're currently running Windows NT, your up-to-date Emergency Repair Disk.

As noted earlier, the chances are small that you'll be responsible for installing Windows 2000 Pro if you're on a corporate network. But if it falls to you for some reason, consult your network administrator for the key pieces of information you'll need during the installation process: your computer's name, domain or workgroup name, and *IP address*. Before you install Windows 2000, the administrator may also take this opportunity to connect your PC to the network and create a domain account for you.

Tip: Keep a computer journal to record all the major changes you make to your computer. While you're going through the Windows 2000 Setup process, for example, write down the steps you take, any difficulties you have, and how you resolve them. This record is extremely helpful when troubleshooting a problem. There's no phrase a tech-support person dreads more than, "Well, right before it crashed, there was a message about disks, or maybe it was memory or something...."

Disconnect the UPS

One last thing before you install: Disconnect your UPS (uninterruptible power supply), if you have one. The Windows 2000 Setup program may have problems detecting it. You can reconnect it after Windows 2000 Setup is finished.

Installing Windows 2000

Once you've completed that elaborate checklist on the previous pages, you'll be delighted to hear that the Windows 2000 Setup program usually runs very smoothly. All of the preceding warnings and preparatory steps are tantamount to wearing a belt *and* suspenders: It's better to be safe than sorry.

Upgrading To Windows 2000

To upgrade from a previous operating system, follow these steps:

1. **Start your computer.**

   The Windows 2000 Setup process is simplest when you start up from within some version of Windows.

2. **Insert the Windows 2000 CD-ROM.**

   If you're asked, "Would you like to upgrade to Windows 2000?" click Yes, even if you plan to perform a clean install.

   In any case, now the Welcome screen appears.

Note: You can also install Windows 2000 across a network—just run the Winnt.exe program (if you're running Windows 95, 98, or Me) or the Winnt32.exe program (if you're running Windows NT or 2000) from the I386 folder, wherever on the network where the Windows 2000 Setup files are located.

---

3. **Click Upgrade.**

See Figure A-1 for an illustration; see page 411 for help in choosing between these options.

4. **Click Next; accept the License Agreement.**

If you don't click "I accept this agreement," you're kicked out of the installation process, so it's really no decision at all.

5. **Choose whether or not to upgrade to NTFS (Figure A-2).**

Choose Yes to upgrade the drive to NTFS, or choose No to leave it with the current file system.

6. **Click Next. Enter the Product Key.**

In the Product Key box, enter the long string of letters and numbers on the back of your Windows 2000 CD-ROM case, and then click Next.

Now Setup copies files to your hard drive, restarts your computer into a text-mode Setup, copies some more files, restarts into Windows 2000, detects your hardware, configures your PC's components, copies some more files, and then restarts again into Windows 2000, for real this time.

Performing a Clean Install

There are two ways you can start the clean install process—either from an already installed version of Windows, or by booting your system with the Windows 2000 CD-ROM or setup disks.

Figure A-1:
Click Next in the first screen of the Windows 2000 Setup Wizard to confirm your choice to upgrade. If Setup doesn't launch automatically when you insert the Windows 2000 CD-ROM, click Start→Run, type D:\setup.exe (replacing D with your CD-ROM's drive letter), and click the Install Windows 2000 link to begin Setup.

Installing from Windows

If you already have a version of Windows, follow steps 1 and 2 of the preceding instructions. Then, at the Welcome screen:

1. **Click "Install a new copy of Windows 2000 (Clean Install)." Click Next. Accept the License Agreement, then click Next again. Type your Product Key, then click Next.**

   For help finding the Product Key, see Step 6 of the previous instructions.

   If your hard drive has several partitions, you can click the Advanced Options button at this point, turn on "Choose installation partition during setup," and then click OK.

2. **Click Next.**

   Setup copies files to your hard drive, then restarts your computer into a text-mode Setup.

3. **Press Enter.**

   If you selected "Choose installation partition during setup" in step 1, select the partition you want for Windows 2000 and press Enter. To delete a partition, select it, press D, Enter, and then L.

Note: Be careful; deleting a partition *deletes everything on it.*

Figure A-2:
Unless your system is already using NTFS, Windows 2000 will pester you to upgrade the drive to NTFS. See page 413 for a discussion of NTFS's considerable pros and very few cons.

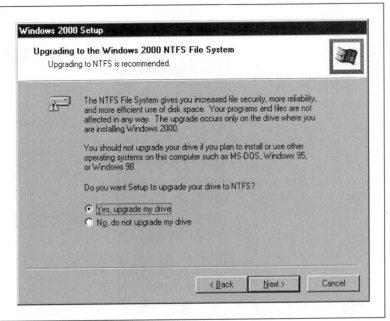

To create a new partition, select one of the unpartitioned disk space entries in the partition list, press C, enter the size of the partition in megabytes, and then press Enter.

4. **Choose your file system.**

If you chose an unformatted partition, you can now choose which file system to use (see page 412). If you chose an existing partition that doesn't use the NTFS file system, you can choose to convert it to NTFS (nothing will be harmed in the process).

5. **Press Enter.**

Setup may format or convert your selected partition, copy a bunch of files, and then restart your computer. All of this takes nearly an hour.

Before long, you come face-to-face with the Setup Wizard, described below.

Installing Directly from CD or Floppy Disks

If some version of Windows isn't already on the computer, start your PC from the Windows 2000 CD-ROM or from the four setup boot disks. To do so, use the following steps:

1. **Insert the Windows 2000 CD-ROM and turn on your computer.**

If you see a prompt asking you to press any key to boot from the CD-ROM, press a key. To boot from the floppy disks, insert the first disk before starting your computer. Insert and remove the disks as requested, until you're finally prompted to press Enter to begin Setup. (Do so).

Tip: Most modern PCs can start up from a CD, but you may first have to change the Boot Order setting (or something similar), which involves working with your BIOS settings. Your computer's manufacturer can help you with this technical step.

---

2. **Accept the License Agreement by pressing F8.**

(If you don't agree, you can't install Windows 2000.)

At this point, continue with Steps 3, 4, and 5 of the preceding instructions.

The Setup Wizard

After your computer finishes the Text mode phase, Setup restarts your computer into the Windows 2000 Setup Wizard. You'll be asked to specify your geographical region, your name, organization, computer name, administrator password (see page 369), dialing location and prefixes, date and time, network settings, and workgroup or domain name (if any). As noted earlier, your network administrator can guide you with these technical settings.

When you click the final Next button, Setup does some more file copying; shows you a list of any problems it encountered; and finally, restarts your computer, which is now a full-fledged Windows 2000 Professional workstation.

The Network Identification Wizard

If your computer is not part of a network, the first time you log on to Windows 2000, the Network Identification Wizard starts and offers you an important choice:

- **Users must enter a user name and password to use this computer.** This is the standard setting. Nobody can use the PC at all without logging on to it, as described on page 19.

- **Windows always assumes the following user has logged on.** If you use your Windows 2000 machine at home or in a one-person office, and you don't much care about security, select this option; type in your name and password. You've gained some convenience, because Windows 2000 won't ask you for your name and password every time you turn on the machine. But you've also disabled most security features of Windows 2000, and turned off the profiles feature that preserves separate settings for each person who uses this PC (see page 374).

Tip: You can change your mind about the choice you make here at any time. To do so, choose Start→Settings→Control Panel. Double-click Users and Passwords. Click the checkbox at the top of the window, and then click OK.

Once you've made a selection, click Finish.

Adding or Removing Windows 2000 Components

You're not obligated to live with the software the Windows 2000 Pro installer dumps onto your hard drive. In fact, many megabytes of it may be accessories that you never use. On the other hand, the Windows 2000 default installation *doesn't* include a number of software morsels that you may decide you'd like to try out. Fortunately, it's easy to add or remove these optional components without disturbing the rest of your Windows 2000 installation:

1. **Choose Start→Control Panel. Double-click the Add/Remove Programs icon.**

   The Add/Remove Programs applet opens.

2. **Click Add/Remove Windows Components at the left side of the dialog box.**

   Now the Windows Components Wizard appears.

3. **Click Next.**

   You've arrived at the master list of optional Windows 2000 components, as shown in Figure A-3.

4. **Turn on a checkbox to request the installation of that component; turn off a checkbox to have the corresponding software removed from your system. Then click Done.**

You may be asked to insert the Windows 2000 CD-ROM as your computer completes the transaction.

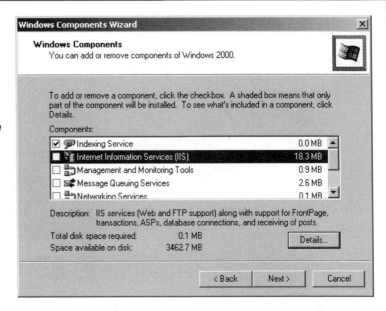

Figure A-3:
To find out what something is, click its name once. And if the Details button appears, you've clicked something that contains several other somethings. Click Details to see a list of the software modules within this category.

What to Do If Setup Fails

What do you do if Setup hangs, shuts off your computer, or displays a STOP error (the infamous Blue Screen Of Death)? Here are a few suggestions:

- **Try again.** Sometimes Setup is smart enough to avoid whatever it was that caused the problem in the first place.

- **Update your BIOS, or disable ACPI.** As noted earlier, ACPI is Windows's advanced power-saving technology. To turn it off, at the beginning of text-mode setup, ignore the prompt to press F6 to install third-party storage drivers; press F5 instead, and then select Standard PC from the list that appears.

- **Try one of the Windows 2000 Help System's Troubleshooters.** The Windows 2000 Help menu has some useful suggestions in its System Setup Troubleshooter. (At the desktop, press F1; in the Help window, click Contents; click Troubleshooting and Maintenance; click "Windows 2000 troubleshooters.") On the other hand, this tip is no help if you don't have access to an operating Windows 2000 machine.

- **Check the Knowledge Base.** The definitive source for troubleshooting any Microsoft product is the Knowledge Base at *http://search.support.microsoft.com* (although once again, you'll need *some* functioning computer to get online).

Windows 2000 Pro, Menu by Menu

E very window in Windows, and every window in software written to run *in* Windows, has a menu bar. Menu bars usually have a menu named File at the left end, and Help at the far right. What comes between depends on the type of software and its functions.

This appendix covers the commands in the Windows 2000 Professional desktop windows.

Tip: Frequently, you'll find that some menu commands are grayed out, meaning that they're not available for use. You can usually figure out why. For example, the Copy command is grayed out unless you've highlighted something to copy. Other reasons for inaccessible commands can be a little more difficult to parse; this appendix also addresses what to do to make grayed out commands available.

File Menu

Along with the Help menu, the File menu is the most universal one in Windows and Windows applications. Its commands may vary depending on whether or not you've highlighted an icon in the window.

Open
Opens the selected icon:

- If the icon is a drive or a folder, this command opens a window that displays the drive/folder's contents.

- If the icon is a program file, the program opens.

- If the icon is a data file, it opens in the program that created it.

If grayed out: Select an icon.

New

Opens a submenu of choices for new icons you can create in the window (see Figure B-1).

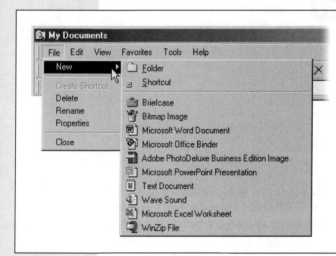

Figure B-1:
The submenu for the New command includes basic Windows elements (folder, shortcut, and so on), plus any that your programs have added. For instance, installing Microsoft Office adds Microsoft Word Document and Microsoft Excel Worksheet commands to the submenu.

Create Shortcut

Creates a *shortcut* to the selected icon (see page 101). For folders and files, the shortcut is placed in the current window, right next to the original icon, where the shortcut isn't especially useful. Drag the shortcut to the desktop or the Quick Launch toolbar. If the selected icon is a drive, Windows 2000 displays a message telling you that you can't create a shortcut to a drive on the drive, and asks if you want to put the shortcut on the desktop.

If grayed out: Select an icon.

Delete

Deletes the selected folder or file. (The command is not available if the selected icon is a drive). Windows 2000 asks you to confirm the fact that you are deleting the icon.

If grayed out: Highlight the file or folder you want to delete.

Rename

Lets you change the name of the selected icon (see page 90).

If grayed out: Select the file or folder you want to rename.

Close

Closes the window. If you're working in a program, closes the document you're working on.

Explore

Opens Windows Explorer (page 86) to display the contents of the selected folder or disk. (If you select a *file* instead of a drive or folder, this command doesn't appear on the menu at all.)

Search

Opens a Search window that's configured to look in the selected drive or folder (page 36). (Again, this command doesn't appear on the menu at all unless you've highlighted a drive or folder.)

Sharing

Opens the Sharing tab for a selected drive, folder, or printer where you can enable or disable sharing (page 295). This command appears only when a folder, drive, or printer icon is highlighted.

Send To

Selecting this command (which is available only for files and folders, not drives) displays a submenu that lists the choices on your system for Send To. See page 97 for details on using this command.

Properties

Opens the Properties dialog box for the selected icon. See page 91 for details on the resulting dialog box.

Edit Menu

When you work in, say, your word processor, you use the Edit menu quite a bit—its Cut, Copy, and Paste commands are very useful for moving bits of text. At the desktop, these commands operate on icons, providing an easy way for you to move files and folders from one window or disk to another.

The menu's commands vary, depending on whether an icon in the window is selected.

Undo

Reverses the last action you performed. The name of the command changes to describe what you did; if you delete a file, for example, the command name becomes Undo Delete.

Cut, Copy

You can cut or copy any selected icon except a drive. As you'd expect, Cut removes the original icon from its current folder location; Copy leaves the original icon in place. (See page 93 for details on cutting and copying icons.)

If grayed out: Select an icon to cut or copy.

Paste, Paste Shortcut

Once you've cut or copied an icon, you can click in a new folder or disk window and select Paste. The icon reappears in that location. (Paste Shortcut creates a shortcut to the original icon.) The keyboard shortcut is Ctrl+V.

If grayed out: The Clipboard is empty. Cut or copy an icon.

Copy to Folder, Move to Folder

These commands offer another way to move a folder or file to another folder. When you choose either command, a dialog box opens so you can select the target folder (see Figure B-2).

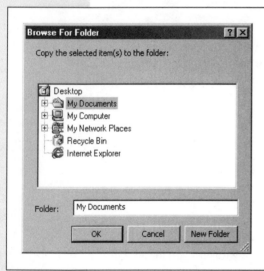

Figure B-2:
Click the + button to expand the folder or drive; select a folder into which you want to copy or move the selected icon. You can create a new folder under the selected folder by clicking the New Folder button.

Select All

Highlights all of the icons in the open window (or, if no window is open, on the desktop). Windows applies any subsequent command (Copy, Delete, Print, or whatever) to all of them at once. If you're editing an icon's name, and your cursor is blinking in the renaming rectangle, this command highlights the entire file name instead. Keyboard equivalent: Ctrl+A.

Invert Selection

This is a quick way to select everything in the window *except* one icon. Click the icon you want to *exclude,* and then use this command to select everything else. Windows highlights the icons that weren't selected, and vice versa.

View Menu

Use the commands on this menu to change the look of the currently open window.

Toolbars

This command offers a submenu of toolbars you can add to the window. For details on these toolbars and their functions, see page 70.

Status Bar

Makes the status bar appear or disappear at the bottom of the window. The status bar displays information about the contents of the current window, or the selection you've made inside of it. (It may say, for example, "3 object(s) selected" or "Type: Microsoft Word Document.")

Explorer Bar

Splits the window, creating a new left-side pane that shows the kind of extra information you choose using the View→Explorer Bar submenu. The choices are:

- **Search.** Lets you enter criteria for searching your system (see page 36).

- **Favorites.** Shows a list of your favorite Internet sites for one-click access (see page 233).

- **History.** Shows a list of Web sites and desktop folders you've had open recently. Click an item to return to the same place.

- **Folders.** Turns any window into a Windows Explorer-like view, with a folder hierarchy on the left side, folder contents on the right.

- **Tips.** Offers a new Windows 2000 tip every day (at the bottom of the window, not the left side).

- **Discuss.** Connects you to a Discussion Server, *if* one is configured on your network.

Large Icons, Small Icons, List, Details, Thumbnails

These commands let you view the files in a window as icons (which you move by dragging freely), as a neat list view that's automatically sorted, or as thumbnails (large buttons that reveal what's in graphics files). Page 37 offers a complete description of these views and their relative advantages.

Arrange Icons, Line Up Icons

These commands are useful for tidying a window filled with randomly spaced icons.

If you choose View→Line Up Icons, all icons in the window jump to the closest positions on the invisible underlying grid. This is a temporary status, however—as soon as you drag icons around, or add more icons to the window, the newly moved icons wind up just as sloppily positioned as before you used the command.

If you choose View→Arrange Icons, on the other hand, all icons in the window snap to the invisible grid *and* sort themselves according to your choice from the submenu (by size, name, date, and so on). Use this method to place the icons as close as possible to each other within the window, rounding up any strays. (In a list view, these commands simply sort the list according to the criterion you specify in the submenu.)

If grayed out: Line Up Icons is available only when the window is in Large Icons or Small Icons view.

Choose Columns

In a list view, Windows 2000 shows the details of each file in Name, Size, Type, and Modified columns. But using this command, you can choose from an enormous list of additional columns that you'd like displayed (in the frontmost window): Company Name, Product Version, Sender Name, and so on. You can also specify how wide you'd like each column to be, and (using the Move Up and Move Down buttons) where you'd like it to appear in the left-to-right order.

Customize This Folder

This command launches a wizard that walks you through the process of changing the folder window's background (such as the identifying text and graphics that appear on the left side of the window). See page 70 for details.

Go To

This command's submenu lets you move forward or backward through desktop windows you've recently opened, much like the Back and Forward buttons in your Web browser. (The View→Go To→Home Page launches your Web browser, connects to the Internet, and takes you to the page you've designated as your home page.)

Refresh

Updates the contents of the window. Use this command if you've just cut, pasted, or deleted icons, and the window doesn't yet reflect the changes. Keyboard equivalent: F5.

Favorites Menu

The Favorites menu stores locations you visit frequently, whether folders on your PC or Web sites on the Internet.

Add to Favorites

Adds the currently open Web page or desktop window to the Favorites list.

Organize Favorites

Opens a dialog box where you can organize your favorite places. For example, you may want a folder for all the favorite places on your computer, another folder for all the Internet sites related to cooking, and another folder for all the Internet sites you visit to get help on computing. See page 234 for more on organizing your Favorites.

Tools Menu

This menu offers a handful of miscellaneous commands, most of which pertain to networking.

Map Network Drive

This command lets you assign a drive letter to a disk or folder to which you've connected over the network, as described on page 292.

Disconnect Network Drive

This command summons a dialog box that lets you *delete* a drive mapping you've established using the Map Network Drive command.

Synchronize

You use this command in conjunction with the Offline Files feature described on page 315; it brings your computer's documents up to date with the copies on the network. Synchronization also works with Web sites—you can update your laptop's copy of certain Web pages, for example, for reading on the train ride home.

Folder Options

The dialog box summoned by this command lets you change several global desktop-window options. You can read about these settings in detail starting on page 74.

Help Menu

This menu has two commands: Help Topics, which opens the Windows 2000 Help system discussed in Chapter 6; and About Windows, which displays your license information, along with information about your computer's memory.

Index

Colophon

The book was created in Microsoft Word, whose revision-tracking feature made life far easier as drafts were circulated from author to technical and copy editors. Inner Media's Collage captured illustrations; Adobe Photoshop and Macromedia Free-Hand were called in as required for touching them up.

The book was designed and laid out in Adobe PageMaker 6.5 on a Power Mac 8500 and Power Mac G3. The fonts used include Formata (as the sans-serif family) and Minion (as the serif body face). Index entries were typed into a custom FileMaker database, then collated and formatted by EZ Index, a shareware program. The book was then generated as an Adobe Acrobat PDF file for proofreading, "beta reading," and final transmission to the printing plant.